Visitation
of
England and Wales

VOLUME 11
1903

Edited by
Joseph Jackson Howard, LL.D.,
Maltravers Herald Extraordinary
and Frederick Arthur Crisp

HERITAGE BOOKS
2013

HERITAGE BOOKS

AN IMPRINT OF HERITAGE BOOKS, INC.

Books, CDs, and more—Worldwide

For our listing of thousands of titles see our website
at
www.HeritageBooks.com

A Facsimile Reprint
Published 2013 by
HERITAGE BOOKS, INC.
Publishing Division
100 Railroad Ave. #104
Westminster, Maryland 21157

Originally privately printed
1903

International Standard Book Numbers
Paperbound: 978-0-7884-0435-1
Clothbound: 978-0-7884-6977-0

LIST OF PEDIGREES.

LIST OF PLATES.

~~~~~~~~~~~

Pedigrees.

VIRTUTE ET VALORE

ROBERTS.

Arms on record in the College of Arms.—Azure, three estoiles or, on a chief wavy of the last an Eastern crown gules.

Crest.—A lion rampant or, holding in the dexter paw a sword, the blade wavy argent, pommel and hilt gold, and charged on the shoulder with an Eastern crown as in the arms.

Motto.—Virtute et valore.

Supporters.—Dexter: A soldier of the 92nd (Gordon Highlanders) Regiment of Foot, holding in his exterior hand a musket; Sinister: A soldier of the Goorka Infantry, holding in his exterior hand a rifle, both habited and accoutred proper.

Roberts.

Rev. John Roberts (2nd son of John Roberts of the City of Waterford, Architect of both Cathedrals and of the Leper Hospital at Waterford [who died 23 May 1796, aged 84, and was bur. at the French Church, Waterford. M.I.], by Mary Susanna his wife [who died 21 January 1800, aged 84, and was bur. at the French Church, Waterford. M.I.], dau. of Major Francis Sautelle, Architect of the Town Hall, Chamber of Commerce and other public buildings at Waterford [of a French Refugee family settled in that city]); born 24 January 1745; of Trinity College, Dublin, B.A. 1766; Rector of the united parishes of Crooke and Kill St. Nicholas, Rector of Dunhill, all co. Waterford, and of Ballymacward, co. Galway; Chaplain to the Military Barracks of Geneva, co. Waterford, collated Provost of the Diocese of Kilmacduagh, co. Galway, 20 July 1813, Domestic Chaplain to the 1st and 2nd Marquesses of Waterford; presented to the living of Drumcondra, near Dublin, in 1814, by the Duke of Richmond, Lord-Lieutenant of Ireland, which he exchanged soon after for that of Ballymacward; J.P. for co. Waterford; died at Ballinasloe, co. Galway, in 1815. Will dated 22 March 1814, proved 12 May 1815.

—Anne, dau. of the Rev. Abraham Sandys of Dublin, B.A., Minor Canon of St. Patrick's Cathedral, Dublin; marr. at St. Ann's, Dublin, 23 January 1771; died, aged 78, 7 May 1833, and bur. at the French Church, Waterford. M.I.

A

Hester, born 27 January 1772; marr. 1stly 10 January 1793, Lieutenant Molloy; marr. 2ndly Commander Charles Tulloch, R.N., who died s.p. She died at Cheekpoint, co. Waterford, and was bur. in the churchyard at Faithleg, near Waterford.

John Roberts of Waterford; born at Waterford 14 April 1773; Attorney, Court of Chancery; died 2 February, bur. in the church at Ballynakill, co. Waterford, 4 February 1837.

—Grace, eldest dau. of William Dobbyn of Waterford; marr. at Waterford 18 May 1796; died, aged 89, 18 August 1854, and bur. in Shankill Graveyard, Belfast.

B

William Roberts, born at Waterford 29 June 1797, bapt. at Waterford Cathedral 8 July 1826; of the Excise Office, London; died at 96 Ladbroke Grove Road, London, aged 79, on Sunday, 29 October, bur. in Highgate Cemetery, London, 2 November 1876. Will dated 19 December 1866, with codicil dated 4 April 1876, proved (Prin. Reg., 936, 76) 29 December 1876, by Anna Maria Roberts of 96 Ladbroke Grove Road, co. Middlesex, the relict, the sole Executrix. (*See page 5.*)

—Anna Maria (his cousin), 2nd dau. of Captain Thomas Roberts of Waterford, R.N., by Katherine his wife, dau. of James Hackett of Fethard, co. Tipperary, a Major in the Army; born at Waterford 19 February 1807, bapt. at Waterford Cathedral 24 June 1813; marr. by licence at Ballynakill (by the Rev. John Cooke) 16 July 1827; died at 96 Ladbroke Grove Road, London, aged 85, on Thursday, 28 January, bur. in Highgate Cemetery, London, 3 February 1892. Will dated 21 May 1885, proved (Prin. Reg., 359, 92) 17 March 1892, by Samuel Roberts and Abraham Francis Roberts, the Exors.

C

Anna Grace, born 6 November, bapt. at St. Mary's, Islington, London, 5 December 1828; died, aged 14, 7 May, bur. in Highgate Cemetery, London, 13 May 1843.

John William Roberts of Wilderspool House, Warrington, co. Lancaster; born at Canonbury, in the parish of Islington, London, 7 February, bapt. at St. Mary's, Islington, 9 April 1830; educated at the Endowed School, Waterford.

—Lavinia Elizabeth, only dau. of Captain John Brittain, Queen's Messenger, by Louisa his wife, dau. of Robert Wilkins; born in the parish of Islington, London, 2 December 1836, bapt. at St. Mary's, Islington, 8 February 1837; marr. at St. Pancras', London (by the Rev. Charles Henry Andrews, the senior Curate), on Tuesday, 19 January 1858; died at High Barnet, co. Middlesex, aged 57, on Wednesday, 28 November, bur. in the Great Northern Cemetery, New Southgate, co. Middlesex, 3 December 1894. Will dated 4 February 1891, proved (Prin. Reg., 1225, 94) 31 December 1894, by John William Roberts, gent., and William Brittain Roberts, the son, the Exors.

D

I

Abraham Roberts, born 10 August 1774, and died young.

B   B

Thomas Roberts, born 28 October 1800, = Harriett, 3rd dau. of William Lowndes of Chesham, bapt. at Waterford Cathedral 23 April 1819; of the Honble East India Co.'s Service; Captain 51st Bengal Native Infantry; died at his residence in Montpellier Square, Knightsbridge, London, aged 50, on Tuesday, 29 October, bur. at Holy Trinity, West Brompton, London, 8 November 1850. Will dated 17 February 1848, proved (P.C.C., 64, 51) 6 January 1851, by Harriett Roberts, the relict, the sole Executrix.

co. Buckingham, J.P., by Harriet Wilson his wife, dau. of John Kingston of Rickmansworth, co. Hertford; born at Chesham 23 December 1811, bapt. there 7 April 1812; marr. at St. Mary's, Bath, co. Somerset, 8 April 1835; died at 30 Kensington Square, London, aged 70, on Thursday, 6 April, bur. in West Brompton Cemetery, London, 11 April 1882. Will dated 21 June 1881, proved (Prin. Reg., 585, 82) 17 July 1882, by Arthur Roberts of 30 Kensington Square, co. Middlesex, the son, the sole Exor.

E

Harriett, born at Mussoorie, North-West Provinces, India, 29 May 1836; marr. at Waterford Cathedral (by the Very Rev. the Dean of Waterford, assisted by the Rev. William John Price), on Friday, 6 March 1857, Major-General George Ricketts Roberts of 35 Lee Park, Lee, co. Kent, formerly of the Bengal Staff Corps (elder son of General Sir Abraham Roberts, G.C.B., by Frances Isabella his 1st wife, dau. of George Poyntz Ricketts of the Bengal Civil Service); born at Meerut, North-West Provinces, India, 8 February 1827; entered the Army as Ensign 7 June 1844, Lieutenant 1 July 1846, Captain 22 November 1856, Major 7 June 1864, Lieut.-Colonel 7 June 1870, Brevet-Colonel 7 June 1875, and Deputy Commissary-General; retired with hon. rank of Major-General 15 December 1880. (See page 10.)

C   C

Thomas Clarence Roberts, born at St. Paul's = Jane Elizabeth, youngest dau. of Francis Terrace, Camden Town, London, 23 January, bapt. at Camden Chapel, London (since 1851, Camden Town Parish Church), 26 April 1832; died at the Farm House, Ferring, co. Sussex, aged 64, on Monday, 27 January, bur. at Ferring 30 January 1896. Will dated 1 December 1865, proved (Prin. Reg., 182, 96) 17 February 1896, by Jane Elizabeth Roberts, the relict, the sole Executrix.

Coham Kelly of Houghton Place, Harrington Square, London, by Jane his wife, dau. of Thomas Young of King's Lynn, co. Norfolk; born at Robert Street, St. Pancras, London, 15 February, bapt. at Holy Trinity, Marylebone, London, 21 October 1838; marr. at St. Margaret's, Plumstead, co. Kent (by the Rev. James Adair McAllister, the Vicar), on Friday, 1 December 1865.

Pembroke Roberts, born at Bromley, co. Kent, on Thursday, 25 October 1866, bapt. at the parish church, Bromley, 15 February 1867; educated at Kelly College, Tavistock, co. Devon.

                                                          F

D

William Brittain Roberts, born = Hilda Marian, eldest dau. of John French of New Barnet, co. at Camden Town, London, 3 January, bapt. at Camden Town Parish Church 2 March 1859.

Hertford; born at 7 Hillmarton Villas West, Camden Road, London, on Sunday, 27 December 1863; marr. at Holy Trinity, Lyonsdown, co. Hertford (by the Rev. George Yeats, assisted by the Rev. William John Hocking), on Saturday, 7 June 1884.

Victor George Roberts, born at 190 Upper Parliament Street, Liverpool, on Friday, 27 February, bapt. at Holy Trinity, New Barnet, 11 May 1885; educated at Boteler Grammar School, Warrington, co. Lancaster.

A ——— A

Mary, born 3 May 1783; died unmarried 28 July 1801,
and bur. at the French Church, Waterford.

B ——— B

Arthur Roberts of "Oakleigh," Court Road, Eltham, co.=Margaret Frances, dau. of John
Kent; born 30 April 1838, bapt. at Missouri, East India, 27 | Hughes of London, Barrister-at-
February 1839; educated at Kensington Grammar School; | Law, by Elizabeth his wife, dau.
M.R.C.S. Eng. 1859, L.M. 1860, L.R.C.P. Lond. 1861. | of William Jones of Bath, co.
Somerset; born in London 6 July
1834; marr. at St. Mary's, Dover,
co. Kent (by the Rev. Charles
Lowndes, Vicar of Hartwell, co.
Buckingham), 26 September 1868.

[signature: Arthur Roberts]

E

Arthur Francis Lowndes Roberts, born at 30 | Frances Dorothea Lowndes, born at 30
Kensington Square, London, on Thursday, | Kensington Square, London, on Monday,
5 December 1872; died there, aged 9, on | 29 January, bapt. at St. Barnabas', West
Saturday, 1 April, bur. in Brompton Cemetery, | Kensington (by the Rev. Francis Hessey,
London, 5 April 1882. | D.C.L.), 20 March 1877.

C ——— C

Emily Catharine, born in London 21 June, bapt. | Augustus Henry | Samuel Roberts, born 15
at Camden Chapel, London (since 1851, Camden | Roberts, born | March, bapt. at Camden
Town Parish Church), 26 December 1833; marr. | 11 March 1835; | Chapel, London (since
at St. Stephen's, Westbourne Park, co. Middlesex | died unmarried | 1851, Camden Town Parish
(by the Rev. Harvey Brooks), on Saturday, 2 June | 5 March 1865, | Church), 17 June 1838.
1866, James Crowder Eastcott of 35 St. Ronan's | and bur. in the
Road, Southsea, co. Hants (son of Richard Ducke | Happy Valley,
Eastcott, by Catherine Dyball his wife); born in | Hong Kong, | Abraham Francis Roberts,
London 25 April, bapt. at Camden Chapel, | China. | born 12 September 1839.
London (since 1851, Camden Town Parish
Church), 18 June 1829; educated at University
College, London; M.R.C.S. Eng. 1852; Surgeon
R.N., Deputy-Inspector-General 1884 (retired
1884).

F ——— F

Walter Roberts, born at Bromley,=Harriett Silver, youngest dau. of George Blackford Silver
co. Kent, on Tuesday, 18 Feb- | Darter of Fitzroy Square, London, by Mary Elizabeth
ruary, bapt. at the parish church, | Underhill his wife; marr. at the Old Mission Church,
Bromley, 29 July 1868; educated | Calcutta, India (by the Rev. Arthur Herbert Bowman, the
at Holborn Grammar School. | Incumbent), on Monday, 17 September 1900.

Mary Elizabeth, born at | Gladys Margaret, born at Calcutta 11 November
Calcutta 24 September, | 1902, bapt. there 5 February 1903; died at
bapt. there 5 December | Darjeeling, Bengal, India, 2 June 1903, and
1901. | bur. there.

3

Alice, born 1 August 1787, and died young.

B

John Dobbyn Roberts, born 1 April ⊤ **Mary, dau. of George Symes of Wicklow,**   **Samuel Roberts,**
1802, bapt. at Waterford Cathedral | M.D.; born 27 July 1798; marr. at   died in Jamaica,
8 July 1826; died at Belfast 25 | Rathasput, co. Wexford, 1 September 1828;   West Indies.
January, bur. in Shankhill Grave- | died at Belfast 19 September 1840, and
yard, Belfast, 27 January 1887. | bur. in Shankhill Graveyard, Belfast.

John Symes Roberts, born 26   **Samuel Thomas Roberts** ⊤ **Jane Hudson, dau. of Dr. Christopher**
August 1830, and bapt. at   of Belfast; born at | Leycester Malet, formerly of Brazil; born
Waterford; died unmarried   Belfast 25 November, | at Castletownsend, co. Cork, 30 November
12 May 1866, and bur. in   bapt. at St. Anne's, | 1843, and bapt. there; marr. at Holy
Shankhill Graveyard, Belfast.   Belfast, 28 December | Trinity, Belfast, 4 February 1865; died
    —   1838. | 7 October 1870, and bur. in Balmoral
George Alcock Roberts, born   Cemetery, Belfast.
20 July 1833, and bapt. at
Waterford; died 1 November,
bur. in Shankhill Graveyard,   **John Leycester Roberts,**   **Martha Symes, born in Belfast**
Belfast, 3 November 1903.   born in Belfast 19 De-   24 November 1867, bapt. at St.
    —   cember 1865, bapt. at   Anne's, Belfast; marr. at Knock-
Ann Sophia, born 23 December   Holy Trinity, Belfast, 28   breda, near Belfast, 11 September
1835, and bapt. at Belfast;   January 1866; died 30   1901, William McConbrie Bell
died 24 November 1844, and   March 1869, and bur.   (son of William and Elizabeth
bur. in Shankhill Graveyard,   in Balmoral Cemetery,   Bell); born at Clanvaraghan, co.
Belfast.   Belfast.   Down, 1 January 1866.

C

Frederick James Roberts of   **James Hackett Roberts, born 23** ⊤ **Clara Fannie Adelaide, only dau.**
Grove Lodge, Weybridge,   November 1843, bapt. at Camden | of Arthur Wood, M.D., formerly
co. Surrey; born 20 October   Chapel, London (since 1851, | Surgeon to 9th and 16th Lancers,
1841, bapt. at Camden   Camden Town Parish Church) | by Clara Martha his wife; born
Chapel, London (since 1851,   24 January 1844; died at Southsea, | at Manchester, and bapt. there;
Camden Town Parish   co. Hants, 24 June, bur. in Highland | marr. at St. Philip's, Kensington,
Church), 20 February 1842;   Cemetery, Southsea, 29 June 1902. | London (by the Rev. Robert
matriculated at London   Will dated 23 June 1902, proved | Towers, Vicar of St. Andrew and
University 1860, from King's   (Prin. Reg., 12, 1902) 7 August | St. Philip's, Upper Westbourne
College; a Student of the   1902, by Clara Fannie Adelaide | Park, London, assisted by the
Middle Temple 22 October   Roberts, the relict, the sole Executrix. | Rev. William Smale, the Vicar),
1861, called to the Bar 17   on Wednesday, 8 April 1885.
November 1865; marr. at
All Saints', Finchley Road,
St. John's Wood, London,   **Evelyn Clara, born at Streatham**   **Hilda Frances, born**
on Tuesday, 6 October   Hill, co. Surrey, 11 January, bapt.   29 February, bapt. at
1874, Isabella, widow of   at St. Thomas', Streatham Hill,   St. Thomas', Streatham
J. Capel Hanbury.   28 March 1886.   Hill, 25 April 1888.

F   F

Percy Heriot Roberts, born at Bromley, ⊤ **Isobel Marie, elder dau. of Charles Montague Hailes**
co. Kent, 27 November 1869, bapt. there | of Hampstead, co. Middlesex; born 21 October 1879;
7 April 1870; educated at Kelly College, | marr. at St. Stephen's, Hampstead (by the Rev. Joshua
Tavistock. co. Devon.   Kirkman), on Tuesday, 18 June 1901.

John Heriot Roberts, born at 78 Milton Park, Highgate, co. Middlesex,
on Tuesday, 25 March, bapt. at St. Michaels', Highgate, 7 June 1902.

Captain Thomas Roberts of Waterford, R.N.; born at Waterford═Katherine, dau. of 12 January 1778; entered the Navy in February 1790, as a Supernumerary on board the "Swallow," 14, lying at Plymouth; served in the Mediterranean as Midshipman 1793–96, in the "Cyclope," frigate, and "Bedford" and "Audacious," 74's, all commanded by Captain Davidge Gould; in the "Cyclope" he assisted at the reduction of Bastia in May 1795, and in the "Bedford" he fought in Hotham's actions 14 March and 13 July 1795; he was made Lieutenant 24 December 1796 in the "Serpent" sloop (Captain Richard Buckall); from 5 January to 5 July 1797 he was employed on the coast of Africa, and during that period he aided in taking a felucca which had been despatched from Cadiz for the purpose of apprising the South American trade of the commencement of hostilites between France and Spain, and afterwards contributed to the capture, among other vessels, of a French transport laden with naval stores; appointed Commander of the "Serpent" by Sir Hyde Parker, and sanctioned by the Admiralty 23 July 1798; in the following year, owing to ill health, was sent home as whipper-in to a fleet of 113 West Indiamen, under the protection of the "Regular," 44, bearing the flag of Vice-Admiral Richard Rodney Bligh; on the renewal of hostilities in 1803, he was one of the first appointed to raise sea fencibles in Ireland, and remained on that service until it was abolished in 1810; Post-Captain 1840; appointed Receiver of the Leper Hospital Estate in the county and city of Waterford 10 September 1840; died 16 February 1855, and bur. at the French Church, Waterford. Will dated 9 October 1850, proved 16 March 1855.

James Hackett of Fethard, co. Tipperary, a Major in the Army; marr. at Waterford 25 June 1804; died at 44 Grosvenor Square, Rathmines, Dublin, aged 82, on Thursday, 24 January, bur. in Mount Jerome Cemetery, Harold's Cross, Dublin, 28 January 1867.

                         G

Anna Maria, born at Waterford 19 February 1807, bapt. at Waterford Cathedral 24 June 1813; marr. by licence at Ballynakill, co. Galway (by the Rev. John Cooke), 16 July 1827, her cousin, William Roberts (eldest son of John Roberts of Waterford, by Grace his wife, eldest dau. of William Dobbyn of Waterford); born 29 June 1797, bapt. at Waterford Cathedral 8 July 1826; of the Excise Office, London; died at 96 Ladbroke Grove Road, London, aged 79, on Sunday, 29 October, bur. in Highgate Cemetery, London, 2 November 1876. Will dated 19 December 1866, with codicil dated 4 April 1876, proved (Prin. Reg., 936, 76) 29 December 1876, by Anna Maria Roberts of 96 Ladbroke Grove Road, co. Middlesex, the relict, the sole Executrix. She died at 96 Ladbroke Grove Road, London, aged 85, on Thursday, 28 January, and was bur. in Highgate Cemetery, London, 3 February 1892. Will dated 21 May 1885, proved (Prin. Reg., 359, 92) 17 March 1892, by Samuel Roberts and Abraham Francis Roberts, the Exors. (*See page 1.*)

Alice Dorothea, born at 94 Gaisford Street, London, on Monday, 14 August, bapt. at St. Luke's, Kentish Town, London, 9 November 1871.

—

Herbert Roberts, born at 94 Gaisford Street, London, on Wednesday, 18 February, bapt. at St. Thomas', Camden Town, London, 21 May 1874; educated at Holborn Grammar School; served in South African War 1900–1901, as Lieutenant Duke of Edinburgh's Volunteer Rifles (medal with one clasp, Cape Colony).

Gerald Roberts, born at 94 Gaisford Street, London, on Friday, 14 July 1876, bapt. at St. Thomas', Camden Town, London, 2 February 1877; educated at Kelly College, Tavistock, co. Devon.

—

Violet Kathleen, born at 94 Gaisford Street, London, on Thursday, 27 June, bapt. at St. Thomas', Camden Town, London, 12 September 1878.

Anne, born 8 May 1789; marr. Lieut.-Colonel Thomas J. Maling, Private Secretary to General Rowland Hill (afterwards Viscount Hill), Commander-in-Chief of the British Army. She died at Whitehaven, co. Cumberland, 28 May 1843. Will dated 7 May 1839, proved (P.C.C., 499, 43) 5 July 1843, by John Greensill and John Roberts Price, the Exors.

G

Katherine, born at Waterford 12 August 1810, bapt. at Waterford Cathedral 24 June 1813; marr. at Purfleet, co. Essex, 23 May 1844, Lieut.-Colonel Jonas Pasley Hardy (son of William Samuel Hardy, by Mary his wife, dau. of William Price); born in Dublin 31 August 1806; served with the 58th Regiment in New Zealand, and was present at the attack and repulse of the hostile natives on the settlement and stockades of Wanganui 19 May, and action of 19 July 1847 (medal); died at 50 Clarinda Park, Kingstown, co. Dublin, aged 64, 27 April, bur. in Mount Jerome Cemetery, Harold's Cross, Dublin, 29 April 1872. Will proved in the Principal Registry, Dublin, 23 May 1872, by William Roberts of 16 George's Street, Mansion House, London, and by the affirmation of George Roberts Price of 84 Lower Leeson Street, Dublin, Barrister-at-Law, the Exors. She died at 31 Morehampton Road, Donnybrook, co. Dublin, 29 January, and was bur. in Mount Jerome Cemetery, Harold's Cross, Dublin, 1 February 1883.

Matilda, born at Waterford 19 April 1812, bapt. at Waterford Cathedral 22 September 1814; died, aged 86, 10 October, bur. in Mount Jerome Cemetery, Harold's Cross, Dublin, 14 October 1898.

Thomas Sautelle Roberts, born 26 May, bapt. at Waterford Cathedral 24 June 1813; died unmarried, aged 46, 27 April, bur. in Mount Jerome Cemetery, Harold's Cross, Dublin, 29 April 1861.

G

B

Abraham Roberts, born at Waterford 7 December 1804; marr. 2ndly 11 September 1850, Elizabeth Yearing, born at Dover, Ills., U.S.A., and died there, leaving issue. He died 2 May 1869, and was bur. at Dover, Ills., U.S.A.

Katherine, 2nd dau. of Nicholas Goodall of Wexford; born at Bath, co. Somerset, 6 June 1807; marr. at Rathaspeck, co. Wexford, 6 June 1828; died 8 July 1849, and bur. at Dover, Ills., U.S.A. 1st wife.

Anne, born 28 January 1807; marr. at Toronto, Canada, John Hurst; died s.p. at Barrie, Ontario, Canada, 16 January 1882, and bur. there. She died at Peterborough, Ontario.

John Roberts, born at Wexford 17 September 1829; died 22 May 1837.

James G. Roberts, born at Wexford 26 November 1830; died at Helena, Wis., U.S.A., 25 June 1854.

Isabella, born at Wexford 1 May 1832; marr. 8 July 1850, Judge E. Penington.

Abraham Roberts, born at Pittsburg, Pa., U.S.A., 6 October 1834; died in California in 1902.

Thomas H. G. Roberts, born at Vicksburg, Miss., U.S.A., 1 February 1837; died 15 September 1838.

B

Grace, born at Vicksburg, Miss., U.S.A., 24 October 1838, and bapt. there; marr. at Fremont, U.S.A., 5 January 1857, G. W. Dunton. She marr. 2ndly at Council Bluffs, Ia., U.S.A., 10 January 1899, to Samuel Alban; born at Muscatine, Ia., U.S.A., 6 July 1844.

Emily, born at Trenton, Mo., U.S.A., 10 July 1840; died 5 July 1844.

Ann M., born 10 January 1843, and died 10 February following.

William Roberts, born at Trenton, Mo., U.S.A., 10 July, and died 9 August 1844.

Letitia, born at Peoria, Ills., U.S.A., 23 September 1845; died 9 July 1849.

A

A

Harriet, born 22 May 1790; marr. Frederick Pennell (son of William Pennell of Waterford, Consul-General of Brazil, by his wife, Elisabeth Carrington of Topsham, co. Devon); died at Gloucester 23 December, bur. there 30 December 1852. She died at her residence, 32 Richmond Terrace, Everton, co. Lancaster, in her 73rd year, on Saturday, 12 July, and was bur. at Gloucester, near her husband, 16 July 1862. (*See page 9.*)

G

G

Emily, born at Waterford 24 July, bapt. at Waterford Cathedral 22 September 1814; died unmarried 12 October 1853, and bur. at the French Church, Waterford. Memorial tablet in Waterford Cathedral.

—

Flora Augusta, born at Waterford 20 April, bapt. at Waterford Cathedral 28 May 1816; died, aged 82, 6 June, bur. in Mount Jerome Cemetery, Harold's Cross, Dublin, 10 June 1898.

Rosamond, born at Waterford 7 May, bapt. at Waterford Cathedral 21 May 1818; marr. at Clonmore, co. Kilkenny, 4 January 1840, her cousin, the Rev. William John Price (son of William Price by Lucinda his wife); born at Waterford 18 September 1810; Lecturer of St. Olave's, Waterford; Vicar of Killelan, co. Kildare; died, aged 49, 27 March 1863, and bur. at the French Church, Waterford. She died 27 April 1854, and was bur. at the French Church, Waterford.

James Hackett Roberts, born at Waterford 13 February, bapt. at Waterford Cathedral 24 February 1820; died 21 December, bur. in the cemetery at Everton, co. Lancaster, 26 December 1886.

Harriet, dau. of Francis Owens by Margaret his wife; born at Penley, co. Salop, 7 May, bapt. there 28 May 1815; marr. at the Registry Office, Liverpool, 7 June 1852; died 26 September 1885, and bur. in Necropolis Cemetery, Low Hill, Everton.

James Roberts, born at College Street, East Liverpool, and bapt. at St. Nicholas', Liverpool, 30 April 1854.

Katherine, born at Sheriffe Street, Everton, co. Lancaster, 27 March 1857; marr. at St. Peter's, Everton, 27 October 1881, Charles Moody (son of Thomas Moody, by Margaret his wife); born at Leeds, co. York, 18 February 1856, and bapt. at Christ Church, Leeds.

B

Elizabeth, born 9 November 1808; marr. 10 October 1846, Henry John Willett of Dublin (eldest son of Henry John Willett of Castlefield, co. Kilkenny); died s.p. 29 May 1872. She died at 116 Rosslyn Street, Toxteth Park, Liverpool, aged 95, 27 January, and was bur. in Toxteth Park Cemetery, Smithdown Road, Liverpool, 30 January 1903.

Michael Roberts of Newtown, Waterford; born 18 July 1811; marr. at Ballynakill, co. Waterford, 10 September 1845, Letitia, younger dau. of Benjamin Roberts of Wexford. He died s.p. by an accident on a yacht, aged 57, on Monday, 3 August, and was bur. at Ballynakill 8 August 1868. Will proved at Waterford 25 August 1868, by Letitia Roberts of Newtown, Waterford, the relict, and sole Executrix.

Hester, born at Waterford 1 February 1813; marr. at Ballynakill 4 January 1841, Thomas Pyne of Waterford, M.D.; born at Waterford; died at Belgrove, Canada, 3 January, bur. at Toronto, Canada, 5 January 1883. She died at Toronto 10 February, and was bur. there 12 February 1896.

Betsy, born 26 June 1792,
and died young.

William Roberts, born at Waterford 4 December ╤ Emily, 3rd dau. of William Henry Hamerton
1823; died at "Rosenberg," Fox Grove Road, | of Dublin; born in Dublin, 12 June 1823,
Beckenham, co. Kent, aged 74, on Thursday, | and bapt. at Queen Anne's Church, Dublin;
16 December, bur. in the cemetery at Shirley, co. | marr. at Calcutta, India, 10 July 1848;
Surrey, 20 December 1897. Will dated 24 | died at her residence "Rosenberg," Fox
January 1893, with codicil dated 16 February | Grove Road, Beckenham, on Tuesday, 13
1897, proved (Prin. Reg., 81, 98) 31 January | October, bur. in the cemetery at Shirley on
1898, by Frederick Arthur Roberts and David | Friday, 16 October 1903.
Alan Stevenson, two of the Exors.

William Thomas Roberts, born 19 May | Emily, born 19 April 1853, | Henry Roberts (twin
1849, and bapt. at Calcutta; died unmarried | and bapt. at Calcutta; marr. | with Catherine Anna),
at Brighton, co. Sussex, aged 42, on Thursday, | at St. John the Evangelist's, | born 29 May 1855,
21 January, bur. at Shirley 26 January 1892. | Bromley, co. Kent (by | and died in 1857.
| the Rev. Stanley Arthur |
— | Vardon, Vicar of All Saints', | —
| Langton Green, co. Kent, |
Letitia Whiteway, born 18 April 1851, and | cousin of the bridegroom), | Catherine Anna (twin
bapt. at Calcutta; marr. at the British | on Saturday, 17 October | with Henry), born
Embassy, Brussels (by the Rev. William | 1891, Arthur Hitchcock | 29 May 1855.
Drury), on Wednesday, 1 September 1869, | of Bettysground, Shute, |
William Cunningham Fairley (son of | co. Devon (youngest son | —
Edward Fairley of Glasgow); he died at | of Edward Hitchcock of |
Burnford House, Bramshaw, co. Hants, | St. Clement's, Paignton, | Ellen, born 17 August,
aged 56, on Tuesday, 21 October, bur. in | co. Devon). | bapt. at St. Peter's,
Brookwood Cemetery, Woking, co. Surrey, | | Notting Hill, London,
27 October 1890. | | 13 October 1858.

Mordaunt Roberts, | Frances Eliza, born 22 August 1824; marr. at Meerut, North-West
died in infancy. | Provinces, India, 20 October 1842, General Charles Grant, C.B. (son of
| Robert Grant of the Bengal Civil Service); of the Royal (late Bengal
— | Horse) Artillery, Ensign 22 April 1819, Lieutenant 2 August 1822,
| Brevet Captain 22 April 1834, Captain 17 January 1836, Brevet Major
Frances   Sophia, | 30 April 1834, Major 5 July 1846, Brevet Lieut.-Colonel 19 June 1846,
died in infancy. | Lieut.-Colonel 5 May 1849, Brevet Colonel 20 June 1854, Colonel
| 18 February 1861, Colonel-Commandant 11 December 1868, Major-
| General 14 October 1858, Lieut.-General 14 December 1868, General
| 1 October 1877; created C.B. 9 June 1849; died at 3 Suffolk
| Square, Cheltenham, co. Gloucester, on Friday, 13 January 1882.
| Will dated 12 February 1875, proved at Gloucester 9 February
| 1882, by Elizabeth Charlotte Grant of 3 Suffolk Square, Chelten-
| ham, co. Gloucester, spinster, and Isabella Caroline Thomas (wife
| of Tudor Vaughan Howell Thomas) of Lampeter House, Narbeth, co.
| Pembroke, the daughters, two of the surviving Exors. She died
| 15 October 1852, and was bur. at Mean Meer, India.

Eliza, born 2 July 1795; marr. at Waterford Cathedral (by the Very Rev. Ussher Lee, Dean of Waterford), 24 February 1827, John Greensill, Inspector of Ordnance Accounts, Halifax, Nova Scotia, and afterwards Storekeeper H.M. Ordnance at Purfleet, co. Essex; died at the Rectory, Helensburgh, co. Dumbarton, aged 77, 17 May 1874, and bur. in the cemetery at Helensburgh. She died at Osnaburgh Street, Regent's Park, London, 17 October, and was bur. in Kensal Green Cemetery, London, 24 October 1851.

G

Mary, born at Waterford 25 January, bapt. at Waterford Cathedral 2 June 1825; died unmarried at Orchardstown, Rathfarnham, co. Dublin, aged 32, 5 June, bur. in Mount Jerome Cemetery, Harold's Cross, Dublin, 9 June 1858. Admͦn was granted at the Principal Registry 3 August 1858, to Katherine Roberts of 9 Henrietta Street, Waterford, the mother and next of kin.

Elizabeth, born at Waterford 5 February, bapt. at Waterford Cathedral 18 February 1830; marr. there 4 July 1854, her cousin, Spencer Perceval Pennell of 77 Marlborough Road, Donnybrook, co. Dublin (son of Frederick Pennell, by Harriet his wife, dau. of the Rev. John Roberts); born at Waterford 5 February 1823; died s.p. at Calcutta, India, 1 June 1863, and bur. there. (See page 7.)

H

Frederick Arthur Roberts, born at Kensington, London, on Monday, 30 April, bapt. at St. Peter's, Notting Hill, London, 25 July 1860; of Trinity Hall, Cambridge, matriculated Michaelmas Term, 1878, B.A. 1882.

Adah Felicitas, 6th dau. of the Honble James Dever of St. John, New Brunswick, Canada, Senator, by Margaret his wife, dau. of James Morris; born at St. John, New Brunswick, and bapt. there; marr. at the Pro-Cathedral, Kensington, London (by the Rev. Father Gavin, assisted by the Rev. Father Bloomfield), on Thursday, 10 September 1891.

Annie, born at 34 Kensington Park Gardens, London, on Thursday, 1 May, bapt. at St. Peter's, Notting Hill, London, 10 September 1862; marr. at St. Paul's, New Beckenham, (by the Rev. Robert Bolton Ransford, Vicar of St. Jude's, Herne Hill, co. Surrey), on Wednesday, 20 January 1892, David Alan Stevenson (son of David Stevenson); born 21 July 1854; M.Inst. C.E.; Engineer to the Commissioner of Northern Lights.

Frederick William Sautelle Roberts, born at 37 De Vere Gardens, Kensington, London, on Monday, 19 June, bapt. at St. Paul's, New Beckenham, co. Kent, 26 July 1899.

I

I

Maria Isabella, born 22 August 1825; marr. at Meerut, North-West Provinces, India, 20 October 1842, Lieut.-Colonel William Maximilian George Maconochie-Welwood of Meadowbank House, co. Midlothian, and of Garvoch, co. Fife (4th son of Alexander Maconochie-Welwood, D.L., Senator of the College of Justice in Scotland, as Lord Meadowbank, by Anne his wife, eldest dau. of the Rt. Honble Lord President Robert Blair of Avontown); of the Honble East India Co.'s Service; formerly Captain 2nd Bengal Light Cavalry, Lieut.-Colonel Edinburgh Artillery and Major Fife Artillery Militia, retired in 1873; died at Brighton, co. Sussex, aged 65, on Friday, 22 December 1882, and bur. in the family vault at Kirknewton. Will dated 1 February 1874, proved (Prin. Reg., 862, 83) 6 October 1883, by Maria Isabella Maconochie-Welwood of "Edgehill," Sydenham, co. Kent, the relict, the surviving Exͦor for England. She died at "Stellenburg," Tunbridge Wells, co. Kent, aged 61, on Christmas Day, Saturday, 25 December, and was bur. in the cemetery at Tunbridge Wells 31 December 1886. Will dated 30 October 1884, with two codicils dated respectively 6 March 1885 and 10 September 1886, proved (Prin. Reg., 296, 87) 17 March 1887, by David Duncan of 10 Hill Street, in the City of Edinburgh, Advocate, the surviving Exͦor.

A

A

Frances Isabella,⹂General Sir Abraham Roberts, G.C.B.; born at⹂Isabella, dau. of Abraham
dau. of George | Waterford 11 April 1784; joined the Waterford | Bunbury of Kilfeacle, co.
Poyntz Ricketts | Militia 1801, appointed to the 48th Regiment of Foot | Tipperary, Captain 62nd
of the Bengal | 1 January 1803, and joined the Honble East India | Regiment of Foot; born at
Civil Service, by | Co.'s Service 1804; Lieutenant 13th Bengal Native | Cathlaw, co. Linlithgow,
Sophia Sarah Jane | Infantry 19 March 1805, Brevet Captain 1 January | 19 January 1799; marr.
his wife, youngest | 1818, Major 27th Native Infantry 24 September 1826 | at Benares, India, 2 Au-
child of Captain | to 28 September 1831, Lieut.-Colonel 28 September | gust 1830. She marr.
Richard Pierce of | 1831, Colonel 10 November 1843, Major-General 20 | 1stly Hamilton George
the "Halsewell" | June 1854, Lieut.-General 13 October 1857, General | Maxwell of Ardwell, N.B.,
East Indiaman, | 3 October 1864; Colonel 101st Regiment (Royal | Major Bengal Army, who
and cousin of | Bengal Fusiliers) 30 September 1862–73; served under | died 17 June 1829. She
Robert Banks, | Lord Lake in the Sutlej Campaign 1805, in Bundelcund, | died at Hampton Court
2nd Earl of | against the Pindarees, and acted as Brigade-Major at | Palace, aged 83, on Tuesday,
Liverpool; marr. | the sieges of Komona and Gunowrie 1806–7; served | 7 March, and was bur. in
at Moydapore, | under Sir William Richards in the Nepaul War | the churchyard at Hampton,
India, 20 July | 1814–15, at the storming of the fort of Kalunga (war | co. Middlesex, 11 March
1820; died, aged | medal); commanded his regiment at Birla Ke Tehee | 1882. Will dated 1 No-
24, 14 May 1827, | in December 1814, where he successfully engaged | vember 1880, proved (Prin.
and bur. at | and captured the chief and many others, completely | Reg., 722, 82) 2 Septem-
Subathu, India. | routing the enemy; appointed Brigadier-General in the | ber 1882, by Jonas Stawell
1st wife. | first Afghan War 1838–42; commanded Shah Shuja's | of 23 Victoria Square,
force in 1840, and was present at the storming and | Clifton, in the City and
capture of Ghuznee (medal and 2nd-class Dooranee | County of Bristol, a Major
Order); commanded the Peshawar division in India 1852–54; | in Her Majesty's Army,
created C.B. 20 December 1839, K.C.B. 28 March 1865, G.C.B. | and Thomas Parr of 41
8 December 1873; died at his residence, 25 Royal York Crescent, | Broad Street, Bristol, the
Clifton, co. Gloucester, in his 90th year, on Sunday 28 December | Exors. 2nd wife.
1873, bur. at the parish church, Clifton, 2 January 1874. M.I.
Will dated 8 January 1873, proved at Bristol 14 January 1874, by
John Davis Sherston of the parish of Bramshaw, co. Southampton,
and Bunbury Taylor of 23 Stanley Gardens, Notting Hill, in the
parish of Kensington, co. Middlesex, the Exors.

K

I

Major-General George Ricketts Roberts of 35 Lee Park, Lee, co. Kent,⹂Harriett, only dau. of
formerly of the Bengal Staff Corps; born at Meerut, North-West Provinces, | Thomas Roberts of
India, 8 February 1827; educated at Clifton, Woolwich and Addiscombe; | the Honble East India
entered the Army as Ensign 7 June 1844, Lieutenant 1 July 1846, Captain | Co.'s Service, Captain
23 November 1856, Major 7 June 1864, Lieut.-Colonel 7 June 1870, Brevet | 51st Bengal Native
Colonel 7 June 1875, and Deputy Commissary-General; retired with hon. | Infantry, by Harriett
rank of Major-General 15 December 1880; served with the 41st Bengal | his wife, 3rd dau. of
Native Infantry at Moodkee, Ferozeshah and Aliwall, with the reserve of the | William Lowndes of
Sutlej Army and at the battle of Sabraon 1845–46 (medal with clasp), with the | Chesham, co. Buck-
force that took possession of the Jullundhur Doab in 1846, and with that | ingham, a Commis-
which marched the same year to coerce Shiekh Imuum-u-Deen of Cashmere; | sioner of Excise, J.P.;
Interpreter and Quarter-Master of the regiment when sent from Delhi to | born at Mussoorie,
Moultan across the Desert via Hansi Hisser Rohtuk and Bahawalpore in 1849, | North-West Provinces,
also when it formed part of the Moultan Brigade that in 1852 proceeded | India, 29 May 1836;
against Ameer Ally Murad of Scinde; appointed to the Commissariat | marr. at the Cathedral,
Department 8 October 1852, and in 1858 in charge of Sir Edward Lugard's | Waterford (by the
Force at Benares (medal, mentioned in despatches); in 1858–59 served as | Very Rev. the Dean
Commissariat Officer with the Brigade under Colonel R. Taylor, 79th | of Waterford, assisted
Highlanders, which formed part of Sir Hope Grant's Force in Oudh; present | by the Rev. William
at the taking of Jugdespore and other Tram Gogra operations; twice thanked | John Price), on
by Government of India for services during | Friday, 6 March 1857.
cholera epidemics, and for his conduct of | (See page 2.)
the duties of Principal Executive Com-
missariat Officer with the camp assembled
at Delhi in 1876 for H.R.H. the Prince
of Wales (now King Edward VII.)

L

10

A

Captain Sir Samuel Roberts of Belmont, co. Waterford, C.B., R.N.; born═Rosamond, eldest
2 July 1785; joined the Navy November 1797, as first-class Volunteer on | dau. of Benjamin
board the "Expedition" (Lieut.-Commander John Hinton) lying at | Roberts of Wex-
Waterford, and was on continuous service for 21 years; engaged with and | ford; marriage
under fire of the enemy 53 times; in Sir John Warren's action at the | licence dated 30
capture of the Loire frigate; in command (at 15 years of age) of the boats | May 1818; died,
manned with 25 men, and with small arms only, captured at Leogan, five | aged 46, 3 No-
well-armed French schooners, having on board 250 soldiers; promoted | vember 1844, and
Lieutenant in the "Superb" 22 May 1806, 1st Lieutenant to the | bur. at the French
"Unicorn" at the destruction of the French shipping in Aix Roads in | Church, Waterford.
April 1809; in January and February 1810 he commanded the boats of | M.I.
the "Armide," in conjunction with those of a squadron, at the capture and
destruction of 15 of the enemy's coasting vessels near Rochelle; on 4 May
1810, with the boats of the "Armide," "Monkey" and "Daring" brigs
under his orders, he effected the destruction of 13 out of a convoy of 17
sail; defended, at the Ile de Ré, by batteries on shore, two armed luggars
and several pinnaces; promoted Captain 6 December 1813, in command
of the "Meteor" bomb 19 February 1814; in that vessel he accompanied
a detachment of troops under Major-General Ross to North America,
serving in the expeditions against Alexandria, Baltimore and New Orleans,
and prior to the attack on the latter place he commanded a division of
boats at the capture on Lake Borgue, 14 December 1814, of five American
gun vessels; advanced to post rank 4 and 13 June, and nominated C.B.
August 1815; Senior Officer in Court of Portugal during war between
Don Pedro and Don Miguel; knighted by the Lord-Lieutenant of Ireland
23 June 1833; died 16 December 1848, and bur. at the French Church,
Waterford. M.I. Will dated 10 August 1846, proved 14 February 1850.

Henry Paget Roberts, died
young, and bur. at the French
Church, Waterford. M.I.

K   K

Harriett Amy Lowndes,	George Grant Roberts,	Arthur Roberts, born	Frances, born 19
born at 24 Montpellier	born 4 January 1860;	9 June 1861, died	September, died 23
Square, Knightsbridge,	died 4 September 1861,	the following day,	September 1862, and
London, on Friday, 30	and bur. at Nyne Tal,	and bur. at Nyne	bur. at Agra, North-
December 1857.	India.	Tal.	West Provinces, India.

Catherine Isabella, born at Agra, North-West Provinces, on | Frederick Roberts, born
Saturday, 26 November 1864; marr. at St. Michael and All Angels', | 28 August, died 25 Sep-
Blackheath Park, co. Kent (by the Rev. Arthur Evelyn Barnes- | tember 1866, and bur. at
Lawrence, the Vicar, assisted by the Rev. Baring Baring-Gould), | Darjeeling, Bengal, India.
on Saturday, 4 July 1896, Arthur Beresford Dowling (son of the
Rev. Barré Beresford Dowling, Rector of Brown-Candover with ────
Chilton-Candover, co. Hants, by Mary Ursula his wife, dau. of the
Rev. Henry George Wells, Rector of Kingsworthy, co. Hants); | Thomas Roberts, born at
born on Christmas Day, 25 December 1865, bapt. at Brown- | Lucknow, India, 14 Sep-
Candover 8 April 1866; educated at Winchester College. | tember, and bur. there
                                                              | 18 September 1878.

L

Field-Marshal the Rt. Honble Sir Frederick Sleigh Roberts, Earl Roberts, and Viscount St. Pierre of Kandahar in Afghanistan, and Pretoria in the Transvaal Colony, and of the City of Waterford, and Baron Roberts of Kandahar in Afghanistan and of the City of Waterford, all in the peerage of the United Kingdom, and a Baronet, K.G., K.P., P.C., G.C.B., G.C.S.I., G.C.I.E., O.M., V.C., D.C.L., Lit.D., LL.D.; born at Cawnpore, North-West Provinces, India, 30 September 1832, and bapt. there; educated at Eton, Sandhurst and Addiscombe; entered the Bengal Artillery as 2nd Lieutenant 12 December 1851, Lieutenant 3 June 1857, Captain 12 November 1860, Brevet Major 12 November 1860, Brevet Lieut.-Colonel 15 August 1868, Brevet Colonel 30 January 1875, Major-General 31 December 1878, Lieut.-General 26 July 1883, General 28 November 1890, Field-Marshal 25 May 1895; served throughout the Indian Mutiny 1857–58, at the siege and capture of Delhi (wounded, horse shot), actions of Bolundshuhur (horse shot), Allyghur, Agra, Kunoj (horse wounded) and Bundhera; skirmishes during the operations connected with the relief of Lucknow; operations at Cawnpore, defeat of the Gwalior contingent, action of Khodagunge, re-occupation of Futtehghur, storming of Meeangunga, action of Koorsee, and operations ending with the capture of Lucknow (mentioned in despatches, "London Gazette," 15 December 1857, 16 January, 29 January, 22 February, 25 May, 31 May and 8 June 1858; received the thanks of the Governor-General of India, medal with three clasps, Brevet of Major, V.C.); served in the North-West Frontier of India Expedition 1863, at the storming of Laloo, capture of Umbeylah, and destruction of Mulkah (medal with clasp); served in the Abyssinian Expedition 1868, and superintended the re-embarkation of the entire army (mentioned in despatches, "London Gazette," 30 June, 3 July and 10 July 1868 (medal, Brevet of Lieut.-Colonel); served in the Looshai Expedition 1871–72, at the capture of Kholel villages and attack on the Northlang range, commanded the troops engaged at the burning of the village of Taikoom (mentioned in despatches, "London Gazette," 21 June 1872); served in the Afghan War 1878–80, commanded Kuram Valley Field Force at capture of Peiwar Kotal, reconnaissance to summit of Shutar Garden Pass, attack by Mangols in Sapari Pass, occupation of the Khost district and reconnaissance up Khuram river; commanded Kabul Field Force at occupation of Kabul, battle of Charasiah, commanded the whole force in march from Kabul to the relief of Kandahar and battle of 1 September 1880 (mentioned in despatches "London Gazette," 4 February, 21 February, 21 March, 13 May and 7 November 1879, 16 January, 4 May and 3 December 1880; received thanks of both Houses of Parliament 4 August 1879 and 5 May 1881, and created a Baronet; thanked by Government of India, and Governor-General in Council; medal with four clasps, bronze star, K.C.B., G.C.B.); served in Burmese Expedition 1886, commanded the Army in Burma after capture of Mandalay (thanked by Government of India, mentioned in despatches, "London Gazette," 2 September 1887, clasp); served as Field-Marshal Commanding-in-Chief the Forces in South Africa 1899–1900, at the operations in the Orange Free State February to May 1900, including operations at Paardeburg 17 to 26 February; relieved Kimberley 15 February, took Commandant Cronje and the Western Army prisoners 27 February 1900; actions at Poplar Grove, Driefontein, Vet River (5 and 6 May) and Zand River; operations in the Transvaal in May and June 1900, including actions near Johannesburg, Pretoria and Diamond Hill (11 and 12 June); operations in the Transvaal, East of Pretoria, July to 29 November 1900, including action at Belfast (26 and 27 August) (medal with six clasps); Colonel-Commandant Royal Artillery 1896–1900, Colonel Irish Guards from 1900, Hon. Colonel 10th Volunteer Battalion (2nd London) King's Royal Rifle Corps from 1887, of the 3rd Battalion Sherwood Foresters (Nottinghamshire and Derbyshire Regiment) from 1888, of the 1st Newcastle-on-Tyne Volunteer Artillery (Western Division R.A.) from 1894, of the Waterford Artillery Militia (Southern Division R.A.) from 1896, of the 3rd Battalion Loyal North Lancashire Regiment (Militia) from 1898, of the City of London Imperial Volunteers 1900, of the 3rd Battalion Gloucestershire Regiment (Militia) from 1900, and of the 2nd Hampshire Volunteer Artillery, R.G.A. (Militia); admitted to the Freedom of the Cities of London, Edinburgh, Glasgow, Bristol, Birmingham, Newcastle-on-Tyne, Dundee, Waterford, Cardiff and Chesterfield, and to the Royal Boroughs of Inverness, Wick, Dunbar and Windsor; Member of Council of Government of Madras from November 1881 to August 1885; Commander-in-Chief in India November 1885 to April 1893; Commander of the Forces in Ireland 1 October 1895 to December 1899; Commander-in-Chief of the Army since 1901; bore Second Sword at Coronation of H.M. King Edward VII. 1902; Hon. D.C.L. Oxford and LL.D. Dublin 1881, Hon. LL.D. Cambridge 1893, Hon. D.Lit. Dublin 1901 (degree conferred at Dublin 30 June 1903); a Knight of Justice of the Order of St. John of Jerusalem in England; a Knight of the Order of the Black Eagle of Prussia; C.B. (mil.) 1872, K.C.B. (mil.) 1879, G.C.B. (mil.) 1880, G.C.I.E. 1887, G.C.S.I. 1893, P.C. 1895, K.G. 1901, Order of Merit 1902; created a Baronet 1881, Baron Roberts of Kandahar in Afghanistan and of the City of Waterford 1892, Viscount St. Pierre and Earl Roberts of Afghanistan, and of Pretoria in the Transvaal Colony, and of the City of Waterford 1901, all in the Peerage of the United Kingdom; Author of "Rise of Wellington," 1895, "Forty-one Years in India," 1897.

=Norah Henrietta (C.I. and Member of the Order of the Royal Red Cross), youngest daughter of John Bews, Captain 73rd Regiment of Foot, and Paymaster-General of Royal Irish Constabulary, co. Mayo, by Mary Elizabeth his wife; born 17 March, bapt. at Castlebar, co. Mayo (by the Rev. Thomas Atkinson), 15 April 1838; marr. at St. Patrick's, Waterford (by the Rev. H. Ryland, Chancellor of the Cathedral), on Tuesday, 17 May 1859.

K

M

K
|

Harriet Mercer, born at Calcutta, India, 16 December 1833; died unmarried at Hampton Court Palace, aged 47, on Friday, 8 October, bur. at Hampton, co. Middlesex, 12 October 1880. Will dated 23 January 1874, proved (Prin. Reg., 252, 81) 1 March 1881, by Sir Frederick Sleigh Roberts of " Edgehill," Sydenham, co. Kent, G.C.B., V.C., C.I.E., the brother, the sole Exor.

M
|

Nora Frederica, born 10 March 1860, and bapt. at Simla, Punjab, India; died 3 March 1861, and bur. at Simla.	Eveleen Sautelle, born at Royal York Crescent, Clifton, co. Gloucester, on Saturday, 18 July, bapt. at Llandaff, co. Glamorgan, 29 August 1868; died 8 February 1869, and bur. at sea.	Frederick Henry Roberts, born at Simla 27 July 1869; died at Simla 20 August 1869, and bur. there.	Aileen Mary, born 20 September 1870, and bapt. at Simla.

Frederick Hugh Sherston Roberts, V.C.; born at Simla, Punjab, India, 8 January 1872; entered the Army as 2nd Lieutenant King's Royal Rifle Corps 10 June 1891, Lieutenant 22 June 1894, A.D.C. to General Officer Commanding the Forces, Ireland, 14 December 1895; served in Isazai Expedition 1892; served in the Waziristan Expedition 1894–95 as Orderly Officer to General Officer Commanding (mentioned in despatches); served with the Chitral Relief Force 1895; served in Nile Expedition 1898, present at the battle of Omdurman (mentioned in despatches, "London Gazette," 30 September 1898); served in South African War 1899, present at the battle of Colenso, where for conspicuous bravery the V.C. was awarded after his death; died of wounds received at that battle 17 December 1899, and bur. at Chieveley, Natal. M.I.	Ada Edwina Stewart, born at Simla 28 March 1875, and bapt. there.

Teague.

John Teague (son of John Teague, Governor of Giltspur Compter Prison, ⊤ Sophia Ann, dau. London); born 14 January, bapt. at St. Olave's, Silver Street, London, 8 February 1779; succeeded his father at the Poultry Compter 26 April 1803, and was appointed to Giltspur Street Compter and Ludgate (then debtors' prisons) 25 September 1804, and to the House of Correction in December 1815, on the removal of the debtors from Giltspur Street and Newgate to the new prison in Whitecross Street, and the removal of the House of Correction prisoners from Newgate to Giltspur Street; died at the Governor's House, Compter, Giltspur Street, West Smithfield, London, aged 62, 17 July, bur. in the East vault at St. Sepulchre's, London, 24 July 1841. *Memorial ring to him and his wife, inscribed "*SOPHIA TEAGUE OB: 5 JUNE 1840, ÆT. 63, JOHN TEAGUE OB: 17 JULY 1841, ÆT. 62," *in the possession of their great-grand-daughter, Gertrude Clara Harker. Miniature portrait in the possession of his grandson, George Fletcher Teague, and a silhouette in the possession of his great-grand-daughter, Gertrude Clara Harker.* Will dated 16 July 1834, proved (P.C.C., 648, 41) 20 September 1841, by James Thomson, one of the surviving Exors. Power reserved to Joseph Payne the other surviving Exor.

Sophia Ann, dau. of Nicholas Alexander; marr. at St. Botolph's, Bishopsgate, London, 28 February 1807; died at Giltspur Street, West Smithfield, London, aged 63, on Friday, 5 June, bur. in the East vault at St. Sepulchre's, London, 11 June 1840.

A

Sophia Ann, born 12 September, bapt. at St. Sepulchre's, London, 20 November 1808; died at Giltspur Street, West Smithfield, London, aged 19 months, 22 April, bur. at St. Sepulchre's, London, 27 April 1810.

—

John James Teague, born 6 February, bapt. at St. Sepulchre's, London, 4 March 1810; died at Giltspur Street, West Smithfield, London, aged 12 months, 19 February, bur. at St. Sepulchre's, London, 24 February 1811.

James Alexander Teague ⊤ Harriette, only dau. of Charles Fletcher of of 28 Spencer Street, Goswell Road, Clerkenwell, London; born 5 December 1811, bapt. at St. Sepulchre's, London, 5 January 1812; died, aged 40, 14 February, bur. in Nunhead Cemetery, co. Surrey, 19 February 1852. *Oil painting in the possession of his son, George Fletcher Teague, and a silhouette in the possession of his grand-daughter, Gertrude Clara Harker.*

Harriette, only dau. of Charles Fletcher of Upper Belgrave Terrace, Pimlico, London, by Harriet Elms his wife; born 23 July, bapt. at St. Mary-le-Strand, London, 28 August 1813; marr. at St. Mary's, Islington, London, 14 June 1838; died, aged 39, 28 September, bur. at Woodford, co. Essex, 2 October 1852. *Oil painting in the possession of her son, George Fletcher Teague.* Admon was granted (P.C.C.) 29 January 1853, to Caroline Frances Teague, spinster, the lawful aunt and curatrix or guardian lawfully assigned to Harriette Sophia Teague, spinster, Clara Champney Teague, spinster, and George Fletcher Teague, minors, and Alexander Crichton Teague, an infant, the natural and lawful children of deceased, for use and benefit until age of 21; Harriet Champney, widow, the grandmother and only next of kin, having first renounced their curation or guardianship.

B

Harriette Sophia, born 10 August, bapt. at St. James', Clerkenwell, London, 8 September 1839; died unmarried at 19 Hilldrop Crescent, Camden Road, London, aged 40, 6 February, bur. in Nunhead Cemetery 11 February 1880. Will dated 28 February 1879, proved (Prin. Reg., 328, 80) 11 March 1880, by George Fletcher Teague of 19 Hilldrop Crescent, Camden Road, London, the brother, the sole Exor.

Caroline Frances, born 2 January, bapt. at St. Sepulchre's, London, 30 January 1814; died unmarried at 12 Hillmarten Road, Camden Road, London, aged 81, on Saturday, 27 April, bur. in Highgate Cemetery, London, 1 May 1895. M.I. *Silhouette as a child, in the possession of her great-niece, Gertrude Clara Harker.* Admͦn was granted at the Principal Registry 19 June 1895, to George Fletcher Teague, the nephew.

C. F. Teague.

Harriet, born 13 September, bapt. at St. Sepulchre's, London (by the Rev. Charles Cornelius Chambers), 17 October 1815; died unmarried at 12 Hillmarten Road, Camden Road, London, aged 79, on Sunday, 16 September, bur. in Highgate Cemetery, London, 19 September 1894. M.I. *Silhouette as a child, in the possession of her great-niece, Gertrude Clara Harker.* Admͦn was granted at the Principal Registry 5 July 1895, to George Fletcher Teague, the nephew.

Sophia, born 23 December 1817, bapt. at St. Sepulchre's, London (by the Rev. Thomas Harrison), 1 April 1818; died unmarried, aged 33, 25 July, bur. in Nunhead Cemetery, co. Surrey, 30 July 1851. *Silhouette as a child, in the possession of her great-niece, Gertrude Clara Harker.*

A

Sophia Caroline, born at 28 Spencer Street, Goswell Road, Clerkenwell, London, 21 August, bapt. at St. James', Clerkenwell, 16 September 1840; marr. at St. Luke's, West Holloway, co. Middlesex (by the Rev. Sparks Bellett Sealy, assisted by the Rev. George Albert Rogers, the Vicar), on Thursday, 17 October 1867, John Cooke Harker of "Danehurst," Champion Hill, co. Surrey; born 22 August 1831. She died at "Fernside," Hornsey Lane, co. Middlesex, aged 38, on Sunday, 29 December 1878, and was bur. in Highgate Cemetery, London, 2 January 1879. M.I. He marr. 2ndly at St. Giles', Camberwell, co. Surrey (by the Rev. James Henry Hazell, Vicar of St. Andrew's, Peckham, co. Surrey), on Wednesday, 19 April 1882, Caroline Sarah, younger dau. of Thomas Goodman of Islington, co. Middlesex; born 3 July 1844.

Sophia Caroline Teague

B

Clara Champney, born 20 November, bapt. at St. James', Clerkenwell, London, 28 December 1842; died unmarried at 19 Hilldrop Crescent, Camden Road, London, aged 26, 14 July, bur. in Nunhead Cemetery, co. Surrey, 20 July 1869. Will dated 12 July 1869, proved (Prin. Reg., 674, 69) 23 October 1869, by George Fletcher Teague of 19 Hilldrop Crescent, Camden Road, London, the brother, the sole Exͦr.

Clara. C. Teague.

George Fletcher=Eliza Louisa Emma, Teague of 32 Hilldrop Road, Camden Road, London; born 19 January, bapt. at St. James', Clerkenwell, London, 16 February 1844.

Eliza Louisa Emma, only child of John Sheldrick of Camden Town, co. Middlesex, by Eliza his wife, dau. of Thomas Hacker; born at King Square, Goswell Road, London, 12 November 1856, bapt. at St. Barnabas', King Square, 14 January 1857; marr. at the parish church, Kentish Town, co. Middlesex, 12 August 1882.

Alexander Crichton Teague, born 28 December 1846, bapt. at St. James', Clerkenwell, London, 9 April 1847; died, aged 10, bur. in Nunhead Cemetery 2 March 1857.

George F. Teague

Fac-simile of a Portrait of John South of Little Bentley, co. Essex; baptised at Little Bentley 25 March 1792, died 9 March 1857; in the possession of John Arthur South, his grandson.

South of Little Bentley, co. Essex.

Rebecca, dau. of John Lord [bur. at Dovercourt, co. Essex, 24 March 1852, aged 84], by Elizabeth Inman his wife [bur. at Dovercourt 5 August 1851, aged 77]; marr. by licence at Little Bentley, co. Essex, 28 December 1820; bur. there 4 February 1825. 1st wife.

═ John South of Little Bentley, afterwards of Foulton Hall, Ramsey, both co. Essex (son of Thomas South of Little Bentley, by Martha his wife); bapt. at Little Bentley 25 March 1792; died, aged 65, 9 March, bur. at Little Bentley 14 March 1857. M.I.

═ Sarah, dau. of Thomas Burrows of Little Oakley, co. Essex, by Sarah Lord his wife; born 21 January, bapt. privately at Little Oakley 24 January 1796, and received into the church there 6 August 1797; marr. by licence at Little Oakley (by the Rev. J. Thomas Scott) 20 May 1825; marr. 1stly at Little Oakley 28 August 1818, Edward Rayner of Little Oakley (son of John Rayner of Great Oakley, co. Essex, by Elizabeth his wife); bapt. at Great Oakley 11 January 1790; died, leaving issue, aged 36, 27 September, bur. at Great Oakley 30 September 1824. Will dated 25 September 1824, proved in the Archdeaconry Court of Colchester 29 May 1825. She died at Manningtree, co. Essex, aged 78, 17 March, and was bur. at Little Bentley 22 March 1875. M.I. 2nd wife.

E Rayner

Sarah South

A

J South

Thomas South, bapt. at Little Bentley 3 December 1822; died, aged 19, 7 April, bur. at Little Bentley 5 March 1841. M.I.

Thomas South

Clementina, born at Little Bentley 3 March, bapt. there 9 May 1824; marr. at Ramsey 11 November 1843, George Blumer of Hartlepool, co. Durham, and of Harwich, co. Essex (eldest son of Luke Blumer of Harwich, afterwards of Hartlepool, by Margaret Wheatley of South Shields, co. Durham, his 1st wife); born at South Shields 24 October, bapt. at St. Hilda's, South Shields, 19 November 1817. Clementina, his wife, died at Hartlepool, aged 24, 3 March, and was bur. in the churchyard at Hartlepool 8 March 1848. M.I. He marr. 2ndly at Chapter Row Chapel, South Shields, 17 July 1849, Elizabeth, dau. of William Garritt of South Shields; born at South Shields 12 January, bapt. at St. Hilda's, South Shields, 16 February 1820; died at York 28 July, bur. in the cemetery at West Hartlepool on Monday, 31 July 1893. Will dated 27 March 1889, proved at Durham 15 September 1893, by Francis Yeoman, the sole Exor. He died at Hartlepool, aged 50, 27 December, and was bur. in the churchyard at St. Hilda's, Hartlepool, 30 December 1867. M.I. Will dated 11 April 1866, proved at Durham 12 March 1868, by William Gray of Greatham, co. Durham, Robert Brewis of Hartlepool, co. Durham, and John George Blumer of Hartlepool, the son, the Exors.

Luke Blumer

Elizabeth Blumer

Clementina South

George Blumer

(See Pedigree of Blumer, Vol. 9, page 76.)

Elizabeth, marr. at Ramsey, co. Essex, 22 August 1849, Leonard Roach of Melbourne, Australia (son of James Roach); she died in Melbourne in 1887. ⊤⊥

John South of Ramsey, co. Essex,⊤Sarah, 2nd dau. of Edward Cooper of and afterwards of Alton Hall, Stutton, co. Suffolk (twin with Maria); born 24 June 1828; died at Alton Hall, Stutton, on Sunday, 30 October, bur. in the churchyard at Stutton on Thursday, 3 November 1892. M.I. Will dated 6 July 1889, proved at Ipswich 24 December 1892, by Cyril Frederick South, the son, Henry Spurling and Sarah South, the relict, the Exors.

Great Oakley, co. Essex, by Sarah his wife, dau. of James Allsop of Great

Oakley (see *Pedigree of Cooper, Vol. 5, page 112*); born 20 September, bapt. at Great Oakley 3 November 1837; marr. there by licence (by the Rev. John Howard Marsden, B.D., Rural Dean), 11 February 1857.

Sarah Kate, born at Ramsey 15 November, bapt. there 11 December 1857.

John Arthur South, born at Ramsey 11 February, bapt. there 9 March 1859.

Gertrude, born at Ramsey 9 April, bapt. there 9 May 1860; marr. by licence at Stutton on Thursday, 21 October 1880 (marriage settlements dated 14 October 1880, Trustees, John South of Alton Hall, Stutton [who died 30 October 1892, his son, John Arthur South, being appointed in his stead 12 December 1893], and William Henry Crisp [who died 1 June 1902, Cooper South being appointed in his stead]), to Frederick Arthur Crisp of Grove Park, Denmark Hill, and of "Broadhurst," Godalming, both co. Surrey (eldest son of Frederick Augustus Crisp of Playford Hall, co. Suffolk, by Sarah his wife, 4th dau. of John Steedman of Walworth, co. Surrey [see *Pedigree of Steedman, page 89*]); born at Walworth 27 June, bapt. at St. Mary, Newington, co. Surrey, 29 October 1851. ⊤⊥

Maria (twin with John), born 24 June 1828; marr. at Llandaff Cathedral 3 December 1856, Edward Cooper of St. Osyth, co. Essex (son of Edward Cooper of Great Oakley, co. Essex, by Sarah his wife, dau. of James Allsop of Great Oakley [see *Pedigree of Cooper, Vol. 5, page 112*]); born 10 June, bapt. at Great Oakley 21 June 1833; died s.p. at Little Oakley Lodge, aged 58, 17 January, bur. at Great Oakley 22 January 1892. Will dated 19 December 1891, with codicil dated 13 January 1892, proved at Ipswich 18 February 1892, by Russell Wontner of Little Oakley and Amis Hempson of Ramsey, the Exōrs. She died at Little Oakley Lodge 3 November, and was bur. at Little Oakley 7 November 1891.

Anna, born 1 June 1830, bapt. at Ramsey, co. Essex (by the Rev. Thomas Greene Hickman) 11 February 1832; marr. by licence at Ramsey (by the Rev. William Bull) 5 October 1849, the Rev. Edwin Fice (son of Samuel Fice); appointed first Rector of Canton, co. Glamorgan, 1858; died at Cwmbran, co. Monmouth, aged 42, 21 August, bur. there 26 August 1863. Memorial tablet to his memory in the church at Canton. Will dated 7 October 1862, proved at Llandaff 28 November 1863, by William Rice of Tewkesbury, co. Gloucester, and Richard Rice of Tewkesbury, the Exōrs. She died at St. George's Hospital, Hyde Park Corner, London, 14 October, and was bur. in Kensal Green Cemetery, London, 17 October 1870. Admōn was granted at the Principal Registry 24 October 1871, to Samuel Edwin Fice of Great Malvern, co. Worcester, the son, and one of the next of kin.

Edward Stanley South, born at Ramsey 28 December 1861, bapt. there 28 January 1862; died 31 May, bur. at Ramsey 4 June 1863. M.I.

Cyril Frederick=Ellen Maria, only dau. of George Mumford Sexton of South, born at Ramsey 16 January, bapt. there 8 February 1863.

Wherstead, afterwards of Sproughton, both co. Suffolk, by Ellen Matilda his wife, dau. of William Stutter Frost of Brent Eleigh, co. Suffolk; born at Wherstead Hall 26 March, bapt. at Wherstead 24 April 1866; marr. at St. Peter's, Ipswich, co. Suffolk (by the Rev. William Berry, the Vicar, and the Honble and Rev. Walter William Brabazon Ponsonby, Rector of Stutton, co. Suffolk), on Wednesday, 11 October 1893.

(See *Pedigree of Sexton, Vol. 6, page 21.*)

Winifred, born at Uttoxeter, co. Stafford, at 9 p.m., 17 April, bapt. there 26 June 1895.

John Mumford South, born at Uttoxeter on Thursday, 25 August 1898, bapt. there 15 March 1899.

Enid, born at Uttoxeter at 5.15 a.m. on Sunday, 19 October 1902, bapt. at Dunston, co. Stafford, on Tuesday, 24 March 1903.

A

Samuel South, bapt. privately (by the Rev. Thomas Greene Hickman), 11 February 1833 (baptism registered at Ramsey, co. Essex); died at Ramsey, aged 19, 7 June, bur. at Little Bentley, co. Essex, 13 June 1851. M.I.

James South (twin with Mahala), bapt. privately (by the Rev. Thomas Greene Hickman) 6 March 1834 (baptism registered at Ramsey); died, aged one week, bur. at Ramsey 12 March 1834.

—

Mahala (twin with James), bapt. privately (by the Rev. Thomas Greene Hickman) 6 March 1834 (baptism registered at Ramsey); died, aged one week, bur. at Ramsey 12 March 1834.

Frederick South, bapt. at Ramsey (by the Rev. John Adeney) 10 April 1837; died, aged 18 months, bur. at Ramsey 8 October 1839.

—

James South, bapt. at Ramsey (by the Rev. John Adeney) 28 June, and bur. at Ramsey 4 July 1839.

B

Maude, born at Ramsey 4 October, bapt. there 5 November 1865.

—

Marion Edith, born at Ramsey 18 December 1867, bapt. there 23 February 1870; marr. at St. Peter's, Ipswich, co. Suffolk (by the Rev. William Berry, the Vicar) on St. Valentine's Day, Thursday, 14 February 1895 (marriage settlements dated 13 February 1895, Trustees, John Arthur South and Harold Percy Mason), to George Godson Mason of Ipswich (eldest son of George Calver Mason of Broadwater, Ipswich, by Lætitia Maria his wife, dau. of Charles Williams); born at Ipswich 18 May, bapt. at St. Peter's, Ipswich, 21 June 1869.

Edward Percy South, born at Ramsey 24 January, bapt. there 23 February 1870; died at Tunbridge Wells, co. Kent, aged 32, on Friday, 22 August, bur. in the churchyard at Stutton, co. Suffolk, on Wednesday, 27 August 1902. Will dated 17 August 1902, proved (Prin. Reg., 53, 1902) 23 October 1902, by John Arthur South, the brother, the sole Exor.

Cooper South, born at Ramsey 10 July, bapt. there 10 August 1873.

Goddard of The Lawn, Swindon, co. Wilts.

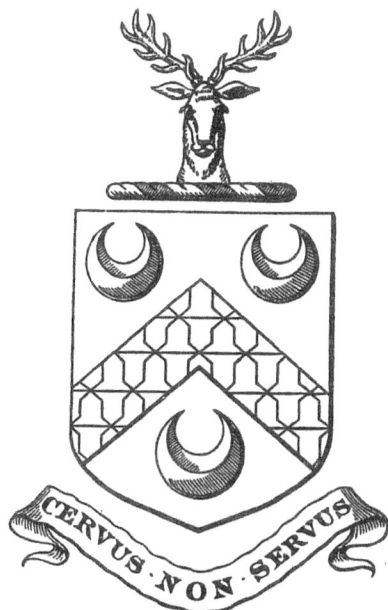

Arms on record in the College of Arms.—Gules, a chevron vair between three crescents argent.

Crest.—A stag's head affrontée, couped at the neck gules, attired or.

Motto.—Cervus non servus.

Ambrose Goddard of The Lawn, Swindon, co. Wilts (2nd son of Ambrose Goddard of The Lawn, Swindon, M.P. for co. Wilts, by Sarah his wife, only dau. and heiress of Thomas Williams of Pilrowth, co. Carmarthen); born 12 October, bapt. at Swindon 13 November 1779; of Christ Church, Oxford, matriculated 24 June 1798, aged 18, B.A. 1802; of the 10th Hussars, Lieutenant 22 November 1804, Captain 21 August 1806, resigned 1812; served in the Peninsular War; J.P. and D.L. for co. Wilts, High Sheriff 1819–20, M.P. for the Hundreds of Cricklade 1837 –41; died at The Crescent, Bath, co. Somerset, aged 75, on Wednesday, 29 November, bur. at the parish church, Swindon, 5 December 1854. M.I. Admon was granted (P.C.C.) 30 June 1855, to Ambrose Lethbridge Goddard, the son. ═ Jessie Dorothea, eldest dau. of Sir Thomas Buckler Lethbridge of Sandhill Park, co. Somerset, 2nd Bart., by Jessie Catherine his 1st wife, 3rd dau. of Thomas Hesketh, and sister of Sir Thomas Dalrymple Hesketh of Rufford Hall, co. Lancaster, 3rd Bart.; marr. at Bishop's Lydiard, co. Somerset (by the Rev. Lord William Somerset), 1 August 1818; died at Brighton, co. Sussex, aged 43, on Monday, 6 March, bur. at the parish church, Swindon, 16 March 1843. M.I.

A

Ambrose Lethbridge Goddard of The Lawn, Swindon; born in London on Thursday, 9 December 1819; educated at Harrow and at St. John's College, Cambridge; J.P. and D.L. for co. Wilts, M.P. for the Hundreds of Cricklade 1847–68, and 1874–80, when he retired; Major Royal Wiltshire Yeomanry Cavalry; Lord of the Manor of Swindon; died at the Manor House, Bournemouth, co. Hants, aged 79, 15 November, bur. at the Old Church, Swindon, 19 November 1898. Will dated 31 May 1898, proved (Prin. Reg., 1353, 98) 15 December 1898, by FitzRoy Pleydell Goddard and the Rev. Charles Frederick Goddard, the sons, the Exors. ═ Charlotte, elder dau. of Edward Ayshford Sanford of Nynehead Court, M.P. for co. Somerset, J.P. and D.L., F.R.S., by Henrietta his 1st wife, only surviving dau. of Sir William Langham of Cottesbrooke, co. Northampton, 8th Bart.; born 15 October, bapt. privately 17 October 1824 (baptism registered at Nynehead); marr. at Nynehead on Saturday, 14 August 1847.

B

Lieut.-Colonel Ambrose Ayshford Goddard, born at Chester Square, London, on Sunday, 7 May 1848; educated at Eton; entered the Grenadier Guards as Ensign and Lieutenant 16 September 1868, Captain 22 March 1871, Lieut.-Colonel 1879, and appointed Regimental Major 1883; served in the Egyptian Campaign at Suakim (Egyptian medal and clasp, and Khedive's star); died on board H.M.S. "Tyne," on his homeward voyage from Suakim, aged 37 years, on Monday, 25 May 1885, and bur. in the Valetta Military Cemetery, Malta. M.I. Brass tablet on South wall of the parish church, Swindon.

Jessie Henrietta, born at 58 Chester Square, London, on Wednesday, 24 April, bapt. at the parish church, Swindon, 7 June 1850.

John Hesketh Goddard, born 14 September 1821, and bapt. at Bath, co. Somerset ; Major 14th Light Dragoons, with which regiment he served throughout the Punjab Campaign 1848-49, including the action at Ramnuggur (with the charging squadrons), passage of the Chenab, and the battles of Chittian Wallah and Googerat (severely wounded, medal and clasps) ; died at Simla, Bengal, India, aged 32, 31 May 1854.

—

Thomas Henry Goddard, born 17 October 1824 ; died, aged 4 months, 24 February, bur. at the parish church, Swindon, 3 March 1825.

Jessie Dalrymple, born 22 October, bapt. at the parish church, Swindon, co. Wilts, 26 December 1825 ; marr. there (by the Rev. Edward Ayshford Sanford), on Thursday, 15 April 1847, Colonel Henry Hussey Vivian, Baron Swansea, of Singleton, co. Glamorgan (eldest son of John Henry Vivian of Singleton, M.P. for Swansea 1832-55, J.P. and D.L., F.R.S., F.G.S., Major Royal Stannary Artillery [brother of Lieut.-General Sir Richard Hussey, 1st Baron Vivian, G.C.B., &c.], by Sarah his wife, eldest dau. of Arthur Jones of The Priory, Reigate, co. Surrey, and of Caervallack, co. Flint) ; born at Singleton 6 July 1821 ; educated at Eton and at Trinity College, Cambridge ; Colonel 4th Glamorgan Rifle Volunteers ; J.P. and D.L. for co. Glamorgan, M.P. for Truro 1852-57, co. Glamorgan 1857-85, and for Swansea 1885-93, Chairman of Glamorganshire County Council ; F.G.S. ; Author of "Notes of a Tour in America," 1878 ; created a Baronet 13 May 1882, and elevated to the Peerage 9 June 1893, as Baron Swansea of Singleton, co. Glamorgan, in the Peerage of the United Kingdom.   She died, leaving issue a son, Ernest Ambrose, now 2nd Baron Swansea, at Singleton, aged 22, on Monday, 28 February 1848, and was bur. at Sketty, co. Glamorgan.   He marr. 2ndly 14 July 1853, Flora Caroline Elizabeth, only dau. of Sir Montague John Cholmeley of Easton Hall and Norton Place, co. Lincoln, 2nd Bart., M.P. for North Lincolnshire, by Lady Georgiana his wife, 5th dau. of William, 8th Duke of St. Alban's.   She died at Park Wern, Swansea, aged 35, leaving issue, on Saturday, 25 January 1868, and was bur. at Sketty.   He marr. 3rdly at Bretton Park, Wakefield, co. York, the seat of Wentworth Blackett Beaumont, on Thursday, 10 November 1870, Averil, dau. of Captain Richard Beaumont, R.N., by Susan Hussey his wife, 3rd dau. of Major-General Godfrey, 3rd Baron Macdonald, by whom he had issue. He died suddenly at Singleton Swansea, aged 73, on Wednesday, 28 November, and was bur. in Sketty Churchyard 3 December 1894.   Will dated 6 February 1894, proved (Prin. Reg., 336, 95) 21 March 1895, by the Rt. Honble Averil, Baroness Swansea, the relict, the Rt. Honble Ernest Ambrose, Baron Swansea, the Honble John Aubrey Vivian, William Graham Vivian and Arthur Pendarves Vivian, five of the Exors.

FitzRoy Pleydell Goddard of The Lawn, Swindon,═Eugenia Kathleen, dau. of Thomas Richard and of "The Comedy," Christian Malford, co. Wilts ; born at The Lawn, Swindon, on Sunday, 29 August, bapt. at the parish church, Swindon, 17 October 1852 ; of Christ Church, Oxford, matriculated 20 January 1871, aged 18 ; employed by the Indian Government in the Adaman and Nicobar Islands from February 1877 to March 1879, H.B.M.'s Consul in the Cape Verde Islands 10 April 1880, appointed Consul at Ajaccio, Corsica, 15 June 1885, but did not proceed ; appointed a Queen's Foreign Service Messenger 10 December 1885, retired 1 October 1895 ; J.P. for co. Wilts ; Major Royal Wiltshire Yeomanry Cavalry (granted the temporary rank of Major in the Army while serving with the Imperial Representative Corps in Australia November 1900), resigned his commission 13 March 1903 ; Lord of the Manor of Swindon and Wanborough.

Merry of Twyford Lodge, East Grinstead, co. Sussex, by Eugenia Mary Wallace his wife ; born at Twyford Lodge 12 October 1867, and bapt. at East Grinstead ; marr. at the parish church, Chippenham, co. Wilts, 1 June 1895 ; marr. 1stly at St. Peter's, Colchester, co. Essex (by the Rev. Henry Caddell, the Vicar), 12 June 1885, Alexander George Sutton of Christian Malford (3rd son of Sir Richard Sutton of Norwood Park, co. Nottingham, 4th Bart., by Harriet Anne his 2nd wife, eldest dau. of William Fitz-William Burton of Burton Hall, co. Carlow) ; born 19 August 1862 ; died, leaving issue, on the yacht "Creole" off Cowes, Isle of Wight, aged 30, 25 July, bur. in the cemetery at Ryde, Isle of Wight, 28 July 1893.

A | A

Charles Richard Goddard, born 12 April, bapt. at St. Peter's, Brighton, co. Sussex, 11 May 1831 (baptism entered in the Register of the parish church, Swindon, co. Wilts, 2 January 1832); Midshipman R.N.; "September 30, 1849. At Hong Kong, aged 18, Charles Richard, third son of Ambrose Goddard, esq. of the Lawn, Swindon. As one of the pirates was boarded by the Columbine's boats, Mr. Goddard, a midshipman, observed one of the enemy's crew descending into the hold with a lighted match. Guessing his purpose, Mr. Goddard leapt down after him, and lost his own life in attempting to arrest him. The fatal match had already been applied, and before another instant, the explosion had destroyed the vessel, Mr. Goddard, and eight or ten English seamen." (*Gent.'s Mag., Vol. 33, 1850, page 341.*)

Emma Caroline, born 19 July, bapt. at the Chapel of Ease, old church, Brighton, 14 August 1832 (baptism entered in the Register of the parish church, Swindon, 31 December 1832); marr. at the parish church, Swindon, on Thursday, 16 April 1857, the Rev. Greville Phillimore (5th son of Joseph Phillimore of Shiplake House, co. Oxford, M.P. for St. Mawes and Yarmouth, D.C.L., J.P., Chancellor of the dioceses of Oxford, Gloucester and Bristol, by Elizabeth his wife, dau. of the Rev. Walter Bagot, Rector of Blithfield and Leigh, co. Stafford); born in London 5 February 1821; educated at Westminster 1831, at Charterhouse 1832-38, and at Christ Church, Oxford, matriculated 30 May 1838, aged 17, Student 1838-52, B.A. 1841, M.A. 1845; Vicar of Down Ampney, co. Gloucester, 1851-67, Henley-on-Thames, co. Oxford, 1867-83, and of Ewelme, co. Oxford, July 1883 until his death; died at the Rectory, Ewelme, aged 62, on Monday, 21 January, bur. in the churchyard at Shiplake 25 January 1884. Will dated 9 January 1866, proved (Prin. Reg., 244, 84) 8 March 1884, by Emma Caroline Phillimore of Ewelme Rectory, Wallingford, co. Oxford, the relict, and Walter George Frank Phillimore of 4 Paper Buildings, Temple, co. Middlesex, D.C.L., the nephew, two of the Exors.

Edward Hesketh Goddard of 37 Elvaston Place, South Kensington, London; born at The Lawn, Swindon, on Friday, 19 October 1855, bapt. privately the same day (baptism registered at the parish church, Swindon); entered the Royal Glamorgan Militia 17 February 1875, and the Army as 2nd Lieutenant 31 January 1877, Lieutenant Royal Dublin Fusiliers 1 April 1880, Acting Adjutant 102nd Regimental District 1883-86, Adjutant 1st Battalion Royal Dublin Fusiliers 20 January 1886 to 13 April 1887, Captain the Cheshire Regiment 17 August 1887, and of the 2nd Battalion The Dorsetshire Regiment 5 October 1887; Adjutant 2nd Volunteer Battalion Essex Regiment 1 June 1891, retired 26 October 1895; Captain Royal Southern Reserve Regiment 1 June 1900 resigned 15 February 1901.

Dulcie Gwendoline, 3rd dau. of William Jones Loyd of Langleybury, co. Hertford, M.A., J.P., High Sheriff 1861, by Caroline Gertrude his wife, 2nd dau. of John Henry Vivian of Singleton, co. Glamorgan, M.P.; born at 77 Eaton Square, London, on Wednesday, 6 October, bapt. at St. Peter's, Eaton Square, 6 November 1858; marr. at St. Paul's, Knightsbridge, London (by the Rev. Edward Thomas Vaughan, Vicar of Langleybury, assisted by the Rev. Edgar Sheppard, D.D., Sub-Dean of the Chapels Royal, and the Rev. Charles Frederick Goddard, brother of the bridegroom), on Monday, 13 April 1891.

Rev. Charles Frederick Goddard, born at The Lawn, Swindon, on Wednesday, 25 November 1863, bapt. at Swindon 1 January 1864; educated at Wellington College and at Chancellor's School, Lincoln, 1887; Curate-in-Charge of Swindon, co. Wilts, 1892-95, Vicar of Clearwell, co. Gloucester, since 1895.

Ambrose William Goddard, born at 131 Sloane Street, London, 19 March, bapt. at St. Paul's, Knightsbridge, London, 13 April 1892.

Hesketh Pleydell Goddard, born at 50 Montagu Square, London, on Saturday, 25 August 1894, and bapt. there privately; died 6 September, bur. at Swindon 10 September 1894.

A

Lucy Clarissa, born 13 October 1833; marr. at Swindon, co. Wilts, on Thursday, 18 December 1856, Lieut.-Colonel Henry William Verschoyle of Kilberry, co. Kildare (youngest son of Robert Verschoyle of Kilberry, by Catherine his wife, dau. and heiress of Thomas A. Curtis of Mountown, co. Dublin); of the Grenadier Guards; served throughout the Crimean War, wounded (medal), carried the Guard's Colours at the Battle of Inkerman; died at Cowes, Isle of Wight, aged 36, on Saturday, 20 August, bur. in Kensal Green Cemetery, London, 25 August 1870. M.I. in Royal Military Chapel, Wellington Barracks, London. Will proved in the Principal Registry, Dublin, 5 October 1870, by John James Verschoyle of Tassaggard, co. Dublin, and William Armitage Moore of Aramore, co. Cavan, two of the Exors. She died at 6 Wilton Crescent, London, aged 67, on Palm Sunday, 31 March, bur. in Kensal Green Cemetery, London, 4 April 1901. Will dated 17 December 1900, proved (Prin. Reg., 7, 1901) 2 May 1901, by Theresa Blanche Verschoyle, spinster, the daughter, and Henry Fuller Acland Hood, the Exors.

Colonel Frederick Fitz-Clarence Goddard of 1 Maida Vale Mansions, Maida Vale, London; born 4 April 1836; entered the Army as Ensign in the 80th Regiment September 1854, retired 8 March 1867; appointed 9 March 1867 to Barrack Department, Colonel Army Service Corps and A.A.G. North-Eastern District 11 December 1888 until 15 September 1895, when placed on retired list; served in Indian Mutiny (medal) and in Egyptian Expedition 1885.

= Hannah Lucy, 3rd dau. of James Chisholm Gooden-Chisholm, The Chisholm, of 33 Tavistock Square, London, by Anne Elizabeth his wife, dau. of John Lambert of Banstead, co. Surrey; born 9 July 1855, and bapt. at St. Pancras, London; marr. at St. George's, Hanover Square, London (by the Rev. Henry Luke Paget), on Wednesday, 22 March 1899; marr. 1stly at St. Pancras, London, on Tuesday, 24 November 1891, Shirley Baker of Surbiton, co. Surrey (only son of John Strange Baker of Surbiton), who died at Southwold, co. Suffolk, aged 35, on Monday, 21 August, and was bur. in Norbiton Cemetery, co. Surrey, 24 August 1893.

Julia Margaret, born 14 April 1840, bapt. at the parish church, Swindon, 8 August 1843; died at Montagu Square, London, aged 12 years and 8 months, on Monday, 20 December, bur. in Kensal Green Cemetery, London, 28 December 1852.

—

Sara Adelaide, born 26 January, bapt. at the parish church, Swindon, 8 August 1843; marr. at Henley-on-Thames, co. Oxford, 26 June 1872, John Mair (son of John Mair of Phyllis Court, Henley-on-Thames); born 12 December 1847; died at Buckland House, Lymington, co. Hants, on Tuesday, 28 January, bur. at Lymington 31 January 1902. Will dated 13 December 1901, proved (Prin. Reg., 33, 1902) 12 March 1902, by Alfred Henry Arnould and Arthur Robert Verschoyle, the Exors.

24

Harrison.

Arms.—Or, on a chief sable three eagles displayed argent.
Crest.—Out of a ducal coronet a talbot's head or, guttée de poix.

Thomas Harrison of Esher, co. Surrey (son of Robert Harrison of Esher, and elder brother to Robert Harrison of Hoxton, co. Middlesex, and of Firby, co. York [which estate he had purchased from Humphrey Brooke Osbaldeston, who had purchased it about 1767 from the representative of the last of the Stamper family], and of Chalk Farm, Farnborough, co. Kent); marr. Rachel, dau. of Thomas Simpson, by Rachel his wife; died at Firby Hall, aged 84, and bur. at Westow, co. York, 24 March 1820. He died at Esher, and was bur. there 14 August 1783. Will dated 3 March 1783, proved (P.C.C., 418 *Cornwallis*) 27 August 1783, by Rachel Harrison, the relict, the sole Executrix.

A

Rev. Thomas Harrison of Firby Hall; born at Esher 12 November, bapt. there 11 December 1768; educated at Eton and at Trinity College, Cambridge; inherited Firby Hall in 1802 from his uncle, Robert Harrison of Hoxton, and of Chalk Farm, Farnborough; died at Firby 4 November, bur. in the family vault at Westow 9 November 1838. M.I. Will dated 7 June 1831.

Anna, youngest dau. of Elias Inchbald of Malton and Thorpe Bassett, both co. York, by Mary his wife, dau. of Joseph Rider of Malton, and grand-daughter of William Inchbald of Selby, co. York; born at Malton 14 December 1795; marr. at South Shields, co. Durham, 4 September 1822; died at Scarborough, co. York, in her 90th year, on Thursday morning, 30 April, bur. in the family vault at Westow 4 May 1885. M.I.

B

Robert Harrison, only son, born at Firby 4 March, bapt. at Westow 4 April 1824; died at school at Green Hammerton, co. York, 3 October, bur. in the family vault at Westow 8 October 1833. M.I.

Sophia Mary, born at Firby 30 May, bapt. at Westow 22 July 1825; marr. there 1 September 1848, Edward Clough-Taylor of Kirkham Abbey, co. York (eldest son of Edward Clough-Taylor of Kirkham Abbey, by Emma Georgiana Bentley his wife, dau. of William Badcock); born at Easthorpe, co. York, 25 September, bapt. at Amotherby, co. York, 30 September 1822; of Trinity College, Cambridge, B.A. 1845, M.A. 1848, J.P. and D.L. for co. York; sold Kirkham in March 1878; died at Coneysthorpe, co. York, 13 December, bur. at Westow 17 December 1892. Admon was granted at York 16 January 1893, to Sophia Mary Clough-Taylor, the relict. She inherited the Firby Hall Estate on the death of her father 4 November 1838, and died at Edwinstowe House, co. Nottingham, whilst on a visit to her daughter, Mrs. Byron, at 2.30 p.m. on Monday, 7 July, and was bur. by the side of her husband in the churchyard at Westow, on Thursday, 10 July 1902. Admon (with will dated 3 July 1902) was granted at York 22 September 1902, to Harriet Anna Georgina Clough-Taylor, spinster, the universal legatee.

(*See Pedigree of Clough-Taylor, Vol. 6, page 44.*)

25

A
─┐

Rev. Robert Harrison, born at Esher, co. Surrey,═Mary Lowson of Witton-le-Wear, co. Durham,
2 May 1772; educated at Eton and at Trinity sister of Newby Lowson, the artist (who
College, Cambridge, B.A. 1794; Vicar of travelled with Turner, and who painted a
Blanchland, co. Northumberland, and of water-colour portrait of his brother-in-law, the
Lastingham, co. York, for 25 years; died s.p. Rev. Robert Harrison); died at Lastingham,
at Lastingham, aged 77, on Thursday, 28 aged 64, 13 April, bur. there 17 April 1835.
November, bur. there 3 December 1850. M.I. M.I.

B ─────────────────────────────────┐
│   │

Harriet, born at Firby, co. York, 18 July, bapt. at Frances Matilda, born at Firby 26
Westow, co. York, 22 August 1826; marr. 1stly at November 1827, bapt. at Westow 3
Westow 15 June 1847, George Tomline Gordon of January 1828; marr. at St. George's,
Cuckney, co. Nottingham (eldest son of the Rev. John Hanover Square, London (by the Rev.
Gordon, Vicar of Edwinstowe, co. Nottingham, and George de Hochepied Larpent), on
grandson of The Very Rev. George Gordon, Dean of Wednesday, 18 October 1865, the Rev.
Lincoln); died at New Orleans, U.S.A., on Wednesday, John Acland James (eldest son of the
26 February 1868, and bur. there. M.I. in the church Rt. Rev. John Thomas James, D.D.,
at Westow. She marr. 2ndly at Ealing, co. Middlesex Bishop of Calcutta, and grandson of
(by the Rev. G. Glossop), on Wednesday, 26 October the Rev. Thomas James, D.D., Head-
1870, Captain (afterwards Rear-Admiral) Henry master of Rugby School); born at
Anthony Trollope, R.N. (eldest son of Captain Spencer House, East Sheen, co.
William Henry Trollope of Landford House, co. Surrey, 24 September 1825; educated
Wilts, of the Honble East India Co.'s Service, by at Eton and Fellow of King's College,
Mary Arthur his wife, dau. of John Arthur Worsop of Cambridge, B.A. 1850, M.A. 1853;
Landford House); born 30 September 1837; served Perpetual Curate of Wattisham, co.
in Black Sea during the Crimea War (5th-class Suffolk, 1858–62, Vicar of Dalby Parva,
Medjidie), retired 1887; killed on the railway at co. Leicester, 1882–86, died s.p. at 18
Ganton Station, co. York, after playing golf there, Wilton Place, London, aged 71, on
6 March, bur. in Scarborough Cemetery, co. York, Monday, 9 November, bur. at Dalby,
9 March 1895. Will dated 1 April 1873, with codicil co. Leicester, 13 November 1896. M.I.
dated 6 February 1891, proved (Prin. Reg., 665, 95) Admon was granted at the Principal
4 May 1895, by Harriet Trollope, the relict, the Registry 5 December 1896, to Frances
Executrix.   ═   Matilda Acland James, the relict.
                                                   ⊼

Frances Matilda Acland James

Shedden of Spring Hill, Isle of Wight, and of Paulers Pury Park, co. Northampton.

Arms on record in the College of Arms.—Azure, on a chevron between three griffins' heads erased argent, as many cross-crosslets fitchée gules, on a chief of the second an escallop of the first between two cinquefoils of the third.

Crest.—A hermit proper, couped below the shoulders, vested russet, his hood pendent at the back.

Motto.—Fidem meam observabo.

George Shedden of Paulers Pury Park, co. Northampton, Knockmarloch, co. Ayr, and of Hardmead, co. Buckingham (eldest son of Robert Shedden of London,

(From a letter dated 31 August 1823.)

Merchant, by Agatha Wells his wife, dau. of John Goodrich of Nansemond Plantation, Virginia, North America); born in Virginia 29 June 1769; died at his residence, Spring Hill, East Cowes, Isle of Wight, in his 86th year, on Wednesday, 21 March, bur. at Whippingham, Isle of Wight, 27 March 1855. Will dated 12 August 1842, with five codicils dated respectively 26 February 1845, 5 September 1846, 5 August 1848, 26 June 1852, and 3 March 1854, proved (P.C.C., 359, 55) 18 April 1855, by William George Shedden, the son, one of the Exors. Power reserved to Robert Hawthorn, the other Exor.

= Mary (his cousin), elder dau. and coheir of William Goodrich of Spring Hill, East Cowes, by Catharine his wife, dau. of James Cole; born in Virginia, North America, 2 February 1776; marr. at Whippingham (by the Rev. J. F. F. Gill) on Sunday, 4 September 1796; died at Spring Hill, East Cowes, aged 51, on Sunday, 2 December, bur. at Whippingham 11 December 1827.

A

Robert Goodrich Shedden, born on Friday, 22 September 1797; died 16 March 1798.

—

Catharine Goodrich, born at Spring Hill, East Cowes, 14 October, bapt. at Whippingham 18 November 1798; died unmarried at Spring Hill, East Cowes, aged 57, on Tuesday, 12 June, bur. at Whippingham 16 June 1855. Will dated 10 May 1855, proved (P.C.C., 643, 55) 7 July 1855, by Thomas Francis Wilding, one of the Exors. Power reserved to Robert Hawthorn and John Brown, the other Exors.

John Goodrich Shedden, born in London, "out of hearing of Bow Bells," on Friday, 21 March 1800; died on Sunday, 21 September 1800.

—

George Shedden, born in London 23 February 1801; died at Energlyn, co. Glamorgan, on Thursday, 20 August, bur. at Caerphilly, co. Glamorgan, 26 August 1801.

Agatha Wells Bridger, born in London 9 June 1802; marr. at Whippingham, Isle of Wight (by the Rev. Walter Farquhar Hook, Curate-in-Charge [afterwards Dean Hook]), 2 November 1824, Robert Hawthorn of London (son of John Hawthorn, and grandson of John Hawthorn of Oulton, co. Wigton); born 18 March 1791; died at Gower Street, London, in his 78th year, on Thursday, 4 March, bur. in Kensal Green Cemetery, London, 11 March 1869. Will dated 1 February 1865, proved (Prin. Reg., 258, 69) 2 April 1869, by William Hawthorn of 5 Lime Street Square, in the City of London, the son, one of the surviving Exors. She died at 68 (late 34) Gower Street, London, aged 62, on Sunday, 8 January, and was bur. in Kensal Green Cemetery, London, 14 January 1865.

William George Shedden of=Caroline, youngest dau. of Paulers Pury Park, co. Northampton, Hardmead, co. Buckingham, Knockmarloch, co. Ayr, and of Spring Hill, East Cowes, Isle of Wight; born at 6 Bedford Square, London, 22 July 1803; J.P. for co. Hants; Lord of the Manors of Paulers Pury and Hardmead; died s.p. at his residence, Spring Hill, East Cowes, aged 69, on Tuesday, 3 December, bur. at Whippingham 11 December 1872. Will dated 6 November 1872, proved (Prin. Reg., 59, 73) 7 January 1873, by William Hawthorn of 5 Lime Street Square, in the City of London, the nephew, one of the Exors.

Admiral Sir Graham Eden Hamond of Norton Lodge, Freshwater, Isle of Wight, 2nd Bart., G.C.B., D.L., by Elizabeth his wife, dau. of John Kimber of Fowey, co. Cornwall; marr. at Freshwater 11 September 1861; died at West Malvern, co. Worcester, aged 64, on Thursday, 20 October, bur. at Whippingham 26 October 1881. Will dated 3 April 1873, with three codicils dated respectively 22 July 1873, 18 February 1875, and 21 June 1880, proved at Winchester 19 December 1881, by William George Galloway of Cridland Farm, Spaxton, co. Somerset, the nephew, one of the Exors.

W.G. Shedden

Agatha   *W. B. Hawthorn*

Charlotte Louisa Jessie, born at Fairlee Cottage, Isle of Wight, on Thursday, 19 April, bapt. at Whippingham 31 May 1855; marr. at St. James', East Cowes (by the Rev. George Prothero, Rector of Whippingham, Canon of Westminster, and Chaplain in Ordinary to H.M. Queen Victoria, assisted by the Rev. Robert William Burnaby, the Vicar, and the Rev. Arthur Winthrop Woodruff), on Thursday, 5 April 1883, John Winthrop Woodruff of East Cowes (3rd son of the Rev. John Woodruff, Vicar of Upchurch, co. Kent, by Frances his wife, dau. of the Rev. Edward Winthrop); born at the Vicarage, Upchurch, on Thursday, 5 September, bapt. at Upchurch 10 October 1850; M.R.C.S. Eng. 1881, L.R.C.P. and L.M. Edin. 1881 (retired).

Roscow George Shedden, born at Spring Hill, East Cowes, on Saturday, 13 May, bapt. at Whippingham 24 June 1882; of New College Oxford, matriculated 11 October 1901.

Alice Katharine Beatrix, born at Spring Hill, East Cowes, on Monday, 1 October, bapt. at Whippingham 7 November 1883.

Edward Claude Shedden, born at Spring Hill, East Cowes, on Monday, 12 January, bapt. at Whippingham 19 February 1885; entered Royal Military College, Sandhurst, January 1903.

Margaret Bridger Goodrich, born in London 18 August 1804 ; marr. at St. George's, Bloomsbury, London, on Monday, 2 July 1827, the Rev. James Galloway (only son of James Galloway of Jamaica, West Indies, by Elizabeth his wife) ; born at Falmouth, Trelawney, Jamaica, 4 October 1801 ; of Exeter College, Oxford, matriculated 12 March 1818, aged 16, B.A. 1821, M.A. 1824 ; Rector of Spaxton, co. Somerset, 1846 until his death ; died at the Rectory, Spaxton, aged 73, on Friday, 9 October, bur. at Spaxton 15 October 1874. Will dated 17 April 1872, with codicil dated 5 October 1874, proved at Taunton 16 November 1874, by William George Galloway of Spaxton, co. Somerset, the son, one of the Exors. She died at the Rectory, Spaxton, in her 43rd year, on Tuesday, 8 June, and was bur. at Spaxton 17 June 1847.

Robert John Shedden, born in London 19 February 1806 ; died at West Cowes, Isle of Wight, aged 59, on Wednesday, 5 July, bur. at Whippingham, Isle of Wight, 8 July 1865. Will dated 24 April 1861, proved at Winchester 5 October 1865, by Thomas Edmund Wood of Northwood, Isle of Wight, and Henry James Damant of West Cowes, Isle of Wight, the Exors.

Mary George, born in London 26 November 1807 ; died unmarried, aged 19, 20 December, bur. at Paulers Pury, co. Northampton, 28 December 1826.

—

Beatrix, born in London 6 March 1809 ; died unmarried at Spring Hill, East Cowes, aged 47, on Tuesday, 20 May, bur. at Whippingham 26 May 1856. Will dated 30 July 1855, proved (P.C.C., 506, 56) 17 June 1856, by William George Shedden, the brother, one of the Exors. Power reserved to Roscow Cole Shedden and the Rev. Edward Cole Shedden, the brothers, the other Exors.

Beatrix Shedden

George Shedden of Spring Hill, East Cowes, Isle of Wight, Paulers Pury Park, co. Northampton, and of Hardmead, co. Buckingham ; born at Fairlee Cottage, Isle of Wight, on Monday, 27 October, bapt. at Whippingham 27 December 1856 ; of Trinity College, Cambridge, matriculated in 1876, B.A. 1881 ; a Student of the Inner Temple 9 November 1878, called to the Bar 17 November 1883 ; J.P. for co. Hants, Lord of the Manors of Paulers Pury and Hardmead.

= Alice Sarah, 3rd dau. of Caleb Hammond Gater of Town Hill Park, co. Hants, by Sarah his wife, dau. of James Warner of Botley, co. Hants ; born 31 December 1855, and bapt. at South Stonham, co. Hants ; marr. at St. Peter's, Southampton (by the Rev. William Dann Harrison, assisted by the Rev. Frederick Hermann Bowden-Smith), on Thursday, 7 October 1880.

C

Graham Percival Shedden, born at Spring Hill, East Cowes, on Tuesday, 27 July, bapt. at Whippingham 20 August 1886 ; entered Royal Military Academy, Woolwich, January 1903.

Constance Evelyn, born at Somerville, Ryde, Isle of Wight, on Wednesday, 28 August, bapt. at Whippingham 2 October 1889.

Mary Eleanor Goodrich, born at Somerville, Ryde, on Friday, 20 March, bapt. at St. John's, Ryde, 10 May 1891.

A ——— A

Louisa, born in London 28 April 1810; died unmarried at Powys House, East Cowes, Isle of Wight, aged 58, on Sunday, 20 September, bur. at Whippingham, Isle of Wight, 24 September 1868. Will dated 21 February 1868, proved (Prin. Reg., 738, 68) 23 November 1868, by William Hawthorn of 5 Lime Street Square, in the City of London, the nephew, one of the Exors.

Louisa Shedden [signature]

Roscow Cole Shedden of Millfield House, East Cowes, Isle of Wight, Paulers Pury Park, co. Northampton, and of Knockmarloch, co. Ayr; born in the Isle of Wight 10 October, bapt. at Whippingham 16 December 1811; J.P. for co. Hants; died at his residence, Millfield House, East Cowes, aged 65, on Saturday, 5 May, bur. at Whippingham 9 May 1877. Will dated 21 August 1874, with codicil dated 13 December 1875, proved (Prin. Reg., 422, 77) 31 May 1877, by Charlotte Joanna Shedden of Millfield House, Whippingham, Isle of Wight, the relict, Thomas Francis Wilding of 5 Lime Street Square, in the City of London, and James Fitchett Burrell of Frimley Manor, co. Surrey, three of the Exors.

═ Charlotte Joanna, eldest dau. of James Fitchett Burrell of Belvoir House, Fareham, co. Hants, and of Frimley Manor, co. Surrey; born at Fareham 2 December, bapt. there privately 4 December 1819; marr. at the parish church, Fareham (by the Rev. Edward Cole Shedden, brother of the bridegroom, assisted by the Rev. Walter Scot Dumergue, the Vicar), on Thursday, 9 March 1854; died at Millfield House, East Cowes, aged 74, on Sunday, 31 December 1893, bur. at Whippingham 4 January 1894. Will dated 9 November 1892, with codicil dated 22 February 1893, proved at Winchester 21 February 1894, by George Shedden and Graham Eden Shedden, the sons, the Exors.

Roscow Cole Shedden [signature]

B ——— B

Roscow James Shedden, born at Fairlee Cottage, Isle of Wight, on Friday, 21 May, bapt. at Whippingham 21 July 1858; died at Millfield House, East Cowes, aged 8, on Wednesday, 27 June, bur. at Whippingham 30 June 1866.

Lavinia, born in London 23 January 1813; died unmarried at 10 Princes Buildings, Clifton, co. Gloucester, on Thursday, 16 November, bur. at Redland Church, Bristol, 21 November 1882. Will dated 18 June 1881, proved at Bristol 9 December 1882, by William George Galloway of Spaxton, co. Somerset, the nephew, one of the Exors.

Lavinia Shedden

Graham Eden Shedden of Knockmarloch, co. Ayr, Millfield House, East Cowes, Isle of Wight, and of Elvington Court, Eythorne, co. Kent; born at Millfield House, East Cowes, on Sunday, 6 November, bapt. at St. James', East Cowes, 5 December 1859; formerly Captain Hants Yeomanry Cavalry.	Margaret, dau. of George Henry Gater of Winslowe, Southampton, by Sarah his wife, dau. of John Robert Cozens of Wallingford, co. Oxford, J.P.; born 4 February 1863, and bapt. at Westend, co. Hants; marr. at St. Peter's, Fareham, co. Hants (by the Rev. Canon George Prothero, assisted by the Rev. Thirlwall Gore Browne, the Vicar), on Wednesday, 30 March 1892.	Mary Constance, born at Millfield House, East Cowes, on Tuesday, 29 October, bapt. at St. James', East Cowes, 26 November 1861.

Graham Eden Shedden

B

Harold Roscow Graham Shedden, born at Elvington Court, Eythorne, on Sunday, 3 September, bapt. at Eythorne 10 October 1899.	George Eden Graham Shedden, born at Elvington Court, Eythorne, on Sunday, 13 January, bapt. at Eythorne 26 February 1901.

A

Rev. Edward Cole Shedden, born in London 9 August 1815 ; of University═Mary, 2nd dau. of
College Oxford, matriculated 5 June 1833, aged 17, B.A. from St. Mary Joseph Hall of
Hall, Oxford, 1837, M.A. 1840 ; Rector of Clapton, co. Northampton, 1845 Castleton, co.
until his death ; died at the Rectory, Clapton, aged 61, on Sunday, Derby, by Hannah
17 September, bur. at Clapton 20 September 1876. Will dated 2 October Lax his wife,
1875, proved at Peterborough 1 November 1876, by William Hawthorn, dau. of the Rev.
the nephew, and Thomas Francis Wilding, both of 5 Lime Street Square, Thomas Brown,
in the City of London, and the Rev. Joseph Hall of Edensor, co. Derby, Vicar of Tides-
the Exors. well, co. Derby ;
marr. at Castleton
6 July 1842.

Edward C. Shedden

Octavia, born in London 18 April 1817 ; died at Powys House, East Cowes, Isle of Wight, aged
82, 15 March, bur. at Whippingham, Isle of Wight, 19 March 1900. Will dated 6 July 1885,
with two codicils dated respectively 23 July 1895 and 24 October 1899, proved at Winchester
22 May 1900, by the Rev. Joseph Hall, Rowland Edmund Prothero, and William George
Galloway, the Exors.

George Shedden

A CLEAN HEART AND A CHEERFUL SPIRIT

PORTMAN.

Arms.—Quarterly: 1st and 4th, Or, a fleur-de-lis azure, PORTMAN; 2nd and 3rd, Gules, a chevron ermine between ten crosses pattée, six in chief and four in base, argent, BERKELEY.

Crests.—1, A talbot sejant or, PORTMAN; 2, An unicorn passant gules, armed, crined and unguled or, BERKELEY.

Supporters.—Dexter: A savage, wreathed around the head and loins with ivy, in his dexter hand a club resting on the shoulder proper; Sinister: A talbot or.

Motto.—A clean heart and a cheerful spirit.

Portman.

Lucy, 2nd dau. of the Rev. Thomas Whitby of Cresswell Hall, co. Stafford, and of Portland Place, London, High Sheriff for co. Stafford, *temp.* George III., by Mabella his wife, dau. of John Turton of Orgreave, co. Stafford; marr. at Walcot, Bath, co. Somerset, 28 August 1798; died at Bryanston, co. Dorset, 20 March, bur. there 31 March 1812. 1st wife.

═Edward Berkeley Portman of Bryanston, co. Dorset, and of Orchard Portman, co. Somerset (2nd son and eventual heir of Henry William Portman of the same, by Anne his wife, dau. of William Wyndham of Dinton, co. Wilts); born at Bryanston 31 January, bapt. there 24 February 1771; M.P. for Boroughbridge 1802-6, and for co. Dorset 1805-23; died at Rome, Italy, aged 52, 19 January, bur. in the church at Bryanston 16 April 1823. Will dated 28 July 1821, with codicil dated 9 July 1822, proved (P.C.C., 236 *Richards*) 22 April 1823, by Edward Berkeley Portman, the son, the sole Exor.

of═Mary, eldest dau. of Sir Edward Hulse of Breamore House, co. Hants, 3rd Bart., by Mary Lethieullier his wife, and heir of her uncle, Smart Lethieullier of Aldersbrook, co. Essex; marr. 16 March 1816; died s.p. at the Rectory, Buckland, co. Surrey, in her 79th year, on Sunday, 31 October, bur. at Bryanston 9 November 1852. Will dated 2 August 1837, with codicil dated 29 March 1851, proved (P.C.C., 947, 52) 9 December 1852, by the Rev. Thomas Hulse, the brother, one of the Exors. Power reserved to the Rt. Honble Edward, Baron Portman, the other Exor. 2nd wife.

A

Edward Berkeley Portman, Viscount Portman of Bryanston, co. Dorset, and Baron Portman of Orchard Portman, co. Somerset; born at Bryanston 9 July, bapt. privately 11 July 1799 (baptism registered at Bryanston); educated at Eton 1814, and at Christ Church, Oxford, matriculated 20 October 1817, aged 18, B.A. 29 October 1821, M.A. 1 June 1826; M.P. for co. Dorset 1823, 1826, 1830 and 1831-32, and for Marylebone, London, 12 December 1832 to March 1833; created Baron Portman of Orchard Portman, co. Somerset, 21 January 1837, and Viscount Portman of Bryanston, co. Dorset, 28 March 1873; Major 1st Somersetshire Regiment of Militia 13 March 1839; Lord-Lieutenant for co. Somerset 22 May 1839 to June 1864; a Commissioner and Councillor of the Duchy of Cornwall 19 August 1840, a Councillor of the Duchy of Lancaster 13 February 1847; Vice-Lieutenant for co. Dorset; President of the Royal Agricultural Society in 1846, 1856 and 1862; appointed one of the Council to H.R.H. the Prince of Wales (now King Edward VII.) in 1863; Lord Warden of the Stannaries, Rider and Master Forester of Dartmoor, and High Steward of the Duchy of Cornwall 20 January 1865 till his death; died at Bryanston, in his 90th year, on Monday, 19 November, bur. there 24 November 1888. Will dated 5 November 1869, with codicil dated 13 January 1881, proved (Prin. Reg., 153, 89) 20 February 1889, by the Rt. Honble William Henry Berkeley, Viscount Portman of Durweston, co. Dorset, the son, the sole Exor.

═Lady Emma, 3rd dau. of Henry, 2nd Earl of Harewood, by Henrietta his wife, dau. of Sir John Saunders Sebright, Bart.; born at Harwood House, co. York, 16 March 1809; marr. at St. George's, Hanover Square, London (by the Dean of Carlisle), on Saturday, 16 June 1827; Lady of the Bedchamber to H.M. Queen Victoria 1837-51, and an Extra Lady of the Bedchamber 15 July 1851; died at Bryanston House, aged 56, on Wednesday, 8 February, bur. at Bryanston 16 February 1865.

B

William Henry Berkeley Portman, Viscount Portman of Bryanston, co. Dorset, and Baron Portman of Orchard Portman, co. Somerset; born 12 July, bapt. privately 14 July (baptism registered at St. James', Westminster), and received into the church at Bryanston 25 August 1829; educated at Eton and at Merton College, Oxford, matriculated 15 Oxford 1847, aged 18; D.L. for co. Somerset, J.P. for the counties of Somerset and Dorset; M.P. for Shaftesbury 1852-57, and for co. Dorset 1857-85; succeeded his father as 2nd Viscount Portman 19 November 1888; Hon. Colonel West Somersetshire Yeomanry Cavalry since 1896; Chairman and Alderman of Dorset County Council.

═Honble Mary Selina Charlotte, posthumous and only child of William Charles, Viscount Milton, eldest son and heir of Charles William, 5th Earl Fitzwilliam, K.G.; born at Fife House, Whitehall, London, 9 January 1836, bapt. privately the same day (baptism registered at St. Martin-in-the-Fields, London); marr. at the Chapel Royal, Whitehall, London (by the Rev. James Samuel Upton), on Thursday, 21 June 1855; died suddenly at Bryanston, aged 62, on Wednesday morning, 4 January, bur. in the South-East corner of the churchyard at Durweston, co. Dorset, next to the grave of her daughter Constance, on Saturday, 7 January 1899. Will dated 29 July 1895, proved (Prin. Reg., 342, 99) 25 March 1899, by the Honble Henry Berkeley Portman, the sole Exor.

C

Henry William Berkeley Portman of Dean's Court, co. Dorset; born at Bryanston, co. Dorset, 8 May, bapt. privately 10 May 1801 (baptism registered at Bryanston); Major 6th (Inniskilling) Dragoons, formerly 7th Hussars, and Lieutenant Dorsetshire Yeomanry Cavalry; J.P. for co. Dorset; died at Red Hill, Lydney, co. Gloucester, in his 78th year, on Monday, 31 March, bur. at Pylle, co. Somerset, 5 April 1879. Will dated 5 June 1869, with two codicils dated respectively 24 June 1871 and 26 June 1871, proved (Prin. Reg., 659, 79) 18 July 1879, by the Rev. Henry Fitzhardinge Portman of the Rectory, Pylle, co. Somerset, the son, one of the Exors. ＝ Harriet Emily Cavendish, dau. of Thomas Lennox Napier Sturt of Buckshaw House, co. Dorset, a Puisne Judge in the Honble East India Co.'s Service, by Jannette his wife, dau. of Andrew Wilson, M.D.; born at Compton Castle 25 February 1813; marr. at Compton Pauncefoot, co. Somerset (by the Rev. Napier Sturt), on Tuesday, 8 May 1832; died at "Avonside," Fordingbridge, co. Hants, aged 77, on Saturday, 23 August, bur. in the cemetery at Wimborne, co. Dorset, 28 August 1890. Will dated 16 December 1889, proved (Prin. Reg., 879, 90) 19 September 1890, by George Henry Sawtell of 23 Red Lion Square, co. Middlesex, the sole Exor.

A ─ Edith Grace, born at Child Okeford, co. Dorset, 18 February, bapt. there 2 March 1837; marr. at Sherborne Minster, co. Dorset (by the Rev. Fitzhardinge Berkeley Portman, uncle of the bride, assisted by the Rev. Henry Fitzhardinge Berkeley Portman, brother of the bride, and the Rev. William Hector Lyon, the Rector), on Thursday, 11 April 1872, George Stanley Orred of Hayward Lodge, Child Okeford (2nd son of George Orred of Tranmere, co. Chester, by Matilda his wife, dau. of Thomas Thistlethwayte of Southwick Park, co. Hants, M.P.); formerly Lieutenant 7th Royal Fusiliers and 2nd Battalion Royal Highlanders (Black Watch), afterwards Captain 1st Volunteer Battalion Dorchester Regiment, and of the Army Reserve.

Edwin Berkeley Portman of 46 Cadogan Place, London; born at Bryanston 3 August 1830, bapt. privately the next day (baptism registered at Bryanston); educated at Rugby and at Balliol College, Oxford, matriculated 17 March 1847, aged 16, S.C.L. and B.A. 1850, B.C.L. 1854, Fellow of All Souls' College 1850-57; a Student of Lincoln's Inn 10 July 1848, went to the Inner Temple 1 June, and called to the Bar there 7 June 1852; Private Secretary to 1st Commissioner of Public Works; M.P. for Northern Division co. Dorset December 1885-92. ＝ Caroline Ella, 2nd dau. of David Ward Chapman, by Caroline Mary his wife, dau. of Charles Phelips of Briggins Park, co. Hertford; marr. at St. Andrew's, Ashley Place, London (by the Rev. Boswell Chapman), on Saturday, 14 May 1887.

E. B. Portman

B ─ Violet Guendolen, born at 46 Cadogan Place, London, on Thursday, 9 May 1889.

Edward William Berkeley Portman of Hestercombe, co. Somerset, and of 33 Great Cumberland Place, London; born at Fife House, Whitehall, London, on Wednesday, 30 July 1856, and bapt. there; educated at Eton and at Christ Church, Oxford, matriculated 15 January 1875, aged 18; formerly Major Dorsetshire Yeomanry Cavalry; J.P. for co. Dorset, J.P. and D.L. for co. Somerset, High Sheriff 1898. ＝ Honble Constance Mary, 3rd dau. of Beilby Richard, 2nd Baron Wenlock, by Lady Elizabeth Grosvenor his wife, 3rd dau. of Richard, 2nd Marquis of Westminster, K.G.; born at Escrick Park, co. York, on Wednesday, 4 October 1854; marr. at East Clandon, co. Surrey (by the Honble and Rev. Algernon Lawley), on Thursday, 7 July 1892. She marr. 1stly at St. George's, Hanover Square, London (by the Honble and Rev. Stephen Lawley, and the Honble and Rev. Sidney Meade), on Tuesday, 19 June 1877, the Honble Eustace Vesey (3rd son of Thomas, 3rd Viscount De Vesci); born 31 January 1851; Captain 9th Lancers 1879; died at Abbeyleix, Queen's County, on Thursday, 18 November 1886, leaving issue.

Captain Wyndham Berkeley Portman of Hare═Sarah, only dau. of Thomas Thornhill of
Park, co. Cambridge, R.N.; born at Bryanston, │ Fixby, co. York, and of Riddlesworth, co.
co. Dorset, 4 June, bapt. privately 10 June │ Norfolk, by his wife, Sarah Sober of
1804 (baptism registered at Bryanston); │ Southampton; marr. at Riddlesworth 28
Commander R.N. (retired); died at Hinxton │ September 1829; died at Hare Park on
Hall, co. Cambridge, in his 79th year, on │ Whit-Sunday, 16 May 1880.
Saturday, 7 July 1883.

Wyndham Berkeley Portman of Richmond Hill, co.═Emily Charlotte, dau. of George
Surrey; born 15 May 1831; died at Alipore House, │ Newton of Croxton Park, co.
Worcester Road, Sutton, co. Surrey, 18 September, bur. │ Cambridge, by Charlotte his wife,   E
in Brookwood Cemetery, co. Surrey, 20 September 1890. │ dau. of General Denzil Onslow of
Will dated 22 April 1879, proved (Prin. Reg., 959, 90) │ Stoughton House, co. Huntingdon;
16 October 1890, by Emily Charlotte Portman of Alipore │ marr. at St. George's, Hanover
House, Sutton, co. Surrey, the relict, the sole Executrix. │ Square, London, 24 March 1854.

Arthur Fitzhardinge Berkeley
Portman, born 22 August 1861.

D

Alice Elizabeth, younger dau. of═Rev. Henry Fitzhardinge═Gertrude, dau. of John Frederick
John Mainwaring Paine of │ Berkeley Portman, born │ Norman of Staplegrove, co.
Farnham, co. Surrey, by Caroline │ at Child Okeford, co. │ Somerset, by Emma his wife, dau.
his wife, dau. of William │ Dorset, 18 October, │ of the Rev. John Haydon Cardew,
Newnham, M.D., F.R.C.S.; │ bapt. there 15 November │ Rector of Curry Mallet, co.
born at Farnham 18 June 1845, │ 1838; of Magdalen │ Somerset; born at Staplegrove
bapt. there 19 July 1846; marr. │ College, Oxford, matricu- │ 19 August, bapt. there 21 September
at Holy Trinity, Eastbourne, co. │ lated 9 June 1857, aged │ 1854; marr. at St. Mary Magdalen's,
Sussex (by the Rev. John │ 18, B.A. 1863; Rector │ Taunton, co. Somerset (by the Rev.
Frederick Denison Maurice, │ of Pylle 1866–85, and │ Fitzhardinge Berkeley Portman,
assisted by the Rev. Charles │ of Orchard Portman, │ uncle of the bridegroom, assisted
Edward Steward), on Thursday, │ with Thurlbeare and │ by the Rev. Edward Imber Gardiner,
11 October 1866; died 13 April, │ Stoke, co. Somerset, │ brother-in-law of the bride, and   D
bur. at Pylle, co. Somerset, │ since 1885. │ the Rev. Dr. Finch), on Wednesday,
17 April 1877. 1st wife. │ │ 20 April 1887. 2nd wife.

Frederick Arthur Berkeley   Blanche Ethel,   Cicely Joan, born at   Isabel Grace, born at the
Portman, born at the   born 28 Feb-   Orchard Portman on   Rectory, Thurlbeare, on
Rectory, Pylle, on Monday,   ruary, bapt. at   Saturday, 16 Novem-   Monday, 13 July, bapt. at
28 October, bapt. at Pylle   Pylle 19 April   ber, bapt. there 31   Thurlbeare 8 September
7 June 1868.   1870.   December 1889.   1891.

B   B

C   C

Walter George Berkeley Portman, born at 8 Rutland Gate, London, on Wednesday, 2 June
1858, and bapt. there; died at Bournemouth, co. Hants, aged 7 years and-a-half, on Wednesday,
13 December, bur. at Bryanston 20 December 1865.

38

A

A

Lucy Mabella, born at Bryanston, co. Dorset, 1 September 1805; marr. 26 May 1824, George Digby Wingfield-Digby of Sherborne Castle, co. Dorset, and of Coleshill, co. Warwick (eldest son of William Wingfield, M.P., a Master in Chancery, by his 1st wife, Lady Charlotte Mary, dau. and, in her issue, sole heiress of Henry, 1st Earl Digby); born 1 June 1797; of Christ Church, Oxford, matriculated 14 April 1815, aged 17, B.A. 1819; Barrister-at-Law of the Inner Temple 1821; J.P. and D.L. for co. Dorset, High Sheriff 1860; assumed the additional name of Digby in 1856; died s.p. at Sherborne Castle, in his 86th year, on Monday, 7 May, bur. at Sherborne 11 May 1883. Will dated 2 June 1881, with two codicils dated respectively 5 July 1881 and 3 March 1882, proved (Prin. Reg., 887, 83) 5 November 1883, by the Rev. Fitzhardinge Berkeley Portman of Staple Fitzpaine, co. Somerset, and Wadham Knatchbull of Sherborne, co. Dorset, two of the Exors.

E

E

Mary, marr. at St. George's, Hanover Square, London (by the Rev. Fitzhardinge Berkeley Portman, uncle of the bride), on Monday, 7 June 1852, George Onslow Newton of Croxton Park, co. Cambridge, and of Pickhill Hall, co. Denbigh (son of George Newton of Croxton Park, by Charlotte his wife, dau. of General Denzil Onslow of Stoughton House, co. Huntingdon); born at Croxton Park on Monday, 22 February 1830; of Trinity College, Cambridge, matriculated Michaelmas Term 1848, B.A. 1852, M.A. 1861; J.P. and D.L. for the counties of Cambridge and Huntingdon, High Sheriff for the former county 1864. She died s.p. at Croxton Park, aged 22, on Thursday, 6 September, and was bur. at Croxton 13 September 1855. He marr. 2ndly at St. Peter's, Eaton Square, London, 24 June 1858, Cecilia Florence, 2nd dau. of Edwyn Burnaby of Baggrave Hall, co. Leicester, J.P. and D.L., by Anne Caroline his wife, dau. of Thomas Salisbury; she died at Florence, Italy, leaving issue two daughters, on Sunday, 7 February 1869. He marr. 3rdly, 27 July 1878, Lady Alice Laura Sophia, 2nd dau. of Thomas Barnes, 11th Earl of Dundonald, by Louisa Harriet his wife, dau. of William Alexander Mackinnon of Mackinnon; born 8 September 1849; a Lady of Grace of Order of St. John of Jerusalem in England. George Onslow Newton died at 18 Queen's Gate Terrace, South Kensington, London, the residence of his daughter, the Countess of Dysart, on Friday, 7 December 1900. Will dated 20 July 1887, with five codicils dated respectively 19 January 1888, 28 February 1891, 29 December 1893, 21 January 1895 and 5 September 1900, proved (Prin. Reg., 79, 1901) 28 January 1901, by Arthur Fitzhardinge Berkeley Portman, the Exor named in will, Edmund Bourke, the Exor named in 4th codicil, Rear-Admiral in the Royal Navy, and George Douglas Cockrane Newton, the Exor named in 5th codicil.

D

D

B

Lucy Ella, born at Bryanston on Sunday, 20 November, bapt. privately 22 November 1831 (baptism registered at Bryanston).

C

Henry Berkeley Portman of Buxted Park, co. Sussex; born at 8 Rutland Gate, London, on Thursday, 16 February 1860, and bapt. there; educated at Eton and Non-Collegiate of Oxford, matriculated 17 October 1879, aged 19; formerly Major Dorsetshire Yeomanry Cavalry; J.P. for co. Sussex.

Emma Andalusia Frere, only surviving child of Lord Nigel Kennedy (brother of Archibald, 2nd Marquess of Ailsa, M.P.); born on Sunday, 20 October 1861; marr. at St. George's, Hanover Square, London (by the Rev. Edgar Sheppard, D.D., Sub-Dean of the Chapels Royal, assisted by the Honble and Rev. Walter Berkeley Portman, Rector of Corton-Denham, co. Somerset, uncle of the bridegroom), on Wednesday, 25 September 1901. She marr. 1stly 25 October 1881, George Lionel Henry Seymour, 5th Earl of Portarlington; born 19 August 1858; died at Ostend on Friday, 31 August, bur. at Coolbanagher, Queen's County, on Thursday, 6 September 1900. Will dated 23 January 1893, with codicil dated 2 August 1900, proved (Prin. Reg., 1550, 1900) 14 November 1900, by the Rt. Honble Emma Andalusia Frere Dawson-Damer, Countess of Portarlington, the relict, the sole Executrix.

Selina Lusia, born at Buxted Park on Friday, 11 September, bapt. at Buxted on Thursday, 22 October 1903.

Marianne, born 1 September, bapt. privately 3 September 1806 (baptism registered at Bryanston, co. Dorset); marr. at St. Mary's, Bryanston Square, London (by the Rev. Thomas Hulse), on Thursday, 14 April 1831, George Drummond of Stanmore, co. Middlesex (son of George Harley Drummond of Stanmore, by Margaret his wife, dau. of Alexander Munro of Glasgow); born 12 February 1802; died at Wilton Crescent, London, on Sunday, 5 January 1851. Will dated 5 November 1845, proved (P.C.C., 188, 51) 12 March 1851, by Andrew Mortimer Drummond, the uncle, Andrew Robert Drummond and Charles Drummond, the Exors. She died at Wilton Crescent, London, 1 December 1842.

Sarah, born at 49 Berkeley Square, London, 17 October 1834.	Seymour Berkeley Portman-Dalton of Sleningfield Park, co. York, of Fillingham Castle, co. Lincoln, and of 18 Eccleston Square, London; born at 49 Berkeley Square, London, 12 January 1838, and bapt. at Riddlesworth, co. Suffolk; assumed by Royal Licence dated 10 December 1887, the additional name of Dalton; J.P. and D.L. for co. Lincoln.	=Georgiana Isabella, eldest dau. of John Dalton of Sleningford Park, co. York, and of Fillingham Castle, co. Lincoln, J.P. and D.L., Captain 1st Royal Dragoons, by Georgiana Isabella his wife, dau. of Colonel Henry Tower; born at Sleningford Grange, Ripon, co. York, 2 September 1845, bapt. privately the next day (baptism registered at North Stainley-cum-Sleningford, co. York); marr. at St. Gabriel's, Warwick Square, London, on Wednesday, 2 June 1880.	Alice, born in London 22 August 1846; died 12 February 1898, and bur. at Dullingham, co. Cambridge.

Colonel Augustus Berkeley Portman of Priestwood House, Bracknell,=Mary Frances Lovett, co. Berks; born at Weymouth, co. Dorset, 14 June, bapt. at Child Okeford, co. Dorset, 22 July 1840; entered the Honble East India Co.'s Service 9 December 1859 as Lieutenant in Bombay Artillery, and in the Royal Artillery (Bo.) 18 February 1861; served with B/18 Battery Royal Artillery, and appointed to Royal Horse Artillery in 1866; transferred to Bombay Staff Corps 16 April 1866; served in the Police Department of the Bombay Presidency, and acted for three and-a-half years as Inspector-General of Registration and Stamps, Bombay; rejoined the Police, and retired from the service 9 December 1890; promoted Captain 9 December 1871, Major 9 December 1879, Lieut.-Colonel 9 December 1885, and Colonel 9 December 1889; J.P. for co. Dorset.

Mary Frances Lovett, 2nd dau. of William Lochiel Cameron of the Honble East India Co.'s Service, by Jane Rose his wife, dau. of Dr. Daniell of Dublin; born at Poona, Bombay Presidency, India, 30 September 1844, and bapt. there; marr. at Kirkee, Bombay Presidency, 21 January 1864.

Helen Cavendish, born at Baroda, Punjab, India, 10 May 1865, and bapt. there; died at Gunnish Khired House, near Kirkee, Bombay Presidency, 26 September 1886, and bur. in the cemetery at Kirkee the next day.

Emma Selina, born at 42 Portman Square, London, on Easter Sunday, 5 April 1863, and bapt. there privately; marr. at St. Mary's, Bryanston Square, London, 7 May 1885, the Rt. Honble Ronald Ruthven, Earl of Leven and Melville, P.C. (3rd son of John Thornton Leslie, 9th Earl of Leven and 8th Earl of Melville, by Sophia his 2nd wife, dau. of Henry Thornton, M.P.); born at Roehampton, co. Surrey, 19 December 1835, bapt. at the parish church, Putney, co. Surrey, 13 February 1836; educated at Eton and at Christ Church, Oxford, matriculated 8 June 1854, aged 18, B.A. 1858, M.A. 1865; D.L. for co. Nairn; one of H.M. Lieutenants for the City of London; Keeper of the Privy Seal of Scotland; Lord High Commissioner of Church of Scotland for five years from 1898; succeeded his half-brother, Alexander, as 10th Earl of Leven and 9th Earl of Melville 22 October 1889.

Harriet Ella, born 27 April, bapt. privately 29 April 1807 (baptism registered at Bryanston, co. Dorset); marr. at St. Mary's, Bryanston Square, London, 1 March 1827, William Stratford Dugdale of Blyth Hall and Merevale, co. Warwick (only son of Dugdale Stratford Dugdale of Merevale Hall, M.P., by the Hon[ble] Charlotte his 1st wife, dau. of Assheton, 1st Viscount Curzon); born 1 April 1800; J.P. and D.L. for co. Warwick; M.P. for Shaftesbury 1830–31, Bramber 1831–32, and for North Warwickshire 1832–47; died at Blyth Hall, aged 71, 15 September, bur. at Merevale 22 September 1871. Will dated 10 March 1870, with codicil dated 5 August 1871, proved at Birmingham 11 December 1871, by William Stratford Dugdale of Merevale Hall, co. Warwick, John Stratford Dugdale of the Inner Temple in the City of London, and Henry Charles Geast Dugdale of Blyth Hall, a Captain in Her Majesty's 2nd Battalion Rifle Brigade, the sons, three of the Exors. She died at Blyth Hall, aged 95 years and 355 days, on Friday, 17 April, and was bur. at Merevale 21 April 1903.

Frederick William Berkeley Portman, born at Langton Lodge, Blandford, co. Dorset, 15 March 1842; Ensign 15th Regiment Bombay Native Infantry; died at Ahmednagar, Bombay, India, aged 18, on Wednesday, 1 August 1860, and bur. in the cemetery at that station.

Aileen Ethel, born at Satara, Bombay Presidency, 31 July 1866, and bapt. there; marr. at Kirkee, Bombay Presidency, on Saturday, 10 October 1885, William Yorke Foster of "The Grove," Hardingham, co. Norfolk (eldest son of Sir William Foster of Norwich, Bart., by Georgina his 1st wife, dau. of Richard Armit of Monkstown, co. Dublin); born at Upper St. Giles' Street, Norwich, on Sunday, 1 April 1860, and bapt. there; entered the Army as Lieutenant Royal Artillery 18 February 1880, Captain 1 April 1888, Major 20 November 1897, Staff-Captain Royal Artillery, Bengal, 23 May 1892 to 31 March 1895, D.A.A.G. for Royal Artillery, Bombay, 1 April 1895 to 14 May 1897; served in South African War 1899–1900, with the Ladysmith Relief Force, including action at Colenso, in command of the 66th Royal Field Artillery; at the operations in the Transvaal in May and June 1900 (medal and clasps).

Mary Ada, only dau. of Major Francis Hastings Toone Gordon-Cumming; marr. at Birdsall, co. York, 9 February 1888; divorced on her petition 1897; marr. 2ndly (by the father of the bridegroom) on Wednesday, 7 June 1899, Ralph Assheton Harbord (eldest son of the Hon[ble] and Rev. John Harbord, Rector of South Repps, co. Norfolk). She died 13 May 1900, and was bur. at Salisbury, Rhodesia, British South Africa. 1st wife.	Claud Berkeley Portman of Child Okeford, co. Dorset; born at Durweston, co. Dorset, on Tuesday, 1 November 1864, bapt. privately the next day, and received into the church at Bryanston 19 January 1865; educated at Eton; formerly Captain Dorsetshire Imperial Yeomanry 1896; J.P. for co. Dorset.	Harriette Mary, 2nd dau. of William Stevenson; marr. at the British Consulate, Rome, and afterwards at Holy Trinity, Rome, on Saturday, 12 March 1898. She marr. 1stly John Dutton Hunt, Captain Highland Light Infantry, who divorced her in 1897, and changed his name to Hopton in 1898. 2nd wife.

Guinivere, born at The Manor House, Child Okeford, at 3.45 p.m., on Saturday, 5 January, bapt. at Bryanston 30 July 1889.	Joan, born at 4 Lower Berkeley Street, Portman Square, London, on Sunday, 24 August, died there 12 September 1890, and bur. in Brookwood Cemetery, co. Surrey, the next day.	Edward Claud Berkeley Portman, born at Child Okeford on Friday, 8 July, bapt. there 28 July 1898.	Sylvia Grace, born at Child Okeford 19 March, bapt. at St. George's Chapel, Albemarle Street, London, 25 April 1900.
			Jocelyn, born at Child Okeford on Wednesday, 27 May, bapt. at St. George's Chapel, Albemarle Street, London, 22 June 1903.

41

A _____

┌─────────┐

Rev. Fitzhardinge Berkeley Portman of Orchard Portman House, ╤ Frances Anne, eldest dau. of
co. Somerset; born 23 January, bapt. privately 25 January │ the Rev. William Nicholas
1811 (baptism registered at Bryanston, co. Dorset); of Christ │ Darnell, Rector of Stanhope,
Church, Oxford, matriculated 20 May 1828, aged 17, Fellow │ co. Durham, and Prebendary
of All Souls' College 1831–40, B.A. 1832, M.A. 1836; Rector │ of Durham, by Elizabeth
of Staple Fitzpaine and Orchard Portman, co. Somerset, 1840, │ Bowe his wife; born 3 De-
Prebendary of Wells 1841, and Rural Dean; died at Orchard │ cember 1818; marr. at
Portman, aged 82, on Monday, 6 March, bur. at Staple │ Stanhope 24 August 1840;
Fitzpaine 10 March 1893. Will dated 4 June 1889, with two │ died at the Rectory, Staple
codicils dated respectively 18 March 1890 and 8 February 1892, │ Fitzpaine, on Sunday, 19 May,
proved (Prin. Reg., 381, 93) 6 April 1893, by Charles Edward │ bur. at Staple Fitzpaine
Lance and Edmund Mainley Awdry, the Exors. │ 23 May 1889.

G

┌──

Mary Elizabeth, born 23 May, bapt. at Staple Fitzpaine 20 June 1841; marr. at Calcutta, India,
on Monday, 5 November 1866, Charles Edward Lance of Stoke Court, Taunton, co. Somerset
(3rd son of the Rev. Edwin Lance, Rector of Buckland St. Mary, co. Somerset, by Madeline
Monica his wife, dau. of Josias du Pré Porcher of Wirishead, co. Devon); born 3 June 1827;
educated at East India College, Haileybury; formerly of the Bengal Civil Service.

☥

D _____

┌─────────────────────────────┐   ┌─────────────────

Evelyn Harriet Lavinia, born at Langton Lodge, Blandford,   Geraldine Blanche, born at
co. Dorset, 26 September, bapt. at Pimperne, co. Dorset,   Dean's Court, Wimborne, on
30 October 1843; marr. at Wimborne Minster, co. Dorset   Friday, 29 June, bapt. at Wim-
(by the Rev. Fitzhardinge Berkeley Portman, uncle of the   borne Minster 30 August 1855;
bride, assisted by the Rev. Henry Fitzhardinge Berkeley   marr. at Ditcheat, co. Somerset
Portman, brother of the bride, and the Rev. Henry Parker   (by the Rev. Fitzhardinge
Cookesley), on Thursday, 3 October 1867, as his 2nd wife,   Berkeley Portman, uncle of the
the Honble Maurice Berkeley Portman, her cousin (3rd son   bride, assisted by the Rev.
of Edward Berkeley Portman, 1st Viscount Portman); born   William Marriatt Leir, the
at Bryanston on Friday, 18 January 1833, bapt. privately the Rector), on Wednesday, 25
next day (baptism registered at Bryanston); J.P. for co.   June 1884, Blanchard Reginald
Somerset; Attaché at Mexico 1853–56; Member of the   Toogood Coward, Commander
Canadian Parliament 1861–64; died at Ashfield House, North   R.N. (retired 27 May 1896).
Petherton, co. Somerset, aged 54, at 2 p.m. on Thursday, 12   She died 16 March, and was
January, bur. in the cemetery at North Petherton 17 January   bur. at Newton Abbot, co.
1888. (See page 43.)   Devon, 20 March 1900.
                                ☥
F _____   ☥

┌────────────────┐

William Aubrey Fitzhardinge Berkeley Portman, born at Ahmednagar, Bombay Presidency,
India, 19 October 1870, and bapt. there; died at " Brookfield," Keynstone, co. Dorset, on
Monday, 5 June 1871, and bur. in the churchyard at Keynstone.

B _____ B

C _____ C

┌─────────────────────────────┐   ┌─┐ ┌──

Susan Alice, born at 42 Portman Square, London,   Seymour Berkeley Portman, born at 42
30 March 1866, and bapt. there privately;   Portman Square, London, on Wednesday,
marr. at St. Mary's, Bryanston Square, London,   19 February 1868, and bapt. there
8 August 1893, Alan William Heber-Percy of   privately.
Durweston, co. Dorset (youngest son of Algernon
Charles Heber-Percy of Hodnet Hall, co. Salop,   ―
and of Airmyn, co. York, by Emily his wife, eldest
dau. of the Rt. Rev. Reginald Heber, D.D.,   Frances Maud, born at 42 Portman Square,
Bishop of Calcutta); born 27 March 1865;   London, on Tuesday, 2 July 1872, and
educated at Eton and at Trinity College, Cam-   bapt. there privately; died at Durweston,
bridge; J.P. and County Councillor (Pimperne   aged 10 months, on Monday, 12 May,
Division) co. Dorset. ╤   bur. at Bryanston 16 May 1873.
              ☥

Emma Lucy, born at Staple Fitzpaine, co. Somerset, 21 April, bapt. there 13 August 1843; marr. at Staple Fitzpaine (by the Rev. William Henry Lance) on Thursday, 4 May 1865, Daniel Mildred of Preston, Cirencester, co. Gloucester (son of Daniel Mildred of Woodford, co. Essex, by Emily his wife, dau. of Brice Pearse of Woodford); born at Hale End, Woodford, on Wednesday, 11 July 1838; died at Preston, Cirencester, 28 December 1873. Will dated 6 November 1872, proved at Gloucester 31 January 1874, by Henry Mildred of 8 St. Helen's Place, in the City of London, Frederick Mildred, the younger, of 73 Lombard Street, in the said City, and the Rev. Oswald Smith of Crudwell, co. Wilts, Rector of Crudwell, three of the Exors.

Helen Vidal, dau. of Captain John Harris of London, Canada West; born 25 July 1834; marr. at London, Canada West, 4 June 1856; died at London, Canada West, on Friday, 30 March 1860, and bur. there. 1st wife.	Maurice Berkeley Portman of "Ashfield, North Petherton, co. Somerset; born at Bryanston, co. Dorset, on Friday, 18 January 1833, bapt. privately the next day (baptism registered at Bryanston); J.P. for co. Somerset; Attaché at Mexico 1853–56; a Member of the Canadian Parliament 1861–64; died at "Ashfield," North Petherton, aged 54, at 2 p.m. on Thursday, 12 January, bur. in the cemetery at North Petherton 17 January 1888. Will dated 1 June 1883, proved (Prin. Reg., 269, 88) 3 March 1888, by the Honble Evelyn Harriet Lavinia Portman of "Ashfield," North Petherton, Bridgwater, co. Somerset, the relict, the sole Executrix.	Evelyn Harriet Lavinia (his cousin), eldest dau. of Henry William Berkeley Portman of Dean's Court, Wimborne, co. Dorset; born at Langton Lodge, Blandford, co. Dorset, 26 September, bapt. at Pimperne, co. Dorset, 30 October 1843; marr. at Wimborne Minster (by the Rev. Fitzhardinge Berkeley Portman, uncle of the bride, assisted by the Rev. Henry Fitzhardinge Berkeley Portman, brother of the bride, and the Rev. Henry Parker Cookesley) on Thursday, 3 October 1867. 2nd wife. (See page 42.)

(See page 42.)

Berkeley Portman of West Stratford House, Micheldever, co. Hants; born 8 April 1857.	Jessie Campbell, 3rd dau. of General Sir Robert Percy Douglas, 4th Bart., by Louisa his 2nd wife, youngest dau. of Robert Lang of Moor Park, co. Surrey; marr. at Bradford, co. Somerset (by the Rev. Fitzhardinge Berkeley Portman, assisted by the Rev. Hugh Jenison Adair, the Vicar), on Tuesday, 6 February 1883.

Maurice Percy Berkeley Portman, born 8 August 1884; entered the Royal Navy 15 September 1900, Mipshipman H.M.S. "Cressy" 19 August 1901.

Gerald Berkeley Portman of Healing Manor, co. Lincoln; born at Montagu House, 22 Portman Square, London, on Saturday morning, 23 January 1875; entered the Army as 2nd Lieutenant 10th Hussars 28 September 1895, Lieutenant 5 October 1896, Captain 11 June 1901; A.D.C. to Lord Curzon, Viceroy of India, during 1901.	Dorothy Marie Isolde, youngest dau. of Sir Robert Sheffield of Normanby Park, co. Lincoln, 5th Bart., by Priscilla Isabella Laura his wife, 3rd dau. of Lieut.-Colonel Henry Dumaresq, R.E.; marr. at St. Andrew's, Burton-on-Stather, co. Lincoln (by the Rt. Rev. Edward King, D.D., Bishop of Lincoln, assisted by the Rev. George Marriott, Rector of Sigglesthorne, co. York), on Wednesday, 16 July 1902.

Gerald William Berkeley Portman, born at Healing Manor on Thursday, 20 August, bapt. at St. Andrew's, Burton-on-Stather, on Wednesday, 23 September 1903.

G   G

Katherine Ella, born at Staple Fitzpaine, co. Somerset, 1 November 1844, bapt. privately 11 February, and received into the church at Staple Fitzpaine 3 August 1845; marr. at Sydney, New South Wales, 22 May 1873, Charles Alexander John Woocock of Nerada, Queensland, Australia.

B

Louisa Mary, born at Bryanston House, co. Dorset, on Sunday, 15 June 1834, and bapt. privately the same day (baptism registered at Bryanston); died unmarried at 5 Prince's Gate, Hyde Park, London, aged 36, 7 July, bur. at Bryanston 14 July 1870. Will dated 3 June 1865, with codicil dated 10 June 1870, proved (Prin. Reg., 500, 70) 30 July 1870, by the Hon[ble] William Henry Berkeley Portman of 42 Portman Square, co. Middlesex, and the Rev. Walter Berkeley Portman, Rector of Corton-Denham, co. Somerset, the brothers, the Exors.   B

I

Cecil Berkeley Portman, born at = **Florence Wyndham,** 4th dau. of Lachlan Forbes of Eversley House, Brooklands, co. Shillingstone, co. Dorset, Major 31st Regiment of Foot, Chester, on Sunday, 12 September, J.P. for co. Dorset, by Julia his wife, dau. of Alexander bapt. at Brooklands 26 September Wyndham of West Loope, co. Dorset; marr. at Shilling-1869; formerly 2nd Lieutenant 3rd stone (by the Rev. Arthur Gordon Deedes, Curate of Battalion (Prince Albert's) Somerset-St. John the Divine, Kennington, co. Surrey) on Saturday, shire Light Infantry (Militia).   6 December 1902.

H

Maurice William Portman of Organ = **Mary,** dau. of Captain Hudson   **Maurice Vidal Portman,** Ford Manor, Wareham, co. Dorset; of Flixton, co. Suffolk, R.N.;   born at London, Canada born at London, Canada West, marr. at St. Peter's, Eaton   West, on Wednesday, 10 October 1858, and bapt. there; Square, London, 12 September   21 March 1860. educated at Repton and H.M.S. 1889. She marr. 1stly Herbert "Britannia"; Commander R.N. Wybault Colvin. (retired).

Guy Maurice Berkeley Portman, born at "Grey Friars," Ringwood, co. Hants, on Monday, 4 August 1890, and bapt. at Ringwood.   I

C

Mary Isabel, born at Montagu   **Constance,** born at Montagu House, 22 Portman Square, House, 22 Portman Square, London, at 11.20 a.m., on Tuesday, 11 July 1882; died London, on Thursday, 12 there, at 2 p.m., on Friday, 14 July, bur. in the churchyard April 1877, and bapt. there at Durweston, co. Dorset, on Tuesday, 18 July 1882. privately.

Frances Blanche, born at Staple Fitzpaine, co. Somerset, on Saturday, 30 May, bapt. there 9 September 1846; marr. at All Saints', Knightsbridge, London (by the Rev. William Cavington, assisted by the Rev. Edward Pattinson Cole), on Thursday, 9 December 1869, the Rev. Thomas Henry Cole (eldest son of Thomas Bullman Cole of Yeovil, co. Somerset); born 16 May 1831; of Exeter College, Oxford, matriculated 7 June 1854, aged 19, B.A. 1858, M.A. 1861; Chaplain of H.M. Prison, Lewes, co. Sussex, 1871; died at Malling Deanery, Lewes, aged 58, on Tuesday, 4 April 1893. Will dated 6 August 1892, proved (Prin. Reg., 432, 93) 30 May 1893, by John Currey and the Rev. Gerald Henry Moor, the Exors. She died s.p. 2 November, and was bur. in Highgate Cemetery, London, 7 November 1870.

Rev. Walter Berkeley Portman, born at Bryanston Square, London, 1 December 1836, bapt. privately the next day (baptism registered at Bryanston, co. Dorset); educated at Eton and at Christ Church, Oxford, matriculated 30 May 1855, aged 18, B.A. 1859; Rector of Corton-Denham, co. Somerset, for 40 years; died at Corton-Denham, aged 66, on Sunday, 22 March, bur. there 26 March 1903. Will dated 14 May 1880, with two codicils dated respectively 27 June 1889 and 11 February 1895, proved (Prin. Reg., 57, 1903) 23 May 1903, by the Honble Alice Portman, the relict, and the Rev. Alan Berkeley Portman, the son, the Exors.

Alice, youngest dau. of Sir John Mordaunt of Walton, co. Warwick, 9th Bart., by Caroline Sophia his wife, 2nd dau. of the Rt. Rev. George Murray, D.D., Bishop of Rochester; born at Walton on Saturday, 17 February, bapt. at Walton D'Eivill, co. Warwick, 17 March 1844; marr. there (by the Rev. Francis Murray) on Wednesday, 5 October 1864.

Ethel, born at 5 Prince's Gate, Hyde Park, London, on Friday, 26 October, bapt. there privately 29 October 1866, and received into the church at Corton-Denham, co. Somerset, 3 February 1867.

Rev. Alan Berkeley Portman, born at Corton-Denham on Saturday, 17 February, bapt. there 7 April 1872; educated at Wellington and at University College, Oxford, matriculated 11 October 1890, aged 18, B.A. 1894, M.A. 1902; Curate of Sampford Courtenay, co. Devon, 1898, Rector of Corton-Denham since May 1903.

Gertrude Emma, born at Eversley House, Brooklands, co. Chester, on Monday, 15 May, bapt. at Brooklands 27 July 1871; marr. at St. Mary's, North Petherton, co. Somerset (by the Rev. Henry Fitzhardinge Berkeley Portman, uncle of the bride, assisted by the Rev. Prebendary Robinson, uncle of the bridegroom, and the Rev. Percy Turner Mitchell, the Vicar), on Wednesday, 30 July 1902, William Hunter Gandy of Bradley Court, Micheldean, co. Gloucester (son of the Rev. James Hunter Gandy, M.A., Rector of Stanwick, co. Northampton, by Marian Jane his wife, dau. of the Rev. W. Robinson, Vicar of North Petherton); born at the Rectory, Stanwick, 13 April, bapt. at Stanwick 23 June 1867; educated at Thames Nautical Training College, and H.M.S. "Worcester"; Int. B.Sc. (London), F.R.G.S., F.C.S.; of the Royal Naval Reserve.

G

Gertrude Agnes, born 27 December 1850, bapt. at Staple Fitzpaine, co. Somerset, 20 February 1851; marr. there (by the Ven^ble George Anthony Denison, Archdeacon of Taunton, assisted by the Rev. William Neville) on Thursday, 24 April 1879, Robert Neville Grenville of Butleigh, co. Somerset (eldest son of Ralph Neville Grenville of Butleigh Court, M.P., D.L., by Julia Roberta his wife, dau. of Sir Robert Frankland Russell, Bart., M.P.); born at Windsor, co. Berks, on Wednesday, 16 December 1846; educated at Eton and at Magdalene College, Cambridge, B.A. 1869, M.A. 1878; Civil Engineer; Captain West Somersetshire Yeomanry Cavalry 1878-85; J.P., D.L., and County Alderman for co. Somerset, High Sheriff 1900.

Reginald Fitzhardinge Berkeley=Carrie, dau. of John Portman of Decorah, Iowa, U.S.A.; born at Staple Fitzpaine 20 February, bapt. there 13 April 1853; educated on H.M.S. "Britannia" 1864-65; Midshipman R.N., invalided 1869.

Carrie, dau. of John Stewart of Decorah, Iowa, by Catherine his wife, dau. of Frederick Fox, Barrister-at-Law; born at Brownsville, N.Y., U.S.A., 11 February 1849, and bapt. there; marr. at Decorah 6 November 1878.

G

Frances Catherine, born at Decorah, Iowa, on Monday, 9 August, bapt. there 21 November 1880.

John Fitzhardinge Berkeley Portman, born at Decorah, Iowa, 6 November, bapt. there 27 December 1885.

K

Lionel Portman, born at Corton-Denham, co. Somerset, on Friday, 26 December 1873, bapt. there 10 February 1874; educated at Wellington and at University College, Oxford, matriculated 15 October 1892, aged 18; Coxswain of the University Eight 1893.

Francis John Portman, born at the Rectory, Corton-Denham, on Sunday, 24 March, bapt. at Corton-Denham 5 May 1878; educated at Radley and at Christ Church, Oxford, B.A. 1900.

I

Montagu Berkeley Portman of "Ashfield," Bridgwater, co.=Jessie Elizabeth, youngest dau. Somerset; born at Eversley House, Brooklands, co. Chester, on Saturday, 6 July, bapt. privately 15 July 1872 (baptism registered at Brooklands); educated privately at Southbourne, co. Hants, and at the Military College, Oxford; formerly Lieutenant 3rd Battalion (Prince Albert's) Somersetshire Light Infantry.

Jessie Elizabeth, youngest dau. of George Edwin Lance of the Bengal Civil Service; born 12 November 1876; marr. at St. George's, Hanover Square, London, 13 December 1899.

Gerald Berkeley Portman, born 11 February 1903.

46

Alma Beatrice, born 15 October, bapt. at Staple Fitzpaine, co. Somerset, 13 December 1854; died, aged 4, 2 March, bur. at Staple Fitzpaine 5 March 1859.

Mabel Georgina, born 10 May, bapt. at Staple Fitzpaine 20 July 1856; marr. at Butleigh, co. Somerset (by the Rev. William Henry Lance), on Saturday, 26 August 1893, the Rev. William Henry Box (son of Stephen Thomas Box, by Hannah his wife); of St. John's College, Cambridge, matriculated Michaelmas Term, 1886, B.A. 1889, M.A. 1893; Chaplain King's College, Taunton, co. Somerset, 1890–93, and Rector of Puckington, co. Somerset, 1894–98.

Arthur Fitzhardinge Berkeley Portman of Chevy Chase, Maryland, U.S.A.; born at Staple Fitzpaine 18 November 1859, bapt. there 6 January 1860; educated at St. Andrew's College, Chardstock, co. Somerset.
═══
Adeline, dau. of Samuel Bealls Elwell of Serena, Illinois, U.S.A., by Elizabeth Katherine Dolph his wife; born at Serena, Illinois, 27 February 1860; bapt. at Iowa City, Iowa, U.S.A.; marr. at Las Vegas, New Mexico, U.S.A., 20 August 1893.

Philip Neville Berkeley Portman, born 30 October, bapt. at Staple Fitzpaine 7 December 1864; died at Staple Fitzpaine, aged 17 months, 7 April, bur. there 10 April 1866.

Portman

Freeman of Combs, co. Suffolk.

Edmund Freeman of "The Cedars," Combs, co. Suffolk (3rd son of the=Margaret, dau. of Rev. John Freeman, Rector of Creeting All Saints' and St. Peter's, co. Suffolk, by Elizabeth his wife, eldest dau. of Sir Philip Broke of Nacton, co. Suffolk, Bart.); born 27 February, bapt. at Combs 16 March 1782; Captain in the West Suffolk Militia and in the Hon[ble] East India Co.'s Service; succeeded to the Combs family estates in 1810, after the deaths of his elder brothers, John Freeman, who died in 1795, and Philip Freeman, who died in 1810; died at Combs, aged 39, 5 March, bur. in the family vault in the church at Combs 12 March 1821. Will dated 7 November 1820, proved (P.C.C., 664 *Mansfield*) 31 December 1821, by Margaret Freeman, the relict, Edmund Jenney, Horatio George Broke and William Pearson, the Exors.

Margaret, dau. of William Hughes of Mulgannon, co. Wexford; marr. at Augha-loo, co. Wexford, 20 October 1813; died, aged 64, 22 January, bur. in St. Nicho-las' Churchyard, Chichester, co. Sussex, 27 January 1849.

Edm? Freeman *Margaret Freeman*

A

Edmund Freeman (twin with Margaret); born 29 June 1814, bapt. privately at Tullamore, King's County, and received into the church at Combs 30 April 1816; bur. at Combs 21 October 1819.

—

Margaret (twin with Edmund); born 29 June 1814, bapt. privately at Tulla-more, and received into the church at Combs 30 April 1816; bur. at Combs 3 May 1828.

Rev. John Freeman, born in July, bapt. at=Lucy Charlotte, dau. of Combs 31 July 1815; educated at Dedham Grammar School, co. Suffolk, and at St. Peter's College, Cambridge, B.A. and Senior Optime 1837, M.A. 1840; Rector of Ashwicken with Leziate, co. Norfolk, 1840, Rural Dean 1846; J.P. for co. Norfolk 1855; died s.p. at Ashwicken Rectory, aged 61, on Thursday, 4 January, bur. at Ashwicken 10 January 1877. M.I. Will dated 17 January 1876, with codicil dated 29 December 1876, proved at Norwich 12 March 1877, by James Inglis of Colchester, co Essex, gent., Lucy Charlotte Freeman of Ashwicken, co. Norfolk, the relict, and the Rev. William Maundy Harvey Elwyn of Waresley, co. Huntingdon, the Exors.

John Freeman

Lucy Charlotte, dau. of Robinson Kittoe, R.N.; marr. at Barham, co. Suf-folk (by the Rev. William Kirby, F.R.S.), on Wednes-day, 22 April 1840; died at Seckhams, Lindfield, co. Sussex, in her 70th year, on Wednesday, 3 Decem-ber, bur. at Ashwicken 8 December 1884. Will dated 28 November 1883, proved (Prin. Reg., 29, 85) 20 January 1885, by George Dominicus Kittoe of 47 Aynhoe Road, West Kensington, co. Middlesex, the brother, and Mary Ann Elwyn (wife of the Rev. William Maundy Harvey Elwyn) of the Vicarage, Waresley, co. Huntingdon, the Exors.

B

Mary, born 20 May, bapt. at Subdeanery Church, Chichester, 6 June 1847; marr. at Exeter Cathedral (by the Ven[ble] Archdeacon Woollcombe) on Wednesday, 6 August 1879, the Ven[ble] William Andrewes Fearon, D.D. (3rd son of the Rev. Daniel Rose Fearon, Vicar of Assington, co. Suffolk, by Frances Jane his wife, dau. of the Rev. Charles Andrewes); born at the Vicarage, Assington, 4 February 1841; of New College, Oxford, matriculated 13 October 1859, aged 18, Scholar 1859, B.A. 1864, Fellow 1864–80, M.A. 1866, B. and D.D. 1884; Tutor 1865; Head-Master Durham Cathedral School 1882–84, Assistant-Master Winchester College 1868–82, Head-Master 1884–1901; Hon. Canon of Winchester since 1889, Archdeacon of Winchester 1903.

William Freeman, born 19 November 1816, bapt. at Combs, co. Suffolk, 11 September 1817; educated at Dedham Grammar School, co. Suffolk; Lieutenant Royal Artillery; died unmarried at Coddenham, co. Suffolk, and bur. in the family vault at Combs 3 August 1837.

Ven^ble Philip Freeman, born at "The Cedars," Combs, 8 February, bapt. at Combs 15 February 1818; educated at Dedham Grammar School, under Dr. George Taylor, and Scholar of Trinity College, Cambridge, 1835, awarded, in 1837 and 1838, Sir William Browne's medals for a Latin ode and epigrams, elected Craven University Scholar 1838, B.A. and Senior Classic 1839, M.A. 1842, Fellow of St. Peter's College, Cambridge, 1839; Principal of Chichester Theological College 1846–48, Canon and a Reader in Theology of Cumbrae College (the college built by the Earl of Glasgow in the Island of Cumbrae, co. Bute) 1852–58, having at the same time charge of the Episcopal Church of that island; Vicar of Thorverton, co. Devon, 1858 –74, Prebendary of Exeter Cathedral November 1861–64, Archdeacon of Exeter and Canon of Exeter April 1864 to death; Author of "The Principles of Divine Service," 1855, and numerous other works; died from the result of an accident on the railway, 18 February, at the residence of Thomas Gambier, Surgeon, 1 Northumberland Terrace, Primrose Hill, co. Middlesex, aged 57, on Wednesday, 24 February, bur. in the churchyard at Thorverton 2 March 1875. Will dated 4 February 1868, proved (Prin. Reg., 300, 75) 3 April 1875, by the Rev. Harry Baber of Ramsbury, co. Wilts, and James Inglis of Colchester, co. Essex, the Exors.

Ann, youngest dau. of the Rev. Henry Hervey Baber, F.R.S., Rector of Stretham, co. Cambridge, and Keeper of the Printed Books at the British Museum 1812–37; born at the British Museum 11 February 1821; marr. at Stretham (by the Rev. Dr. Mill, Chaplain to the Archbishop of Canterbury) on Tuesday, 18 August 1846; died at Exmouth, co. Devon, aged 76, on Thursday, 14 October, bur. at Thorverton 18 October 1897. Will dated 4 November 1895, proved (Prin. Reg., 1209, 97) 27 November 1897, by George Broke Freeman and the Rev. Edward Vere Freeman, the sons, the Exors.

Philip Freeman [signature]

George Broke Freeman, born 12 November, bapt. at Old Subdeanery Church, Chichester, co. Sussex, on Advent Sunday, 3 December 1848; educated at Uppingham School and at Trinity College, Cambridge, Declamation Prize 1870, B.A. (2nd-class Classical Tripos) 1871, M.A. 1874; a Student of Lincoln's Inn 28 January 1870, called to the Bar 17 November 1873; Equity Draftsman and Conveyancer; Original Member of London Diocesan Conference.

Horatia, youngest dau. of Horace Dobell of 84 Harley Street, London, M.D., by Elizabeth Mary his wife, dau. of George Fordham; born 18 January 1855; marr. at St. Andrew's, Wells Street, London (by the Rev. Benjamin Webb, the Vicar, and the Rev. Harry Baber, Vicar of Ramsbury, co. Wilts, uncle of the bridegroom), on Saturday, 14 April 1877.

Philip Horace Freeman, born at 60 Cornwall Road, Bayswater, London, on Monday, 27 May, bapt. at All Saints', Notting Hill, London, 29 June 1878; educated at Marlborough College and at Trinity College, Cambridge, B.A. (3rd-class Historical Tripos) 1901.

George Sydney Freeman, born at 60 Cornwall Road, Bayswater, London, on Wednesday, 19 November, bapt. at All Saints', Notting Hill, London, 16 December 1879; educated at Bradfield College (Exhibitioner), and Scholar of Pembroke College, Oxford, 2nd-class Classical Mods. 1900, B.A. (3rd-class Final Classical Schools) 1902.

A

Elizabeth Mary, born 4 February, bapt. at Combs, co. Suffolk, 7 February 1820; died at Woodbridge, co. Suffolk, aged 9, and bur. in the family vault at Combs 15 December 1829.

Edmund Freeman, born in 1821; died, aged 7 months, and bur. in the family vault at Combs 15 April 1822.

B

Edith, born 13 May, bapt. at Sub-deanery Church, Chichester, co. Sussex, 29 May 1850.

Rev. Edward Vere Freeman, born 30 January, bapt. at New Subdeanery Church, Chichester, 20 February 1853; educated at Winchester and at Brasenose College, Oxford, 2nd-class Natural Science Honour Schools 1875, B.A. 1875, M.A. 1878; Vicar of West Anstey, co. Devon, 1885, of St. James', Exeter, 1893, and of Exmouth, co. Devon, 1897; Rural Dean of South Molton 1892–93.

Honor Henrietta, youngest dau. of the Rev. John Drake Becher of Hill House, Southwell, co. Nottingham, by Elizabeth Susannah his wife, dau. of Henry Vesey Machin; marr. at Southwell Minster (by the Rev. Harry Baber, Vicar of Ramsbury, co. Wilts, assisted by the Rev. William Becher) on Wednesday, 15 January 1879.

Margaret Mary Vere, born at 10 Beacon, Exmouth, on Tuesday, 18 November, bapt. at Exmouth 14 December 1879; marr. at Holy Trinity, Exmouth, 10 December 1901, Thomas Gosselin Elliott of Delpotonoya, Ceylon (son of Nicholas Gosselin Elliott of Kellistown, co. Carlow, by Anna his wife, dau. of Captain Sir Thomas Ross, R.N.); born 6 February 1870.

C

Kenneth John Freeman, born at 60 Cornwall Road, Bayswater, London, on Monday, 19 June, bapt. at All Saints', Notting Hill, London, 31 July 1882; educated at Winchester (Scholar), and Scholar of Trinity College, Cambridge; awarded, in 1903, Sir William Browne's medal for a Greek epigram, and elected Browne University Scholar same year.

Percy Broke Freeman, born at 30 Bassett Road, London, on Monday, 29 August, bapt. at All Saints', Notting Hill, London, 29 September 1887; educated at Bradfield College (Exhibitioner).

Dorothy, born at 30 Bassett Road, London, on Friday, 30 May, bapt. at All Saints', Notting Hill, London, 5 July 1890.

G. Broke Freeman

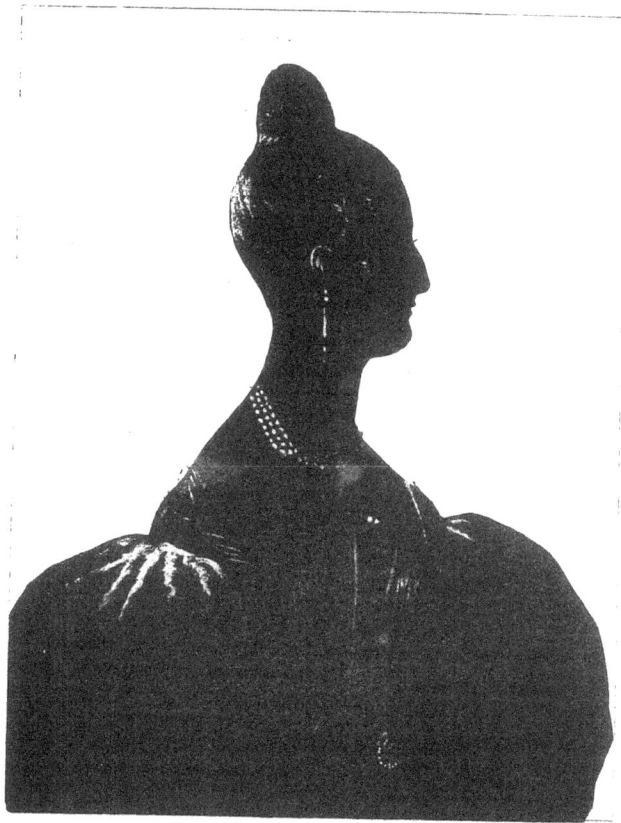

Fac-simile of a Silhouette of Susanna, daughter of John Spencer of Wrotham, co. Kent, and wife of James Hackett Hodsoll of Loose Court, co. Kent; born 10 May 1812, died 8 May 1874; in the possession of Charles Maxfield Hodsoll, her son.

Hodsoll of Loose, co. Kent.

Arms.—Azure, three wells argent.

James Hodsoll of Wrotham, co. Kent (only surviving son of Maxfield Hodsoll of Wrotham, by Sarah his wife, dau. of James Hackett); born at Wrotham 13 October, bapt. there 5 November 1788; died, aged 25, 27 September, bur. at Wrotham 4 October 1813. = Caroline, dau. of Joseph Spencer of Wrotham, by Susanna Woodhams his wife; born at Hartfield, co. Sussex, 25 December 1789, bapt. there 10 February 1790; marr. at Wrotham 10 June 1812; marr. 2ndly Edward Munk of Maidstone, co. Kent, who died, aged 63, and was bur. in the churchyard of the parish church, Maidstone, 7 December 1841. Will dated 9 July 1841, proved (P.C.C., 823, 41) 30 December 1841, by Abraham Spencer and George Spencer, two of the Exors. Power reserved to William Wickham, the other Exor. She died, aged 76, 8 October, and was bur. in the churchyard of the parish church, Maidstone, 13 October 1866.

Fac-simile of an impression of a seal from a deed dated 1690.

James Hackett Hodsoll of Loose Court, co. Kent; born at Wrotham 13 May 1813, bapt. there 18 April 1814; Lord of the Manor of Loose, Patron of the living of Dennington, co. Suffolk; died at the Rectory, Dennington, the residence of his son-in-law, aged 74, on Sunday, 19 February, bur. in the cemetery at Maidstone 23 February 1888. Will dated 27 March 1879, with codicil dated 13 May 1882, proved (Prin. Reg., 343, 88) 26 April 1888, by Charles Maxfield Hodsoll of Loose Court, in the parish of Loose, co. Kent, the son, one of the Exors. = Susanna, dau. of John Spencer of Wrotham, by Hester Hooker his wife; born at Mayfield, co. Sussex, 10 May, bapt. there 19 June 1812; marr. at St. Bride's, Fleet Street, London, 27 May 1839; died at 2 Oak Villas, Haverstock Hill, London, aged 61, on Friday, 8 May, bur. in the cemetery at Maidstone 15 May 1874.

Jas H. Hodsoll

A

Laura, born 17 July, bapt. at the parish church, Maidstone, 12 August 1840; marr. at the parish church, Loose, 26 October 1870, the Rev. George Castleden (son of George Castleden of Canterbury, co. Kent, by his wife, Jane Packman Smith of Canterbury); born at St. Dunstan's, Canterbury, 9 May 1842; of Queen's College, Cambridge, matriculated Michaelmas Term, 1862, B.A. 1866, M.A. 1869; Rector of Dennington since 1879.

Caroline, born 2 March, bapt. at the parish church, Maidstone, 27 April 1842; marr. at New College Chapel, St. John's Wood, London (by the father of the bridegroom), on Wednesday, 12 July 1871, Edward Hill Mannering (elder son of the Rev. Edward Mannering, Minister of Holywell Mount Chapel, and afterwards of Bishopsgate Chapel, London, by Mary his wife, dau. of John Hill of London); born 22 January 1830; educated at Mill Hill School, co. Middlesex; Secretary of the Sun Fire Office, London; died at his residence, 11 Arkwright Road, Hampstead, co. Middlesex, aged 67, on Sunday, 13 June, bur. in Abney Park Cemetery, London, on Wednesday, 16 June 1897. Will dated 7 May 1897, proved (Prin. Reg., 922, 97) 13 August 1897, by Walter Mannering, the brother, and Charles Price, the Exors. She died, aged 47, on Friday, 11 January, and was bur. in Abney Park Cemetery, London, 15 January 1889.

B

Julia Henrietta, born at Loose Court on Friday, 7 October, bapt. at the parish church, Loose, 1 November 1870; marr. at St. Jude's, South Kensington, London (by the Rev. George Castleden, uncle of the bride), on Thursday, 9 June 1898, the Rev. George Douglas Castleden (only son of the Rev. George Castleden, Rector of Dennington); born 12 March 1875; of Pembroke College, Cambridge, matriculated Michaelmas Term, 1894, B.A. 1897, M.A. 1901; Curate of the Cathedral and Abbey Church of St. Albans, co. Hertford, since 1900, and Chaplain of H.M. Prison at St. Albans.

A

Charles Maxfield Hodsoll of Loose, co. Kent, formerly of Loose Court, and Lord of the Manor of Loose; born 15 November 1843, bapt. at the parish church, Maidstone, co. Kent, 17 April 1844.

=

Georgiana Mary, eldest dau. of George Kennet Pollock (eldest surviving son of Sir David Pollock, Chief Justice, Bombay, India), by Julia his wife, youngest dau. of Joseph Wood of Manadon Park, co. Devon; born at Calverley Park, Tunbridge Wells, co. Kent, on Saturday, 17 January, bapt. at Holy Trinity, Tunbridge Wells, 13 March 1846; marr. at the parish church, Loose, on Tuesday, 12 October 1869.

Georgiana Katharine, born at Loose Court on Saturday, 21 October, bapt. at the parish church, Loose, 15 November 1871.

Charles Wilfred Pollock Hodsoll, born at Loose Court on Saturday, 29 November, bapt. at the parish church, Loose, 22 December 1873; of University College, Oxford, matriculated 15 October 1892, aged 18, Exhibitioner 1892, graduated with honours (in classics) July 1896.

George Bertram Pollock Hodsoll, born at Loose Court on Friday, 18 June, bapt. at the parish church, Loose, 20 July 1875; Lieutenant 4th Battalion The Suffolk Regiment (Militia).

B

Harold Edward Pollock Hodsoll, born at Loose Court on Monday, 30 April, bapt. at the parish church, Loose, 4 June 1877; 2nd Assistant Surveyor to the Admiralty.

Laura Caroline Ethel, born at Loose Court on Sunday, 2 March, bapt. at the parish church, Loose, 24 April 1879.

Arthur Maxfield Pollock Hodsoll, born at Loose Court on Saturday, 18 December 1880, bapt. at the parish church, Loose, 16 February 1881.

Charles M. Hodsoll

Taylor of Manningtree, co. Essex.

Thomas Taylor of Ipswich, co. Suffolk ;═══Ann, dau. of William Tidyman
born at Ipswich in 1788 ; died, aged | of Ipswich ; born at Needham
64, 1 November, bur. at Mistley, co. | Market, co. Suffolk, in 1786 ;
Essex, 5 November 1852. | marr. 9 October 1810 ; died,
aged 88, 23 January, bur. at
Mistley 29 January 1874.

J. Taylor

A

Elizabeth, born at Bank House, Manningtree, co. Essex, 1 August 1814, bapt. at Manningtree (by the Rev. James Salisbury Dunn) 17 August 1841 ; marr. there 19 March 1842, Anthony Simpson (3rd son of Ralph Simpson of Darlington, co. Durham) ; born 5 March 1813 ; of St. Mary Hall, Oxford, matriculated 28 May 1841, aged 28 ; died at Brixton, co. Surrey, 28 October, bur. at the parish church, Brixton, 2 November 1847. She died at Manningtree, aged 41, 18 December, and was bur. in the cemetery at Manningtree 24 December 1855.

William Taylor of═══Susannah, dau. Manningtree ; born | of Philip Pearce at Bank House, | Trusson, by Sarah Manningtree, 16 | his wife, dau. of April 1816 ; died at | Philip Aldrich of Manningtree, aged | Framlingham, co. 55, 1 April, bur. in | Suffolk ; born at the cemetery at | Darsham, co. Suf-Manningtree 6 April | folk, 27 May, 1871. Admon was | bapt. there 5 June granted at Ipswich | 1826 ; marr. at 24 April 1871, to | St. Peter's, Col-Susannah Taylor of | chester, co. Essex, Manningtree, co. | 13 April 1852. Essex, the relict.

Martha, born at Bank House, Manningtree, 23 January 1821, bapt. at Manningtree (by the Rev. James Salisbury Dunn) 17 August 1841 ; died unmarried at Dulwich, co. Surrey, 16 September 1896.

Sarah, born at Mistley 26 January 1853.

———

Philip Taylor, born at Mistley 7 February 1854 ; died, aged 2 years and 3 months, 6 May, bur. at Manningtree 10 May 1856.

———

Alfred Taylor, born at Mistley 3 March 1855 ; died, aged 11 months, 13 February, bur. at Manningtree 18 February 1856.

Catherine Ann, born at Mistley 2 May 1856 ; died 21 February 1900.

———

Matilda, born at Mistley 30 August 1857 ; died, aged $8\frac{1}{2}$, 2 February, bur. at Manningtree 9 February 1866.

———

Harriett (twin with Caroline), born at Mistley 2 September 1858 ; died, aged $7\frac{1}{2}$, 6 February, bur. at Manningtree 9 February 1866.

Caroline (twin with Harriett), born at Mistley 2 September, died, aged 7 weeks, 22 October, bur. at Manningtree 27 October 1858.

———

Thomas Trusson Taylor, born at Mistley 1 October 1859.

———

Elizabeth, born at Mistley 24 June, died 27 June, bur. at Manningtree 29 June 1861.

B

A

Charles Taylor of Manningtree, co. Essex; born at Bank House, Manningtree, 3 June 1826, bapt. at Manningtree (by the Rev. James Salisbury Dunn) 9 January 1852. = Ellen, dau. of John Deane of Wix, co. Essex, by Mary his wife, dau. of John Constable of Wix; born at Wix 15 February, bapt. there 23 February 1823; marr. at St. James', Colchester, co. Essex, 26 January 1852.	Thomas Taylor, born at Bank House, Manningtree, 5 July 1828; marr. Kate Sexton of Wherstead Hall, Ipswich, co. Suffolk. He died s.p., aged 30, 9 October, and was bur. in the cemetery at Ipswich 15 October 1858. M.I.	A son died young.

C

Charles Walter Taylor of Mistley, co. Essex; born 27 December 1852, bapt. at Manningtree 13 February 1853; died at 50 Kepple Road, East Ham, co. Essex, aged 47, 11 March, bur. in Woodgrange Cemetery, co. Essex, 15 March 1900. Will dated 28 October 1891, proved at Ipswich 27 April 1900, by Charles Maurice Stanford, the sole Exor. = Frances, dau. of William Rees of Stepney, co. Middlesex, by Hannah Paddon his wife; born 2 April, bapt. at St. Dunstan's, Stepney, co. Middlesex, 27 August 1854; marr. at Napier, New Zealand, 28 July 1879; died, aged 37, 12 October, bur. in Woodgrange Cemetery 14 October 1891.	John Harry Taylor, born 25 July, bapt. at Manningtree (by the Rev. Henry John Dodsworth) 23 September 1854; died 18 November following, and bur. in the cemetery at Manningtree.

Chas Taylor

Charles Deane Taylor, born 25 December 1882, bapt. at the parish church, Leyton, co. Essex, 28 January 1883.	Florence Ellen, born 20 November 1885, bapt. at the parish church, Leyton, 28 February 1886.	Sydney Albert Taylor, born 26 October 1887, bapt. at the parish church, Leyton, 22 January 1888.

B

George Frederick Taylor, born 11 July, bapt. at Manningtree 24 December 1862.	Ellen, born at Mistley 4 June 1865; died, aged 8 months, 22 January, bur. at Manningtree 27 January 1866.	Herbert Charles Taylor, born at Mistley 27 December 1868.
—	—	—
William Tydeman Taylor, born 12 December 1863, bapt. at Manningtree 10 March 1864.	Charlotte, born at Mistley 24 December 1866.	Jane, born at Mistley 1 May 1870; died 16 August 1871, and bur. in the cemetery at Ipswich.

c

Ellen Agnes, born at Bank House, Manningtree, co. Essex, 11 January, bapt. there privately (by the Rev. William Peile Babington) 4 February 1856 (baptism registered at Manningtree).

Mary, born at Bank House, Manningtree, 8 April, bapt. there privately (by the Rev. William Peile Babington) 20 April 1857 (baptism registered at Manningtree); marr. at Mistley, co. Essex, 23 June 1885, Christopher George Battiscombe (son of the Rev. Henry Battiscombe, Minister of St. German's Chapel, Blackheath, co. Kent, by Eliza Susan Crickmer his wife); born at 18 Lee Park, Blackheath, 31 January 1857.

Deane Taylor, born 8 September 1858, bapt. at Manningtree (by the Rev. William Peile Babington) 20 February 1859; died, aged 23 weeks, 20 February, bur. in the cemetery at Manningtree 23 February 1859.

Anna Elizabeth, born at Bank House, Manningtree, 10 February, bapt. at Manningtree (by the Rev. William Peile Babington) 1 April 1860; marr. at Mistley 1 July 1891, Robert Henry Lingwood (son of Henry Lingwood of Needham Market, co. Suffolk, by his wife, Elizabeth Anne Roberts of Alderton, co. Suffolk); born at Needham Market on Christmas Day, 25 December 1861.

Louisa Blanche, born at Bank House, Manningtree, 5 July, bapt. at Manningtree (by the Rev. William Peile Babington) 25 August 1861; marr. at Mistley (by the Rev. Leighton George Hayne, D.Mus.) 1 December 1881, Charles Maurice Stanford of Braiswick House, Colchester, co. Essex (4th son of Frederick Stanford of Houbridge Hall, Great Oakley, co. Essex, by Anna Sophia his wife, 2nd dau. of Edwards Crisp of Rendlesham, co. Suffolk); born at Houbridge Hall, Great Oakley, 28 February, bapt. at Great Oakley 26 March 1846.

(See Pedigree of Stanford, Vol. 9, page 93.)

VIVE · UT · VIVAS

ABERCROMBY.

Arms on record in the College of Arms.—Argent, a fesse embattled gules, and in chief, issuing out of the embattlements of the fesse, a dexter arm embowed in armour proper, garnished or, the cubit part of the arm encircled by a wreath of laurel, and the hand grasping a French Republican military flag in bend sinister; ancient arms, argent, a chevron indented gules, between three boars' heads erased azure.

Crest.—A bee erect proper.

Supporters.—Two greyhounds per fesse, argent and or, each plain collared with line reflexed over the back gules, and charged on the shoulder with a thistle proper.

Abercromby.

George Abercromby, Baron Abercromby (eldest son of the Rt. Honble Major-General Sir Ralph Abercromby of Tullibody, co. Clackmannan, K.B., P.C., M.P. [Commander-in-Chief against the French, was mortally wounded at the battle of Alexandria March 1801, monument in St. Paul's Cathedral, London, by grant of the House of Commons], by Mary Anne his wife, 2nd dau. and coheir of John Menzies of Fernton, co. Perth, who was created Baroness Abercromby of Aboukir and of Tullibody, co. Clackmannan, in recognition of her husband's services, 28 May 1801); born at Tullibody 17 October 1770; Advocate 5 July 1794, M.P. for Edinburgh 1805–6, and for co. Clackmannan 1806–7 and 1812 until Escheator of Munster 1815; succeeded his mother as 2nd Baron 11 February 1821; died 14 February 1843, and bur. in Tullibody Church. Will dated 16 December 1841, proved (P.C.C., 225, 43) 19 April 1843, by the Rt. Honble George Ralph, Lord Abercromby, the son, the sole Exor. = Honble Montagu, 3rd dau. of Henry, 1st Viscount Melville, by Elizabeth his 1st wife, dau. of David Rennie of Melville Castle, Lasswade, Edinburgh; born 29 April 1772; marr. at Edinburgh 25 January 1799; died 10 March 1837, and bur. in Tullibody Church.

A

Colonel George Ralph Abercromby, Baron Abercromby of Aboukir and of Tullibody; born at Edinburgh 30 May 1800; Major 3rd Dragoon Guards 22 June 1826 to 21 November 1828; M.P. for Clackmannan and Kinross 13 July 1824 to 2 June 1826 and 10 August 1830 to 23 April 1831, for co. Stirling 30 April 1838 to 23 June 1841, and again for Clackmannan and Kinross 6 July 1841 to 18 February 1842; Lord Lieutenant and Sheriff-Principal of co. Clackmannan 1843 until his death; succeeded his father as 3rd Baron 14 February 1843; died at Airthrey Castle, Stirling, 25 June 1852, and bur. in Tullibody Church. Will dated 23 July 1844, proved (P.C.C., 679, 52) 23 September 1852, by the Rt. Honble James Abercromby, Baron Dumferline, one of the Exors. Power reserved to the Rt. Honble Louisa Penuel Forbes, otherwise Abercromby, Baroness Abercromby, the relict, the Rt. Honble Fox Maule, Baron Panmure, the Rt. Honble Robert Saunders Dundas, commonly called Viscount Melville, the Honble Ralph Abercromby, the Honble Henry Dundas and Henry Dundas, the other Exors. = Louisa Penuel, 3rd dau. of John Hay Forbes of Medwyn, co. Peebles, Lord Medwyn, a Senator of the College of Justice, by Louisa his wife, dau. of Sir Alexander Penrose Gordon-Cumming of Altyre and Gordonstown, co. Elgin, 1st Bart.; marr. at 17 Ainslie Place, Edinburgh, 3 April 1832; died at her house, 21 Chapel Street, Belgrave Square, London, on Thursday, 20 April 1882, and bur. in Tullibody Church. Will dated 24 November 1875, proved (Prin. Reg., 521, 82) 17 July 1882, by Elizabeth Forbes of 4 Shandwick Place, Edinburgh, in North Britain, spinster, the sister, and the Honble John Abercromby and the Honble Ralph Abercromby, both of 21 Chapel Street, Belgrave Square, co. Middlesex, the sons, the Exors.

B

Montagu, born 11 August 1835, and bapt. at the parish church, Denny, co. Stirling; marr. at Stirling 29 April 1856, George Frederick, Earl of Glasgow (4th son of George, 4th Earl of Glasgow, by Julia his 2nd wife, dau. of the Rt. Honble Sir John Sinclair of Ulbster, co. Caithness, P.C., 1st Bart.); born 9 October 1825; of Christ Church, Oxford, matriculated 31 May 1844, aged 18, B.A. 1847, M.A. 1852; M.P. for co. Bute February to July 1865; Principal Keeper of the Signet; Founder of Cumbrae Cathedral; D.L. for the counties of Renfrew and Fife; succeeded his brother James as 6th Earl 11 March 1869; Lord Clerk Register of Scotland 1879 until his death; died at 32 Palmerston Place, Edinburgh, aged 64, 23 April, bur. at Cumbrae 30 April 1890.

A

Montagu, born 25 May 1807; marr. 4 August 1836, the Rt. Honble Fox Maule-Ramsay, afterwards Baron Panmure of Brechin and Navar, co. Forfar, and Earl of Dalhousie (eldest son of William, 1st Lord Panmure, by Patricia Heron his 1st wife, dau. of Gilbert Gordon of Halleaths, co. Dumfries); born at Brechin Castle, co. Forfar, 22 April 1801; educated at Charterhouse; an Officer in the 79th Highlanders; M.P. for co. Perth 1835-37, Edinburgh 1838-41, and again for co. Perth 1841-52; Under Secretary of Home Department 1835-41, Vice-President of Board of Trade June to September 1841, Secretary of State for War 1846-52 and 1855-58, being President of Board of Control for a few weeks in February 1852; P.C. 1841; Lord Rector of the University of Glasgow 1842, Lord Lieutenant of co. Forfar 1849, Privy Seal 1853; succeeded his father as 2nd Baron 13 April 1852, and his cousin, James Andrew, as 11th Earl of Dalhousie 19 December 1860; K.T. 1853, G.C.B. 1855; took the additional name of Ramsay after that of Maule in 1851; died s.p. at Brechin Castle, aged 73, 6 July, bur. at Panbride 14 July 1874. Confirmation of the Commissariot of Forfar dated 4 November 1874, of Major Thomas Young of Linchiden, co. Dumfries, and George Dalhousie Ramsay of the War Office, the nephews, and the Honble Arthur Kinnaird, Thomas Brodie, Writer to the Signet, Edinburgh, and John Shiell of Dundee, as Exors nominate of the Rt. Honble Fox Maule-Ramsay, Earl of Dalhousie, Baron Panmure of Brechin and Navar. Sealed 12 November 1874. She died at Pitfour Castle, co. Perth, 11 November, and was bur. at Panbride 19 November 1853.

Mary Anne, born 7 December 1811; marr. at St. James', Piccadilly, London (by the Rev. John Vane), on Monday, 13 July 1857, Colonel Nicholas Robert Brown; of the 34th Regiment of Foot; died at 4 Cleveland Row, St. James', London, aged 62, on Friday, 4 March, bur. in Kensal Green Cemetery, London, 10 March 1870. Will dated 27 February 1862, proved (Prin. Reg., 245, 70) 28 April 1870, by the Honble Mary Anne Brown of 4 Cleveland Row, St. James' Street, co. Middlesex, the relict, the sole Executrix. She died at 36 James Street, Buckingham Gate, London, in her 87th year, on Saturday, 24 September, bur. in Kensal Green Cemetery, London, on Wednesday, 28 September 1898. Will dated 30 May 1885, proved (Prin. Reg., 1094, 98) 11 October 1898, by Henry George Swayne Williams, the surviving Exor.

B

George Ralph Campbell Abercromby,═Lady Juliet Janet Georgina, V.A., only dau. of Adam, Baron Abercromby of Aboukir and of Tullibody, co. Clackmannan; born at Leamington, co. Warwick, 23 September, bapt. at the parish church, Leamington, 2 November 1838; J.P. and D.L. for the counties of Stirling and Clackmannan; succeeded his father as 4th Baron 25 June 1852.

2nd Earl of Camperdown, by Juliana Cavendish his wife, eldest dau. of Sir George Richard Philips of Weston, co. Warwick, Bart., M.P.; born 24 January 1840; marr. at Camperdown House, co. Forfar, 6 October 1858; one of the Ladies of the Bedchamber-in-Ordinary to H.M. Queen Victoria, and Member of the Royal Order of Victoria and Albert (3rd-class).

John Abercromby of═Adèle Wilhelmine Marika, 62 Palmerston Place, Edinburgh; born 15 January 1841; educated at Harrow; formerly Lieutenant Rifle Brigade and Captain Highland Borderers Militia.

his cousin, dau. of Chevalier Charles von Heidenstam, Chamberlain to the King of Sweden; marr. at Athens, Greece, 26 August 1876; marriage dissolved at his suit by Court of Session 1879.

Ralph Abercromby, born 11 February 1842; Lieutenant 60th Rifles; Member of the Royal Meteorological Society; died at Sydney, New South Wales, aged 54, on Monday, 21 June 1897, and bur. there. Confirmation of the Honble John Abercromby, the Honble Thomas Cochrane and John Houblon Forbes. Sealed in London 20 October 1897.

Barlow of Acomb, co. York, and of Warkworth, co. Northumberland.

Arms.—Sable, two bars ermine, on a chief indented per pale, or and argent, an eagle displayed of the first.
Crest.—A mercury's cap or, wings argent, thereon an eagle's head erased proper, gorged with a collar ermine.
Motto.—Hic posuisse gaudet.

Rev. George Francis Barlow (younger son of Francis Barlow of Mitcham, co. Surrey, Deputy Clerk of the Crown in the Court of King's Bench, by Alethea his wife, dau. of Henry Masterman of Settrington, co. York); of Oriel College, Oxford, matriculated 21 April 1785, aged 16, B.A. 1789, M.A. 1791; Curate of Lower Tooting, co. Surrey, Vicar of Edwardstone, co. Suffolk, 17 October 1800; he was presented to the Rectory of Sotterley, co. Suffolk, by Miles Barne of Sotterley 7 February 1805, and to that of Burgh, co. Suffolk, by the same Patron 27 August 1814; died at Burgh, in his 82nd year, 24 March, bur. there 30 March 1850. Will dated 30 July 1847, proved (P.C.C., 340, 50) 23 May 1850, by Francis Barlow Robinson and Edmund Barlow, the son, the surviving Exors.

=Harriet, dau. of John Mount of Wasing Place, co. Berks, High Sheriff 1770, by Christian Hyett his 2nd wife; born 16 February, bapt. at Wasing 15 March 1780; marr. at Lower Tooting 21 May 1798 (marriage settlements dated on or about 20 May 1798); died, in her 70th year, on Sunday, 23 September, bur. at Burgh 28 September 1849.

A

Francis Barlow, born 26 January 1799; of Trinity Hall, Cambridge, B.A. 1821, M.A. 1824; a Student of the Middle Temple 20 June 1820, called to the Bar there 11 November 1825, admitted a Barrister of Lincoln's Inn, *ad eundem*, 9 January 1837; Master and Commissioner in Lunacy 1842–79, Hon. Commissioner in Lunacy 1879, Deputy High Steward of Cambridge University 1856, Secretary of Presentations to Lord Lyndhurst (Lord Chancellor 1841–42); died at 48 Montagu Square, London, aged 88, on Tuesday, 1 February, bur. in Highgate Cemetery, London, 4 February 1887. Will dated 31 March 1883, with two codicils dated respectively 28 March 1885 and 7 April 1886, proved (Prin. Reg., 188, 87) 7 March 1887, by the Rev. John Mount Barlow of Ewhurst, co. Surrey, the brother, and Eustace Hepburn Barlow of 40 Devonshire Street, Portland Place, co. Middlesex, the nephew, the Exors.

=Laura Sarah, youngest dau. of William Mount of Wasing Place, by Jane his wife, dau. of William Page of Poynters, co. Surrey; born at Wasing 19 August 1802, bapt. privately the same day (baptism registered at Wasing); marr. at the parish church, Marylebone, London (by the Rev. Richard Durnford), on Saturday, 7 June 1828; died suddenly at Lewes Crescent, Brighton, co. Sussex, aged 64, on Thursday, 18 April, bur. in Highgate Cemetery, London, 25 April 1867.

Harriet, born 3 November 1800; marr. at Burgh 25 June 1835, Charles Francis Robinson, Master of the Crown Office, King's Bench, of 3 Chandos Street, Cavendish Square, London, and of Effingham, co. Surrey (son of Marmaduke Robinson of Malton, co. York); died suddenly at 3 Chandos Street, Cavendish Square, London, aged 81, on Tuesday, 25 March, bur. at Balcombe, co. Sussex, 1 April 1862. M.I. Will dated 1 February 1860, proved (Prin. Reg., 301, 62) 23 May 1862, by Francis Barlow Robinson of 26 Essex Street, Strand, co. Middlesex, gent., the brother, and Edmund Barlow of the same place, gent., two of the Exors. She died s.p. suddenly at Balcombe, aged 51, on Sunday, 12 June, and was bur. there 19 June 1852. M.I.

B

62

Caroline, born 19 March 1802; died in infancy.

—

William Francis Barlow, born 15 November 1803; Lieutenant and Adjutant 23rd Native Infantry; died at Assurburgh, Bombay, India, 3 August 1827.

George Barne Barlow, born at Sotterley, co. Suffolk, 2 September 1805; Assistant Master of the Crown Office, King's Bench; died at Queen Anne Street, Cavendish Square, London, aged 41, on Sunday, 9 May, bur. in Kensal Green Cemetery, London, 15 May 1847. Will dated 10 July 1846, proved (P.C.C., 456, 47) 2 June 1847, by Edmund Barlow and the Rev. John Mount Barlow, the brothers, the Ex̃ ors.

=Frances Charlotte, youngest dau. of John Gervaise-Maude of Great George Street, Westminster, by Henrietta Hartwell his wife; born 4 November 1814; marr. at St. Margaret's, Westminster (by the Rev. Philip Strong, Rector of St. Michael's, Myland, co. Essex), on Thursday, 19 March 1846; died at 55 Beaumont Street, Marylebone, London, aged 77, on Tuesday, 19 January, bur. in Kensal Green Cemetery, London, 23 January 1892. Will dated 12 June 1891, proved (Prin. Reg., 103, 92) 15 February 1892, by George Barlow, the son, the sole Ex̃ or.

George Barlow of 28 New Cavendish Street, Portland Place, London; born in Great George Street, Westminster, on Saturday, 19 June, bapt. at St. Margaret's, Westminster, 6 August 1847; of Exeter College, Oxford, matriculated 29 May 1866, aged 18.

=Louisa (Violet), dau. of Joseph Fryer, by Hannah his wife, dau. of George Mortimer; born 4 January 1853; marr. by licence at St. Matthew's, Bayswater, London (by the Rev. John Green), on Wednesday, 2 October 1872.

Francis Mount Barlow, born 14 October 1829; of Trinity Hall, Cambridge, B.A. 1852, M.A. 1855; died s.p. at 2 Lewes Crescent, Brighton, co. Sussex, aged 47, on Easter Day, 1 April, bur. in Highgate Cemetery, London, 7 April 1877. Adm̃ on was granted at the Principal Registry 3 July 1877, to Francis Barlow of 48 Montagu Square, co. Middlesex, the father and next of kin.

=Lady Harriet Eliza Danvers (patent of precedence granted in 1866), youngest dau. of Lord Charles Augustus Butler, Captain in the Honble East India Co.'s Service, Madras, by Letitia Rudyerd Ross his wife, youngest dau. of Colonel John William Freese of the Madras Artillery; born 3 November 1847; marr. at St. George's, Hanover Square, London (by the Bishop of Chichester), on Wednesday, 12 July 1876; marr. 2ndly at St. Mary's, Bryanston Square, London (by the Honble and Rev. Canon Leigh, assisted by the Rev. Sir Charles Clarke, Bart.), on Thursday, 7 January 1886, Charles Harrison (3rd son of Frederick Harrison of Sutton Place, Guildford, co. Surrey, by Jane his wife, dau. of Alexander Brice of Belfast); born 1 August 1835; educated at King's College, London, and privately; admitted Solicitor 1858; F.S.A., F.R.G.S.; Member of London County Council (Bethnal Green Division), Vice-Chairman 1892-95; M.P. for Plymouth 15 July 1895-97; died suddenly at 29 Lennox Gardens, Chelsea, co. Middlesex, aged 62, on Friday, 24 December 1897.

Edmund Barlow of Hasketon, co. Suffolk, and of Sigsworth, co. York; born 5 September 1807, bapt. the same day (baptism registered at Sotterley, co. Suffolk); died at his residence, 36 Rutland Gate, Knightsbridge, London, aged 71, on Saturday, 9 August, bur. in the churchyard at Lee, co. Kent, 15 August 1879. Will dated 8 May 1879, with codicil dated 8 August 1879, proved (Prin. Reg., 757, 79) 3 September 1879, by the Rev. John Mount Barlow of Ewhurst, co. Surrey, the brother, and Douglass Round of 9 Old Square, Lincoln's Inn, co. Middlesex, Barrister-at-Law, the nephew, the Exors.

Edmund Barlow (signature)

Henrietta, dau. of John Teesdale of Russell Square, London; born 18 December 1817; marr. at Harrogate, co. York, 5 October 1841; died at 36 Rutland Gate, Knightsbridge, London, aged 73, on Thursday, 2 April, bur. at Lee 8 April 1891. Will dated 6 April 1887, with two codicils dated respectively 20 February 1888, and 18 March 1891, proved (Prin. Reg., 475, 91) 29 May 1891, by Edmund Francis Masterman Barlow, the son, and Douglass Round, Barrister-at-Law, both of 36 Rutland Gate, co. Middlesex, and Henry Paulson Bowling Trevanion of 26 Essex Street, co. Middlesex, the Exors.

Laura Frederica, born at Eliot Place, Blackheath, co. Kent, on Wednesday, 6 Sept. 1848; died at 36 Rutland Gate, Knightsbridge, London, aged 15, on Thursday, 21 April 1864, and bur. at Lee.

Cecilia Katherine, born at Eliot Place, Blackheath, on Sunday, 1 September 1850; marr. 18 November 1875, her cousin, Douglass Round of Birch Cottage, Colchester, co. Essex (3rd son of the Rev. James Thomas Round of "The Holly Trees," Colchester, by Louisa his wife, dau. of the Rev. George Barlow of Burgh, co. Suffolk); born 29 March 1846; of Trinity College, Cambridge, B.A. 1869, M.A. 1873; a Student of Lincoln's Inn 19 April 1869, called to the Bar 6 June 1872. She died at 36 Rutland Gate, Knightsbridge, London, aged 41, on Sunday, 31 January, and was bur. at Birch, co. Essex, 5 February 1892. He marr. 2ndly at All Saints', Colchester (by the Rev. Bixby Garnham Luard and the Rev. Percy Luard, father and brother of the bride, and the Rev. George Gibson Brown, the Rector), on Monday, 12 September 1898, Helen Lucy, 3rd dau. of the Rev. Bixby Garnham Luard, Rector of Birch, by Clara Isabella Sandford his wife, dau. of the Rev. John Bramston, Vicar of Witham, co. Essex.

Edmund Francis Masterman Barlow of Hasketon; born at 36 Rutland Gate, Knightsbridge, London, on Tuesday, 8 March 1859; of Exeter College, Oxford, matriculated 15 October 1879, aged 20; died at his residence, Hasketon, in his 44th year, on Friday, 19 December, bur. in the churchyard at Hasketon 23 December 1902. Will dated 20 September 1900, proved (Prin. Reg., 35, 1903) 10 February 1903, by Arthur Moss and Eustace Hepburn Barlow, the cousin, the Exors.

Louisa, born 21 August, bapt. at Sotterley, co. Suffolk, 17 September 1809; marr. at Burgh, co. Suffolk, 19 January 1836, the Rev. James Thomas Round of "The Holly Trees," Colchester, co. Essex (2nd son of Charles Round of Birch Hall, co. Essex, and of "The Holly Trees," Colchester, by Charlotte his wife, dau. of Joseph Green of Stratford, co. Essex, who was great-grandson of Jane Desborough, sister of Oliver Cromwell); born in the parish of St. James', Colchester, 14 July 1798; educated at Felstead Grammar School 1806-16, and at Balliol College, Oxford, matriculated 13 December 1816, aged 18, Scholar 1817–20, B.A. 1820, Fellow 1820–35, M.A. 1823, Tutor 1824, Senior Dean 1825, Bursar 1827, Proctor 1829 B.D. 1830; Rector of St. Runwald's, Colchester, 1824–51, of St. Nicholas', Colchester, 1830–46, and of All Saints', Colchester, 1851 until his death; Rural Dean of Colchester and Prebendary of St. Paul's Cathedral 1843 until his death; Lord of the Manor and Patron of the living of Woodham Mortimer, co. Essex; died at Hammersmith, co. Middlesex, aged 62, on Monday, 27 August, bur. in the churchyard at Birch 31 August 1860. Will dated 18 December 1856, with codicil dated 2 December 1859, proved at Ipswich 26 October 1860, by Louisa Round of Colchester, co. Essex, the relict, and Charles Gray Round of Birch, co. Essex, the brother, the Exors. She died at "The Holly Trees," Colchester, aged 67, on Whit-Monday, 21 May, and was bur. in the churchyard at Birch 25 May 1877.

Rev. Henry Masterman Barlow, born at Sotterley 9 July 1811, bapt. the next day (baptism registered at Sotterley); of Wadham College, Oxford, matriculated 18 March 1830, aged 18, B.A. 24 April 1834; Minister of Christ Church, Norwich, 1841, Rector of Burgh 1850 until his death; died at the Rectory, Burgh, aged 66, on Thursday, 20 July, bur. at Burgh 24 July 1876. Will dated 27 February 1875, proved at Ipswich 6 September 1876, by Edmund Barlow of Hasketon, co. Suffolk, the brother, and Manfred Biddell and Herman Biddell, both of Playford, co. Suffolk, gents., the Exors.

Elizabeth, dau. of Jonas Briggs of Dunwich, co. Suffolk, by Mary Hudson his wife; born at Dunwich 5 November, bapt. there 6 December 1811; marr. by licence at Sotterley 22 January 1840; died 11 December, bur. at Burgh 17 December 1866.

Harriet, born at Metton, co. Norfolk, 19 May, bapt. there 20 June 1847; marr. at Burgh (by the Rev. Canon Edward James Moor, assisted by the Rev. Christopher Hodgson) on Wednesday, 20 April 1870, Herman Biddell of Playford, co. Suffolk (youngest son of Arthur Biddell of The Hill House, Playford, by Jane his wife, dau. of Robert Ransome of Ipswich, co. Suffolk); born 16 June 1832, bapt. at Playford, aged 19, 18 April 1852.

(*See Pedigree of Biddell, Vol. 3, page 99.*)

Juliana, born at Burgh, co. Suffolk, 27 February, bapt. at Sotterley, co. Suffolk, 18 March 1813; marr. at Burgh 20 August 1840, Francis Barlow Robinson of Balcombe, co. Sussex (son of Marmaduke Robinson of Malton, co. York); born 13 August 1796; died at Balcombe, aged 81, 2 March, bur. there 9 March 1878. M.I. Will dated 3 July 1877, with codicil dated 10 July 1877, proved (Prin. Reg., 342, 78) 3 April 1878, by Edmund Barlow and Henry Paulson Bowling, both of 26 Essex Street, Strand, co. Middlesex, two of the Exors. She died s.p. at Balcombe, aged 60, on Thursday, 30 January, and was bur. there 6 February 1873. M.I.

Rev. John Mount Barlow,═Charlotte Eliza, born at Lowestoft, co. Suffolk, 7 December 1814; of Worcester College, Oxford, matriculated 28 June 1832, aged 17, B.A. 1836, M.A. 1840; Rector of Ewhurst, co. Surrey, for 47 years; died at the Rectory, Ewhurst, aged 77, on Thursday, 24 November, bur. at Ewhurst 29 November 1892. Will dated 21 May 1887, with codicil dated 29 November 1889, proved (Prin. Reg., 1152, 92) 27 December 1892, by Algernon Barlow, Barrister-at-Law, and Lyonell Barlow, two of the Exors.

Charlotte Eliza, youngest dau. of John Clutterbuck of Warkworth, co. Northumberland, Major 65th Regiment, by Mary Anne his wife, youngest dau. of the Honble Thomas Lyon of Hetton House, co. Durham; born at Warkworth 6 June, bapt. there 21 September 1830; marr. there (by the Rev. Henry George Liddell, Rector of Easington, co. Durham) on Thursday, 7 December 1854.

Richard Barlow, born at Burgh 2 September, bapt. there 28 September 1817; died, aged 20, 6 June, bur. at Burgh 12 June 1838.

[signature: J. M. Barlow]

Algernon Barlow of Bossall Hall, York,═Essex Frances, eldest dau. of Major born at Ewhurst 15 January, bapt. there 17 February 1856; educated at Winchester and at Trinity Hall, Cambridge, B.A. 1877; a Student of Lincoln's Inn 8 February 1876, called to the Bar 17 November 1879; Lord of the Manor and Patron of the living of Acomb, co. York.

Essex Frances, eldest dau. of Major Robert Thompson of Walworth Hall, co. Durham, by Essex his wife, dau. of William Gray of East Bolton, co. Northumberland); born at East Bolton 10 April 1864, bapt. privately the next day (baptism registered at East Bolton); marr. at Coniscliffe, co. Durham, on Wednesday, 17 May 1893.

Alethea, born at Ewhurst 13 January, bapt. there 8 February 1857.

Essex Eleanor, born at 37 Brunswick Gardens, Kensington, London, on Sunday, 6 May, bapt. at St. Paul's, Kensington, 24 June 1894.

A

Eleanor, born 29 March, bapt. at Burgh, co. Suffolk, 14 April 1820; marr. there (by the Rev. Henry Masterman Barlow) on Tuesday, 27 May 1851, the Rev. John Montagu Randall (son of James Randall of Hampstead, co. Middlesex, by Emma his wife, dau. of the Rev. Jeremiah Joyce of Highgate, co. Middlesex); born 9 August 1819; Curate of St. Margaret's, Lowestoft, co. Suffolk, 1843–50, then for 44 years Vicar of Langham Bishops, co. Norfolk; died at Lowestoft, aged 76, on Saturday, 2 February, bur. in the cemetery at Lowestoft 5 February 1895. Will dated 31 January 1889, proved (Prin. Reg., 320, 95) 11 March 1895, by Juliana Harriet Randall, spinster, the daughter, the sole Executrix. She died at Worthing, co. Sussex, aged 73, on Friday, 15 December, and was bur. in the cemetery at Broadwater, co. Sussex, 18 December 1893.

Lieut.-Colonel Frederick=Cordelia, only dau. Barlow of "The Shrubbery," Hasketon, co. Suffolk; born at Burgh 8 March, bapt. there 13 April 1823; J.P. for co. Suffolk; Hon. Major Suffolk Artillery Militia, formerly Lieut.-Colonel 3rd Battalion Suffolk Rifle Volunteers; died at Hasketon, aged 74, on Monday, 18 January, bur. there 21 January 1897.

Cordelia, only dau. of the Rev. Thomas Maude of Burley Hall, co. York, Rector of Hasketon; born 26 January 1836; marr. at Spennithorne, co. York (by the Rev. John Mount Barlow, Rector of Ewhurst, co. Surrey, brother of the bridegroom), on Tuesday, 26 September 1854.

Eustace Hepburn Barlow of Sigsworth, co. York; born at the Parsonage, Hasketon, on Sunday, 26 August, bapt. at Hasketon 4 November 1855; educated at Westminster; J.P. for the West Riding, co. York.

Sybilla Harriet, born at Hasketon 12 July, bapt. there 7 November 1858.

—

Mary Cordelia, born at Hasketon on Monday, 14 May 1860.

Henrietta Rosamund, born 20 September 1862, bapt. at Hasketon 11 January 1863.

Mark Masterman Barlow, born at Hasketon 9 June, bapt. there 9 October 1864.

C   C

Lyonell Barlow of=Sophia Sidney, dau. of "Formosa," Malvern, co. Worcester; born at Ewhurst 12 February, bapt. there 3 April 1859; educated at Haileybury and at Trinity Hall, Cambridge, B.A. 1881, LL.M. 1895.

Sophia Sidney, dau. of Richard Chaloner Lindsey, Major Bengal Staff Corps, by Florence his wife, dau. of George Henry Pentland of Black Hall, Drogheda, co. Louth; born at Black Hall, Drogheda, on Monday, 13 April, bapt. at Termonfeckin, co. Louth, 14 May 1868; marr. at Upton, co. Worcester, 25 April 1900.

Harold Barlow,=Millicent Alice, younger born at Ewhurst 24 October, bapt. there 23 November 1860; educated at Charterhouse and at the Royal Indian Engineering College, Cooper's Hill; P.W.D., Bengal, India.

Millicent Alice, younger dau. of Frederick Barnes Peacock, C.S.I., by Christine his wife, dau. of Frederick Christian Lewis; born at Calcutta, India, 9 November 1873, and bapt. at the Fort, Calcutta; marr. at the Cathedral, Calcutta, 7 March 1896.

(*See Pedigree of Peacock, Vol. 10, page 119.*)

Florence Marion Rose, born at "Formosa," Malvern, on Wednesday, 13 February, bapt. at the Priory Church, Malvern, 13 May 1901.

Violet Norah, born at "Formosa," Malvern, on Tuesday, 8 April, bapt. at the Priory Church, Malvern, 21 May 1902.

Montague Frederick Harold Barlow, born at Midnapore, Bengal, India, 25 November 1896, and died there 6 October 1897.

Lance Mount Barlow (twin with Vernon Harold), born at Cuttack, Bengal, 8 November 1899, and bapt. there in February 1900.

Vernon Harold Barlow (twin with Lance Mount), born at Cuttack, Bengal, 8 November 1899, and bapt. there in February 1900.

c

Charles John Barlow=Edith Mary, dau. of John Cates
of Westbury House, Collier of Godalming, co. Surrey;
Guildford, co. Surrey; by Harriett his wife, dau. of
born at Ewhurst, Edward Browne Kirbell; born at
co. Surrey, 3 De- Godalming 8 March, bapt. there
cember 1862, bapt. 25 April 1869; marr. at St.
there 16 January Andrew's, Westminster, 7 June
1863; educated at 1900.
Charterhouse.

George Thomas Barlow, born at
Ewhurst 11 March 1864, bapt.
there 25 April 1865; P.W.D.
North-West Provinces, India; marr.
at Almora, North-West Provinces,
India, 7 September 1891, Amelia
Sophia Anthony.

Harold Everard Barlow (twin
with Eleanor Mary), born at
Darjeeling, Bengal, India,
12 May 1892.

Eleanor Mary (twin with
Harold Everard), born
at Darjeeling, Bengal,
12 May 1892.

Laura, born at Ewhurst 8 October, bapt. there 4 November
1866; marr. at the Priory Church, Malvern, co. Worcester,
on Tuesday, 21 July 1896, Frederick Peacock of Holmbury,
Alipur, Calcutta, India (only son of Frederick Barnes Peacock,
C.S.I., by Christine his wife, dau. of Frederick Christian
Lewis); born at Mentone, France, on Tuesday, 10
December 1867; educated at Eton and at New College,
Oxford, matriculated 18 January 1887, aged 19;
Barrister-at-Law of the Inner Temple 1889.

(See Pedigree of Peacock, Vol. 10, page 119.)

Francis John Barlow, born at
Ewhurst 27 May, bapt. there
12 July 1869.

—

Marion, born at Ewhurst 1 April,
bapt. there 28 May 1871.

—

Charlotte, born at Dalton Hill,
Albury, co. Surrey, 1 October,
bapt. at Ewhurst 31 October
1873.

Algernon Barlow

68

Hamilton.

John Hamilton (3rd son of John Hamilton of Christchurch Priory, co. Hants, and of Riseland, Tobago, West Indies, by Mary Susannah Anne his wife, dau. of William Wilson of Soonhope, co. Lanark, Writer to the Signet); born at Riseland, Tobago, 12 April, bapt. at the Protestant Church, Tobago, 16 June 1782; educated at Eton and at Trinity College, Cambridge; died at Guildford Lawn, Dover, co. Kent, in his 77th year, on Tuesday, 11 January, bur. in the cemetery at Dover 18 January 1859. M.I. Will dated 31 October 1855, with codicil dated 30 April 1857, proved (Prin. Reg., 59, 59) 2 February 1859, by the Rev. John Hamilton of Lynsted, near Sittingbourne, co. Kent, and Henry Rose Hamilton of 8 Guildford Lawn, the sons, the Exors.

== Elizabeth Anna, eldest dau. of John Trayton Fuller of Ashdown House, co. Sussex, by the Honble Anne his wife, only dau. of Major-General Sir George Augustus Eliott, K.B., created Lord Heathfield, Baron Heathfield of Gibraltar, 6 July 1787, A.D.C. to H.M. King George II.); born 4 July, bapt. at Heathfield, co. Sussex, 24 July 1780 marr. at the parish church, Marylebone, London, 18 January 1805; died, aged 59, 29 August, bur. in a vault at the old church of St. James', Dover, 4 September 1840.

(*See Pedigree of Fuller-Eliott-Drake, Vol. 10, page 2.*)

John Hamilton

A

Rev. John Hamilton, born at Weyhill, co. Hants, 14 December 1806, bapt. there 12 April 1807; educated at Eton and at Brasenose College, Oxford, matriculated 11 October 1824, aged 17, B.A. 1828, M.A. 1832; Vicar of Lynsted 1837–39; died at Lynsted, in his 85th year, on Monday, 25 May, bur. there on Friday, 29 May 1891. Will dated 1 March 1890, proved (Prin. Reg., 742, 91) 14 July 1891, by John Hamilton of 93 Elm Park Gardens, co. Middlesex, and George Trayton Eliott Hamilton of Newton-next-Castleacre, co. Norfolk, the sons, two of the Exors.

== Augusta Harriet, 4th dau. of Sir Henry Hawley of Leybourne Grange, co. Kent, 2nd Bart., by Catherine Elizabeth his wife, eldest dau. of Sir John Gregory Shaw of Kenward, co. Kent, Bart.; born at Eltham, co. Kent, 20 April, bapt. there (by the Rev. John Kenward Shaw-Brooke, the Vicar), 20 May 1812; marr. at Frant, co. Kent (by the Rev. James Hawley), on Tuesday, 6 August 1839.

Henry Rose Hamilton, formerly of the Island of Tobago, West Indies; born at Weyhill 7 February, bapt. there 6 March 1808; educated at Eton; died suddenly at Sunningdale House, Silverhill, St. Leonard's-on-Sea, co. Sussex, unmarried, aged 70, on Sunday, 7 April, bur. in the cemetery at Hastings, co. Sussex, 12 April 1878. Will dated 16 May 1873, with two codicils dated respectively 29 May 1873 and 23 June 1874, proved at Lewes 24 May 1878, by the Rev. John Hamilton of Lynsted, co. Kent, the brother, and Euphemia Hamilton of Sunningdale, spinster, the sister, two of the Exors.

John Hamilton

B

Susannah Anne, born at Weyhill, co. Hants, 3 June, bapt. there 30 June 1809; died unmarried at 8 Guildford Lawn, Dover, co. Kent, aged 60, on Wednesday, 3 November, bur. in the cemetery at Dover 9 November 1869. M.I. Will dated 10 November 1864, proved (Prin. Reg., 768, 69) 10 December 1869, by the Rev. John Hamilton of Lynsted Vicarage, Sittingbourne, co. Kent, and Henry Rose Hamilton of Guildford Lawn, Dover, co. Kent, the brothers, the Exors.

Eliza Euphemia, born at Weyhill 7 September, bapt. there 4 December 1811; marr. at Dover 27 July 1843, the Rev. Frederick Thornton Raikes (younger son of Richard Mee Raikes of London, Governor of the Bank of England 1833–34, by Jane his wife, dau. of Samuel Thornton); born 20 February 1819; sometime Captain in the 62nd Regiment; Vicar of Milnthorpe, co. Westmoreland, 1860, Vicar of Heversham, co. Westmoreland, and Chaplain of Milnthorpe Union. She died at Meerut, North-West Provinces, India, 15 March, and was bur. there 16 March 1845. He marr. 2ndly at Burham, co. Kent, 29 January 1849, Harriet, youngest dau. of James Hobbs of London. He died, leaving issue, at Milnthorpe, aged 76, on Tuesday, 26 March, and was bur. there 30 March 1895. Will dated 15 March 1881, proved at Carlisle 23 April 1895, by William Stavert, the son-in-law, and Arthur Hamilton Raikes, the son, the Exors.

Elizabeth Anna, born at Lynsted, co. Kent, 29 September, bapt. there 29 October 1841; marr. at St. George's, Hanover Square, London (by the Rev. Charles Hawley, Rector of Leybourne, co. Kent, uncle of the bride, assisted by the Rev. Frederick Parr Phillips, Rector of Stoke d'Abernon, co. Surrey, brother-in-law of the bridegroom), on Tuesday, 20 September 1870, as his 2nd wife, Walter James McGrigor (younger son of Sir James McGrigor, 1st Bart., K.C.B., F.R.S., Physician Extraordinary to H.M. Queen Victoria, and Fellow of the College of Physicians of London and Edinburgh, and Director-General of the Army Medical Department, by Mary his wife, youngest dau. of Duncan Grant of Lingeistone, co. Moray); born at Camden Hill, Kensington, London, 18 March 1817; of Trinity College, Cambridge, B.A. 1840, M.A. 1843; a Student of Lincoln's Inn 29 April 1840, called to the Bar 4 May 1843; Hon. Major 2nd Battalion Queen's Own Cameron Highlanders. He marr. 1stly at All Soul's, Langham Place, London (by the Rev. Henry Neave, the Rector, cousin of the bride, assisted by the Rev. Frederick Parr Phillips), on Wednesday, 29 August 1849, Maria Anne, eldest dau. of Vice-Admiral Joseph Digby, R.N., by Ann his wife, 2nd dau. of Josias Jackson, M.P. for Southampton, and grand-daughter of the Honble and Very Rev. William Digby, D.D., Dean of Durham. She died, leaving issue, at 53 Upper Seymour Street, Portman Square, London, aged 23, on Thursday, 25 September, and was bur. in Kensal Green Cemetery, London, 30 September 1851. He died at 3 Upper George Street, Bryanston Square, London, aged 74, on Sunday, 7 June, and was bur. in Kensal Green Cemetery, London, 12 June 1891. Will dated 2 July 1879, proved (Prin. Reg., 766, 91) 29 July 1891, by Elizabeth Anna McGrigor of 3 Upper George Street, Bryanston Square, co. Middlesex, the relict, the sole Executrix. Elizabeth Anna McGrigor marr. 2ndly at the British Consulate, Rotterdam, and afterwards at SS. John and Philip's, The Hague (by the Rev. Isaac Herbert Ratford), on Wednesday, 20 August 1902, Randolph Richards Luscombe (son of Commissary-General Thomas Popham Luscombe of Killester, co. Dublin, by Catherine his wife, eldest dau. of William Robinson, Governor of the Bank of England); formerly Captain 4th Dragoon Guards. Elizabeth Anna Luscombe died at Durward House, Kensington Court, London, on Saturday, 14 November, and was bur. in the Luscombe family vault in Mount Jerome Cemetery, Harold's Cross, Dublin, on Thursday, 19 November 1903.

Euphemia, born at Winterborne-Herringstone, co. Dorset, 7 October, bapt. there 14 November 1812; died at Sunningdale, Silverhill, St. Leonard's-on-Sea, co. Sussex, in her 78th year, on Thursday, 16 January, bur. in the cemetery at Hastings, co. Sussex, 22 January 1890. M.I. Will dated 1 December 1884, proved at Lewes 17 February 1890, by the Rev. John Hamilton of Lynsted Vicarage, co. Kent, the brother, John Hamilton, the younger, of 93 Elm Park Gardens, Chelsea, co. Middlesex, the nephew, Mary Grace Woodruffe (wife of Charles Sheldon Pearce Woodruffe) of Old Roar, Silverhill, St. Leonard's-on-Sea, co. Sussex, the niece, and Octavius Roper Tyler of Eastbourne, co. Sussex, the Exors.

James Hamilton, born at Winterborne-Herringstone 30 December 1813, bapt. there 31 January 1814; Lieutenant R.N.; died unmarried at Dover, co. Kent, aged 28, 25 December, bur. in St. James' Church, Dover, 30 December 1842.

Augusta Christina, born at Lynsted 22 September, bapt. there 19 October 1843; marr. at Lynsted 29 September 1869, William Gordon Trevor (son of Colonel Samuel Smith Trevor, by Frances his wife, dau. of the Rev. James Randolph, Curate-in-Charge of Lyme Regis, co. Dorset, and of Bagborough, co. Somerset); born in Burmah 21 January 1835; Captain 80th Regiment and of the Bombay Staff Corps; died at Cumballa Hotel, Bombay, India, on Wednesday, 8 October, bur. in the cemetery at Bombay 9 October 1884. She died at Matharan, India, aged 27, on Monday, 24 April, and was bur. there 25 April 1871.

Cordelia Eleanor, born at Lynsted 10 December 1845, bapt. there 27 January 1846; marr. at Lynsted (by the Rev. Harris Jervoise Bigg-Wither, Rector of Worting, co. Hants) on Thursday, 25 October 1877, Robert Evans Montgomery of Tunbridge Wells, co. Kent (3rd son of Andrew Castle Montgomery, Resident Magistrate, Ballymena, co. Antrim, by Helen Nagle Hill his wife, dau. of Henderson Boyle of Durnafland, Derry, Captain 18th Hussars); born at Bray, co. Wicklow, 1 December 1845; entered the Royal Marine Light Infantry as 2nd Lieutenant 24 June 1863, Lieutenant 4 January 1867, Captain 6 January 1879, Major 22 September 1884 (retired 10 March 1890); Lieutenant of "Charybdis" during operations in the Lingie and Lukat Rivers, against Malays, in the Straits of Malacca, 1874 (Perak medal and clasp); served with the Royal Marine Battalion at the defence of Suakin, during the operations in the Eastern Soudan 1884–85 (Egyptian medal and Khedive's bronze star).

Mary Grace, born at Lynsted 7 July, bapt. there 10 August 1847; marr. at Lynsted (by the Rev. Harris Jervoise Bigg-Wither, Rector of Worting on Thursday, 3 December 1874, Captain Charles Sheldon Pearce Woodruffe, R.N., of Old Roar, Silverhill, St. Leonard's-on-Sea (son of Daniel Woodruffe, Lieutenant R.N., by Maria his wife, dau. of Charles Hewitt of Mancetter, co. Warwick, and widow of – Adcock); born at West Bromwich, co. Stafford, 12 May 1839, bapt. at Christ Church, West Bromwich, 12 May 1846; entered the Royal Navy June 1853, Sub-Lieutenant 31 December 1859, Lieutenant 2 November 1860, Commander 17 February 1874, retired as Captain 13 May 1887; served in boats of "Agamemnon" in landing troops in the Crimea; present at the bombardment of Sebastopol and under fire at Balaclava; several times under fire in boats whilst reconnoitring; in "Royal Albert" at captures of Kinburn and Kertch (Crimean and Turkish medals, Sebastopol clasp); served in boats of "Magicienne" on several expeditions against pirates 1858, in the China seas; present with the landing party at the storming of the Peiho forts June 1859; served in boats of "Imperieuse" in the Peiho River 1860 (China medal).

A

George Thomas Hamilton, born 1 March 1815; Lieutenant, Interpreter and Quartermaster 24th Bengal Native Infantry; killed, unmarried, at Moodkee, India, 18 December 1845.

Margaret Louisa, born 9 October, bapt. at Wherwell, co. Hants, 18 October 1818; marr. Florian Glüber of Darmstadt, Germany, who died at Darmstadt 2 June 1892. She died at Darmstadt 5 December 1892, and was bur. there.

B   B

Adela Louisa, born at Lynsted, co. Kent, 22 April, bapt. there 22 May 1849; marr. at St. James', Piccadilly, London (by the Rev. George William Waller Minns), on Thursday, 14 May 1874, Octavius Roper Tyler of Spring Lodge, Cheltenham, co. Gloucester (younger son of Colonel Charles Henry Tyler of Lynsted Lodge, Sittingbourne, co. Kent, D.L. for co. Kent, and Lieut.-Colonel East Kent Militia, by Delilah Benwell his wife); born at Lynsted 21 May, bapt. there 19 August 1848.

John Hamilton of Sorbie, Broadwater Down, Tunbridge Wells; born at Lynsted 15 October, bapt. there 17 November 1850; educated at Marlborough; Fellow Royal Geographical Society.

═Helen, 3rd dau. of General Charles Crutchley of Sunninghill Park, co. Berks, Colonel of the Royal Welsh Fusiliers, J.P., by Eliza Bayfield his wife, dau. of Captain John Harris, R.N., of Eldon House, London, Ontario, Canada; born at Cliftonville, Belfast, co. Antrim, on Monday, 4 October 1858; marr. at Sunninghill (by the Rev. Beauchamp Kerr Pearse, Rector of Ascot, co. Berks, assisted by the Rev. Lewis William Girardot, Curate of Sunninghill) on Tuesday, 24 July 1883.

John Hamilton, born at 24 Upper Berkeley Street, Portman Square, London, on Thursday, 5 June, bapt. at St. Mary's, Marylebone, London, 11 July 1884; educated at Eton; appointed to the Transvaal Civil Service at Pretoria, South Africa.

Julia Helen, born at 93 Elm Park Gardens, Chelsea, London, on Monday, 4 January, bapt. at St. Luke's, Chelsea, 3 March 1886.

Charles Eliott Hamilton, born at 93 Elm Park Gardens, Chelsea, London, on Monday, 27 February, bapt. at St. Luke's, Chelsea, 11 April 1888; educated at Harrow.

George Frederick Hamilton, born at 93 Elm Park Gardens, Chelsea, London, on Sunday, 30 March, bapt. at St. John's, Hollington, co. Sussex, 31 May 1890.

Margaret Euphemia, born at 93 Elm Park Gardens, Chelsea, London, on Thursday, 4 June, bapt. at St. Luke's, Chelsea, 15 July 1896.

B

George Trayton Eliott Hamilton, ⊤ Anna, only dau. of William Money Farrer of Kempstone
born at Lynsted, co. Kent, | Lodge, co. Norfolk, by Anna his wife, dau. of Herring
27 June, bapt. there 28 July | Beck; born at Kempstone Lodge, and bapt. at Kempstone
1854; educated at Haileybury. | 9 December 1855; marr. there (by the Rev. Augustus
| Wenman Langton, the Rector) on Saturday, 8 June 1878.

Reginald George Eliott Hamilton (twin   Elinor Grace (twin with   Henry Francis Trayton
with Elinor Grace), born at Newton-by-   Reginald George Eliott),   Hamilton, born at Newton-
Castleacre, co. Norfolk, on Monday, 21   born at Newton-by-   by-Castleacre on Tuesday,
April, bapt. there 15 May 1879; bur.   Castleacre on Monday,   14 March, bapt. there 16
at Newton-by-Castleacre 27 August 1880.   21 April, bapt. there   April 1882.
                                      15 May 1879.

Anna Christina, born at Newton-by-Castleacre   Archibald George Fuller Hamilton, born at
on Thursday, 4 September, bapt. there 28   Newton-by-Castleacre on Friday, 10 June,
September 1884.   bapt. there 10 July 1887.

John Hamilton.

73

Clark.

Peter Clark of Earl's Terrace, Kensington, and Mincing Lane, London (son of Peter Clark, by his wife, Magdalen Morell of Jersey; born 21 September 1765; died at St. Leonard's-on-Sea, co. Sussex, aged 77, 16 September, bur. at All Saints', Hastings, co. Sussex, 16 September 1842. ═ Mary Dodd, born 11 February 1768; marr. at St. Dunstan-in-the-East, London, 25 June 1791; died at Sandgate, co. Kent, in her 84th year, on Friday, 19 December, bur. at All Saints', Hastings, 24 December 1851. Will dated 6 November 1842, with two codicils dated respectively 9 August 1843 and 13 June 1851, proved (P.C.C., 18, 52) 13 January 1852, by John Nassau Clark, Edward Clark and Henry Bingley Clark, the sons, the Exors.

A

John Nassau Clark of Mincing Lane and of 26 Tavistock Square, London; born in London 7 February 1793; died at 26 Tavistock Square, London, in his 64th year, on Tuesday, 3 February, bur. in Highgate Cemetery, London, 9 February 1857. Will dated 21 June 1850, proved (P.C.C., 181, 57) 14 March 1857, by Edward Clark and Henry Bingley Clark, the brothers, two of the Exors. Power reserved to Frederick Le Gros Clark, the brother, the other Exor. ═ Louisa, eldest dau. of John Bridgman of London, by Sophia Halk his wife; born 3 October 1800; marr. in Paris on Thursday, 5 July 1827; died at Rome, aged 67, on Tuesday, 4 February 1868, and bur. in the English Cemetery there. Will dated 14 August 1865, proved (Prin. Reg., 249, 68) 1 April 1868, by Henry Bingley Clark of Merrow, co. Surrey, and Frederick Le Gros Clark of Lee, co. Kent, the Exors.

Rev. Nassau Clark, born at 17 Guildford Street, Russell Square, London, 10 April, bapt. at St. Dunstan-in-the-East, London, 8 June 1835; of Magdalene College, Cambridge, matriculated Michaelmas Term, 1866, B.A. 1871, M.A. 1874; Vicar of Yeadon, co. York, 1879–86, and Rector of Sawtry, co. Huntingdon, since 1887; formerly of the 89th Regiment and 4th Hussars; died, aged 68, on Friday, 3 July 1903. ═ Sophie, dau. of John Cunningham, by Sophia Burdett his wife; born 6 October 1843; married at St. George's, Bloomsbury, London, 19 March 1864.

Perceval Perceval-Clark, born at 17 Guildford Street, Russell Square, London, 22 August 1837, bapt. at St. Dunstan-in-the-East, London, 23 January 1838; of Worcester College, Oxford, matriculated 27 February 1856, aged 18, B.A. 1860, M.A. 1868; of the Inner Temple 1859; formerly Captain 9th Lancers; assumed by Deed Poll registered in the Court of Chancery June 1885, the additional surname of Perceval before that of Clark. ═ Alice Margaret, 2nd daughter of William Richards of Ely Rise, Llandaff, co. Glamorgan; born 21 March 1843; marr. at Stoke Bishop, co. Gloucester (by the Rev. David Wright, the Vicar, assisted by the Rev. William Richards Watson, Rector of St. Peter's, Saltfleetby, co. Lincoln, cousin of the bride), on Tuesday, 6 December 1864.

B

C

Evelyn Perceval, born at Ryde, Isle of Wight, on Monday, 16 July, bapt. at St. Mary's, Boltons, West Brompton, London, 4 November 1866.

Alice Margaret Perceval, born at 8 The Boltons, West Brompton, London, on Tuesday, 31 December 1867, bapt. at St. Mary's, Boltons, West Brompton, 18 March 1868; marr. at Witley, co. Surrey, 30 August 1898, Cyril Bowman of Longridge, Earl's Court, London (son of John Eddowes Bowman); born at 14 St. Mary Abbott's Terrace, Kensington, London, on Tuesday, 2 January 1849.

Mildred Perceval, born at 7 Clarendon Road, Kensington, London, on Tuesday, 29 December 1868.

—

Louise Perceval, born 22 August 1870.

Peter Clark, born at 40 Philpot Lane, in the parish of St. Andrew Hubbard, London, 21 February 1795; died at Leghorn, Italy, 24 June 1855, and bur. in the English Cemetery there. Will dated 17 November 1854, proved (P.C.C., 591, 55) 16 July 1855, by Edward Clark and Henry Bingley Clark, the brothers, two of the Exors. Power reserved to Eliza Clark, the relict, the other Exor.

A ═══ Eliza, dau. of Captain George Suter, R.N.; born at Malta 13 May 1805; marr. at Corfu, Greece, 21 March 1829; died at Leghorn, aged 85, on Easter Monday, 7 April 1890, and bur. in the English Cemetery there. Will dated 13 December 1887, proved (Prin. Reg., 25, 91) 9 January 1891, by William Thomas Samuel Rae of 21 Marlborough Road, St. John's Wood, co. Middlesex, one of the Exors.

Edward Clark of Sandgate, co. Kent; born at 40 Philpot Lane, in the parish of St. Andrew Hubbard, London, 22 September 1797; died at the residence of his brother, Henry Bingley Clark, at Merrow, co. Surrey, on Thursday, 12 November 1863. Will dated 6 October 1860, proved (Prin. Reg., 693, 63) 10 December 1863, by Henry Bingley Clark of Merrow, near Guildford, co. Surrey, and the Rev. George Clark of Tenby, co. Pembroke, the brothers, the Exors.

Mary Esther, born at 40 Philpot Lane, in the parish of St. Andrew Hubbard, London, 15 May 1801; died at 39 Piccadilly, London, aged 80, on Tuesday, 15 November, bur. in Brompton Cemetery, London, 19 November 1881. Will dated 5 January 1877, with two codicils dated respectively 18 March 1878 and 28 September 1878, proved (Prin. Reg., 16, 82) 4 January 1882, by Gerard Collingwood Clark of 9 Clarendon Road, Kensington, co. Middlesex, and Alfred Ashley Clark of 17 St. Swithin's Lane, in the City of London, the nephews, the Exors.

D

George Dodd Clark, born at Corfu 15 February 1830; died at Zante, Greece, 30 January 1849, and bur. there.

Edward Nassau Clark, born at Zante 6 November 1831; died at Calcutta, India, 13 November 1860, and bur. there.

Amy Henrietta Mary, born at Zante 30 April 1834.

B

Louisa Maria, born 17 October 1840, bapt. at St. Dunstan-in-the-East, London, 20 February 1841; marr. at St. Mary's, West Brompton, London (by the Venble George Clark, Archdeacon of St. David's, uncle of the bride, assisted by the Rev. James Palmer Nash), on Wednesday, 7 October 1868, Norcliffe Gilpin of Palewell Lodge, East Sheen, co. Surrey (eldest son of Henry Gilpin); born 14 February 1840; formerly Captain 84th Regiment of Foot. She died at Chislehurst, co. Kent, 27 April, and was bur. at the Church of the Annunciation, Chislehurst, 30 April 1900. M.I. at St. Bartholomew's, Brighton, co. Sussex. Admon (with will dated 25 April 1900) was granted (Prin. Reg., 753, 1900) 25 May 1900, to Norcliffe Gilpin, late a Captain in H.M. 84th Regiment, the lawful husband.

C

Muriel Perceval, born at 9 Cottesmore Gardens, Kensington, London, 21 July 1874; marr. at St. Michael and All Angels', Bedford Park, Chiswick, co. Middlesex (by the father of the bridegroom, assisted by the Rev. Reginald Thomas Heygate and the Rev. Alfred Wilson, the Vicar), on Tuesday, 18 October 1898, the Rev. John Michael Stanhope Walker (4th son of the Rev. Joseph Walker, Rector of Averham, co. Nottingham); born at the Rectory, Averham, on Saturday, 6 May, bapt. at St. Michael's, Averham, 25 June 1871; educated at Repton School and at Brasenose College, Oxford, matriculated 15 October 1890, aged 19, B.A. 1892, M.A. 1893; Curate of Honley, co. York, 1895–98, Milnsbridge, co. York, 1898–1900, and of Chapel Allerton, co. York, since 1900.

Perceval Perceval-Clark, born at 9 Queen Anne's Gardens, Bedford Park, co. Middlesex, on Friday, 25 November 1881; 2nd Lieutenant 4th Battalion The East Surrey Regiment (Militia) 28 February 1902.

Isabella March, born at 40 Philpot Lane, in the parish of St. Andrew Hubbard, London, 3 January 1803; marr. at St. Dunstan-in-the-East, London, 28 January 1835, the Rev. Gerard Edwards Smith (6th son of Henry Smith of Camberwell, co. Surrey); born 28 January 1804; of St. John's College, Oxford, matriculated 1 July 1822, aged 18, B.A. 1829, Vicar of St. Peter-the-less, Chichester, co. Sussex, 1835–36, Rector of North Marden, co. Sussex, 1836–43; Vicar of Cantley, co. York, 1844–46, Perpetual Curate at Ashton Hayes, co. Chester, 1849–53, and Vicar of Osmaston, co. Derby, 1854–70; died at Ockbrook, co. Derby, aged 77, on Wednesday, 21 December, bur. there 27 December 1881. Will dated 30 September 1881, proved (Prin. Reg., 66, 82) 28 January 1882, by Gerard Collingwood Clark of Market Buildings, 26 Mark Lane, in the City of London, one of the Exors. She died at Hillside, Ockbrook, aged 72, on Thursday, 25 February, and was bur there 2 March 1875. Will dated 30 April 1842, proved at Derby 9 April 1875, by the Rev. Gerard Edwards Smith of Ockbrook, co. Derby, the sole Exor. Probate granted under certain limitations.

—

Elizabeth Ann, born at 39 Mincing Lane, London, 21 April 1804; died at Earl's Terrace, Kensington, London, aged 47, and bur. in Brompton Cemetery, London, 22 May 1851.

Henry Bingley Clark,=Julia, eldest dau. of born at 39 Mincing Thomas Staveley Lane, London, 5 April of Earl's Terrace, 1808; died at Merrow, Kensington, Lon- co. Surrey, aged 63, don; born 7 June on Monday, 1 May, 1823; marr. at St. bur. there 5 May MaryAbbott's, Ken- 1871. Will dated 3 sington, London May 1866, proved (by the Rev. George (Prin. Reg., 385, 71) Clark), on Thurs- 3 June 1871, by Julia day, 29 August Clark of Merrow, co. 1844; died at Surrey, the relict, the Merrow, aged 76, sole Executrix. and bur. there 30 March 1900.

Louisa Suter, born at Zante, Greece, 12 February 1836; marr. at Florence, Italy, 19 November 1856, the Rev. Henry John Huntington (son of Charles Huntington); born at Hull, co. York, 1 August 1821; of Christ's College, Cambridge, B.A. 1846; Consular Chaplain at Leghorn, Italy, afterwards at Marseilles, South of France, and at Malaga, Spain; died suddenly at Malaga, aged 67, on Wednesday, 13 July, bur. there 15 July 1887. Will dated 12 July 1887, proved (Prin. Reg., 858, 87) 26 October 1887, by Henry Edward Huntington of Wellington College, Wokingham, co. Berks, the son, the sole Exor.

Ellen Elizabeth, born at Earl's Terrace, Ken- sington, London, 11 January 1838; died at Leghorn, 24 June 1855.

—

Frederick Henry Clark, born at Zante 4 June 1839; died at Zante 3 October 1844, and bur. there.

Frederica Henrietta Anne, born at Zante 18 July 1844.

—

Frances Leonard Clark, born at Zante 20 February 1846.

Ven^ble George Clark, born at 39 Mincing Lane, London,—Anna Eliza Frances, dau. of the
8 July 1809; of University College, Oxford, matriculated | Rev. John Raven Senior of Iron
29 June 1827, aged 17, Bennett Scholar, B.A. 1831 | Acton, co. Gloucester; born 27
(2nd-class Lit. Hum), M.A. 1834; Vicar of Cantley, co. | May 1808; marr. at St. Mary
York, 1845–54, Prebendary of Hereford 12 December | Abbott's, Kensington, London,
1848 until his death, Rector of Tenby, co. Pembroke, | 1 August 1837; died at Robeston
1854–66, Archdeacon of St. David's 1864; died at | Wathen, aged 88, on Wednesday,
the Rectory, Lampeter Velfrey, co. Pembroke, in his | 16 December 1896, and bur.
66th year, on Friday, 11 December, bur. at Robeston | there. Will dated 20 June 1888,
Wathen, co. Pembroke, 16 December 1874. Will dated | proved (Prin. Reg., 257, 97)
30 January 1872, proved (Prin. Reg., 14, 75) 9 January | 31 March 1897, by Anna Duke
1875, by Anna Eliza Frances Clark of Robeston Wathen, | Clark, spinster, the daughter, one
co. Pembroke, the relict, the sole Executrix. | of the Executrixes.

Emily Adelaide, born at Alton, co. Hants, 26 June, bapt. there 1 August 1838; marr. at Tenby (by the father of the bride) on Tuesday, 3 August 1858, William Hastings Hughes, 4th son of the Rev. John Hughes of The Priory, Donnington, co. Berks, and of The Boltons, West Brompton, London. She died at Puerto de Santa Maria, Spain, 10 January 1864, and was bur. at Cadiz, Spain.

Mary Senior, born at Alton 22 November 1839, bapt. there 6 March 1840.
—
Anna Duke, born at High Street, Hastings, co. Sussex, 4 January 1843.

Colonel Gerard Collingwood Clark, born at the Parsonage, Cantley, 6 November, bapt. at Cantley 21 December 1845; of University College, Oxford, matriculated 28 January 1865, aged 19, B.A. 1869 (2nd-class Law and Modern History), M.A. 1873; of Lincoln's Inn 1867; Lieut.-Colonel Commanding (Hon. Colonel) 1st Volunteer Battalion Royal Fusiliers (City of London Regiment) 1883–96.

—Harriet Delamain, 3rd dau. of the Rev. Peter Thomas Ouvry of East Acton, co. Middlesex, formerly Vicar of Wing, co. Buckingham, by Jane his 1st wife, dau. of Sir George Nicholls, K.C.B., of Hyde Park Street, London (see Pedigree of Nicholls, Vol. 2, page 49); born at the Vicarage, Wing, at 10 a.m., on Saturday, 10 January, bapt. there 15 February 1852; marr. at Wing (by her father), on Thursday, 24 May 1883.

(See Pedigree of Ouvry, Vol. 3, page 167.)

Peter Senior Clark, born at Ford Place, Grays, co. Essex, on Wednesday, 10 September 1884; died 27 July 1885.

Mary Francisca, born at 9 Clarendon Road, Kensington, London, on Wednesday, 5 May 1886; died at 9 Cottesmore Gardens, Kensington, London, aged 2 years and 11 months, on Monday, 15 April 1889.

Hester Anita, born at 9 Cottesmore Gardens, Kensington, London, on Thursday, 8 September 1887.

Aimée Harriet, born at 1 Hyde Park Street, London, on Wednesday, 29 May 1889.

A

Harriet Ann, ══ Frederick Le Gros Clark of ══ Harriet, dau. of John ══ Henrietta, younger dau.
dau. of Henry │ "The Thorns," Sevenoaks, │ Brewer of Swanscombe, │ of Henry Andrew Drum-
Willmer of │ co. Kent; born at 39 Mincing │ and of The Grove, Lee, │ mond of Tenby, co.
Down Place, │ Lane, London, 7 February │ both co. Kent; born │ Pembroke, Captain in
Harting, co. │ 1811; Consulting Surgeon │ at 10 Saville Row, │ the Honble East India
Sussex, and │ at St. Thomas' Hospital, │ Walworth, co. Surrey, │ Co.'s Service, by Maria
of "The Fish- │ London, formerly President │ 5 April 1832; marr. at │ his wife, dau. of Captain
eries," Wind- │ of the Royal College of │ the parish church, │ William James Tur-
sor, co. Berks; │ Surgeons, F.R.S.; died at │ Swanscombe (by the │ quand, R.N.; born 1
born at 101 │ "The Thorns," Sevenoaks, in │ Rev. Ralph Raisbeck │ June 1826; marr. at
High Street, │ his 82nd year, on Tuesday, │ Tatham, Vicar of Dal- │ Tenby (by the Rev.
Marylebone, │ 19 July, bur. at Riverhead, │ lington, co. Sussex) on │ George Clark, the Rector,
London, 6 │ co. Kent, 23 July 1892. │ Thursday, 1 May 1856; │ brother of the bride-
August 1818; │ Will dated 25 July 1887, │ died, aged 24, on Thurs- │ groom) on Tuesday, 15
marr. at Stoke │ with codicil dated 4 August │ day, 5 March, bur. at │ June 1858; died 9 June
Poges, co. │ 1887, proved (Prin. Reg., │ St. Margaret's, Lee, 10 │ 1903, and bur. at River-
Buckingham, │ 824, 92) 16 August 1892, │ March 1857. 2nd wife. │ head. 3rd wife.
15 September │ by Frederick Willmer Clark,
1841; died on │ gent., and Alfred Ashley   E
Saturday, 29 │ Clark, the Exors.
June 1850.
1st wife.

F. LeGrosClark (signature)

Herbert Brewer Clark, born at
Linden House, Lee, on Wednesday, 18 February, bapt. at St.
Margaret's, Lee, 21 April 1857;
died, aged 3½ years, on Saturday,
4 August, bur. at St. Margaret's,
Lee, 8 August 1860.

                                                                                             F

Frederick Willmer Clark, ══ Helen Christine, 3rd dau. of Francis Crawshay of Bradbourn Hall,
born at 27 Finsbury Place, │ Sevenoaks, co. Kent, and of 14 Eccleston Square, Belgravia,
London, on Saturday, 19 │ London, by Laura his wife, dau. of Richard Crawshay of Ottershaw
December 1846, and bapt. │ Park, co. Surrey; born 1 November 1851; marr. at Riverhead, co.
at Highgate, co. Middlesex; │ Kent (by the Rev. James McGibbon Burn-Murdoch, the Vicar),
educated at Blackheath │ on Wednesday, 23 April 1873.
Proprietary School.

Annie Christine, born at │ Helen Mabel Sophonisba, │ Charles Nevill Clark, born at Brasted,
"Rosecroft," St. Mary Cray, │ born at St. Mary Cray 24 │ co. Kent, 14 October 1886, and bapt.
co. Kent, on Friday, 24 │ December 1876, bapt. there │ there; died at Brasted 22 January,
April, bapt. at St. Mary │ 21 January 1877. │ bur. there 26 January 1889.
Cray 24 May 1874.

Mary Edith, born at Linden House, Lee, co. Kent, on Wednesday, 9 November 1859, bapt. at St. Margaret's, Lee, 7 January 1860.

Henry Drummond Clark, born at Linden House, Lee, on Friday, 20 December 1861, bapt. at St. Margaret's, Lee, 14 February 1862; died on Thursday, 1 June, bur. at St. Margaret's, Lee, 5 June 1865.

E

Alfred Ashley Clark=Kate, 2nd dau. of Andrew Swanzy of "The of Linden Cottage, Quarry," Sevenoaks, F.R.G.S., by Emma his Sevenoaks, co. Kent; wife, youngest dau. of William Jones of born at 24 Spring Peckham Rye, co. Surrey; born at 5 Glebe Gardens, London, on Terrace, Lee, on Tuesday, 31 July, bapt. Friday, 27 October at St. Margaret's, Lee, 12 September 1855; 1848; educated at marr. at Riverhead, co. Kent (by the Rev. Haileybury. Thomas Biddall Swanzy, assisted by the Rev. James McGibbon Burn-Murdoch, the Vicar), on Wednesday, 9 September 1874.

Walter Constable Clark born at 24 Spring Gardens, London, on Friday, 21 June 1850; died, aged 10½ years, on Christmas Day, Tuesday, 25 December, bur. at St. Margaret's, Lee, 28 December 1860.

(See Pedigree of Swanzy, "Visitation of Ireland," Vol. 4, page 13.)

F

Andrew Le Gros Clark, born at Bromley, co. Kent, on Friday, 12 May 1876, and bapt. at Riverhead.

Willmer Le Gros Clark,=Ethel Mary Dora, younger dau. of Charles born at Linden Cottage, Young of Sevenoaks; born 7 October Sevenoaks, on Saturday, 1871; marr. at St. John's, Dunton Green, 29 December 1877, bapt. co. Kent (by the Rev. Percy Frederick at St. John's, Sevenoaks, Young, brother of the bride), on Wednesday, 10 February 1878. 2 April 1902.

Ethel Kate Le Gros, born at Linden Cottage, Sevenoaks, on Saturday, 31 July, bapt. at St. John's, Sevenoaks, 15 August 1880; marr. at Riverhead (by the Rev. Canon James McGibbon Burn-Murdoch), on Tuesday, 16 April 1901, Ernest Augustus Young (3rd son of Charles Young of "The Thorns," Sevenoaks); born at Laleham House, Isleworth, co. Middlesex, on Monday, 29 September 1873.

Mildred Le Gros, born at Linden Cottage, Sevenoaks, on Friday, 2 May, bapt. at St. John's, Sevenoaks, 29 June 1884.

E

Rev. Edward Travers Clark, ⊤ Ethel May, eldest dau. of Edward Clapton of Towercroft,
born at Linden House, Lee, │ Lee, and of St. Thomas'
co. Kent, on Tuesday, 26 Jan- │ Street, Southwark, by
uary, bapt. at St. Margaret's, │ Mary his wife, eldest
Lee, 13 April 1864; of Trinity │ dau. of John Churchill
Hall, Cambridge, matriculated │ of Oakfield, Wimbledon
Michaelmas Term, 1882, B.A. │ Park, co. Surrey, J.P.;
1887, M.A. 1891; Vicar of St. │ born at 1 Torrington
Thomas', Southwark, co. Surrey, │ Villas, Lee, on Thursday, 4 August, bapt. there privately
1896–98, Curate-in-Charge of St. │ 20 August 1864, and received into the church at Holy
Aldate's, Gloucester, 1898–1902, │ Trinity, Lee, 30 March 1867; marr. there (by the Rev.
Chaplain to Worshipful Com- │ Benjamin Walter Bucke, the Vicar, assisted by the Rev.
pany of Salters', and Diocesan │ Edward Louis Churchill Clapton, Vicar of St. Michael's,
Missioner of the Diocese of │ Wandsworth Common, co. Surrey, brother of the bride,
Gloucester; Vicar of Newnham- │ and the Rev. Josias Grant Mills, Hospitaller of St. Thomas'
on-Severn, co. Gloucester, since │ Hospital, London) on Tuesday, 10 November 1891.
July 1902, Surrogate for the │
diocese of Gloucester 1902.

Edward Clapton

(*See Pedigree of Clapton, Vol. 10, page 10.*)

Frederick Le Gros Clark, │ Cyril Drummond Le Gros │ Wilfrid Edward Le │ Edith Elsie Le Gros,
born at Ivy House, │ Clark, born at Clyde │ Gros Clark, born │ born at Alexandra
Chislet, co. Kent, on │ Street, South Kensington, │ at Alexandra Road, │ Road, Hemel Hemp-
Saturday, 3 September, │ London, on Sunday, 20 │ Hemel Hempstead, │ stead, 18 February,
bapt. at St. John's, │ May, bapt. at St. Paul's, │ co. Hertford, 5 June, │ bapt. at Holy Trinity,
Marshside, Chislet, 9 │ Onslow Square, London, │ bapt. at Boxmoor, │ Lee, 24 May 1897.
October 1892. │ 18 June 1894. │ co. Hertford, 10 │
│ │ July 1895. │

Jones of Kelston Park, co. Somerset.

Arms on record in the College of Arms.—Ermine, a lion rampant azure, within a bordure of the last, charged with eight mullets, or.

Crest.—A lion rampant azure, resting the sinister fore-paw upon an antique shield or, charged with a spear-head proper, and the dexter hind paw upon a mullet, also or.

Motto.—Æquo animo.

Rev. Inigo William Jones of Chobham Place, in the parish of Chobham, co. Surrey, formerly of Turnham Green, co. Middlesex, and of Oakley Hall, Marsham, co. Berks (youngest and only surviving son of Henry Jones of Bloomsbury Square, London, Conveyancer, by Harriet his wife, dau. of Alderman Nathaniel Thomas of Ratton Lodge, co. Sussex); Fellow Commoner of Trinity College, Cambridge, B.A. 1803; died at Chobham Hall, aged 29, 30 October, bur. in a vault at St. Stephen's, Walbrook, London, 8 November 1809. Will dated 8 February 1806, proved (P.C.C., 830 *Loveday*) 23 November 1809, by Margaret Elizabeth Jones, the relict, the Executrix. ⊤ Margaret Elizabeth, only dau. of Lieut.-General Henry Richmond Gale of Bardsea Hall, in the parish of Urswick, co. Lancaster; born at Urswick 3 October, bapt. there 15 October 1786; marr. at Urswick 19 November 1804; marr. 2ndly, General Francis Newbery, Colonel 3rd Dragoon Guards, who died s.p. at Wiesbaden, Nassau, aged 70, 9 November 1848. She died at Earl's Terrace, Kensington, London, aged 73, 12 December, and was bur. in Kensal Green Cemetery, London, 17 December 1859. Admon was granted at the Principal Registry 9 January 1860, to Inigo William Jones of Kelston Park, co. Somerset, and Henry Richmond Jones of Calderstones within Allerton, co. Lancaster, Lieut.-Colonel of Her Majesty's 6th Regiment of Dragoon Guards, or Carabineers, and a Colonel in Her Majesty's Army, C.B., the only children.

A

Lieut.-Colonel Inigo William Jones of Kelston Park, co. Somerset, formerly of Ludford House, Ludlow, co. Salop; born at Gower Street, London, 25 April, bapt. at St. Giles-in-the-Fields, London, 21 May 1806; of Trinity College, Cambridge, B.A. 1830, M.A. 1836; Lieut.-Colonel 1st Battalion Somersetshire Volunteers, formerly Major 11th Hussars; J.P. and D.L. for co. Somerset, High Sheriff 1868; died at Nice, France, in his 73rd year, on Saturday, 5 October, bur. at Kelston 14 October 1878. Will dated 11 June 1856, with six codicils dated respectively 8 October 1845, 17 November 1857, 17 November 1857, 25 January 1859, 26 April 1872, and 25 January 1878, proved (Prin. Reg., 875, 78) 4 November 1878, by Henry Richmond Jones of 45 Clarendon Square, Leamington, co. Warwick, C.B., a General in Her Majesty's Army, Colonel of Her Majesty's 6th Dragoon Guards, or Carabineers, the brother, the surviving Exor. ⊤ Ann Maria, dau. of Joseph Neeld of Grittleton, co. Wilts, M.P. for Chippenham; marr. at St. Mary's, Bryanston Square, London (by the Rev. Thomas Wyld, Rector of North Wraxall, co. Wilts), on Wednesday, 14 August 1844; died at Kelston Park on Friday, 30 August, bur. at Kelston 3 September 1889. Will dated 15 October 1881, proved (Prin. Reg., 837, 89) 28 October 1889, by Inigo Richmund Jones of 10 South Audley Street, co. Middlesex, a Lieut.-Colonel in Her Majesty's Scots Guards, the son, the sole Exor.

B

A
_____
|

General Henry Richmond Jones, C.B., born in Hereford Street, Mayfair,═┬═Harriet Elizabeth, 2nd
London, 25 August, bapt. at St. George's, Hanover Square, London, | dau. of Joseph Need
16 October 1807; entered the Army as Cornet in 1825, a Lieutenant | Walker of Calderstone,
the following year, Captain 1830, Major 1850, Lieut.-Colonel 1851, | co. Lancaster, by
Colonel 1854; commanded the 6th Dragoon Guards (Carabineers) in | Katherine his wife,
the Crimea, and was present at the battle of the Tchernaya and the siege | dau. of Samuel Parker
and fall of Sebastopol; served in the Indian Campaign, commanding | of Scots House,
General Penny's Column in the action of the Kirkrowlie, and commanded | co. Northumberland;
a brigade of cavalry at the capture of Bareilly, for which service he was | marr. at Childwall, co.
nominated a C.B. in 1858, afterwards commanded the left column with | Lancaster (by the
Lord Clyde's force in the attack on Benhi Madho's force at Dunderkera, | Rev. Joseph Walker),
and subsequently the cavalry with Lord Clyde's force in the Trans-Gogra | on Thursday, 28 Oc-
Campaign, including the affairs of Magedia, Chundal and Bankee, taking | tober 1852.
part in the pursuit of the rebels to the Raptee; Major-General 1865,
Lieut.-General 1873, General 1877; appointed Colonel of the 14th
Hussars in 1869, and of the 6th Dragoon Guards in 1873; died at the
Royal York Hotel, Brighton, co. Sussex, aged 73, on Sunday, 3 October,
bur. at Kelston, co. Somerset, 8 October 1880. Will dated 23 June 1880,
proved (Prin. Reg., 872, 80) 12 November 1880, by Inigo Richmund
Jones of 10 South Audley Street, co. Middlesex, a Captain in Her
Majesty's Scots Guards and a Lieut.-Colonel in the Army, the nephew,
and Henry Walker of Perdiswell House, co. Worcester, the Exors.

|

Caroline Harriet Margaret, born at Hounslow, co. Middlesex, on Tuesday, 15 August, bapt.
at Childwall 25 October 1854; marr. at the parish church, Leamington, co. Warwick
(by the Honble and Rev. James Wentworth Leigh, assisted by the Rev. Joseph Walker,
uncle of the bride), on Thursday, 22 July 1880, Robert Oswald Milne, only son of William
Henry Milne of "Woodville," Leamington.

B _____ B
|

Mabel Margaret, born at Coventry, co. Warwick, on Sunday, 11 October, bapt. at St. Michael's,
Coventry, 17 December 1846.

C

| Gladys Agnes Margaret Inigo, born at Kelston Park on Sunday, 4 May, bapt. at Kelston 30 May 1879; died, aged 18, on Wednesday, 16 June, bur. at Kelston 19 June 1897. | Eva Adela Mabel Inigo, born at 10 South Audley Street, London, on Monday, 1 January, bapt. at St. Mary's, Bourdon Street, Berkeley Square, London, 7 March 1883. | Allix Doreen Inigo, born at 10 South Audley Street, London, on Sunday, 22 February, bapt. privately 26 March, and received into the church at St. Mary's, Bourdon Street, Berkeley Square, London, 13 April 1885. |

Alice Charlotte Matilda, only dau. of the Rev. Jonathan Dawson of Rollesby Hall, co. Norfolk, by Alice his wife, dau. of the Rev. George Pearse; marr. at St. George's, Hanover Square, London (by the Rev. Joseph John Gurney, Rector of St. John de Sepulchre, Norwich), 14 January 1878; died, aged 34, on Thursday, 26 March, bur. at Kelston, co. Somerset, 31 March 1885. 1st wife. ═ Major-General Inigo Richmund Jones of Kelston Park, co. Somerset, C.B.; born at Worton Hall, near Isleworth, co. Middlesex, on Saturday, 23 September, bapt. at Isleworth 14 November 1848; entered the Scots Guards as Ensign 18 December 1866, Captain 4 February 1871, Lieut.-Colonel 15 March 1879, Regimental Major 1 July 1886, Colonel 1 July 1890; served in the Soudan Expedition 1885, at Suakim (medal with clasp and bronze star), also on the Staff in the South African War 1899–1900, Commanding Guards Brigade since 10 April 1900, appointed to command the Scots Guards Regiment and Regimental District 1903; J.P. for co. Somerset. ═ Elinor Margaret, elder dau. of the Honble Richard Charteris of Cahir Lodge, co. Tipperary, D.L. (2nd son of Francis, 9th Earl of Wemyss), by Lady Margaret his wife, dau. and heiress of Richard, last Earl of Glengall; born at Lower Grosvenor Street, London, 1 September 1859; marr. at St. Mark's, North Audley Street, London (by the Rev. Joseph Watson Ayre, the Vicar), on Thursday, 12 July 1888. 2nd wife.

Maud Evelyn Inigo, born at 10 South Audley Street, London, on Thursday, 18 April, bapt. at St. Mark's, North Audley Street, 18 May 1889.

Henry Richmund Inigo Jones, born at 10 South Audley Street, London, on Thursday, 17 December 1891, bapt. at St. Mark's, North Audley Street, 20 January 1892.

B

Alice Josephine, born at Lampton Hall, near Hounslow, co. Middlesex, on Wednesday, 8 May, bapt. at Isleworth 11 June 1850.

Ralph William Jones (twin with Christopher Neeld); born at Nottingham on Saturday, 2 August, bapt. privately 31 August, and received into the church at Lenton 24 December 1851.

—

C

Christopher Neeld Jones (twin with Ralph William); born at Nottingham on Saturday, 2 August, bapt. privately 31 August, and received into the church at Lenton, co. Nottingham, 24 December 1851; Captain 94th Regiment (Connaught Rangers); volunteered for service with the Royal Irish Regiment, and was killed at the Battle of Tel-el-Kebir 13 September 1882.

Agnes Ann, born at Montpellier Hill, Dublin, on Wednesday, 20 October, bapt. at St. Paul's, Dublin, 11 December 1852; died at Cannes, France, on Tuesday, 7 March, bur. there 10 March 1882.

—

Ida, born at Ludford, co. Salop, on Wednesday, 8 February, bapt. there 26 March 1854.

Miniature Portrait of John Steedman of Walworth, co. Surrey; baptised at Barnes, co. Surrey, 31 July 1786; died 17 November 1846; in the possession of his grandson, Frederick Arthur Crisp.

Leah, daughter of John Steedman, and wife of Albinus Roberts of St. Albans, co. Hertford, born 27 February 1817, died 10 April 1847.

Elizabeth Martha, daughter of John Steedman, born 8 May 1818, died unmarried 5 March 1899.

Emma, daughter of John Steedman, born 20 June 1825, died unmarried 12 December 1854.

Mary, daughter of John Steedman, and wife of Robert Stephen Faulconer of Clapham Park, co. Surrey, born 31 January 1820, died 30 January 1903.

Sarah, daughter of John Steedman, and wife of Frederick Augustus Crisp of Playford, co. Suffolk, born 24 April 1822, died 15 August 1881.

Steedman.

Thomas Steedman of Barnes, co. Surrey (eldest son of Thomas Steedman of Islington, co. Middlesex, Citizen and Carpenter of London, Master of the Carpenters' Company 1776, by Mary his wife, dau. of Abraham and Anne Redfern); bapt. at St. Mary Somerset, London, 18 March 1753; Citizen and Carpenter of London; admitted a Freeman of the City of London 2 May 1775; bur. at St. Mary Somerset, London, 21 July 1808. Will dated 21 September 1799, proved (P.C.C., 690 *Ely*) 3 August 1808, by Elizabeth Martha Steedman, spinster, the daughter and substituted Executrix, Martha Steedman, wife of the Testator and Executrix named in the will, dying in the lifetime of Testator.

═ Martha, dau. of William Bryant of St. Peter's, Paul's Wharf, London, by Mary his wife; bur. at St. Mary Somerset, London, 10 May 1803. Admon was granted (P.C.C.) 2 June 1803, to Thomas Steedman, the husband.

Elizabeth Martha, bapt. at St. Mary Somerset, London, 19 March 1777; died, aged 63, and bur. at St. Mary Somerset, London, 24 September 1846. Will dated 22 September 1824, proved (P.C.C., 948, 46) 20 October 1846, by John Steedman, the brother, the sole Exor.

John Steedman of Walworth, co. Surrey; born at Barnes, bapt. there (by the Rev. H. Pugh, the Curate) 31 July 1786; Citizen and Carpenter of London, and a Citizen of Rochester; admitted a Freeman of the City of London 13 January 1818, and of Rochester 17 June 1816; died at Walworth, in the 61st year of his age, on Tuesday, 17 November, bur. in Norwood Cemetery, co. Surrey, 24 November 1846. M.I. *Portrait in the possession of Frederick Arthur Crisp, his grandson.* Will dated 12 November 1846, proved (P.C.C.) 9 December 1846, by Leah Steedman, the relict, and Elizabeth Martha Steedman, the daughter, the Executrixes.

═ Leah, dau. of Richard Badcock of Chipping Wycombe, co. Buckingham, by Martha his wife, dau. of Edward Humfrey of Blewbury, co. Berks; born 5 June 1796, bapt. privately at Blewbury the same day (registered 8 June), and received into the church 7 July following; marr. by licence at Chipping Wycombe (by the Rev. James Price, the Vicar) 20 February 1816; died at "Fairlawn," Clarence Road, Clapham Park, co. Surrey, aged 80, on Sunday, 19 November, bur. in Norwood Cemetery on Saturday, 25 November 1876. *Portrait in oils at "Broadhurst," Godalming, co. Surrey, by Sydney Hodges, and a Memorial Ring inscribed:* "IN MEMORY OF LEAH STEEDMAN, BORN 5TH JUNE 1796, DIED 19TH NOV: 1876," *is in the possession of Frederick Arthur Crisp, her grandson.* Will dated 28 May 1875, proved (Prin. Reg.) 16 January 1877, by Elizabeth Martha Steedman and Mary Faulconer, the daughters, and Robert Stephen Faulconer, the son-in-law, the Exors.

Other issue.

A

Leah, born at Walworth, co. Surrey, 27 February, bapt. at St. Mary, Newington, co. Surrey, 28 March 1817; marr. at St. Peter's, Walworth, 4 August 1835, Albinus Roberts of St. Albans, co. Hertford (son of John Pelham Roberts, by Mary Anne his wife, dau. of William Borrer of Hurstpierpoint, co. Sussex); born at Hurstpierpoint 24 March, bapt. there 3 June 1814. She died at St. Albans, aged 30, 10 April, and was bur. at St. Peter's, St. Albans, 19 April 1847. M.I. He marr. 2ndly at St. Peter's, St. Albans, 12 September 1850, Sarah Ann, dau. of Edward Langridge of St. Albans. She died at 61 Marine Parade, Brighton, co. Sussex, aged 65, 23 June, and was bur. at St. Peter's, St. Albans, 28 June 1886. M.I. Her will dated 4 October 1883, was proved at Lewes 3 September 1886, by Herbert Roberts of 21 The Avenue, Blackheath, co. Kent, the son, the sole Exor. He died at St. Albans, aged 62, 15 January, and was bur. at St. Peter's, St. Albans, 19 January 1877. M.I. Will dated 11 August 1876, proved (Prin. Reg., 145, 77) 10 February 1877, by Sarah Ann Roberts of St. Albans, co. Hertford, the relict, and Harvey Roberts, the son, two of the Exors.

(*See Pedigree of Roberts, Vol. 7, page 160.*)

—

Elizabeth Martha, born at Walworth 8 May, bapt. at St. Mary, Newington, co. Surrey, 19 June 1818; died unmarried at "Fairlawn," Clarence Road, Clapham Park, co. Surrey, in her 81st year, on Sunday, 5 March, bur. in Norwood Cemetery, co. Surrey, on Thursday, 9 March 1899. *Portrait in oils at "Broadhurst," Godalming, co. Surrey, by Sydney Hodges, in the possession of Frederick Arthur Crisp, her nephew.* Will dated 6 December 1878, proved (Prin. Reg., 362, 99) 24 March 1899, by Mary Faulconer, the sister, and Frederick Arthur Crisp, the nephew, the Exors.

Mary, born at Walworth 31 January, bapt. at St. Mary, Newington, 1 March 1820; marr. at Holy Trinity, Tunbridge Wells, co. Kent (by the Rev. Edward Hoare, the Incumbent), on Thursday, 25 October 1855, Robert Stephen Faulconer of Clapham Park and Walworth (eldest son of William Faulconer of Shermanbury, co. Sussex, by Mary Walder his wife; [*Memorial Rings inscribed:* "IN MEMORY OF WILLIAM FAULCONER, BORN 26TH JANY 1783, DIED 14TH JUNE 1854: MARY FAULCONER, BORN 27TH NOVR 1788, DIED 20TH OCTR 1861," *and* "MARY FAULCONER OBT 20TH OCTR 1861, ÆT: 73 YRS:" *are in the possession of Frederick Arthur Crisp*]); born at Shermanbury 26 October, bapt. there 23 November 1817; Citizen and Carpenter of London, Master of the Carpenters' Company 1874; died s.p. at "Fairlawn," Clarence Road, Clapham Park, aged 60, 22 July, bur. in Norwood Cemetery 27 July 1878. M.I. The Clock Tower on the site of the old church of St. Mary, Newington, bears the following inscription: "This Clock Tower erected Anno Domini 1877 by R. S. Faulconer Esquire formerly a Churchwarden of the Parish of S. Mary Newington probably marks the site of the Saxon Church mentioned in Doomsday Book in connection with Walworth as it certainly does that of several Churches which have been built in succession upon it. The last Church upon this site was erected in 1793 and was removed under the authority of an Act of Parliament in 1876 in which year on May 1st the new Mother Church of S. Mary Newington in the Kennington Park Road was consecrated." *Portrait in oils at "Broadhurst," Godalming, by Sydney Hodges, in the possession of Frederick Arthur Crisp, his nephew.* Will dated 20 February 1878, proved in the Principal Registry 28 August 1878, by Mary Faulconer, Frederick Arthur Crisp and Thomas Faulconer Wisden, the Exors. She died at "Fairlawn," Clarence Road, Clapham Park, in her 83rd year, on Friday night, 30 January, and was bur. in Norwood Cemetery on Wednesday, 4 February 1903. M.I. *Portrait in oils at "Broadhurst," Godalming, by Sydney Hodges, in the possession of Frederick Arthur Crisp, her nephew.* Will dated 10 March 1899, proved (Prin. Reg., 58, 1903) 20 February 1903, by Frederick Arthur Crisp, the nephew, the sole Exor.

(*See Pedigree of Faulconer, Vol. 4, page 83.*)

A

Sarah, born at Walworth, co. Surrey, 24 April, bapt. at St. Mary, Newington, co. Surrey, 22 May 1822; marr. at St. Peter's, Walworth (by the Rev. Francis Freeman Statham), on Wednesday, 30 May 1849 (by licence of the Archbishop of Canterbury 25 May 1849), to Frederick Augustus Crisp of Walworth, co. Surrey, and afterwards of The Hall, Playford, co. Suffolk (son of Edwards Crisp of Rendlesham, and afterwards of Gedgrave Hall, near Orford, co. Suffolk, by Mary his wife, dau. of John and Sarah Mayhew of Orford); born at Rendlesham on Monday, 2 July 1821, bapt. there (by the Rev. C. Henley, the Rector) 30 August 1822; Member of the Royal College of Surgeons 5 October 1844, Licentiate of the Society of Apothecaries 15 January 1846; died at The Hall, Playford, in his 63rd year, on Wednesday, 6 February, bur. at Playford on Monday, 11 February 1884. M.I. Will dated 16 April 1878, proved in the Principal Registry 4 April 1884, by Frederick Arthur Crisp and William Henry Crisp, the sons, the Exors. She died at The Hall, Playford, aged 59, on Monday, 15 August, and was bur. at Playford 22 August 1881. M.I. Will dated 1 September 1877, proved in the Principal Registry 25 October 1881, by Frederick Arthur Crisp and William Henry Crisp, the sons, the Exors.

Emma, born at Walworth 20 June, bapt. at St. Mary, Newington, 15 July 1825; died unmarried at Dulwich, co. Surrey, aged 29, 12 December, bur. in Norwood Cemetery, co. Surrey, 18 December 1854. Admon was granted at the Principal Registry 19 January 1877, to Mary Faulconer, wife of Robert Stephen Faulconer, of "Fairlawn," Clarence Road, Clapham Park, co. Surrey, the sister.

—

Ellen, born at Walworth 25 July, bapt. at St. Mary, Newington, 19 August 1831; died, aged 1 year and 8 months, 3 April 1833, bur. in the ground attached to the Independent Meeting House at Walworth. The remains were afterwards removed to Norwood Cemetery.

Lockett.

Joseph Lockett of Goostrey, and afterwards of Marthall, both co. Chester; marr. at Over Peover, co. Chester, 5 August 1777, Ann, dau. of William Barns of Over Peover; bapt. at Over Peover on Sunday, 26 May 1754. He died at Chelford, co. Chester, in 1834.

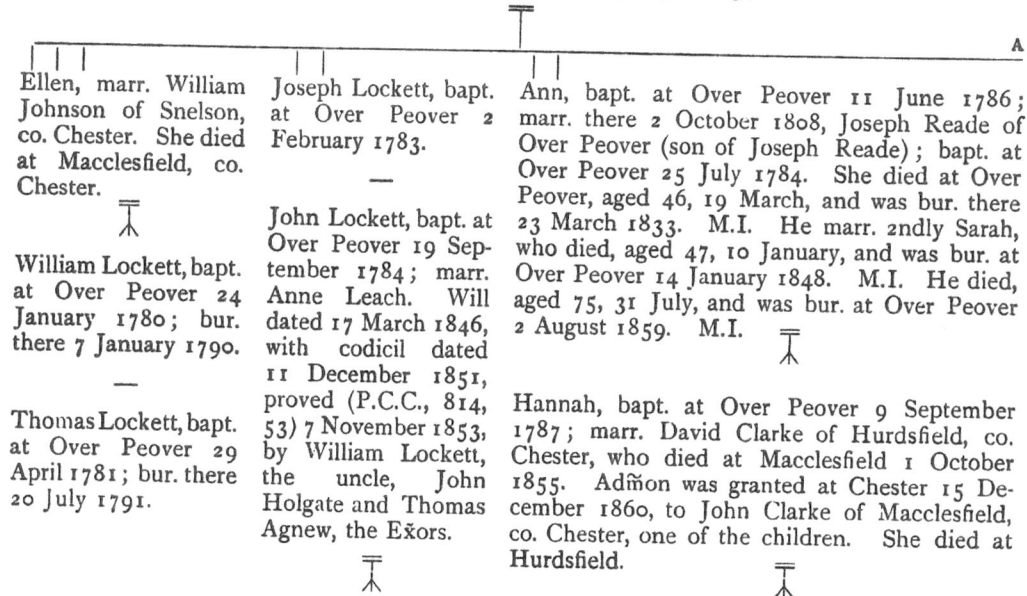

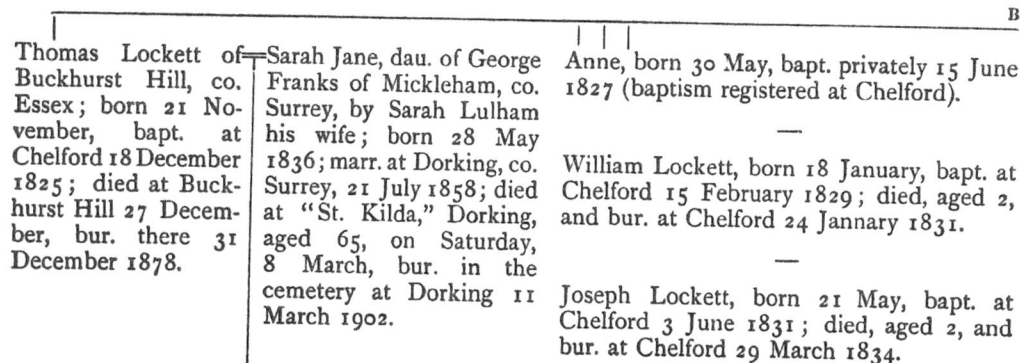

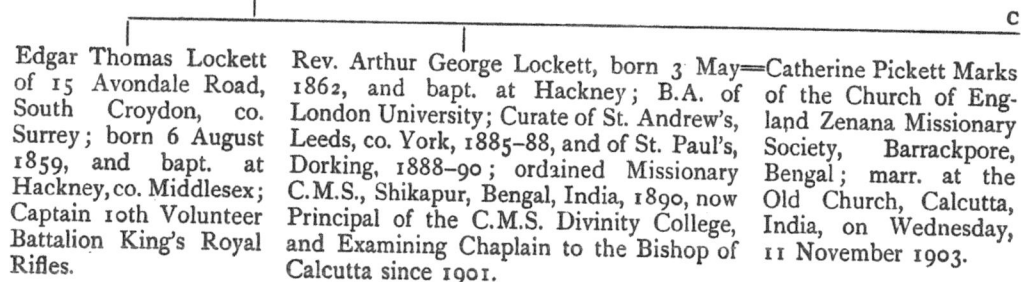

A

Ellen, marr. William Johnson of Snelson, co. Chester. She died at Macclesfield, co. Chester.

William Lockett, bapt. at Over Peover 24 January 1780; bur. there 7 January 1790.

Thomas Lockett, bapt. at Over Peover 29 April 1781; bur. there 20 July 1791.

Joseph Lockett, bapt. at Over Peover 2 February 1783.

—

John Lockett, bapt. at Over Peover 19 September 1784; marr. Anne Leach. Will dated 17 March 1846, with codicil dated 11 December 1851, proved (P.C.C., 814, 53) 7 November 1853, by William Lockett, the uncle, John Holgate and Thomas Agnew, the Exors.

Ann, bapt. at Over Peover 11 June 1786; marr. there 2 October 1808, Joseph Reade of Over Peover (son of Joseph Reade); bapt. at Over Peover 25 July 1784. She died at Over Peover, aged 46, 19 March, and was bur. there 23 March 1833. M.I. He marr. 2ndly Sarah, who died, aged 47, 10 January, and was bur. at Over Peover 14 January 1848. M.I. He died, aged 75, 31 July, and was bur. at Over Peover 2 August 1859. M.I.

Hannah, bapt. at Over Peover 9 September 1787; marr. David Clarke of Hurdsfield, co. Chester, who died at Macclesfield 1 October 1855. Admon was granted at Chester 15 December 1860, to John Clarke of Macclesfield, co. Chester, one of the children. She died at Hurdsfield.

B

Thomas Lockett of Buckhurst Hill, co. Essex; born 21 November, bapt. at Chelford 18 December 1825; died at Buckhurst Hill 27 December, bur. there 31 December 1878. = Sarah Jane, dau. of George Franks of Mickleham, co. Surrey, by Sarah Lulham his wife; born 28 May 1836; marr. at Dorking, co. Surrey, 21 July 1858; died at "St. Kilda," Dorking, aged 65, on Saturday, 8 March, bur. in the cemetery at Dorking 11 March 1902.

Anne, born 30 May, bapt. privately 15 June 1827 (baptism registered at Chelford).

—

William Lockett, born 18 January, bapt. at Chelford 15 February 1829; died, aged 2, and bur. at Chelford 24 January 1831.

—

Joseph Lockett, born 21 May, bapt. at Chelford 3 June 1831; died, aged 2, and bur. at Chelford 29 March 1834.

C

Edgar Thomas Lockett of 15 Avondale Road, South Croydon, co. Surrey; born 6 August 1859, and bapt. at Hackney, co. Middlesex; Captain 10th Volunteer Battalion King's Royal Rifles.

Rev. Arthur George Lockett, born 3 May 1862, and bapt. at Hackney; B.A. of London University; Curate of St. Andrew's, Leeds, co. York, 1885–88, and of St. Paul's, Dorking, 1888–90; ordained Missionary C.M.S., Shikapur, Bengal, India, 1890, now Principal of the C.M.S. Divinity College, and Examining Chaplain to the Bishop of Calcutta since 1901. = Catherine Pickett Marks of the Church of England Zenana Missionary Society, Barrackpore, Bengal; marr. at the Old Church, Calcutta, India, on Wednesday, 11 November 1903.

A

Timothy Lockett, bapt. at Over Peover, co. Chester, 1 August 1789; died, aged 73, and bur. at Chelford, co. Chester, 17 November 1862. M.I. =Elizabeth, dau. of Thomas Darlington of Moulton, co. Chester, by Martha Maydew his wife; born 16 March 1794; marr. at Davenham, co. Chester, 1 March 1825; died, aged 80, and bur. at Chelford 14 May 1874. M.I.

Elizabeth, bapt. at Over Peover 5 February 1792; bur. there 23 September 1803.

—

Samuel Lockett, bapt. at Over Peover 1 April 1798; died at Manchester.

B

John Lockett formerly of Heaton Moor, co. Lancaster; born 21 March, bapt. at Chelford 21 April 1833. =Anne, eldest dau. of William Holland of Macclesfield, co. Chester, by Rebecca his wife, dau. of William and Rachel de Bel; born 23 March, bapt. at Chelford 20 April 1834; marr. at Lingen, co. Hereford, 15 October 1863; died 21 July, bur. in Willow Grove Cemetery, Reddish, co. Lancaster, 25 July 1893.

John Lockett

D

B

Rev. Henry John Lockett, born 14 July, bapt. at St. Paul's, Macclesfield, 27 August 1864; educated at King Edward VI.'s Modern Grammar School, Macclesfield, 1872–78, matriculated at Cambridge University as unattached Student 1886, graduated (2nd-class Honours Theology) June 1889, and spent last term, 1889, at Ridley Hall, Cambridge, M.A. 1893; Curate of the parish church, Bradford, co. York, 1890–94, Vicar of St. Clement's, Bradford, since 1894.

Henry J. Lockett

C

Ethel Annie, born 12 July 1864; died unmarried at "St. Kilda," Dorking, co. Surrey, aged 36, on Wednesday, 21 November, bur. in the cemetery at Dorking 24 November 1900.

Herbert Edward Lockett of Epsom, co. Surrey; born at Buckhurst Hill, co. Essex, 1 November 1867, and bapt. there. =Edith, dau. of Henry Brown of Ealing, co. Middlesex, by Sarah Hannah his wife, dau. of William Henry Pottle; born at Chelsea, co. Middlesex, 7 October 1873; marr. at Ealing 5 November 1900.

Percy Arthur Lockett, born at Epsom 31 January 1902.

Thomas Herbert Lockett, born at Epsom 11 July, bapt. there 13 September 1903.

91

B

Samuel Lockett, born at=Jessie Jane, dau. of Thomas Whitehead of Plymouth Grove,
Chelford, co. Chester, | Manchester, by Margaret Brough his wife; born at Manchester
23 March, bapt. there | 15 August 1833, and bapt. at St. Mary's, Manchester; marr. at
19 April 1835; died at | St. Stephen's, Manchester, 7 March 1859. She marr. 2ndly at
Chelford, aged 36, 27 | St. Alkmund's, Derby, 1 January 1873, William Henry Nicholson
November, bur. there | (son of John Nicholson of Workington, co. Cumberland, by his wife,
1 December 1871. M.I. | Martha Sharrack of Preston, co. Lancaster); born at Manchester
8 April 1840, and bapt. at Gravel Lane Chapel, Salford, co. Lancaster.

Thomas Whitehead Lockett, born at Bolton
Lane, Manchester, 2 October 1869; died at
Plymouth Grove, Manchester, aged 3 months,
and bur. at Chelford 1 January 1870.

D

Walter Holland Lockett of "Perran,"=Katherine Pennington, dau. of Major-General Charles
Hadley Wood, co. Middlesex; born 12 | Gilbert Robinson of the Royal Artillery, by Mina
May, bapt. at St. Paul's, Macclesfield, | Elizabeth his wife, dau. of Edward Richard Purefoy
co. Chester, 13 June 1866; educated at | Colles of Dublin; born at Mean Meer, Punjab, India,
King Edward VI.'s Modern Grammar | 25 June 1871, and bapt. there; marr. at Christ Church,
School, Macclesfield. | Hampstead, co. Middlesex, 13 June 1900.

Emma, born 21 April, bapt. at St. Paul's, | Alice Mary, born 4 April, bapt. at
Macclesfield, 20 May 1868; a Missionary of the | St. Paul's, Macclesfield, 27 May 1873.
C.M.S. at Frere Town, East Africa, since 1895.

—

—

Elizabeth Darlington, born 14 June, bapt. at | Arthur William Lockett, born 13 May,
St. Paul's, Macclesfield, 30 July 1870; Principal | bapt. at St. Paul's, Macclesfield, 25 June
of the Girl's High School, Heaton Chapel, | 1876; educated at King Edward VI.'s
co. Lancaster. | Modern Grammar School, Macclesfield.

Edgar Lockett

Thursby of Ormerod House, co. Lancaster.

Rev. William Thursby of Ormerod House, co. Lancaster (2nd son of John Harvey Thursby of Abingdon Abbey, co. Northampton, M.P., by Emma his wife, dau. of William Pigott of Doddershall, co. Buckingham); born 27 April, bapt. at Pitsford, co. Northampton, 3 May 1795; educated at Harrow and at Oriel College, Oxford, matriculated 27 April 1814, B.A. 1818, M.A. 1820; Vicar of Hardingstone, co. Northampton, 1820, of All Saints', Northampton, 1822–32, and of Worsthorne-next-Burnley, co. Lancaster, 1836–69, Domestic Chaplain to the Duke of Cambridge; J.P. for co. Lancaster; died at 6 Brunswick Terrace, Brighton, co. Sussex, aged 89, on Friday, 10 October 1884, and bur. at Holmes Chapel, co. Lancaster. M.I. in the church at Worsthorne. Will dated 28 October 1881, with two codicils dated respectively 29 December 1883 and 15 January 1884, proved (Prin. Reg., 983, 84) 6 December 1884, by Thomas Hughes of Lincoln's Inn, co. Middlesex, Q.C., Henry Paulson Bowling of 26 Essex Street, Strand, co. Middlesex, and Frederick John Grant of Burnley, co. Lancaster, the Exors.

=Eleanor Mary, elder dau. and coheiress of Colonel John Hargreaves of Ormerod House and Bank Hall, co. Lancaster, by Charlotte Anne his wife, only dau. of Lawrence Ormerod of Ormerod; born 9 February 1803; marr. at St. Peter's, Burnley, 9 September 1824; died at 6 Brunswick Terrace, Brighton, in her 81st year, on Friday, 14 December 1883, and bur. at Holmes Chapel. Admon was granted at the Principal Registry 14 March 1884, to the Rev. William Thursby of 6 Brunswick Terrace, Brighton, co. Sussex.

A

Eleanor Anne, born 12 August 1825; died at Ormerod House, aged 19, on Wednesday, 2 April 1845, and bur. at Holmes Chapel. M.I. in the church at Worsthorne.

B

Sir John Ormerod Scarlett Thursby of Ormerod House and of Bank Hall, co. Lancaster, Bart.; born at Falconer's Hill, Daventry, co. Northampton, on Saturday, 27 April 1861; educated at Eton and at Trinity College, Cambridge, matriculated Michaelmas Term, 1880, B.A. 1884; Barrister-at-Law of Lincoln's Inn 1891; J.P. for co. Lancaster; succeeded his father as 2nd Bart. 16 March 1901.

=Ella Beatrice, 2nd dau. and coheiress of Colonel Thomas Richard Crosse of Shaw Hill, co. Lancaster, J.P., by Lady Mary his wife, eldest dau. of Charles Andrew Knox, 4th Earl of Castlestewart; born 22 September 1861; marr. at St. Peter's, Eaton Square, London (by the Rev. William Ford Thursby, assisted by the Rev. Charles Garnett), on Wednesday, 28 November 1888.

Clara, born at 37 Ennismore Gardens, London, on Wednesday, 13 November, bapt. at St. Peter's, Eaton Square, London, 21 December 1889.

93

Clara, youngest dau. of = Colonel Sir John Hardy Thursby of Ormerod House, = Louisa Harriet, Colonel John Williams, R.E., and niece of the Rt. Honble Sir Edward Vaughan Williams; born 24 March 1839; marr. at St. James', Piccadilly, London (by the Rev. Ford Thursby, assisted by the Rev. Frederick Thursby), on Tuesday, 21 February 1860; died at 16 Eccleston Square, London, aged 28, on Thursday, 21 March, bur. in Brompton Cemetery, London, 25 March 1867. M.I. in St. Peter's, Burnley, co. Lancaster. 1st wife.

Colonel Sir John Hardy Thursby of Ormerod House, co. Lancaster, and of Holmhurst, co. Hants, Bart.; born 31 August 1826; educated at Eton; J.P. and D.L. for co. Lancaster, High Sheriff 1887; Hon. Colonel 3rd Battalion East Lancashire Regiment (Militia), formerly Lieutenant 90th Regiment Light Infantry; created a Baronet 26 July 1887; died at Cannes, France, aged 74, on Saturday, 16 March, bur. at Holmes Chapel 20 March 1901. Will dated 28 August 1899, with three codicils dated respectively 28 November 1899, 13 August 1900 and 24 December 1900, proved (Prin. Reg., 1043, 1901) 10 August 1901, by Sir John Ormerod Scarlett Thursby, Bart., the son, Robert Handsley, and Walter Southern, the Exors.

Louisa Harriet, 2nd dau. of Colonel John George Smyth of Heath Hall, co. York, by the Honble Diana Bosville his wife, dau. of Godfrey, 3rd Baron Macdonald; born 8 March 1840; marr. at Kirkthorpe, co. York (by the Rev. William Thursby, assisted by the Rev. John Pullein), on Thursday, 26 Nov. 1868. 2nd wife.

George James = Mary Augusta, elder dau. of Thomas Hardcastle   Mary Eleanor, Thursby, born at 53 Upper Brook Street, Grosvenor Square, London, on Wednesday, 17 November, bapt. at St. Andrew's, Wells Street, London, 31 December 1869; educated at Radley.

Mary Augusta, elder dau. of Thomas Hardcastle of Bradshaw Hall, Bolton-le-Moors, co. Lancaster, and of Blaston Hall, co. Leicester, J.P., by Emily Augusta his wife, dau. of the Rev. William Purdon, Rector of Seaton, born at Bradshaw Hall, Bolton-le-Moors, on Saturday, 15 June 1872; marr. at All Saints', Ennismore Gardens, London (by the Rev. Frederick Hall, Rector of Friern Barnet, co. Middlesex, uncle of the bride, assisted by the Rev. Ravenscroft Stewart, the Vicar), on Tuesday, 11 December 1894.

Mary Eleanor, born at 10 Green Street, Grosvenor Square, London, on Sunday, 30 April, bapt. at St. Andrew's, Wells Street, London, 27 May 1871.

Gerald Hardy Fitz-Roy Thursby, born at Bronsil, Ledbury, co. Hereford, on Sunday, 15 September 1895; died at Blaston, co. Rutland, aged 13 months, on Monday, 19 October, bur. there 21 October 1896.

B

Violet, born at 12 Hyde Park Place, London, on Wednesday, 12 December 1866, and bapt. at St. Gabriel's, Warwick Square, London; marr. at Highcliffe, co. Hants, on Tuesday, 19 February 1889, Willoughby Aston Littledale (4th son of Henry Anthony Littledale of Bolton Hall, Craven, co. York, by Mary Elizabeth his wife, eldest dau. of John Armytage of Kirklees Park, co. York [see Pedigree of Armytage, Vol. 1, page 235]); born 31 August, bapt. at Bolton-by-Bolland, co. York, 30 September 1857; educated at Marlborough and at Exeter College, Oxford, matriculated 3 June 1876, B.A. 1879, M.A. 1884; Fellow of the Society of Antiquaries since 1897.

(See Pedigree of Littledale, Vol. 1, page 240.)

James Legh Thursby of Craig-le, co. Carnarvon; born 4 February 1828; Major 22nd Regiment of Foot, retired 24 March 1863; served with the 9th Regiment in the Crimea from 27 November 1854, including the siege and fall of Sebastopol and assault of the batteries on 18 June (medal with clasp and Turkish medal); J.P. for co. Carnarvon; died at Harrogate, co. York, aged 58, on Saturday, 31 July, bur. in the Extra Mural Cemetery, Brighton, co. Sussex, 4 August 1886.

=Harriet Matilda, eldest dau. of Edward Johnston of Allerton Hall, Woolton, co. Lancaster, and of Silwood Lodge, co. Berks; born 17 August 1832; marr. at the parish church Brighton (by the Rev. Sir Henry Thompson, Bart., assisted by the Rev. Frederick Thursby) on Thursday, 15 October 1863. She marr. 1stly at St. Catherine's, Liverpool (by the Rev. James North), on Thursday, 19 August 1852, Hardman Earle of Liverpool (2nd son of Sir Hardman Earle of Allerton Tower, Woolton, Bart., by Mary his wife, 2nd dau. of William Langton of Kirkham, co. Lancaster); born 20 January, bapt. at St. Peter's, Liverpool, 27 August 1825; died s.p. at Lisbon, Portugal, on board the s.s. "Tagus," on his return from Malaga, Spain, in his 29th year, on Saturday, 28 May, bur. in the English Cemetery at Lisbon 30 May 1853. She died at Craig-le on Saturday, 30 December 1876.

(See Pedigree of Earle, Vol. 10, page 108.)

Ethelrida, born at 7 Eastern Terrace, Brighton, on Monday, 17 October, died, aged 16 days, 2 November, and bur. in the Extra Mural Cemetery, Brighton, 4 November 1864. —

William Legh Thursby, born at 20 Eaton Place, London, on Monday, 18 December 1865, bapt. at St. Peter's, Eaton Square, London, 27 January 1866; Lieutenant Warwickshire Imperial Yeomanry (Paget's Horse); served in South African War 1900–1901.

Hilda, born at 17 Belgrave Place, Brighton, on Monday, 23 December 1867; marr. at St. Augustine's, Queen's Gate, South Kensington, London, 3 August 1893, Herbert Hodder Roberts (son of Colonel Hodder Roberts, by Jane his wife, dau. of Richard Walter); entered the Royal Marine Light Infantry as Lieutenant 1 February 1879, Captain 23 December 1887, Major 15 October 1895 (retired 6 December 1897); Captain (temporary) Royal Home Counties Reserve Regiment 18 April 1900; Recruiting Officer, Hull District, 1 June 1901. She died at Gad's Hill House, co. Kent, 26 October 1897. Will dated 3 August 1893, proved (Prin. Reg., 205, 98) 2 February 1898, by Herbert Hodder Roberts, Major in the Royal Marine Light Infantry, the husband, the sole Exor.

Winifred, born at Leighton Hall, co. Salop, on Wednesday, 11 November 1868; marr. at the Pro-Cathedral, Kensington, 16 December 1890, Henry Albert de Freyne ffrench, Marchese di Castelthomond, in Rome (5th son of Acheson Jeremy Sidney ffrench of Monivea Hamilton, Victoria, Australia, by Anna his wife, dau. of Dr. John Walton of London) born 6 March 1862.

Rev. William Ford Thursby, born 23 August, bapt. at=Fanny, eldest dau. of Edmund Hardingstone, co. Northampton, 15 October 1830; educated at Rugby and at Emmanuel College, Cambridge, LL.B. 1855; Rector and Patron of Bergh Apton, co. Norfolk, for 29 years, Rural Dean of Brooke; J.P. for co. Norfolk; died at the Rectory, Bergh Apton, aged 62, on Monday, 8 May, bur. at Bergh Apton 12 May 1893. Will dated 2 February 1889, with codicil dated 21 March 1891, proved at Norwich 9 August 1893, by Fanny Thursby, the relict, and Arthur Harvey Thursby, the brother, and John Holmes, the Exors.

Fanny, eldest dau. of Edmund Newman Kershaw, by Mary Anne his wife, dau. of the Rev. William Yates; born at Catton Hall, co. Derby, and bapt. at Croxton, co. Stafford; marr. at Witton, co. Chester, 26 August 1858; Patron of Bergh Apton.

Lieut.-Colonel Arthur Edmund=Maud, 2nd dau. of Thursby of Priors Hardwick, co. Warwick, born at Wormleighton, co. Warwick, on Saturday, 19 January, bapt. there 17 February 1861; educated at Wellington and at Trinity Hall, Cambridge; J.P. for co. Warwick; Major and Hon. Lieut.-Colonel 5th Battalion Warwickshire Regiment (Militia); served in the South African War 1901–1902; died at Sutherland, Cape Colony, 6 March 1902, and bur. there. Will dated 24 April 1901, proved (Prin. Reg., 26, 1902) 17 June 1902, by Maud Thursby, the relict, the Rev. Harvey William Gustavus Thursby, the brother, and Henry Aubrey Cartwright, the Exors.

Maud, 2nd dau. of Lieut.-Colonel Henry Cartwright of Eydon Hall, co. Northampton, of the Grenadier Guards, by Jane his wife, dau. of William Holbech of Farnborough, co. Warwick; born at 46 Park Street, Grosvenor Square, London, on Thursday, 15 January, bapt. at St. Mark's, North Audley Street, London, 27 February 1857; marr. at St. Paul's, St. Leonard's-on-Sea, co. Sussex (by the Rev. Edward Arthur Cartwright, assisted by the Rev. William Digby Cartwright), on Thursday, 21 February 1889.

Eleanor Mary Anne, born 25 March, bapt. at Wormleighton 4 May 1862; marr. at St. Mary's, Burghfield, co. Berks (by the Rt. Rev. James Leslie, D.D., Bishop of Reading, assisted by the Rev. Dallas Oldfield Harington, the Rector), on Wednesday, 24 April 1895, as his 2nd wife, the Rev. Godfrey Armytage Littledale (2nd son of Henry Anthony Littledale of Bolton Hall, co. York, by Mary Elizabeth his wife, eldest dau. of John Armytage of Kirklees Park, co. York [see Pedigree of Armytage, Vol. I, page 235]); born 15 September, bapt. at Bolton-by-Bolland, co. York, 15 October 1854; educated at Winchester and at Brasenose College, Oxford, B.A. 1877, M.A. 1880; Vicar of Chipping Norton, co. Oxford, since 1886; Rural Dean of Chipping Norton, 1903.

(See Pedigree of Littledale, Vol. I, page 239, and Addenda, Vol. 5, page vi.)

Diana Mary, born at Hardwick Hill, co. Warwick, on Wednesday, 1 July, bapt. at Priors Hardwick 2 August 1891.

Piers Henry Thursby, born at Hardwick Hill on Wednesday, 19 December 1894, bapt. at Priors Hardwick 20 January 1895.

Arthur William Charles Thursby, born on Sunday, 2 July, bapt. at Priors Hardwick 1 August 1899.

Mary Anne, dau. of Edmund Newman Kershaw, by Mary Anne his wife, dau. of the Rev. William Yates; born 7 October 1834; marr. at Witton, co. Chester, 28 April 1859; died, aged 65, on Friday, 10 August, bur. at Burghfield, co. Berks, on Wednesday, 15 August 1900. Will dated 26 February 1898, proved (Prin. Reg., 240, 1901) 23 February 1901, by Arthur Harvey Thursby, the husband, and Arthur Edmund Thursby, Lieut.-Colonel in H.M. Warwickshire Regiment, the son, the Exors. 1st wife.

=Arthur Harvey Thursby= of Culverlands, co. Berks, and of Priors Hardwick, co. Warwick; born at Hardingstone, co. Northampton, 25 May 1832, and bapt. there; formerly Lieutenant Warwickshire Yeomanry Cavalry; J.P. for co. Warwick, J.P. and D.L. for co. Berks, High Sheriff for co. Berks 1891.

Catherine, only dau. of the Rev. Harry Holdsworth Minchin, formerly Rector of Little Bromley, co. Essex; born at Woodford Halse, co. Northampton, 30 March 1866, bapt. there privately the same day (baptism registered at Woodford Halse); marr. at the Chapel Royal, Savoy, London (by the Rev. Paul Wyatt, the Chaplain), on Monday, 16 March 1903. 2nd wife.

C

Fanny Charlotte, born 5 January, bapt. at Wormleighton, co. Warwick, 14 February 1864; marr. at Burghfield 30 January 1895, the Rev. Charles Hubert Whitfield (eldest son of Hubert Whitfield); of Pembroke College, Cambridge, B.A. 1889, M.A. 1893; Vicar of Moreton Morrell, co. Warwick, 1895–97, of Grazeley, co. Berks, 1897–1903, and Rector of Elston, co. Nottingham, since 1903.

Emma Harriott, born at Wormleighton on Tuesday, 1 August, bapt. there 1 October 1865; marr. at Burghfield 2 December 1896, the Rev. Thomas Hugh Langford-Sainsbury (only son of the Rev. Sainsbury Langford-Sainsbury of Beckington, co. Somerset, by Mary his wife, dau. of John Blandy of Kingston House, co. Berks); born at Beckington 23 September, bapt. there 24 October 1869; educated at Honiton School and at Trinity College, Oxford, matriculated 15 October 1887, aged 18, B.A. 1892, M.A. 1895; Rector and Patron of Beckington with Standerwick, co. Somerset, since 1896.

Rev. Harvey William Gustavus=Thursby, born at Wormleighton on Saturday, 8 June, bapt. there 28 July 1867; educated at Wellington and at Pembroke College, Oxford, matriculated 25 October 1887, aged 20, B.A. 1893, M.A. 1896; Rector and Patron of Bergh Apton 1897; J.P. for co. Norfolk.

Margaret Emily, 4th dau. of William George Mount of Wasing Place and of Hartley Court, both co. Berks, M.P. for Newbury Division of co. Berks, J.P. and D.L. for co. Berks, by Marianne Emily his wife, 3rd dau. of Robert Clutterbuck of Watford House, co. Hertford; born at Wasing Place on Friday, 3 October, bapt. at St. Nicholas', Wasing, 16 November 1873; marr. there (by the Ven^ble Archdeacon Mount, uncle of the bride, assisted by the Rev. John Butler Burne, the Rector and Rural Dean), on Tuesday, 8 June 1897.

John Harvey Thursby, born at 33 Eccleston Square, London, on Tuesday, 6 January, bapt. at St. Peter's, Eaton Square, London, 10 February 1903.

Piers Thursby of Broadwell Hill,══Mary, 3rd dau. of Joseph Godman of Park Hatch, co. co. Gloucester; born 30 November Surrey, and of Merston, co. Sussex, J.P., by Caroline his 1834; educated at Harrow; Captain wife, dau. of Edmund Smithe of Horsham Park, co. 9th (Queen's Royal) Regiment of Sussex, J.P.; born 2 December, bapt. at Hascombe, co. Lancers; served in Indian Mutiny Surrey, 29 December 1839; marr. there (by the Rev. (medal with clasp); J.P. for co. William Ford Thursby, Rector of Bergh Apton, co. Norfolk, Gloucester. assisted by the Rev. Vernon Musgrave, the Rector), on Wednesday, 17 August 1864.

Lieut.-Colonel Richard Hasell Thursby,══Alice Anne, only dau. of Richard | Sophia Charlotte, born 22 September 1836; educated at | Doncaster of Middlethorpe, co. | born at Ormerod Harrow; Lieut.·Colonel Coldstream | Nottingham, by his wife, Harriette | House, co. Lan- Guards, retired 2 September 1868; died | Beardoe of Ardwick, co. Lancaster; | caster, 18 July at The Quay, Instow, co. Devon, aged | marr. at St. Mary Magdalen's, | 1840, and bapt. at 48, on Sunday, 5 April 1885, and | St. Leonard's-on-Sea, co. Sussex (by | Worsthorne, co. bur. at Holmes Chapel, co. Lancaster. | the Rev. William Thursby and the | Lancaster. Adm͠on was granted at the Principal | Rev. John Doncaster, B.D., Rector Registry 3 June 1885, to Alice Anne | of Navenby, co. Lincoln), on Thursby of Melbury Lodge, Winchester, | Thursday, 28 January 1858. co. Southampton, the relict.

Florence Emma, born at 31 | Mabel Gwendolen, marr. at St. Thomas', Winchester, co. Gloucester Street, South Belgravia, | Hants (by the Rev. William Ford Thursby, assisted by the London, on Thursday, 17 February | Rev. Arthur Baron Sole, the Rector), on Wednesday, 1859. | 2 September 1891, Walter Edward Lascelles (eldest son — | of Colonel Walter Richard Lascelles of Norley Hall, co. | Chester, by Ellen his wife, dau. of Charles Siveright); Arthur Doncaster Thursby, born | born 21 March 1862; Captain 3rd Battalion Rifle Brigade at 1 Eccleston Terrace South, | (The Prince Consort's Own); died at Norley, Frodsham, London, on Sunday, 6 May 1860. | co. Chester, aged 34, 23 January, bur. there 27 January — | 1897. Will dated 8 August 1896, proved (Prin. Reg., | 301, 97) 1 March 1897, by George Reginald Lascelles, Edmund Hasell Thursby, born at | Lieutenant in H.M. Regiment of Royal Fusiliers, one of 1 Eccleston Terrace South, Lon- | the Exͦors. don, on Saturday, 8 March 1862; formerly Sub-Lieutenant R.N.

Ethel Constance Geraldine, born at 11 Belgrave Road, London, on | Charles Augustus Monday, 8 July 1867; marr. at St. Thomas', Winchester, 2 October | Hathorne Thursby, 1889, Lieut.-Colonel Thomas Duncan William Dunn of Standen Manor, | born at 118 Sloane Hungerford, co. Berks (son of Major-General William Dunn of Inglewood | Street, London, on and Wallington, co. Berks, Lieut.-Colonel Royal Artillery, by Margaret | Monday, 19 Feb- Duncan his wife, youngest dau. and coheir of William Williams Brown of | ruary 1872. Allerton Hall, co. York); born 15 October 1846; Lieut.-Colonel Hamp- shire Regiment, retired 21 April 1889; died at the Continental Hotel, Cairo, Egypt, aged 52, on Wednesday, 22 March, bur. in the Protestant Cemetery at Cairo 23 March 1899. Will dated 21 February 1899, proved (Prin. Reg., 713, 99) 13 June 1899, by Robert Henry William Dunn, retired Major in the Royal Welsh Fusiliers, the brother, and John Ormerod Scarlett Thursby, the Exͦors.

MUTARE VEL TIMERE SPERNO

RAGLAN.

Arms on record in the College of Arms.—Quarterly: 1st and 4th, Azure, three fleur-de-lis or, FRANCE; 2nd and 3rd, Gules, three lions passant in pale or, ENGLAND; all within a bordure compony, argent and azure.

Crest.—A portcullis chained or.

Supporters.—Dexter, a panther argent, flames issuing from the ears and mouth proper, plain collared and chained or, semée of bezants, torteaux, hurts, pellets and pomeis, and charged on the shoulder with a rose gules; Sinister, a wyvern vert, in the mouth a sinister hand couped at the wrist gules, and charged on the breast with a rose of the last.

Motto.—Mutare vel timere sperno.

Raglan.

Field-Marshal the Rt. Honble FitzRoy James Henry Somerset, Baron Raglan, K.C.B., G.C.B. P.C. (youngest son of Henry, 5th Duke of Beaufort, K.G., by Elizabeth his wife, dau. of Admiral the Honble Edward Boscawen); born at Badminton, co. Gloucester, 30 September, bapt. privately 12 October, and received into the church at Badminton 27 October 1788; educated at Westminster; entered the Army as Cornet 4th Light Dragoons 9 June 1804, Lieutenant 30 May 1805, Captain 6th Garrison Battalion 5 May 1808, Captain 43rd Regiment 18 August 1808, Captain and Lieut.-Colonel 1st Foot Guards 25 July 1814 to July 1825; A.D.C. and Military Secretary to Field-Marshal the Duke of Wellington in Peninsular War and Belgium, present at Ciudad Rodrigo, Badajoz, Salamanca, Vittoria, Pyrenees, Nivelle, Nive, Orthes, and Toulouse, for which he obtained a cross and five clasps; also at Rolica, Vimiera, Talavera, Busaco (wounded 27 September 1810, medal and five clasps, and created K.C.B. 2 January 1815) and Fuentes de Oñoro; was also present and lost an arm at Waterloo; Secretary of Embassy at Paris 1814–19, and Minister Plenipotentiary there January to March 1815; sent on special embassies to Madrid 1823, and to St. Petersburg 1826; M.P. for Truro 1818–20, and 1826–29; Secretary to the Master-General of the Ordnance 1819–27, Military Secretary to the Commander-in-Chief, the Duke of Wellington, 29 August 1827 to September 1852; Major-General 27 May 1825; Lieut.-General 28 June 1838; Colonel 53rd Regiment 19 November 1830 to 8 May 1854, Master-General of the Ordnance 30 September 1852 till his death, Colonel Royal Horse Guards (Blue) 8 May 1854 till his death; D.C.L. Oxford 1834, G.C.B. 17 September 1847, K.M.T. of Austria, K.S.G. of Russia, K.M. of Turkey, K.M.J. of Bavaria, K.T.S. of Portugal; sworn a Privy Councillor 16 October 1852, and raised to the Peerage as Baron Raglan of Raglan, co. Monmouth, 20 October 1852; assumed the command of the British Army in the Crimea in February 1854, which under his lead shared in the victories of the Alma and Inkerman; General 20 June 1854, Field-Marshal 5 November 1854; died in the camp before Sebastopol, about 9 p.m., aged 66, 28 June, bur. in the church at Badminton 26 July 1855. Will dated 7 April 1854, proved (P.C.C., 59, 56) 17 January 1856, by the Rt. Honble Emily Harriet, Baroness Raglan, the relict, Berkeley Drummond, and the Honble Robert Dundas, the Exors.

= Lady Emily Harriet, 2nd dau. of William, 3rd Earl of Mornington, by Elizabeth his wife, dau. of Admiral the Honble John Forbes; marr. at her father's house, 3 Savile Row, St. James', Westminster, by special licence, 6 August 1814; died at 5 Great Stanhope Street, London, aged 87, 6 March, bur. at Badminton 10 March 1881. Will dated 29 February 1868, with codicil dated 12 October 1876, proved (Prin. Reg., 336, 81) 6 April 1881, by the Rt. Honble Robert, Viscount Melville of Melville, co. Edinburgh, in North Britain, and 7 Portugal Street, Grosvenor Square, co. Middlesex, and Robert Nigel Fitzhardinge Kingscote of 34 Charles Street, Berkeley Square, co. Middlesex, C.B., a Lieut.-Colonel in Her Majesty's Army, the surviving Exors.

A

Charlotte Caroline Elizabeth, born at Brussels 16 May 1815.

Arthur William FitzRoy Somerset, born in Paris 6 May 1816; Captain and Brevet-Major Grenadier Guards; Military Secretary to Lords Ellenborough and Hardinge; mortally wounded at the battle of Feroshah, India, 21 December, and died s.p., aged 30, 25 December 1845; marr. at Calcutta, India, 8 July 1845, Emilie Marie Louise Wilhelmina, dau. of the Baron de Baumbach of Hesse, and widow of Captain Mellish. She marr. 3rdly at the British Embassy, Paris, on Tuesday, 19 March 1850, Henry Boddington Webster, elder son of Colonel Sir Henry Vassal Webster, Knt. K.J.S.; she was divorced 7 August 1851.

B

A son, born at 28 Ebury Street, Pimlico, London, on Saturday, 1 March, died 3 March 1884, and bur. in Brompton Cemetery, London.

FitzRoy Richard Somerset, born 10 June, bapt. at St. Paul's, Knightsbridge, London, 10 July 1885; educated at Eton and at the Royal Military College, Sandhurst; 2nd Lieutenant Royal Monmouthshire Royal Engineers (Militia) 10 June 1902.

Lady Georgiana, 3rd daughter of Henry Beauchamp, 4th Earl Beauchamp, by Susan Caroline his wife, dau. of William, 2nd Earl of St. Germans; born 30 July 1832; marr. at St. Paul's, Knightsbridge, London, 24 September 1856; died suddenly at Richmond House, Wimbledon, co. Surrey, aged 33, 30 September, bur. in Brompton Cemetery, London, 5 October 1865, the remains being subsequently removed to the churchyard at Llandenny, co. Monmouth, 8 May 1884. Will dated 24 February 1864, proved (Prin. Reg., 195, 66) 28 March 1866, by the Rt. Honble Richard Henry FitzRoy, Baron Raglan of Cefntilla Court, Llandenny, co. Monmouth, the sole Ex͠or, probate being granted under certain limitations. Adm͠on of rest of goods passed at the Principal Registry 17 November 1866. 1st wife.

Richard Henry FitzRoy Somerset, Baron Raglan; born in Paris 24 May 1817; of Christ Church, Oxford, matriculated 4 June 1835, aged 18, Student 1835–39; of the Ceylon Civil Service 1842–48; Private Secretary to the last King of Hanover 1849–55; Cornet Gloucestershire Yeomanry Cavalry 1856, Captain 1864–75; Lord-in-Waiting to H.M. Queen Victoria 1858 –59, and 1866–68; succeeded his father as 2nd Baron 28 June 1855; D.L. for co. Monmouth; died at 8 Chesterfield Street, Mayfair, London, in his 67th year, on Saturday, 3 May, bur. in churchyard at Llandenny 8 May 1884. Will dated 23 November 1878, proved (Prin. Reg., 510, 84) 19 June 1884, by the Rt. Honble Frederick, Earl Beauchamp, of Madresfield Court, co. Worcester, one of the Ex͠ors.

Mary Blanche, his cousin, eldest dau. of Sir Walter Rockcliffe Farquhar, 3rd Bart., by Lady Mary Octavia his wife, dau. of Henry Charles, 6th Duke of Beaufort; born in London 1 June 1844; marr. at Great Bookham, co. Surrey (by the Rt. Rev. Samuel Wilberforce, D.D., Bishop of Winchester, assisted by the Rev. William Heberden), on Wednesday, 11 October 1871. 2nd wife.

Katherine Anne Emily Cecilia, born 31 August 1824.

Violet Elizabeth Catherine, born 10 November, bapt. at St. James', Piccadilly, London, 19 December 1874; marr. at Holy Trinity, Sloane Street, London, 3 December 1900, Wilfrid Robert Abel Smith (3rd son of Robert Smith of Goldings, co. Hertford, J.P. and D.L. for co. Hertford, High Sheriff 1869, by Isabel his wife, 5th dau. of Henry John Adeane of Babraham, co. Cambridge, M.P.); born 13 September 1870; entered the Army as 2nd Lieutenant 1st Battalion Grenadier Guards 26 November 1890, Lieutenant 23 July 1894, Captain 3 May 1899; A.D.C. to Governor and Commander-in-Chief, New South Wales, 14 April 1899 to 31 October 1900; served in the Nile Expedition 1898, at the battle of Khartoum (mentioned in despatches, "London Gazette," 30 September 1898, 4th-class Medjidie, Egyptian medal with clasp, medal), and in South African War 1901–1902 (medal).

C

A

Colonel George FitzRoy Henry Somerset, Baron Raglan; born at Grosvenor Place, London, on Friday, 18 September, bapt. at St. Paul's, Knightsbridge, London, 15 October 1857 (Sponsor: H.M. the King of Hanover); Page of Honour to H.M. Queen Victoria 1868 –74; Sub-Lieutenant (unattached) 1875, of the Grenadier Guards 1876, Lieutenant 1877, Captain 1886–87; served in Afghan War 1879–80 (mentioned in despatches, medal); A.D.C. to Governor of Bombay (the Rt. Honble Sir James Fergusson, 6th Bart., K.C.M.G., P.C.) 1880–83; succeeded his father as 3rd Baron 3 May 1884; J.P. and D.L. for co. Monmouth; Under Secretary of State for War November 1900 to August 1902; appointed in August 1902, Lieut.-Governor of the Isle of Man, and sworn in at Castle Rushen on Tuesday, 21 October following; Captain Royal Monmouthshire Royal Engineers (Militia) 1887, Major 1895, Lieut.-Colonel Commanding and Hon. Colonel 1901.

Lady Ethel Jemima, 2nd dau. of the Rev. Walter William Brabazon, 7th Earl of Bessborough, by Lady Louisa Susan Cornwallis his wife, only dau. of Edward Granville, 3rd Earl of St. Germans; born at the Vicarage, Canford, co. Dorset, on Wednesday, 8 April, bapt. at Canford 1 May 1857; marr. at St. James', Piccadilly, London (by her father), on Wednesday, 28 February 1883.

B

B

Wellesley FitzRoy Somerset, born 13 June, bapt. at St. Paul's, Knightsbridge, London, 16 July 1887; educated at Eton.

Ethel Georgiana Frances, born 4 June, bapt. at St. John's, Llandenny, 25 July 1889.

103

Arthur Charles Edward Somerset, born at 58 = Louisa Eliza, dau. of John Grant Rutland Gate, Knightsbridge, London, on Sunday, 11 December 1859, bapt. at St. Paul's, Knightsbridge, 5 January 1860; Captain 2nd Battalion Rifle Brigade (Prince Consort's Own) 1887–95, Adjutant 7th Battalion (Militia) 1890–95; retired 1895.

Louisa Eliza, dau. of John Grant Hodgson of Cabalva, co. Hereford, by Rose his wife, dau. of F. Chinnock; born at Sunnyside, Prince's Park, Liverpool, on Sunday, 8 May 1870; marr. at St. Paul's, Knightsbridge, London, 27 November 1893.

Norman Arthur Henry Somerset, born 8 September, bapt. at St. Paul's, Knightsbridge, 21 October 1894.

Lieut.-Colonel Granville William Richard Somerset, born at 58 Rutland Gate, Knightsbridge, London, on Tuesday, 9 September, bapt. at St. Paul's, Knightsbridge, 29 September 1862; Sub-Lieutenant R.N. 1875–84; served in Egyptian War 1882 (medal and bronze star); afterwards Major Royal Monmouthshire Royal Engineers (Militia), retired with rank of Lieut.-Colonel; died suddenly at 30 Milner Street, Cadogan Square, London, on Monday, 25 November, bur. at Llandenny, co. Monmouth, on Thursday, 28 November 1901. Will dated 26 June 1892, proved (Prin. Reg., 16, 1902) 7 January 1902, by the Honble Malvina Charlotte Somerset, the relict, and Sidney Ernald Ralph Lane, the Exors.

= Malvina Charlotte, eldest dau. of Rear-Admiral Sir Malcolm MacGregor of Mac-Gregor, co. Perth, R.N., 4th Bart., by Helen Laura his wife, dau. and heir of Hugh Seymour, 4th Earl of Antrim; born at Lowndes Square, London, 26 October, bapt. at Holy Trinity, Sloane Street, Chelsea, London, 6 December 1865; marr. at St. Paul's, Knightsbridge, London (by the Rev. George Shaw Munn, Rector of Madresfield, co. Worcester, assisted by the Rev. James Baden Powell), on Saturday, 11 June 1892.

Wellesley Henry Somerset, born on Tuesday, 5 April, bapt. at St. Paul's, Knightsbridge, London, 28 April 1864; died at 58 Rutland Gate, Knightsbridge, aged 4 months, on Monday, 15 August, bur. in Brompton Cemetery, London, 18 August 1864.

—

Richard Henry FitzRoy Somerset, born at 16 Great Cumberland Street, Marylebone, London, on Wednesday, 9 August, bapt. at St. Paul's, Knightsbridge, 12 September 1865; 2nd Lieutenant Royal Monmouthshire Royal Engineers (Militia) 1883, Lieutenant 1885, Lieutenant Grenadier Guards 18 August 1886, Captain 2 March 1898; A.D.C. to General Officer Commanding Forces in Ireland 22 December 1892 to 30 September 1895; died at the Royal Southern Hospital, Liverpool, of fever contracted whilst serving on the Niger with the West African Frontier Force, on Wednesday, 2 March, bur. at Llandenny on Saturday, 5 March 1899. Admon was granted at the Principal Registry 19 May 1899, to the Rt. Honble George FitzRoy Henry Somerset, Baron Raglan, the brother.

Richard Granville Somerset, born 15 August, bapt. at St. Paul's, Wimbledon, co. Surrey, 23 September 1894.

Frederica Susan Katherine, born 31 August, bapt. at St. John's, Llandenny, 5 October 1891 (Sponsor: H.R.H. Princess Frederica of Hanover).

Nigel FitzRoy Somerset, born 27 July, bapt. at St. John's, Llandenny, 30 August 1893.

Ivy Felicia, born 30 March, bapt. at St. John the Baptist's, Felixstowe, co. Suffolk, 1 May 1897.

Hunt of Culpho, co. Suffolk.

Wright Hunt of Culpho, co. Suffolk (son of Wright Hunt of Culpho, by Elizabeth his wife, dau. of William Ling of Otley Hall, co. Suffolk); born at Culpho, and bapt. at St. Botolph's, Culpho, 13 August 1770; died at Culpho, aged 71, 12 July 1841, and bur. at Grundisburgh Chapel, co. Suffolk. M.I. Will dated 18 January 1839, proved at Ipswich 3 August 1841, by Ann Hunt, the relict, James Thompson and John Harris, the Exors.

=Ann, dau. of John Finch of Grundisburgh; born at Grundisburgh 29 May 1786; marr. by licence at Culpho 30 September 1817; died at Newbourne, co. Suffolk, aged 83, 2 August 1869, and bur. in the family vault at Grundisburgh Chapel. M.I. Admon was granted at Ipswich 3 February 1870, to William Hunt of Culpho, co. Suffolk, the son, and one of the next of kin.

A

Wright Hunt [signature]

Mary Ann, born 22 November 1818; marr. at Grundisburgh Chapel in 1837, John Harris of Grundisburgh (son of Joseph Harris of Grundisburgh); born 22 September 1811; died at Grundisburgh, aged 65, 21 October 1876, and bur. at Grundisburgh Chapel. M.I. Will dated 23 August 1869, proved at Ipswich 23 November 1876, by Mary Ann Harris, the relict, and Joseph Harris, the son, both of Grundisburgh, co. Suffolk, and Peter Arthur Damant of Witnesham, co. Suffolk, the Exors. She died, aged 63, 8 October 1882, and was bur. at Grundisburgh Chapel. M.I.

William Hunt of Culpho; born at Culpho 27 February 1821; died there, in his 70th year, 27 August, bur. in the family vault at Grundisburgh Chapel 1 September 1890. M.I. Will dated 2 July 1888, proved at Ipswich 12 December 1890, by Sarah Ann Phillis Hunt of Culpho, the relict, the sole Executrix.

=Sarah Ann Phillis, dau. of George Watkins of Clopton, co. Suffolk, by Sarah his wife, dau. of William Catt of Wadgate, Felixstowe, co. Suffolk; born at Monewden, co. Suffolk, 22 June 1828, and bapt. there; marr. at Clopton 27 February 1848; died at Culpho, in her 73rd year, 27 September, bur. in the family vault at Grundisburgh Chapel 3 October 1900. M.I. Will dated 12 September 1899, proved at Ipswich 20 May 1901, by William Wright Hunt, Arthur Rust Hunt and Joseph Hunt, the sons, and William Edward Kersey, the Exors.

B

William Hunt [signature]

George Hunt, born at Culpho 4 September 1852; died there 11 October 1854, bur. at Grundisburgh Chapel. M.I.

William Wright Hunt of Grundisburgh; born at Culpho 4 July 1855, bapt. at Grundisburgh 29 March 1895.

=Ann Caroline, dau. of Joseph Smith of "The Grange," Walton, co. Suffolk, by Ann Boulter his wife, dau. of Joshua Catt of Clopton Hall; born at Thorpe Hall, Hasketon, co. Suffolk, 11 July 1857; marr. at Hasketon (by the Rev. Arthur Maude) 20 January 1881.

Thompson Hunt of Culpho; born at Culpho 9 January 1857.

Arthur Joseph Hunt, born 4 April 1886, bapt. at Grundisburgh 4 May 1890.

Cyril Ernest Hunt, born 7 January 1888, bapt. at Grundisburgh 4 May 1890.

Eveline Annie, born 1 March, bapt. at Grundisburgh 7 June 1891.

Percy Wright Hunt, born 19 April, bapt. at Grundisburgh 21 May 1893.

Hilda Mary, born 23 April, bapt. at Grundisburgh 23 May 1897.

Wright Hunt of Newbourne, co. Suffolk; born 2 February 1823; died at Newbourne, aged 46, 20 June 1869, and bur. in the family vault at Grundisburgh Chapel, co. Suffolk. M.I. Will dated 21 October 1868, proved at Ipswich 12 August 1869, by Joseph Hunt of the City of Canterbury, and John Hunt of Ipswich, co. Suffolk, the brothers, the Exŏrs.

Samuel Ling Hunt of King's Lynn, co. Norfolk; born at Culpho, co. Suffolk, 11 April 1825, and bapt. there; died at King's Lynn, aged 60, 5 December, bur. in the cemetery there 7 December 1885. Will dated 8 August 1879, with codicil dated 24 November 1883, proved at Norwich 23 February 1886, by Sarah Hunt, the relict, and Charles Theophilus Ives, both of King's Lynn, co. Norfolk, two of the Exŏrs.

Sarah, dau. of Samuel Denny of Combs, co. Suffolk; born 15 November 1825; marr. at Combs 16 September 1848; died, aged 65, 29 July, bur. in the cemetery at King's Lynn 3 August 1891. Will dated 19 March 1889, proved at Norwich 6 February 1892, by Samuel Denny Hunt, the son, and William John Stanton, two of the Exŏrs.

C

Emma Sarah, born 12 July, bapt. at the Independent Chapel, King's Lynn, 14 August 1849; marr. there 7 November 1873, Frederick Smith Flanders of Methwold, co. Norfolk (son of Shrewsberry Flanders of Methwold); born at Methwold 23 May, bapt. there 20 June 1843.

Catherine Ann, born 20 January 1851, and bapt. at the Independent Chapel, King's Lynn; marr. there 3 June 1880, Alfred Fowler of Papley, co. Northampton (son of John Fowler of Papley); born at Papley 28 March, bapt. there 20 April 1850; died at 10 Victoria Street, Spalding, co. Lincoln, 19 October, bur. in the cemetery at Spalding 23 October 1896. She died at 10 Victoria Street, Spalding, 28 June, and was bur. in the cemetery at Spalding 1 July 1898.

George Watkins Hunt of Seckford Hall, Great Bealings, co. Suffolk; born 5 December 1858, and bapt. privately.

Geo W Hunt

Emily Jane, dau. of Joseph Smith of "The Grange," Walton, co. Suffolk, by Ann Boulter his wife, dau. of Joshua Catt of Clopton Hall, co. Suffolk; born at Thorpe Hall, Hasketon, co. Suffolk, 25 April 1861, and bapt. privately; marr. at Hasketon (by the Rev. Arthur Maude) 4 September 1884.

Arthur Rust Hunt, born at Culpho 19 August 1861, died there 15 October following, and bur. at Grundisburgh Chapel. M.I.

William Hunt, born 27 June 1885, and bapt. privately.

—

Christmas Hunt, born 24 December 1886, and bapt. privately; died the following day, and bur. in the cemetery at Woodbridge, co. Suffolk.

Joseph George Hunt, born 16 March 1888, and bapt. privately; died, aged 11 months, 14 February, bur. at Great Bealings 18 February 1889.

—

Emily Marjorie, born 10 July 1889, and bapt. privately.

Ida Mary, born 15 January 1892, and bapt. privately.

—

Herbert Joseph Hunt, born 27 August 1894, and bapt. privately.

Joseph Hunt of "The Pynes," Canterbury, co. Kent,═Georgiana, eldest dau. of John born at Culpho, co. Suffolk, 8 November 1827, and │ Baldwin of North Road, Clapham bapt. privately; J.P. for Canterbury. │ Park, co. Surrey, by Ann his wife, dau. of Samuel Gowers; born at Stockwell, co. Surrey, 5 June 1842; marr. at Tacket Street Chapel, Ipswich, co. Suffolk (by the Rev. Eliazer Jones), on Thursday, 29 September 1864.

D

Wright Hunt of "Redcliffe,"═Elise Philippa Salkeld, 3rd dau. of John Hoby, by Jeanie Wilkie South Canterbury; born at his wife, dau. of Frederick Fleck; born at 29 South Street, 1 Dane John, Canterbury, on Thurloe Square, South Kensington, London, on Monday, Sunday, 10 March, bapt. at 17 November, bapt. at Holy Trinity, Brompton, London, St. Mildred's, Canterbury, 29 December 1879; marr. at St. Peter's, Cranley Gardens, 11 April 1867. South Kensington (by the Rev. William Shuckburgh Swayne, the Vicar), on Wednesday, 10 December 1902.

C   C

Mary Ann, eldest dau. of George═Samuel Denny Hunt═Amelia Turner, only child of Onion Mitchell, by Sarah his wife, │ of King's Lynn; born │ Thomas Robert Billing of dau. of John Freeman; born at King's │ there 9 June, bapt. │ Burnham, co. Norfolk, formerly Lynn, co. Norfolk, 5 December 1858, │ at the Independent │ of King's Lynn, by Mary Ann bapt. at St. Nicholas', King's Lynn, │ Chapel, King's Lynn, │ his wife, dau. of John Turner; 2 January 1859; marr. at St. John's, │ 18 July 1852. │ born 20 December 1858, bapt. King's Lynn, 18 October 1882; died 19 │ │ at South Lynn, co. Norfolk, March, bur. at King's Lynn 24 March │ │ 29 January 1859; marr. there 1891. 1st wife. │ │ 9 November 1892. 2nd wife.

Samuel George Hunt, born 18 August, bapt. at St. John's, King's Lynn, 27 August 1885.	William Leonard Hunt, born 5 April, bapt. at St. John's, King's Lynn, 16 May 1887.	Albert Edward Hunt, born 12 October, bapt. at St. John's, King's Lynn, 19 November 1888.	Hilda Mary, born 12 December 1890, bapt. at St. John's, King's Lynn, 19 January 1891.

B

Arthur Rust Hunt═Marian, youngest dau. of Frederick │ Joseph Hunt of Culpho and of of Homefields, │ Augustus Crisp of The Hall, Playford, │ St. John's, Ipswich; born at near Ipswich; born │ co. Suffolk, formerly of Walworth, co. │ Culpho 21 March 1866, bapt. at at Culpho 16 Au- │ Surrey, by Sarah his wife, dau. of John │ the Tabernacle, Penge, co. Kent gust 1862, bapt. at │ Steedman of Walworth (see Pedigree of │ (by the Rev. John Wesley Bond) Grundisburgh co. │ Steedman, page 89); born at Walworth │ 28 June 1899. Suffolk, 29 March │ 2 November, bapt. at St. Mary, 1895. │ Newington, co. Surrey, 4 December 1861; marr. at Playford (by the Rev. John Major Freeman, the Vicar) on Thursday, 29 August 1895.

Frederick John Hunt, born at Sproughton, co. Suffolk, on Monday, 29 June, bapt. at Playford 20 August 1896.	George Rust Hunt, born at Sproughton on Sunday, 13 June, bapt. there 31 October 1897.	Ambrose Robert Hunt, born at Sproughton on Sunday, 30 April, bapt. at Playford 27 September 1899.	Edmund Crisp Hunt, born at Sproughton on Friday, 12 April, bapt. at Playford 8 August 1901.

John Hunt of Ipswich, co. Suffolk ; ═ Sarah Elizabeth, dau. of the Rev. Eliazer Jones of Ipswich, born at Culpho, co. Suffolk, 13 May | by Elizabeth his wife, and grand-daughter of David Jones, 1831; died, aged 66, 1 November, | D.D., of Carmarthen ; born 11 November 1830; marr. bur. in the family vault at | at Tacket Street Chapel, Ipswich, 25 June 1862 ; died, Grundisburgh Chapel, co. Suffolk, | aged 66, 5 January, bur. in the family vault at Grundis- 5 November 1896. M.I. | burgh Chapel 9 January 1892. M.I.

Lucina, born at Ipswich 11 October, | John Ernest Hunt of ═ Mary, dau. of Thomas Norton, bapt. at Tacket Street Chapel, Ipswich, | Walton, co. Suffolk ; | by Mary his wife, dau. of John 11 November 1864; marr. at Holy | born at Ipswich 18 | Awers ; born at Rochester, co. Trinity, Ipswich, 23 December 1888, | October, bapt. at | Kent, 11 October, bapt. at William Tunstall Trodd of Ipswich | Tacket Street Chapel, | Chatham, co. Kent, 16 No- (son of William Trodd of Ipswich); | Ipswich, 5 January | vember 1868; marr. at Calgary, born at Ipswich 6 May 1864, bapt. | 1868. | Alberta, North America, 21 at Holy Trinity, Ipswich, 6 September | | August 1890. 1888.

Marion Elizabeth Gertrude, born | Ernest Eleazer Cecil Hunt, born at Mount at Calgary, Alberta, North America, | Pleasant, Reydon, co. Suffolk, 26 September 7 January, bapt. at the English | 1895, bapt. at St. Nicholas Street Chapel, church at Calgary 3 February 1892. | Ipswich, 3 January 1896.

Gertrude Mary, born at Canterbury, co. Kent, 22 August, bapt. at St. Mildred's, | Edward Gowers Canterbury, 22 September 1868 ; marr. at St. Mary Bredin's, Canterbury (by | Hunt, born at the Rev. Richard Knott Bolton, uncle of the bridegroom, assisted by the | Canterbury 26 Rev. Joseph John Bambridge, the Vicar), on Thursday, 6 June 1895, Lyndon | May, bapt. at Bolton (only son of Lyndon Bolton of Burren and Cooleague, co. Cavan, by | St. Mildred's, Elizabeth Henrietta his wife, dau. of Edward Creed of Ballyclough, co. | Canterbury, 24 Cork); born in Dublin 31 May, bapt. at St. Luke's, Dublin, 27 June 1860; | June 1870. educated at Clifton College and at Clare College, Cambridge, matriculated Michaelmas Term, 1880, B.A. 1884 ; Assistant Examiner H.M. Patent Office.

Agnes Amelia, born 5 February 1856, and bapt. at King's Lynn, co. Norfolk; marr. at the Independent Chapel, King's Lynn, 9 February 1882, William John Stanton of King's Lynn (son of John Neal Stanton of King's Lynn); born 5 March 1857, bapt. at Stepney Chapel, King's Lynn, as an adult, 26 April 1881 ; died at King's Lynn 18 January, bur. in the cemetery at King's Lynn 21 January 1898. Will dated 18 October 1888, proved at Norwich 26 February 1898, by Agnes Amelia Stanton, the relict, and Charles Bristow, the Exors.

A

Sarah, born at Culpho, co. Suffolk, 28 September 1832; marr. at Grundisburgh Chapel, co. Suffolk, 21 November 1866, Phillip Cutting of Otley, co. Suffolk (son of Phillip Cutting of Abbot's Hall, Pettaugh, co. Suffolk); born at Otley 15 June 1831; died there 30 September, bur. at Otley 4 October 1890. Admͦn was granted at Ipswich 7 November 1890, to Sarah Cutting of Otley, co. Suffolk, the relict.

⊤
人

B

Annie Finch, born at Ipswich, co. Suffolk, 11 January, bapt. at Tacket Street Chapel, Ipswich, 6 March 1871; marr. at St. Nicholas Street Chapel, Ipswich, 9 December 1896, David Scott of Bishop's Stortford, co. Hertford (son of David Scott of Bishop's Stortford, by Margaret his wife, dau. of Richard Ronaldson); born at Bishop's Stortford 25 November 1852.

⊤
人

Marian Elizabeth, born at Ipswich 3 February, bapt. at Tacket Street Chapel, Ipswich, 30 March 1873; marr. at All Saints', Ipswich, 27 December 1898, Ernest Robert Riches of Bishop's Stortford (son of Robert Riches of Bishop's Stortford, by Harriet his wife, dau. of William Jackson of Magdalen, co. Norfolk); born at Wereham, co. Norfolk, 30 August 1873.

Dorothy Ann, born at Canterbury 6 November, bapt. at St. Mildred's, Canterbury, 5 December 1871.

Winnifred, born at Canterbury 8 January, bapt. at St. Mildred's, Canterbury, 27 February 1873.

Beatrice Frances, born at Canterbury 19 March, bapt. at St. George's, Canterbury, 25 April 1874.

Rhoda Georgiana, born at Canterbury 11 January, bapt. at St. Mary Bredin's, Canterbury, 17 February 1878.

D

John Henry Hunt, born 29 November 1858, and bapt. at King's Lynn, co. Norfolk; died at 41 Teviot Street, Poplar, co. Middlesex, 31 October, bur. in the East London Cemetery, Plaistow, 4 November 1897. Admͦn (with will dated 11 April 1889) was granted (Prin. Reg., 1220, 97) 19 November 1897, to Eliza Freeman Hunt, the relict, the residuary legatee.

═

Eliza Freeman, dau. of George Onion Mitchell, by Sarah his wife, dau. of John Freeman; born at King's Lynn 21 January 1859, bapt. at St. Nicholas', King's Lynn, 29 August 1861; marr. at St. John's, King's Lynn, 28 April 1886; died 17 January, bur. in the East London Cemetery, Plaistow, 22 January 1898.

Ethel, born at King's Lynn 7 March, bapt. at St. John's, King's Lynn, 4 April 1887.

C

Ella Rose, born 16 August, bapt. at the Congregational Chapel, King's Lynn, 10 October 1861.

Wright Albert Hunt, born 11 June 1867, bapt. at the Congregational Chapel, King's Lynn, 7 April 1868.

═

Helen Anne, dau. of Alfred Cupit; born at Wellington, co. Salop, 15 May 1869, and bapt. at the parish church, Wellington; marr. at All Souls', Brighton, co. Sussex, 5 May 1902.

Arthur F. P. Hunt.

Wood.

Henry Wood of Woodhill, in Send, co. Surrey (4th son of Thomas Wood of Littleton, co. Middlesex, by Mary his wife, dau. and heir of Sir Edward Williams of Gwernyfed, co. Brecon, Bart. [*see Pedigree of Wood, Vol. IV., page 69*]); born 11 August, bapt. at Missenden Abbey, co. Buckingham, 14 September 1782; of the Bengal Civil Service, Accountant-General, Calcutta, R.E.; died at Torquay, co. Devon, in his 89th year, on Friday, 13 January, bur. at Southborough, co. Kent, 19 January 1871. Will dated 5 October 1865, proved 25 February 1871, by Godfrey Thomas Green, and son, James Templeton Wood, two of the Exors.

— Margaret Elizabeth, dau. of Thomas Templeton, Attorney of the Supreme Court, Calcutta; born 27 November 1789; marr. at Calcutta 7 October 1809; died at Woodhill, in her 90th year, on Thursday, 18 September, bur. at Southborough 27 September 1879. Will dated 18 July 1871, proved 28 November 1879, by Godfrey Thomas Green and the Rev. Henry Christopher Lewis, the Exors.

Arms on record in the College of Arms.— Sable, a bull passant argent.
Crest.—A demi-lion rampant or, gorged with a wreath, azure and gules.
Motto.—Taurus gaudet in silvis.

Henry Wood   *M. Wood*

A

Margaret Sophia, born 20 July 1810, and bapt. at Calcutta; marr. at Bramdean, co. Hants (by the Rev. Charles Walters, the Rector), on Tuesday, 25 January 1842, the Rev. John Bury Bourne (2nd son of John Bourne of Stalmine Hall and Little Walton, both co. Lancaster, J.P. for co. Lancaster, by Mary his wife, dau. of John Bury of Salford, co. Lancaster); born 19 August, bapt. at Childwall, co. Lancaster, 13 September 1809; of Caius College, Cambridge, B.A. 1832, M.A. 1836; Rector of Colmer, with Priors Dean, co. Hants, 1839–53, and afterwards of Colney Horton, co. Hants; died at Sandon Terrace, Liverpool, aged 59, on Thursday, 15 October, bur. in the cemetery at Shrewsbury, co. Salop, 19 October 1868. Will dated 31 December 1864, proved at Liverpool 27 October 1868, by Margaret Sophia Bourne of 6 Sandon Terrace, Liverpool, the relict, the sole Executrix. She died at 18 Hereford Square, South Kensington, London, in her 89th year, on Friday, 2 June, and was bur. in the cemetery at Shrewsbury 6 June 1899.

Mary, born 17 September 1811, and bapt. at Calcutta; died at Holden House, Southborough, co. Kent, aged 46, on Tuesday, 2 February, bur. at Southborough 8 February 1858. Will dated 20 January 1858, proved (Prin. Reg., 94, 58) 17 February 1858, by Margaret Sophia Bourne, wife of John Bury Bourne of the Council House, Shrewsbury, co. Salop, the sister, the sole Executrix.

(*See Pedigree of Bourne, Vol. 3, page 149.*)

Henry Wood of Worthing,┬Emily Kynersley, dau. co. Sussex; born 30 June 1813, and bapt. at Calcutta, India; of the Madras Civil Service; died at Worthing, aged 60, on Friday, 10 October, bur. at Littleton, co. Middlesex, 16 October 1873. Will dated 6 May 1872, proved (Prin. Reg., 804, 73) 1 November 1873, by Edward Morehead Wood of 2 Cloisters, Temple, in the City of London, Barrister-at-Law, the son, the sole Exor.

Emily Kynersley, dau. of Charles Kaye of the Island of Jersey; born 14 March 1819; marr. at Rajamahendri, Madras, India, 5 January 1844; died at Hythe House, Staines, co. Middlesex, aged 39, on Sunday, 23 May, bur. at Littleton 29 May 1858.

Catherine Matilda, born 27 February 1815, and bapt. at Calcutta; died at "Woodhill," Send, co. Surrey, on Tuesday, 8 April, bur. at Southborough, co. Kent, 12 April 1884. Will dated 16 November 1883, proved (Prin. Reg., 449, 84) 20 May 1884, by the Rev. Henry Christopher Lewis of Binsted Rectory, near Arundel, co. Sussex, and Robert William Bourne of 18 Hereford Square, co. Middlesex, the nephew, the Exors.

—

Louisa Frances, born 19 February 1817; died 26 July, bur. at Littleton 1 August 1833.

Emily Charlotte, born at Chingleput, Madras, 26 September 1844, bapt. (by the Bishop of Madras) 12 January 1845; marr. at the parish church, Broadwater, co. Sussex (by the Rev. Edward King Elliott, the Rector), on Thursday, 15 November 1866, Major-General George Edward Henry Beauchamp-Proctor of Hurst Lodge, co. Berks (eldest son of George Thomas Beauchamp-Proctor of the Honble East India Co.'s Service, by Hester Maria Fredericka his wife, dau. of Thomas Daniel); born at Madras 21 March 1834, and bapt. there; of the Madras Infantry; entered the Army 23 July 1854, Major-General 23 September 1890, retired 26 January 1892; died, aged 60, on Thursday, 19 July, bur. at Hurst 23 July 1894. Will dated 13 October 1886, with codicil dated 18 May 1894, proved (Prin. Reg., 890, 94) 1 August 1894, by Emily Charlotte Beauchamp-Proctor, the relict, and Louisa Mary Catherine Beauchamp-Proctor, spinster, a daughter, the Executrixes.

Caroline, born at Madras 29 October, bapt. at Cuddalore, Madras, 31 December 1848.

—

Edward Morehead Wood, born at Cuddalore, Madras, 3 November, bapt. there 9 December 1849; of the Middle Temple, Barrister-at-Law; Procurator and Advocate-General of the Mauritius; died at Mauritius 4 July 1881. Will dated 23 January 1879, proved (Prin. Reg., 703, 81) 29 September 1881, by Caroline Wood of Earley, co. Berks, spinster, the sister, the sole Executrix.

Henrietta, born at Hythe House, Staines, on Sunday, 16 May, bapt. at Southborough 11 July 1858; died at Santa Margherita, Liguro, Italy, aged 22, on Thursday, 7 April, bur. at Littleton 11 June 1881. Will dated 28 October 1880, proved (Prin. Reg., 704, 81) 12 September 1881, by Caroline Wood of the Manor House, Earley, co. Berks, spinster, the sister, the sole Executrix.

James Templeton Wood of 10 Pembridge Gardens, Bayswater, London; born 7 November 1819, and bapt. at Moradabad, North-West Provinces, India; educated at Eton and at Trinity College, Cambridge, B.A. 1841, M.A. 1844; a Student of the Inner Temple 22 January 1838 (then aged 18), called to the Bar 31 January 1845; died at Stradmore, Llandyssil, co. Cardigan, in his 68th year, on Wednesday, 19 October, bur. at Littleton, co. Middlesex, 25 October 1887. Will proved (Prin. Reg., 987, 87) 29 November 1887, by Mary Elizabeth Wood of 10 Pembridge Gardens, co. Middlesex, the relict, the sole Executrix.

= Mary Elizabeth, 4th dau. of Richard Moon of Shaw Street, Liverpool, by Elizabeth his wife, dau. of William Bradley Frodsham of Liverpool (see *Pedigree of Brocklebank, Vol. 9, pages 141 and 142*); born in Liverpool 24 October 1823, bapt. at St. Peter's, Liverpool, 11 October 1824; marr. at Aigburth, co. Lancaster, 10 March 1858.

Edward Wood, died in infancy at Rome.

—

Henrietta, born 11 August 1825, and bapt. at Calcutta, India; died at Holden House, Southborough, co. Kent, aged 31, on Friday, 19 June, bur. at Southborough 27 June 1857. Will dated 29 August 1849, proved (P.C.C., 658, 57) 11 August 1857, by Mary Wood, spinster, the sister, the sole Executrix.

James T Wood

Mary. E. Wood

Henry James Theodore Wood of Fingest Cottage, near High Wycombe, co. Buckingham; born at 42 Inverness Road, Bayswater, London, on Monday, 23 March, bapt. at St. Mary's, Paddington, London, 6 May 1863; Scholar of Eton and of Pembroke College, Cambridge, matriculated Michaelmas Term, 1882, B.A. 1885, M.A. 1889; Barrister-at-Law of the Inner Temple, admitted 8 March 1887, called 17 November 1890, and of Lincoln's Inn; J.P. for co. Buckingham 1899; Member of the Alpine Club; a Director of the French Hospital (La Providence); on the Committee of the Most Honourable and Loyal Society of Ancient Britons.

= Ellen Beatrice, 3rd dau. of Sydney Henry Jones-Parry of Ty-llwydd, co. Cardigan, sometime Captain in the Royal Madras Fusiliers, J.P. and D.L. for co. Cardigan, High Sheriff for co. Cardigan 1871, by Dorothea Anne his wife, only child of Charles Arthur Prichard of Ty-llwydd, J.P. and D.L. for the counties of Brecon and Cardigan; born at St. Leonard's-on-Sea, co. Sussex, on Wednesday, 7 February 1866, and bapt. there; marr. at St. James', Paddington, London (by the Rev. Ernest John Heriz Smith), on Saturday, 27 July 1889.

E Beatrice Wood.

Katherine Margaret Love, born at Molewood House, Hertford, on Monday, 5 December, bapt. at St. Andrew's, Hertford, on the Feast of the Holy Innocents', 28 December 1898.

Nicholas Crispin Wood, born at Fingest Cottage, near High Wycombe, on Thursday, 25 October, bapt. at Lane End, co. Buckingham, 19 November 1900.

H. J T. Wood.

EX·LIBRIS
HENRY·JAMES·
THEODORA·WOOD
1896
TAURUS
GAUDET
SILVIS
IN

Coode.

Charles Coode of Bodmin, co. Cornwall (youngest son of Edward ⊤ Ann, dau. of the Rev.
Coode of Methleigh, co. Cornwall, by Betty his wife, 2nd dau. | Joseph Bennet, Rector
of the Rev. John Penrose, Vicar of St. Gluvias, co. Cornwall | of Wigborough, co. Essex;
[*see Pedigree of Coode of Polapit Tamar, co. Cornwall, Vol. 2,* | marr. at St. Breock, co.
page 18]); born 22 March 1780, and bapt. at St. Gluvias; died at | Cornwall, 31 August 1809;
Bodmin, aged 83, 4 October, bur. there 9 October 1863. Will | died at Bodmin, aged 71,
dated 20 April 1850, proved at Bodmin 14 October 1863, by | 14 March, bur. there 20
Anne Coode of Bodmin, co. Cornwall, spinster, the daughter, | March 1850.
the sole Executrix.

A

Betty Ann, bapt. at Bodmin 28 August 1810; died 16 July 1818, and bur. at Budock, co. Cornwall.

—

Charles Edward Coode, bapt. at Bodmin 26 January 1813; an Officer in the Royal Navy; marr. Jane Fisher. He died s.p. 19 September 1867.

—

Jane, bapt. at Bodmin 10 March 1814; died 25 May 1814, and bur. at Bodmin.

—

Charlotte Frances, bapt. at Bodmin 30 April 1815; marr. there 17 September 1850, the Rev. John Symonds (eldest son of John Symonds of Falmouth, co. Cornwall, by Mary Ann his wife); born 25 November 1815, bapt. at Falmouth 16 April 1816; of Clare College, Cambridge, B.A. 1839; Rector of Baldhu, co. Cornwall, 1855; died s.p. at Baldhu, aged 73, and bur. there 13 March 1888. She died at Truro, co. Cornwall, aged 77, 19 March, and was bur. at Baldhu 22 March 1893. Will dated 5 July 1892, proved at Bodmin 15 June 1893, by William Coode, the cousin, the sole Exor.

Sir John Coode, K.C.M.G.; ⊤ Jane Dod, eldest
born 11 November, bapt. pri- | dau. of William
vately 14 November 1816 | Price of Weston-
(baptism registered at Bodmin); | super-Mare, co.
educated at the Grammar School, | Somerset, by Jane
Bodmin; Civil Engineer; a | his wife; born
Member of the Royal Commis- | 29 April 1816;
sion on Harbours in 1858–59; | marr. at Bath,
Member of the Institution of | co. Somerset, 5
Civil Engineers 1849, President | October 1842;
1889–91; knighted 1872, | died at Cum-
K.C.M.G. 1886; Engineer-in- | berland House,
Chief of the Harbours of | Kensington, Lon-
Portland, Colombo and Table | don, in her 81st
Bay; died at 83 Marine Parade, | year, on Thurs-
Brighton, co. Sussex, in his 76th | day, 16 July, bur.
year, on Wednesday, 2 March, | in Kensal Green
bur. in Kensal Green Cemetery, | Cemetery, Lon-
London, 5 March 1892. Will | don, 20 July
dated 7 November 1884, with | 1896. Admon
two codicils dated respectively | was granted at
30 December 1886 and 22 | the Principal
January 1892, proved (Prin. | Registry 21 Oc-
Reg., 416, 92) 21 April 1892, | tober 1896, to
by John Charles Coode, William | John Charles
Shield and the Rev. Frederick | Coode.
Arthur Cecil Lillingston, three |
of the Exors. |

B

Fanny Jane, born at Taunton, co. Somerset, 4 July 1843; marr. at St. John's, Paddington, London (by the Rev. Sir Emilius Bayley, Bart., the Vicar, assisted by the Rev. Philip Hayman Dod, Master of St. John's, Lichfield, co. Stafford), on Thursday, 30 October 1873, William Shield (elder son of William Shield of Colville Road, London, by Mary his wife, 2nd dau. of John Turner of Morpeth, co. Northumberland, and great-grand-daughter of Sir John Pringle of Stitchill, co. Roxburgh, 2nd Bart.); born at Newcastle-on-Tyne, co. Northumberland, 1 March 1845; educated at the Grammar School, Bath; Member of the Institution of Civil Engineers and a Fellow of the Royal Society, Edinburgh.

A

Lucy, bapt. at Bodmin, co. Cornwall, 30 June 1818; died 23 September 1819, and bur. at Bodmin.

Anne, born 26 February, bapt. at Bodmin 19 April 1820; marr. at St. Michael's, Baldhu, co. Cornwall, 17 June 1869, William Pearce of Bodmin (2nd son of Edward Pearce of Bodmin, Lord of the Manor of Bodwannick, Mayor of Bodmin 1836, by Mary his wife, dau. of the Rev. Richard Eliot, B.A. of Trinity College, Oxford, Vicar of Maker and of St. Teath, co. Cornwall); born at Bodmin 9 January 1820, and bapt. privately (baptism registered at Bodmin); died s.p. 4 February, bur. in the cemetery at Bodmin 9 February 1875. Will dated 29 December 1869, proved at Bodmin 11 March 1875, by Anne Pearce of Bodmin, the relict, the sole Executrix.

B   B

John Charles Coode of 19 Freeland Road, Ealing, co. Middlesex; born 23 November 1844, and bapt. at Plymouth, co. Devon; Member of the Institution of Civil Engineers 1883; Officer of the Belgian Order of Leopold.

=Clara Louisa youngest dau. of Lieut-Colonel Griffiths of the 6th Royal Warwickshire Regiment and 25th King's Own Borderers, by Emma his wife, dau. of Lieut.-Colonel Hugh Maurice Scott of the 6th Royal Warwickshire Regiment; born 19 July, bapt. at St. George's, Douglas, Isle of Man, 17 August 1847; marr. at St. Thomas', Douglas (by the Rev. Samuel Simpson, assisted by the Rev. Francis Pierpoint Burton Norman Hutton, the Vicar), on Thursday, 19 September 1872.

John Griffiths Coode, born at St. Helier, Jersey, on Tuesday, 29 July 1873, and bapt. at St. Mark's, St. Helier.

—

Charles Arthur Penrose Coode, born at St. Helier on Wednesday, 19 August 1874, and bapt. at St. Mark's, St. Helier; of Keble College, Oxford, matriculated 1893, B.A. 1896.

—

Arthur Trevenen Coode, born at 16 Queen's Road, St. Helier, on Saturday, 5 February 1876, and bapt. at St. Mark's, St. Helier; of Jesus College, Cambridge, matriculated 1895, B.A. 1898; Civil Engineer.

Loui Dorothy Scott, born at 7 Alexandra Villas, Uxbridge Road, Shepherd's Bush, co. Middlesex, on Friday, 1 February, bapt. at St. Luke's, Shepherd's Bush, 9 July 1878; marr. at Christ Church, Ealing (by the Rev. Robert Jones, Rector of Banham, co. Norfolk, assisted by the Rev. Septimus Hebert, Vicar of Iver, co. Buckingham, and the Rev. Templeton King, the Vicar), on Thursday, 22 December 1898, Foster Knowles (eldest son of William Knowles of 48 Moorgate Street, London, and of "Ribblesdale," Streatham, co. Surrey, by Emma Lætitia his wife, dau. of William Paxton); born at Clapham Park, co. Surrey, on Tuesday, 26 November 1867; educated at Harrow and at Trinity College, Cambridge, matriculated Michaelmas Term, 1887, B.A. 1890, M.A. 1894.

Maurice William Coode, born at Mecklenburg Lodge, Grange Road, Ealing, co. Middlesex, on Saturday, 1 November 1879, bapt. at Christ Church, Ealing, 9 January 1880; Civil Engineer; Captain 3rd Battalion Wiltshire (The Duke of Edinburgh's) Regiment (Militia) 1902; served during South African War 1901, at St. Helena in charge of Boer prisoners (medal).

Barbara Cecil, born at Mecklenburg Lodge, Grange Road, Ealing, on Tuesday, 25 January, bapt. at Christ Church, Ealing, 30 April 1881.

B

Eleanor Lucy, born at Weymouth, co. Dorset, 3 September, bapt. at St. Mary's, Melcombe Regis, co. Dorset, 2 October 1850; marr. at St. John's, Paddington, London (by the Rev. James Fleming, B.D., Canon of York and Vicar of St. Michael's, Chester Square, London, assisted by the Rev. Sir Emilius Bayley, Bart., the Vicar), on Tuesday, 20 July 1886, as his 2nd wife, the Rev. Frederick Arthur Cecil Lillingston (youngest son of Charles Lillingston of The Chauntry, Ipswich, co. Suffolk, by Harriot his wife, only dau. of the Rev. Charles William Fonnereau of Christchurch Park, Ipswich); born at Christchurch Park, Ipswich, 11 July 1837, bapt. privately (baptism registered at St. Margaret's, Ipswich, 19 April 1840); of Trinity College, Dublin, 1854–60, B.A. 1859, M.A. 1870; Archdeacon of Yass, Goulbourn, New South Wales, 1869–71, Vicar of Broxbourne, co. Hertford, 1872–78, of St. Barnabas', Islington, London, 1878–87, of St. James', Clapham, co. Surrey, 1887–99, and of Havering-atte-Bower, co. Essex, 1899–1902, formerly Chaplain at Christ Church, Madras, India; marr. 1stly, at St. Leonard's, Hythe, co. Kent (by the Rev. Henry Sewell, Vicar of Headcorn, co. Kent, uncle of the bride, assisted by the Rev. Edward Lillingston, Incumbent of St. George's, Birmingham, uncle of the bridegroom), on Wednesday, 5 September 1860, Charlotte Jane, 4th dau. of the Rev. James Isaac Monypenny, Vicar of Hadlow, co. Kent; born 20 March, bapt. at St. Leonard's, Hythe, 26 June 1839; died at Highbury Park, London, leaving issue, on Thursday, 1 May, bur. in Highgate Cemetery, London, 5 May 1884. M.I. Admon was granted at the Principal Registry 4 June 1884, to the Rev. Frederick Arthur Cecil Lillingston of 61 Highbury Park, London, the husband.

(See Pedigree of Lillingston, Vol. 9, page 39).

Clara Penrose, born 28 July, bapt. at St. Mary's, Melcombe Regis, 26 August 1852; marr. by special licence at St. John's, Paddington, London (by the Rt. Rev. Rowley Hill, D.D., Bishop of Sodor and Man, assisted by the Rev. Philip Hayman Dod, Master of St. John's, Lichfield, co. Stafford), on Wednesday, 11 October 1882, Godfrey Massy Molony of 14 Carlton Road, Southampton (son of Chartres Brew Molony of Ennis, co. Clare, by Alice [his cousin] his wife, youngest dau. and coheiress of James Barry of Rockstown, co. Limerick); born at Ennis 11 January 1854, and bapt. there privately.

Edith Constance, born 28 September, bapt. at St. Mary's, Melcombe Regis, 13 November 1863; marr. at Emmanuel Church, Paddington, London (by the Rev. Robert Faraker, the Vicar, brother of the bridegroom, assisted by the Rev. Frederick Arthur Cecil Lillingston, Vicar of Havering-atte-Bower, brother-in-law of the bride), on Tuesday, 23 July 1901, as his 2nd wife, Frederick Faraker of Tottenham, co. Middlesex (youngest son of Robert Faraker of Peel, Isle of Man, by Charlotte his wife, dau. of John Christian); born at Peel, Isle of Man, 17 August 1856. He marr. 1stly at Edmonton, co. Middlesex, by licence, on Friday, 25 July 1884, Clara Maria, dau. of Charles Augustus Page of Baldock, co. Hertford. She died 29 January, and was bur. in the cemetery at Tottenham 1 February 1896.

Roddam of Roddam, co. Northumberland.

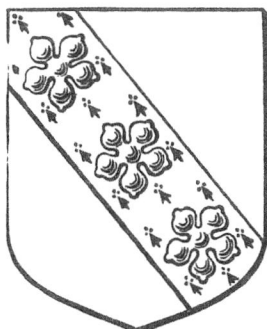

Arms on record in the College of Arms.—Gules, on a bend ermine, three cinquefoils sable.

Roddam John Roddam of Roddam, co. Northumberland (eldest son of Joseph Falder of Alnwick, co. Northumberland [who assumed the name and arms of Roddam on succeeding to the estates, on the death of William Roddam of Roddam, 6 November 1864, in compliance with and under the will of his godfather and kinsman, the late Admiral Robert Roddam], by Elizabeth his wife, dau. of Robert Laing of Birdhopegraig, co. Northumberland); born 26 December 1800, bapt. at St. Michael's, Alnwick, 1 November 1805; J.P. for co. Northumberland, High Sheriff 1872; died at "Tynwald," Grove Park, Chiswick, co. Middlesex, in his 81st year, on Wednesday, 9 March, bur. in the cemetery at Peel, Isle of Man, on Tuesday, 15 March 1881. = Hannah Reed, dau. of Robert Laing of Plenderleith, co. Roxburgh, and widow of Edward Thomas Fairless of Bishop Auckland, co. Durham; marr. 24 July 1821; died at Glasgow, aged 68, 8 August, bur. in Sighthill Cemetery, Glasgow, 13 August 1850.

Will dated 9 November 1880, proved (Prin. Reg., 624, 81) 18 August 1881, by Roddam John Roddam of Swiss Cottage, Addlestone, Weybridge, co. Surrey, gent., the grandson, and James Charles Stevenson of Jedburgh, co. Roxburgh, in North Britain, two of the Exors.

Roddam Falder (twin with Robert); born 23 September 1822; died at Glasgow, aged 37, 8 May, bur. in Sighthill Cemetery, Glasgow, 14 May 1860. = Elizabeth Scott, dau. of William Wyse of Greenock, co. Renfrew, and of Glasgow, by Mary his wife, dau. of William Jamieson; born at Grahamestown, Falkirk, co. Stirling, and bapt. at Greenock; marr. at Kingston, near Glasgow (by the Rev. Dr. Pollock), 18 April 1851.

Robert Falder (twin with Roddam); born 23 September 1822; died at Calcutta, India, 8 August 1855, and bur. there. = Jean, dau. of Robert Scott of Hamburg, Merchant; marr. at Adelaide, New South Wales, 29 April 1855; died 3 October 1862.

Other issue.

Adelaide Robina Winifrede Roddam, born at Edinburgh 22 April 1856, and bapt. there; marr. at Woolston, co. Hants, 12 December 1882, Lieut.-Colonel James Edward Nicholson (eldest son of Edward Nicholson, by Annie Morris Goodbody his wife); born 21 January 1857; Surgeon Royal Army Medical Corps 6 March 1880, Surgeon-Major 6 March 1892, Lieut.-Colonel 4 September 1901; served in South African War 1899–1901; Army Interpreter in French, Lieut.-Colonel Reserve of Officers 26 November 1902.

⊤⋏

A

Mary Wyse, born at Glasgow 18 March, bapt. at Kingston, near Glasgow, 23 May 1852; marr. at St. George's, Hanover Square, London, 13 May 1880, George Drinkwater of Kirby, near Douglas, Isle of Man (eldest son of Sir William Leece Drinkwater of Kirby, H.M. First Deemster of the Isle of Man 1854–97, J.P. and Member of the Council, by Elinor Drinkwater his wife, 3rd dau. of Peter Bourne of Hackinsall, co. Lancaster [*see Pedigree of Bourne, Vol. 3, page 151*]); born 12 October 1852; educated at Eton and at Trinity College, Cambridge, B.A. 1875, M.A. 1878; Barrister-at-Law of Lincoln's Inn 1877; Seneschal and a J.P. for the Isle of Man.

⊤⋏

Hannah Reed Laing, born at Glasgow 10 June, bapt. at Kingston, near Glasgow, 6 August 1854.

Roddam John Roddam⹀Helen Fredericka, youngest dau. of Captain Alexander Taubman Goldie, R.N., of "The Hermitage," Isle of Man, by Mary his wife, youngest dau. of Richard Simpson of Mellor Lodge, co. Chester, and of "The Cliff," Douglas, Isle of Man, J.P. and D.L. (*see Pedigree of Simpson, Vol. 10, page 152*); born at Douglas 22 February 1858, and bapt. at Braddan, Isle of Man; marr. at the parish church, Braddan (by the Ven^ble Archdeacon of the diocese, assisted by the Rev. William Drury, the Vicar), on Tuesday, 1 July 1879.

Roddam John Roddam of Roddam, co. Northumberland; born at 86 West Street, Glasgow, 6 March 1857 (registered at Glasgow 25 March 1857); of Clare College, Cambridge, B.A. 1880; Major 5th Battalion Northumberland Fusiliers (Militia) 26 January 1901; J.P. for co. Northumberland.

Elizabeth Margaret, born at 86 West Street, Glasgow, 6 January 1859 (registered at Glasgow 26 January 1859); marr. at All Saints', St. John's Wood, London, 5 June 1892, Louis Edgar Stevenson of Temple Sowerby, co. Westmoreland (son of James Charles Stevenson of Mount Ulston, Jedburgh, co. Roxburgh, by Sarah Binns his wife); born at Jedburgh 31 January 1864, and bapt. there; of Christ's College, Cambridge, matriculated Michaelmas Term, 1883, B.A. 1886, M.B., B.C. 1889; F.G.S. Lond.; formerly Senior House Surgeon Cumberland Infirmary. She died at Temple Sowerby, aged 43, 29 December 1902, and was bur. there 1 January 1903.

Helen Mary Goldie, born at Swiss Cottage, Addlestone, co. Surrey, on Thursday, 6 May, bapt. at Ottershaw, co. Surrey, 20 June 1880.

Olive Margaret Rickman, born at Swiss Cottage, Addlestone, on Sunday, 8 June 1884.

Robert Collingwood Roddam, born at Roddam Hall on Friday, 10 January, bapt. at Ilderton, co. Northumberland, 24 February 1890.

A

R. J. Roddam

Worsley of Hovingham, co. York.

Sir William Worsley of Hovingham Hall, North Riding, co. York, Bart. (3rd son of the Rev. George Worsley, Rector of Stonegrave and Scawton, co. York, by Anne his wife, 4th dau. of Sir Thomas Cayley of Brompton Hall, co. York, Bart.); born at the Rectory, Stonegrave, on Sunday, 26 August, bapt. privately 28 August 1792 (baptism registered at Stonegrave); J.P. and D.L. for North Riding, co. York; succeeded to the family estates at Hovingham and elsewhere on the death unmarried of his uncle, Edward Worsley of Hovingham, 21 March 1830; created a Baronet 10 August 1838; died at Hovingham, aged 86, on Wednesday, 5 March, bur. in the family vault at Hovingham on Tuesday, 11 March 1879.

= Sarah Philadelphia, 4th dau. of Sir George Cayley of Brompton, co. York, 6th Bart., by Sarah his wife, only dau. of the Rev. George Walker of Nottingham, F.R.S.; born at York 21 Oct. 1803; marr. at Brompton, co. York, 18 Jan. 1827; died at 7 Esplanade Road, Scarborough, co. York, in her 82nd year, on Thursday evening, 23 April, bur. in the family vault at Hovingham on Friday, 1 May 1885. Will dated 31 Aug. 1882, with codicil dated 2 June 1883, proved (Prin. Reg., 84, 86) 15 Jan. 1886, by Sir George Allanson Cayley of Brompton Hall, co. York, Bart., one of the Exors.

A

Thomas Robinson Worsley, born at York 28 Oct., bapt. privately 30 Oct. 1827 (baptism registered at St. Michael's, Spurriergate, York); died at Hovingham, aged 28, on Wednesday, 17 Oct., bur. in the family vault at Hovingham on Monday, 22 Oct. 1855.

Harriet Philadelphia, = his cousin, only child of Captain Marcus Worsley, R.N., of Cliff House, Terrington, and of Conyngham Hall, co. York (brother of Sir William Worsley, 1st Bart.), by Harriet his wife, dau. of Joshua Hamer, and widow of Andrew Barlow; marr. at Knaresborough, co. York, 4 July 1854; died at the residence of Lady Sitwell, "Woodend," Scarborough, on Friday, 11 Aug., bur. in the churchyard at Hovingham on Wednesday, 16 Aug. 1893. Admon (with will annexed, dated 6 May 1878) was granted at York 16 Feb. 1894, to Sir William Cayley Worsley, Bart., the residuary legatee. 1st wife.

Colonel Sir William Cayley Worsley of = Hovingham Hall, Bart.; born at York 6 Dec., bapt. privately 14 Dec. 1828 (baptism registered at St. Michael's-le-Belfry, York); educated at Shrewsbury and at Trinity College, Cambridge; a Student of the Inner Temple 14 Nov. 1850, called to the Bar 30 April 1855; J.P. and D.L. for North Riding, co. York; Hon. Colonel 2nd Volunteer Battalion Yorkshire Regiment; succeeded his father as 2nd Bart. 5 March 1879; died s.p. at Hovingham, in his 69th year, at 1.30. p.m., on Friday, 10 Sept., bur. in the churchyard at Hovingham, by the side of his first wife, on Tuesday, 14 Sept. 1897. Will dated 11 March 1896, with codicil dated 19 Feb. 1897, proved at York 23 Dec. 1897, by Sir William Henry Arthington Worsley, Bart., James Digby Legard, and James Worsley Pennyman, Barrister-at-Law, three of the Exors.

= Susan Elizabeth, youngest dau. of Henry Wyndham Phillips of "Hollowcombe," Sydenham, co. Kent, and of 8 George Street, Hanover Square, London, by Susan Katherine his wife, dau. of the Rev. George Kelly Holdsworth, Vicar of Aldborough, co. York; born at Sydenham on Sunday, 7 April 1861; marr. at the parish church, Brighton, co. Sussex (by Rev. John Julius Hannah, the Vicar), on Wednesday, 11 March 1896. 2nd wife.

Arthington Worsley, ⊤ Marianne Christina Isabella, youngest dau. and coheiress of Colonel
born 21 December │ the Honble Henry Hely-Hutchinson of Weston Hall, co. Northampton,
1830; died at Mal- │ by Harriet his wife (widow of the Honble Frederick Sylvester North
vern, co. Worcester, │ Douglas), eldest dau. of William Wrightson of Cusworth, co. York;
aged 30, on Mon- │ born 5 May 1832; marr. at St. George's, Hanover Square, London
day, 3 June, bur. │ (by the Rev. Henry Howarth, the Rector), on Tuesday, 13 March
in the family vault │ 1860; died at Cliff Hall, Terrington, co. York, on Friday, 11 August,
at Hovingham, co. │ bur. in the family vault at Hovingham on Tuesday, 15 August 1893.
York, 11 June 1861. │ Will dated 15 November 1890, proved at York 9 November 1893, by
│ Sir William Cayley Worsley, Bart., the brother-in-law, the surviving Exor.

A

Sir William Henry ⊤ Augusta Mary Chivers, │ Arthington Worsley ⊤ Helen, dau. of Samuel
Arthington Worsley │ eldest dau. of Edward │ of Mandeville │ Heath Harding, by
of Hovingham Hall, │ Chivers Bower of "Brox- │ House, Isleworth, │ Selina Pomeroy his
co. York, Bart.; born │ holme," Scarborough, co. │ co. Middlesex; born │ wife; marr. in London
at 1 Upper Brook │ York, J.P. and D.L. for │ (posthumous) at the │ 6 January 1900. She
Street, Grosvenor │ West Riding, and J.P. for │ residence of Sir │ marr. 1stly at Bourne-
Square, London, on │ North Riding, co. York, │ William Worsley, │ mouth, co. Hants,
Saturday, 12 January, │ by Amelia Mary his wife, │ Bart., 41 Harley │ 9 August 1886, Frank
bapt. at Hovingham │ 2nd surviving dau. of │ Street, London, on │ Bartlett Thomas Grif-
19 March 1861; │ William Bennet Martin │ Monday, 9 De- │ fiths of Stourbridge, co.
educated at Eton and │ of Worsborough Hall, co. │ cember 1861; Civil │ Worcester, who died,
at New College, Ox- │ York; born at Tickhill │ Engineer. │ aged 30, 21 April, and
ford, matriculated 16 │ Castle, co. York, on │ │ was bur. at Bishop's
October 1880, aged 19, │ Friday, 12 December │ │ Froome, co. Hereford,
B.A. 1884; Major 2nd │ 1862, bapt. at Tickhill │ │ 26 April 1888.
Volunteer Battalion │ 10 January 1863; marr. │
(Princess of Wales' │ at St. Martin's-on-the- │ Marcus Rurik Worsley,
Own) Yorkshire Regi- │ Hill, Scarborough (by │ born at Mandeville
ment 1895–96; J.P. │ the Rev. John William │ House, Isleworth, 28
and County Alderman │ Chaloner, Rector of │ May 1901.
for North Riding, co. │ Newton Kyme, co. York,
York; succeeded his │ great-uncle of the bride,
uncle, Sir William │ assisted by the Rev.
Cayley Worsley, as 3rd │ Robert Henning Parr,
Bart. 10 September │ the Vicar), on Thursday,
1897. │ 13 October 1887.

Winifred Mary, born at Westhorpe │ Edward Marcus Worsley, born at │ Victoria, born at
House, Scarborough, on Sunday, │ Gilling Castle, co. York, on Satur- │ Hovingham Hall
9 December 1888, bapt. at St. │ day, 13 June, bapt. at East Gilling │ on Friday, 23
Martin's-on-the-Hill, Scarborough, │ 17 July 1891. │ February, bapt. at
9 January 1889. │ │ Hovingham (by
│ — │ the Archbishop of
— │ │ York) on Tuesday,
│ Ethel Isabel, born at "The Lodge," │ 13 March 1900.
William Arthington Worsley, born │ Terrington, co. York, on Wednesday,
at Hovingham Hall on Easter Eve, │ 19 October, bapt. at Terrington
Saturday, 5 April, bapt. at Hoving- │ 27 November 1892.
ham 4 May 1890.

A

Sophia Harriet, died at Hovingham Hall, co. York, aged 19, 15 August, bur. in the family vault at Hovingham 20 August 1849.

Catherine Louisa, born at Scarborough 28 July 1832, and bapt. there; marr. at St. James', Piccadilly, London (by the Rev. Thomas Worsley, D.D., Master of Downing College, Cambridge, uncle of the bride), on Tuesday, 5 July 1859, her cousin, Sir George Allanson Cayley of Brompton Hall, co. York, Bart. (eldest son of Sir Digby Cayley, 7th Bart., by Dorothy his wife, 2nd dau. and eventually sole heir of the Rev. George Allanson of Middleton, Quernhow, co. York, Prebendary of Ripon, and Rector of Hodnet, co. Salop); born 31 December 1831; educated at Eton; Lieutenant Yorkshire Hussars Yeomanry Cavalry; Registrar of Deeds for North Riding, co. York, J.P. and D.L. for North Riding, J.P. for the counties of Denbigh and Flint, High Sheriff for co. Denbigh 1883; succeeded his father as 8th Bart. 21 December 1883; died at Port Said, Egypt, in his 64th year, on Thursday, 10 October, bur. at Brompton, co. York, on Monday, 4 November 1895. Will dated 28 October 1891 with three codicils dated respectively 9 November 1891, 19 April 1894, and 12 February 1895, proved at York 29 April 1896, by Sir George Everard Arthur Cayley, Bart., the son, and Richard Frederick Birch of Maes Elwy, St. Asaph, the Exors.

Anne Barbara, born 8 December, bapt. privately 15 December 1833 (baptism registered at Hovingham, co. York).

—

Agnes Isabella, born 21 September, bapt. privately 1 October 1836 (baptism registered at Hovingham).

Emma Frances, born at Hovingham Hall 1 March, bapt. at Hovingham 25 April 1839; marr. there (by the Rev. Thomas Worsley, D.D., Master of Downing College, Cambridge, uncle of the bride, assisted by the Rev. John Pigott Munby), on Tuesday, 20 August 1861, Colonel the Rt. Honble Edward Robert King-Harman of Newcastle, co. Longford, and of Rockingham, co. Roscommon, P.C. (eldest son of the Honble Laurence Harman King-Harman of Newcastle and of Rockingham House, by Mary Cecilia his wife, 7th dau. of James Raymond Johnstone of Alva, co. Clackmannan [see Pedigree of L'Estrange, "Visitation of Ireland," Vol. 3, page 47]); born at Newcastle, Ballymahon, co. Longford, 3 April 1838, and bapt. at Forgney, co. Longford; Hon. Colonel 5th Battalion Connaught Rangers (Militia), formerly Lieutenant 60th (King's Royal Rifle Corps) Regiment, and Captain Royal Longford Militia; J.P. for the counties of Longford, Sligo and Westmeath, M.P. for co. Sligo 1877–80, co. Dublin 1883–85, and for Isle of Thanet 1885–88; Lord-Lieutenant and Custos Rotulorum for co. Roscommon; died at Rockingham, aged 50, on Sunday, 10 June, bur. at Ardcarne, co. Roscommon, 15 June 1888. Will dated 10 November 1886, proved in the Principal Registry, Dublin, 31 August 1888 (and in the Principal Registry, London, 8 September 1888), by Sir George Allanson Cayley of Brompton Hall, Brompton, co. York, Bart., and George Douglas King-Harman of Rockingham, Boyle, co. Roscommon, a Major, the Exors. She died at Geneva, Switzerland, on Monday, 15 May, and was bur. at Ardcarne 23 May 1893.

Landon.

Arms.—Gyronny of eight, or and azure, an inescutcheon argent.
Crest.—A lizard proper.
Motto.—Ma force d'en haut.

Rev. Charles Richard Landon (2nd son of James Landon of⸏Caroline Mann, eldest dau. of
Cheshunt, co. Hertford, by Anna his wife, dau. and eventually
sole heiress of Philip Palmer of Richmond, co. Surrey); born
at Cheshunt 21 February 1766; of Trinity College, Cambridge,
B.A. 1786, M.A. 1789, Fellow of Sydney Sussex College,
Cambridge, 1790, B.D. 1790; instituted to the Rectory of
Vange, co. Essex, in 1809; died at Mill Hill, Billericay, co.
Essex, aged 66, 11 February, bur. at Cheshunt 17 February
1834. Will dated 27 December 1803, proved (P.C.C.)
10 April 1834, by Francis Newcombe Landon, the son.

Josiah Harrop of George Yard,
Lombard Street, London, by
Mary Maria Cantrell his wife;
born 23 July, bapt. at St.
Edmund the King, Lombard
Street, London, 4 September
1771; marr. at St. Clement
Danes', London, 17 June
1802; died at Brentwood,
co. Essex, on Tuesday, 12
March, bur. at Cheshunt
18 March 1844.

A

Charles Ginkell Landon of Tiverton, co. Devon;⸏Louisa, 5th dau. of Benjamin Aislabie of Lee
born 18 August, bapt. at Littlebury, co. Essex,
26 November 1803; of Clare College, Cambridge; Captain 8th Bengal Native Infantry;
died at 18 Woodstock Street, Bond Street,
London, on Friday, 22 February, bur. at
Calverleigh, co. Devon, 1 March 1861. Will
dated 22 July 1847, with codicil dated 26 July
1859, proved (Prin. Reg., 305, 61) 27 May
1861, by the Rev. William John Aislabie of
Alpheton Rectory, Sudbury, co. Suffolk, and
Charles Collier Jones of 28 Mark Lane, in the
City of London, two of the Exors.

Place, co. Kent, by Anne his wife, dau. of
William Hodgson; born 19 February 1809;
marr. at Christ Church, Marylebone, London,
1 August 1837; died at Lyme Regis, co.
Dorset, aged 77, on Saturday, 29 January,
bur. there 2 February 1887. Will dated 16
September 1885, with codicil dated 20 May
1886, proved (Prin. Reg., 245, 87) 14 March
1887, by Edith Landon of Lyme Regis,
co. Dorset, spinster, the daughter, and Frank
Landon of Brentwood, co. Essex, the nephew,
the Exors.

B

Mary, born at Bareilly, North-West
Provinces, India, 23 March, bapt.
there 8 May 1839; died unmarried
at Lyme Regis, aged 52, on
Tuesday, 22 March, bur. there
25 March 1892. Will dated 8
March 1892, proved (Prin. Reg.,
461, 92) 30 April 1892, by Edith
Landon, spinster, the sister, the
sole Executrix.

—

Edith, born at Almorah, North-West
Provinces, India, 4 February, bapt.
at Futtehgurh, North-West Provinces,
India, 12 December 1841.

Katherine (twin with Aislabie), born at Cuttack, Bengal,
India, 29 July 1842, bapt. at Pooree, India, 23 April
1843; marr. at Lyme Regis (by the Rev. George Hilaro
Philip Barlow, the Vicar) on Tuesday, 8 July 1884, as
his 2nd wife, the Rev. Samuel Powning Coldridge of
Ilex House, Dawlish, co. Devon (only son of Samuel
Taylour Coldridge of Exeter, co. Devon); born 14
January 1827; of Christ Church, Oxford, matriculated
15 May 1845, aged 18, B.A. 1849; Vicar of Ide,
co. Devon, 1877-86. He marr. 1stly at St. Sidwell's,
Exeter, on Tuesday, 20 January 1863, Mary, eldest
dau. of John William Wilton of Gloucester; born
31 January 1835. She died, leaving issue, at Highweek,
co. Devon, aged 38, 15 August, and was bur. there
20 August 1873.

Louisa Antoinette, born at Littlebury, co. Essex, 18 September 1804, bapt. there 29 March 1805; died unmarried at Clevedon, co. Somerset, on Tuesday, 10 January 1871, and bur. there. Will dated 20 July 1860, proved (Prin. Reg., 261, 71) 13 April 1871, by Charles Collier Jones of 52 Mark Lane, in the City of London, the surviving Exor.

Caroline Maria (twin with Francis Newcombe), born at Littlebury 14 September, bapt. there 9 December 1806; died unmarried 25 April, bur. at East Horndon, co. Essex, 1 May 1838.

B

Colonel Aislabie Landon (twin with Katherine), born at Cuttack, Bengal, India, 29 July 1842, bapt. at Pooree, India, 23 April 1843; Colonel Retired List Bengal Infantry. = Jane Mary, 2nd dau. of Edward Giffard of the Admiralty, Whitehall, London, by Rosamond Catherine his wife, dau. of William Pennell, Superintendent of Portsmouth Dockyard; born at Hampton, co. Middlesex, 29 November 1848; marr. at St. John's, Secunderabad, India, on Monday, 8 December 1873.

Laura, born at sea 21 December 1843, bapt. at South Weald, co. Essex, 14 July 1844; died at Tiverton, co. Devon, in her 14th year, on Friday, 11 September, bur. at Calverleigh, co. Devon, 17 September 1857.

B

Lucian Giffard Landon, born at Munger, India, 10 January, bapt. there 7 February 1875.

Joan, born at Agra, North-West Provinces, India, on Monday, 15 January, bapt. there 12 February 1877.

Cecily, born at Agra, North-West Provinces, 22 November, bapt. there 13 December 1878.

Anna, born at Dalhousie, Punjab, India, 22 April, bapt. there 18 May 1882.

Roger Palmer Landon, born at Heavitree, co. Devon, 12 August, bapt. there 5 September 1885.

Philip Aislabie Landon, born at Heavitree 5 December 1888, bapt. there 1 January 1889.

Sylvanus Luke Landon, born at Heavitree 16 September, bapt. there 18 October 1891.

Francis Newcombe Landon of Brentwood, co. Essex=Margaret Lætitia, 4th dau. of William
(twin with Caroline Maria); born 14 September, bapt. | Brown of St. Nicholas, Ipswich, co.
at Littlebury, co. Essex, 9 December 1806; died at | Suffolk, by Harriet his wife, dau. of
Brentwood on Tuesday, 10 May, bur. at East Horndon, | George Jermyn; born at Ipswich
co. Essex, 17 May 1859.   Will dated 9 April 1859, proved | 8 July 1823; marr. at St. Nicholas',
(Prin. Reg., 431, 59) 4 July 1859, by Margaret Lætitia | Ipswich (by the Rev. Edward Henry
Landon of Brentwood, co. Essex, the relict, Bridges | Landon), on Wednesday, 25 August
Harvey of Blue Bridge House, Halstead, co. Essex, | 1847; died at 31 Ledbury Road,
and William Brown of Ipswich, co. Suffolk, the Exors. | Bayswater, London, on Tuesday,
| 15 July, bur. at East Horndon
| 19 July 1873. Admon was granted
| at the Principal Registry 13 August
| 1873, to Edward Palmer Landon of
| 16 London Street, in the City of
| London, gent., the son, and one of
| the next of kin.

C

Agnes Mary, born at Brentwood 13 June, bapt. there 9 July 1848; marr. at Hutton, co. Essex
(by the Rev. Henry Holme Westmore, the Rector, assisted by the Rev. William Carus
Wilson), on Thursday, 17 August 1871, Llewellyn Wynn McLeod of Hutton Hall, son of
Bentley McLeod of Clement's Inn, London, by Nancy Bentley his wife, dau. of Bentley
McLeod of Worsell Hall, co. York.

Winifred, born at "Clock House,"	Charles Palmer Landon, born=Caroline, eldest dau. of
Little Burstead, co. Essex, 15 May,	at Heanton Punchardon, co.	Richard Manders of
bapt. at Little Burstead 3 August	Devon, 25 October 1846, bapt.	Brackenstowr House,
1845; marr. at Lyme Regis, co.	there 17 February 1847;	Swords, co. Dublin, by
Dorset (by the Rev. John Curgen-	Chief Superintendent Indian	Caroline his wife, dau.
ven), on Wednesday, 14 January	Telegraph Department; died	of Henry Roe; born
1880, John Gold Philpot (eldest son	suddenly at Lanteglos Rectory,	at Dublin 17 October
of John Philpot of London); born	Camelford, co. Cornwall, in	1852; marr. at the
at 20 Montague Street, Russell	his 47th year, on Tuesday,	parish church, Swords
Square, London, on Saturday, 16	2 October 1894, and bur.	(by the Rev. Robert
December 1848; of Brasenose	at Lanteglos-by-Camelford.	James Roe, Rector of
College, Oxford, matriculated 25	Will dated 5 May 1889, proved	St. Sennen, co. Cornwall,
January 1868, aged 19; a Student	(Prin. Reg., 1206, 94) 21 De-	assisted by the Rev.
of the Middle Temple 13 November	cember 1894, by Caroline	Canon Twigg, the Vicar),
1873, called to the Bar 25 April 1877;	Landon, the relict, the sole	on Wednesday, 28
died at Lyme Regis, aged 46, on	Executrix.	August 1878.
Sunday, 24 November, bur. there 28		
November 1895. =		

Charles Richard Henry Palmer Landon, | Nora, born 13 | John Palmer Landon, born at Calcutta,
born at Brackenstowr House, Swords, | August 1882; | India, 6 August 1883, and bapt. there;
on Friday, 6 June, bapt. at Swords 9 July | died 3 March | entered the Royal Navy as Naval Cadet
1879; Lieutenant 5th Bombay Cavalry | 1883, and bur. | 15 January 1900, Midshipman H.M.S.
(Sind Horse). | at Calcutta. | "Ocean" 15 June 1900.

Augusta Mary, born at Stapleford Tawney, co. Essex, 26 November 1809, bapt. there 28 April 1810; died unmarried at 25 St. Giles' East, Oxford, aged 73, on Tuesday, 9 January, bur. in the Jericho Cemetery at Oxford 12 January 1883. Will dated 14 December 1877, with codicil dated 21 December 1881, proved (Prin. Reg., 55, 83) 25 January 1883, by Edward Palmer Landon of 8 New Broad Street, in the City of London, the nephew, the surviving Exor.

C

Edward Palmer Landon══Mary Rosamond, eldest dau. of Joseph Adolphus Magrath of of Wimbledon, co. Surrey, │ Teignmouth, co. Devon, M.D., by Nony Jane his wife, dau. of formerly of Brentwood, co. │ Lovell Pennell; born at Kingston, Jamaica, 12 December, bapt. Essex; born at Brentwood │ there 24 December 1854; marr. at St. Michael's, Teignmouth (by 27 January, bapt. there │ the Rev. Henry Twells, Rector of Waltham, co. Leicester, assisted 3 March 1850. │ by the Rev. George Staunton Barrow, Rector of Knight's Enham, co. Hants, and the Rev. John Oxenham Bent, Vicar of St. John's, Woolwich, co. Kent), on Thursday, 10 December 1874.

Margaret Josephine, born at Roden House, Shenfield, co. Essex, on Sunday, 13 August, bapt. at Shenfield 1 October 1876.

—

Francis Palmer Landon, born at Roden House, Shenfield, on Friday, 3 August, bapt. at Shenfield 7 October 1877.

Cecil Westmore Landon, born at Roden House, Shenfield, on Wednesday, 5 March, bapt. at Shenfield 14 May 1879; served with Imperial Yeomanry in South African War 1901.

Gladys Mary, born at Roden House, Shenfield, on Sunday, 1 January, bapt. at Shenfield 24 March 1882.

—

Arthur Jermyn Landon, born at Roden House, Shenfield, on Saturday, 4 August, bapt. at Shenfield 10 October 1883; entered the Royal Navy as Naval Cadet 15 January 1900, Midshipman H.M.S. "Formidable" 1902, Sub-Lieutenant 1903.

Kathleen Anna, born at Roden House, Shenfield, co. Essex, on Sunday, 1 March, bapt. at Shenfield 13 May 1885.

—

Edward Guy Landon, born at Roden House, Shenfield, on Friday, 8 October, bapt. at Shenfield 15 December 1886.

Norah Rosamond, born at Roden House, Shenfield, on Friday, 23 December 1887, bapt. at Shenfield 7 March 1888.

—

Herbert Kenelm Landon, born at Roden House, Shenfield, on Wednesday, 20 February, bapt. at Shenfield 17 April 1889.

C

B

Elizabeth, born 8 April, bapt. at Heanton Punchardon, co. Devon, 30 July 1848.

—

Ellen, born at Tiverton, co. Devon, 23 December 1849, bapt. at the parish church, Tiverton, 2 February 1850; died at Tiverton, in her 12th year, on Saturday, 6 July 1861, and bur. there.

John Palmer Landon, born at Tiverton 10 May, bapt. at the parish church, Tiverton, 13 August 1851; died at Tiverton, in his 11th year, on Tuesday, 24 December 1861, and bur. there.

—

Henry Palmer Landon of Gotha, Florida, U.S.A.; born at Tiverton 7 October, bapt. at the parish church, Tiverton, 30 November 1853.

Arthur John Landon, born 18 March, bapt. at Stapleford Tawney, co. Essex, 13 August 1812 ; Barrister-at-Law of Lincoln's Inn ; marr. in May 1851, Charlotte, dau. of George Fortzer ; died at Geelong, Victoria, Australia, in 1872, and bur. there. He died at Lyme Regis, co. Dorset, aged 72, on Thursday, 4 December, and was bur. there 9 December 1884. Will dated 23 August 1880, with codicil dated 11 October 1883, proved (Prin. Reg., 48, 85) 1 January 1885, by Charles Harcourt Landon of 2 Angel Court, Throgmorton Street, in the City of London, the nephew, one of the Exors.

Arthur Landon, born 13 February 1852. ═ Marion, dau. of the Rev. Alexander McNicol ; born at Geelong, Victoria, 1 January 1852 ; marr. at Nyang Station, Moulamein, New South Wales, 23 October 1878.

Edward Landon, born at Melbourne, Australia, 11 September 1854 ; marr. in London 6 June 1886, Mary, dau. of William James of Hereford.

Arthur John Landon, born 5 October 1879, and bapt. at Demilquin, New South Wales.

William Edward Landon, born 15 May 1885, and bapt. at Melbourne, Victoria.

Edith Marion, born 24 September 1886, and bapt. at "Walma," Walgett, New South Wales.

Alexander Charles Landon, born at "Walma," Walgett, New South Wales, 5 October 1889.

Harrop Landon, born at Castlemaine, Victoria, Australia, 27 May 1856. ═ Elizabeth Mackenzie ; born in Scotland ; marr. at Demilquin, New South Wales, in July 1888.

William Mackenzie Landon, born at Demilquin, New South Wales, 1 August 1889.

Harrop Landon, born at Demilquin, New South Wales, 5 September 1890.

Harcourt Percival Landon, born at Essenden, Victoria, Australia, 25 September 1893.

Edward Carlyle Landon.

Arthur Jermyn Landon, born at Brentwood, co. Essex, 29 June, bapt. there 3 August 1851 ; entered the Army Medical Department 1878 ; served in the Zulu War from February 1879, afterwards being attached to General Sir George Colley's force, and was shot at Majuba Hill 27 February 1881 ; died at Camp Prospect, Transvaal, South Africa, 1 March 1881, and bur. at Mount Prospect. Monument erected there to his memory. Will dated 5 September 1875, proved (Prin. Reg., 744, 81) 4 October 1881, by Charles Harcourt Landon of 2 Angel Court, in the City of London, the brother, one of the Exors.

A

Juliana Letitia, eldest dau. of James Birch, Captain R.E., by Nicoletta Letitia his wife, dau. of the Marquis di Mari; born 30 November 1816; marr. at East Horndon, co. Essex, 5 January 1840; died s.p. at Malta, in her 41st year, 26 January, bur. at East Horndon 21 February 1857. Will dated 7 June 1854, proved (P.C.C., 765, 57) 27 October 1857, by Francis Newcombe Landon and Edward Randall Jones, the Exors. 1st wife.	Rev. Edward Henry Landon, born at Stapleford Tawney, co. Essex, 6 November 1813, bapt. there 2 April 1814; of Corpus Christi College, Cambridge, B.A. 1836, M.A. 1839; Perpetual Curate of St. Philip's, Dalston, co. Middlesex; Author of "A Manual of Councils" and other works; died at "Palheiro," Carlton Road, Putney, co. Surrey, 20 March, bur. at Putney 24 March 1877. Will dated 10 May 1870, with codicil dated 1 October 1870, proved (Prin. Reg., 302, 77) 20 April 1877, by Caroline Adelaide Landon of "Palheiro," Carlton Road, Putney, co. Surrey, the relict, Edward Palmer Landon of Brentwood, co. Essex, gent., the nephew, and Charles Collier Jones of 11 Queen Victoria Street, in the City of London, the Exors.	Mary Jane, eldest surviving dau. of John Forbes of Castle Newe and Edinglassie, co. Aberdeen, M.P. for Malmesbury, Director of Honble East India Co., by his wife, Mary Jane Hunter of Beach Hill, co. Berks; born 5 June 1837; marr. at the British Consulate, Funchal, Madeira, and afterwards at the English Church (by the Rev. Thomas Kenworthy Brown), on Thursday, 7 February 1861; died at Madeira on Monday, 2 December 1861, and bur. there. Admon was granted at the Principal Registry 30 June 1862, to the Rev. Edward Henry Landon of St. Leonard's-on-Sea, co. Sussex. 2nd wife.	Caroline Adelaide, dau. of the Honble and Rev. Arthur Philip Perceval, Chaplain to George IV., by Charlotte Anne his wife, dau. of the Honble and Rev. Augustus George Legge, Chaplain to George III. and Chancellor of Winchester; born at East Horsley, co. Surrey, 4 April, bapt. there 18 April 1835; marr. at Bramdean, co. Hants, on Tuesday, 14 February 1865. 3rd wife.

D

[signature: E. H. Landon]

Roger Landon, born at Madeira on Sunday, 1 December 1861; died at Madeira, aged 2 years and 6 months, on Sunday, 26 June 1864, and bur. there.

C   C

Charles Harcourt Landon of East Molesey, co. Surrey; born at Brentwood 30 December 1852, bapt. there 6 February 1853.	Katherine Maude, 3rd dau. of the Rev. Edward Banister, Vicar of Besthorpe, co. Norfolk, by Eliza Anne his wife, dau. of Litchfield Tabrum; born at the Rectory, Chiddingfold, co. Surrey, on Friday, 17 October, bapt. at Chiddingfold 16 November 1856; marr. at West Molesey, co. Surrey (by the Rev. Charles Litchfield Banister, brother of the bride, assisted by the Rev. Thomas Meymott Tidy), on Tuesday, 5 February 1884.

Geoffrey Harcourt Landon, born at Hutton, East Molesey, co. Surrey, on Tuesday, 2 December 1884, bapt. at St. Paul's, East Molesey, 11 January 1885.	Olive Margaret (twin with Hilda Margaret), born at Hutton, East Molesey, on Friday, 17 August, bapt. at St. Paul's, East Molesey, 7 October 1888.	Hilda Margaret (twin with Olive Margaret), born at Hutton, East Molesey, on Friday, 17 August, bapt. at St. Paul's, East Molesey, 7 October 1888.

Rev. Guy Landon, born at ⟶ Mary Frances, only dau. of Frank Maude Taylor Jones (now Eastbourne, co. Sussex, on Jones-Balme) of High Close, co. Westmoreland, J.P. and D.L. Friday, 24 November, bapt. for co. Westmoreland, High Sheriff 1899, and County Councillor, at St. Mary's, Old Eastbourne, by Hannah Wraith his wife; born at Rydal, co. Westmoreland, 24 December 1865; of on Tuesday, 25 June, bapt. at Langdale, co. Westmoreland, Lincoln College, Oxford, 21 July 1867; marr. at Ambleside, co. Westmoreland (by the B.A. 1889, M.A. 1892; Vicar Rev. Walter Michael Tomlinson, Vicar of All Saints', Pontefract, of Evington, co. Leicester, co. York, assisted by the Rev. Henry James Sibthorp and the 1900–1902, and of St. Rev. Arthur Aubert Jackson), on Tuesday, 15 April 1890. Stephen's, Portsea, co. Hants, since 1902.

Evelyn Mary, born at Lesketh How, Ambleside, on Wednesday, 20 May, bapt. at St. Mary's, Ambleside, 17 June 1891.

Cicely Mary, born at South End, Midhurst, co. Sussex, on Tuesday, 28 March, bapt. at Midhurst 10 May 1893.

D

Lionel Landon, born at Kilve, co. Somerset, 27 February, bapt. at Over Stowey, co. Somerset, 21 April 1867; of the Royal Indian Engineering College, Staines, co. Middlesex, 1886–89.

—

Perceval Landon, born at Hastings, co. Sussex, on Monday, 29 March, bapt. at Christ Church, St. Leonard's-on-Sea, co. Sussex, 15 May 1869; of Hertford College, Oxford, 1888–92, B.A. 1893; called to the Bar at the Inner Temple 1895; acted as War Correspondent to "The Times" in South Africa 1899–1900.

Ruth Mary, born at Shanklin, Isle of Wight, on Sunday, 14 April, bapt. at St. Saviour's, Shanklin, 19 May 1872.

—

Godfrey Edward Landon, born at "Arnewood," Lymington, co. Hants, on Thursday, 7 August, bapt. at Hordle, co. Hants, 4 September 1873; of the Royal Indian Engineering College, Staines, 1893–95; of the Indian Telegraph Department.

C   C

Frank Landon of Brentwood, co. ⟶ Eva Mary, only dau. of Joseph Earle of "The Priory," Essex; born at Brentwood 5 April, Brentwood, by Anne his wife, dau. of the Rev. Charles bapt. there 7 May 1854. Smith, Vicar-General of Elfin, Armagh and Ardagh; born at Brentwood on Thursday, 5 March, bapt. there 5 April 1863; marr. at Shenfield, co. Essex (by the Rev. William Earle, uncle of the bride, assisted by the Rev. Henry Holme Westmore, and the Rev. Charles Earle, brother of the bride), on Thursday, 4 August 1881.

Frank Landon (signature)

Dorothy Margaret, born at "The Lodge," Shenfield, on Thursday, 21 June, bapt. at Shenfield 29 July 1883.

Joseph Herbert Arthur Landon, born at Shenfield, on Monday, 13 December 1886, bapt. there 16 February 1887.

Phyllis Mary, born at Brentwood on Wednesday, 16 March, bapt. there 22 May 1892.

c

Harcourt Palmer Landon of Shenfield, co. Essex; born at Brentwood, co. Essex, 12 September, bapt. there 14 October 1855.

[signature]

═ Charlotte Elizabeth Bell, eldest dau. of Surgeon-General William Munro, C.B., M.D., LL.D., by Dora Laidlaw his wife, dau. of James Bell of Menslaws, Jedburgh, co. Roxburgh; born at 10 Pembroke Road, Dublin, on Monday, 14 December 1857; marr. at St. Barnabas', Kensington, London (by the Rev. George Ruthven Thornton, the Vicar, assisted by the Rev. Henry Holme Westmore), on Saturday, 7 July 1883.

Mary Margaret, born at Romford, co. Essex, 9 April bapt. there 4 May 1884.

—

Violet, born at Western Road, Romford, on Thursday, 8 October, bapt. there 31 October 1885.

William Harcourt Palmer Landon, born at Romford 23 December 1886, bapt. there 23 January 1887.

—

John Robert Landon, born at Romford 27 April, bapt. there 20 May 1888.

James Munro Palmer Landon, born at "The Lodge," Shenfield, co. Essex, on Thursday, 17 April, bapt. at Shenfield 7 June 1890.

—

Helen Frances, born at "The Lodge," Shenfield, on Wednesday, 12 October, bapt. at Shenfield 12 November 1892.

—

Victor George Palmer Landon, born at Shenfield 5 March, bapt. there 9 May 1897.

Herbert Landon, born at Brentwood, co. Essex, on Friday, 25 September, bapt. there 1 November 1857; died at Brentwood, aged 5 months, on Saturday, 6 March, bur. there 11 March 1858.

Herbert John Landon, born at Brentwood on Sunday, 3 October, bapt. there 21 November 1858; of the Royal Indian Engineering College, Staines, co. Middlesex, 1877–80; formerly Executive Engineer Bombay P.W.D. (retired 1895).

═ Beryl, dau. of Atherton Edward Ashley, by Sarah Emily his wife, dau. of Dr. William Davy; born at Blackheath, co. Kent, 3 September 1876; marr. at Christ Church, Westminster, 14 June 1900.

[signature] Lionel Landon

PRO REGE · LEGE · GREGE

DE MAULEY.

Arms on record in the College of Arms.—Quarterly: 1st and 4th, Gules, a chevron between three combs argent, PONSONBY; 2nd and 3rd, Sable, a lion passant guardant argent, a chief engrailed or.

Crest.—Out of a ducal coronet or, three arrows, points downwards, one in pale and two in saltire, entwined at the intersection by a snake proper.

Supporters.—Dexter: A lion reguardant proper; Sinister: A bull sable, armed, unguled, and gorged with a ducal coronet or.

Motto.—Pro rege, lege, grege.

De Mauley.

William Francis Spencer Ponsonby, Baron de Mauley (3rd son of Frederick, 3rd Earl of Bessborough, by Lady Henrietta Frances his wife, dau. of John, 1st Earl Spencer); born at Cavendish Square, London, 31 July, bapt. at the parish church, Marylebone, London, 31 August 1787; M.P. for Poole 1826–31, Knaresborough 1831–32, and for co. Dorset 1832–37; created 10 July 1838, Baron de Mauley of Canford, co. Dorset, his wife being a coheir of the Barony of Mauley, said to have been created by writ 1295; died at his residence, 21 St. James' Place, Westminster, aged 68, on Wednesday, 16 May, bur. at Hatherop, co. Gloucester, 23 May 1855. Will dated 8 January 1855, proved (P.C.C., 597, 55) 14 July 1855, by the Honble Ashley George John Ponsonby, the son, and Henry Frederick Ponsonby, the nephew (eldest son of testator's late brother, Sir Frederick Cavendish Ponsonby), the Exors.

Lady Barbara, only child and heiress of Anthony, 5th Earl of Shaftesbury, by Barbara his wife, only dau. and heiress of Sir John Webb of Canford, Bart.; born 19 October 1788; marr. at the parish church, Marylebone, London, 8 August 1814; died at Albemarle Street, London, on Wednesday, 5 June 1844, and bur. at Canford.

A

Charles Frederick Ashley Cooper Ponsonby, Baron de Mauley; born at George Street, Hanover Square, London, 12 September 1815; educated at Eton; M.P. for Poole 1837–47, and for Dungarvan 1851–52; succeeded his father as 2nd Baron 16 May 1855; died suddenly at "The Knap," Rossie, co. Perth, aged 81, on Monday, 24 August, bur. at Little Faringdon, co. Oxford, on Saturday, 29 August 1896. Will dated 8 December 1890, proved (Prin. Reg., 28, 97) 26 January 1897, by the Rt. Honble Maria Jane Elizabeth, Baroness de Mauley, the relict, the sole Executrix.

Lady Maria Jane Elizabeth (his cousin), 4th dau. of John William, 4th Earl of Bessborough, by Lady Maria his wife, dau. of John, 10th Earl of Westmoreland; born 14 March 1819; marr. at All Souls', Langham Place, London, 9 August 1838; died at Langford House, Lechlade, co. Gloucester, aged 78, on Monday, 13 September, bur. at Little Faringdon 17 September 1897. Will dated 13 April 1897, proved (Prin. Reg., 1201, 97) 3 November 1897, by the Rt. Honble William Ashley Webb, Baron de Mauley, the son, the sole Exor.

B

Alice Barbara Maria, born 26 January 1840; died at 24 George Street, Hanover Square, London, aged 6, on Monday, 8 June, bur. at Wimbledon, co. Surrey, 13 June 1846. —

Emily Priscilla Maria, born at Canford 27 November 1841; marr. at St. Paul's, Knightsbridge, London, 2 June 1870, the Rev. Charles William Norman Ogilvy (youngest son of Sir John Ogilvy, 9th Bart., by Lady Jane Elizabeth his 2nd wife, dau. of Thomas, 16th Earl of Suffolk); born at Baldovan House, co. Forfar, on Sunday, 6 October 1839; of Christ Church, Oxford, matriculated 21 October 1858, aged 19, B.A. 1864, M.A. 1865; Rector of Barton-le-Street, co. York, 1870–78, of Hanbury, co. Worcester, 1878, and Vicar of Oswestry, co. Salop, since 1897, also Rural Dean of Oswestry since 1897; died, aged 63, on Sunday, 7 June, bur. at Oswestry 10 June 1903. Will dated 24 September 1895, proved (Prin. Reg., 6, 1903) 13 August 1903, by the Honble Emily Priscilla Maria Ogilvy, the relict, the sole Executrix.

William Ashley Webb Ponsonby, Baron de Mauley; born at George Street, Hanover Square, London, 2 March 1843; formerly Lieutenant Rifle Brigade; A.D.C. to Governor-General of Canada; succeeded his father as 3rd Baron 24 August 1896.

Frances Anna Georgiana, born at the residence of the Earl of Bessborough, Roehampton, co. Surrey, 24 July, bapt. at the parish church, Putney, co. Surrey, 19 August 1817; marr. at Great Canford, co. Dorset, 14 December 1837, the Rt. Honble George William Fox, Baron Kinnaird of Inchture and Baron Rossie of Rossie, co. Perth, K.T., P.C. (eldest son of Charles, 8th Baron Kinnaird, by Lady Olivia Letitia Katherine his wife, 7th dau. of William Robert, 2nd Duke of Leinster); born 14 April 1807; educated at Eton; M.P., J.P., D.L., and Convenor for co. Perth; of the Diplomatic Service; created a Peer of the United Kingdom as Baron Rossie of Rossie, co. Perth, 11 June 1831, which title became extinct at his death, and also Baron Kinnaird of Rossie, co. Perth, 1 September 1860, with remainder to the issue male of his brother, the Honble Arthur Kinnaird; Master of the Buckhounds 1837–41; Grand Master of Freemasons in Scotland, Lord-Lieutenant for co. Perth 1866–78; died at his residence, Rossie Priory, co. Perth, in his 71st year, on Monday, 7 January, bur. at Old Rossie 12 January 1878. On the 16 July 1878, Confirmation of the Commissariot of Perthshire, dated 9 July 1878, of the Rt. Honble Frances Anna Georgiana, Lady Kinnaird, as Executrix, nominate of the Rt. Honble George William Fox, Lord Kinnaird and Baron Rossie of Rossie in the United Kingdom. His trust disposition and deed of settlement dated 25 November 1871, with four codicils dated respectively, two on 5 June 1873, and two on 20 December 1876.

George Ponsonby, born 6 July 1844; died 24 August 1845.

Rev. Maurice John George Ponsonby, born at Cosgrove, co. Northampton, on Friday, 7 August 1846, and bapt. there; educated at Eton and at Christ Church, Oxford, matriculated 19 May 1865, aged 18, B.A. 1869, M.A. 1873; Vicar of Kirkstall, co. York, 1875–78, of St. Paul's, Chichester, co. Sussex, 1878–79, of St. Mark's, New Swindon, co. Wilts, 1879–1903, and of Wantage, co Berks, since May 1903; Hon. Canon of Bristol since 1890, Rural Dean of Cricklade since 1891, Proctor in Convocation since 1898.

Honble Madeleine Emily Augusta, youngest dau. of Thomas Charles, 2nd Baron Sudeley, by Emily Elizabeth Alicia his wife, 2nd dau. of George Hay Dawkins-Pennant of Penrhyn Castle, co. Carnarvon, M.P.; born at Brighton, co. Sussex, on Tuesday, 22 June 1852, and bapt. at St. George's Chapel, Brighton; marr. at St. Paul's, Knightsbridge, London, 29 December 1875.

Gerald Maurice Ponsonby, born at 19 St. George's Square, London, 7 October, bapt. at St. Saviour's, Pimlico, London, 8 November 1876; entered the Army as 2nd Lieutenant Royal Warwickshire Regiment 7 May 1898, Lieutenant 10 March 1899, Captain 3rd Battalion 19 February 1902; served in South African War 1901–1902 with mounted infantry (slightly wounded).

Hubert William Ponsonby, born at the Vicarage, Kirkstall, on Sunday, 21 July, bapt. at Kirkstall 17 August 1878.

A
A

Henry William George Ponsonby, born 1 September 1819; died 24 November 1821, bur. in the Cavendish vault in the church of All Saints', Derby, 29 December 1821, on which day his grandmother, Henrietta Frances, Countess of Bessborough (who was sister to Georgiana, Duchess of Devonshire), was also buried in this vault.

Anthony Ashley Webb Ponsonby, born 11 April 1828; died at Roehampton, co. Surrey, on Sunday, 29 November 1829.

B

Frederick John William Ponsonby=Margaret Fanny, 2nd dau. of Frederick John Howard of of Langford House, Lechlade, co. | Compton Place, co. Sussex, J.P., M.P., by Lady Fanny Gloucester, and of 14 Chapel Street, | his wife, dau. of William Cavendish; born at 1 Belgrave Grosvenor Place, London; born | Square, London, 24 October, bapt. at St. Peter's, Eaton at Rossie Priory, co. Perth, on | Square, London, 19 November 1844; marr. at the parish Saturday, 28 August 1847; educated | church, Eastbourne, co. Sussex (by the Honble and Rev. at Eton; D.L. for co. Oxford. | Maurice John George Ponsonby, brother of the bridegroom, Vicar of Kirkstall, assisted by the Rev. Thomas Pitman, the Vicar), on Thursday, 1 February 1877.

(See Pedigree of Howard, Vol. I., page 187.)

Mary Fanny Louisa, born at 34 Lowndes Street, London, at 2.15 p.m. on Monday, 21 April, bapt. at St. Peter's, Eaton Square, London, on Friday, 23 May 1879 (Sponsors: William Frederick Howard, her uncle, Lady Frederick Cavendish and the Honble Mrs. Norman Ogilvy).

Evelyn Margaret, born at 14 Chapel Street, Belgrave Square, London, at 10.30 a.m. on Monday, 24 October, bapt. at St. Peter's, Eaton Square, London, on Monday, 12 December 1887 (Sponsors: Honble and Rev. Maurice John George Ponsonby, her uncle, Edith Susan Louisa Howard, her aunt, and the Honble Mrs. Brand).

B

A

Ashley George John Ponsonby, born at St. James' Square, London, on Friday, 25 June 1831; appointed Lieutenant and Captain Grenadier Guards 1854, retired from the Army 1855; J.P. and D.L. for co. Gloucester, J.P. for the counties of Berks, Middlesex, Westminster and London; Member of London County Council (Central Finsbury); M.P. for Cirencester 1852–57 and 1859–65; died at his residence, 39 Hyde Park Gate, London, in his 66th year, on Wednesday, 12 January, bur. in the family vault at Hatherop, co. Gloucester, 18 January 1898. Will dated 7 January 1898, proved (Prin. Reg., 195, 98) 8 February 1898, by the Hon[ble] Louisa Frances Charlotte Ponsonby, the relict, and Charles Ranken Vickerman Longbourne, the Ex̄ors.

=Louisa Frances Charlotte, 2nd dau. of Lord Henry Gordon, Major Hon[ble] East India Co's. Service, 4th son of George, 9th Marquis of Huntly; born 17 December 1829; Maid of Honour to H.M. Queen Victoria; marr. at All Saints', Knightsbridge, London (by the Rev. Sackville Bourke, Rector of Hatherop and cousin of the bridegroom, assisted by the Rev. William Harness, the Vicar), on Tuesday, 21 July 1857.

Florence, born at 29 Rutland Gate, London, on Sunday, 27 June 1858; died at 29 Rutland Gate, aged 23 days, on Tuesday, 20 July, bur. in the family vault at Hatherop 27 July 1858.

Claude Ashley Charles Ponsonby of 33 Queen's Gate Terrace, London; born at 63 Rutland Gate, London, on Tuesday, 16 August, bapt. at All Saints', Ennismore Gardens, Knightsbridge, London, 10 September 1859; educated at Eton and at Trinity College, Cambridge, matriculated Michaelmas Term, 1878, B.A. 1884.

=Haller, youngest dau. of Orville Horwitz of Baltimore, Maryland, U.S.A., by Maria Rives his wife, dau. of Samuel Davis Gross of Philadelphia, U.S.A.; born at Baltimore 11 December 1872, bapt. at Grace Church, Baltimore, in January 1873; marr. at All Saints', Ascot, co. Berks, 28 January 1891.

Eustace Ashley William Ponsonby, born at 9 Prince's Gardens, London, on Wednesday, 30 December 1863, bapt. at Holy Trinity, Brompton, London, 5 February 1864.

Claude. A. C. Ponsonby [signature]

Harold Ashley Curzon Ponsonby, born at 10 William Street, Lowndes Square, London, on Tuesday, 6 October, bapt. there privately in December 1891 (baptism registered at St. Mary Magdalen's, Regent's Park, London).

Eric Ashley Claude Ponsonby, born at the Grosvenor Hotel, Victoria Street, London, on Friday, 28 April, bapt. at Shalford, co. Surrey, 28 September 1893; died at Argelès-Gazost, Hautes Pyrénées, 17 October 1894, and bur. in the Protestant Cemetery at Pau, B.P., France.

Moira Blanche May Diana, born at 33 Queen's Gate Terrace, London, on Tuesday, 3 December 1901, bapt. there privately in January 1902 (baptism registered at St. Mark's, Marylebone, London).

B   B

Mary Alice, born 1 April 1849; died unmarried at Wimbledon, co. Surrey, aged 23, on Saturday, 13 July, bur. at Little Faringdon, co. Oxford, 19 July 1872. Adm̄on was granted at the Principal Registry 17 February 1897, to the Rt. Hon[ble] Maria Jane Elizabeth, Baroness de Mauley, the mother.

Edwin Charles William Ponsonby, of "Woodleys," Woodstock, co. Oxford; born at Hatherop, co. Gloucester, on Monday, 13 October, bapt. there 23 November 1851; educated at Eton; J.P. and D.L. for co. Oxford; Major 2nd Volunteer Battalion Oxfordshire Light Infantry 1886–90.

=Emily Dora, dau. of Octavius Edward Coope of Rochetts, co. Essex, M.P., by Emily his wife, dau. of Captain Fulcher of the Indian Army; born at Rochetts on Friday, 20 May 1859; marr. at St. Mark's, North Audley Street, London (by the Rt. Rev. Thomas Legh Claughton, D.D., Bishop of St. Albans, assisted by the Honble and Rev. Maurice Ponsonby and the Rev. Joseph Watson Ayre), on Tuesday, 10 December 1878; died at "Woodleys," Woodstock, aged 38, on Sunday, 3 October, bur. at Glympton, co. Oxford, 7 October 1897. Will dated 24 December 1886, proved (Prin. Reg., 76, 98) 10 January 1898, by the Honble Edwin Charles William Ponsonby, the sole Exor.

Charles Edward Ponsonby, born at 27 Grosvenor Street, London, on Tuesday, 2 September, bapt. at South Weald, co. Essex, 5 October 1879.

Maurice George Jesser Ponsonby, born at Horsley Manor, co. Gloucester, on Friday, 10 September, bapt. at Horsley 6 November 1880.

Ashley William Neville Ponsonby, born at 27 Grosvenor Street, London, on Wednesday, 1 March, bapt. at St. Mark's, North Audley Street, London, 2 April 1882; entered the Army as 2nd Lieutenant 2nd Battalion Oxfordshire Light Infantry 9 March 1901.

Victor Coope Ponsonby, born at 41 Upper Brook Street, London, on Tuesday, 21 June, bapt. at St. Mark's, North Audley Street, London, 27 July 1887.

Diana Helen, born at "Woodleys," Woodstock, on Wednesday, 2 September, bapt. at Wootton, co. Oxford, 18 October 1891.

Helen Geraldine Maria, born at Down Ampney, co. Gloucester, on Sunday, 12 December 1852, bapt. there 2 February 1853; marr. at St. Mark's, North Audley Street, London (by the Honble and Rev. Maurice John George Ponsonby, brother of the bride, assisted by the Honble and Rev. Walter Ponsonby), on Wednesday, 25 July 1877, Sholto George Watson, Lord Aberdour, afterwards Earl of Morton, Lord Dalkeith and Aberdour (son of Sholto George Watson, 18th Earl of Morton, by Helen his 1st wife, dau. of James Watson of Saughton, co. Midlothian); born at Dalmahoy, co. Midlothian, 5 November, bapt. there 9 December 1844; of Trinity College, Cambridge; formerly Lieutenant Midlothian Imperial Yeomanry; D.L. for co. Argyll; succeeded his father as 19th Earl 24 December 1884.

Diana Isabel Maria, born at Down Ampney on Tuesday, 27 March, bapt. there 3 May 1855; died at St. Leonard's-on-Sea, co. Sussex, on her 20th birthday, on Saturday, 27 March, bur. at Little Faringdon, co. Oxford, 2 April 1875.

REGE LEGE · GREGE

WILLIAM ASHLEY WEBB:
5TH BARON DE MAULEY

H.J.F.B.   1903

Jackson of Wisbech, co. Cambridge.

Arms on record in the College of Arms.—Argent, a greyhound courant erminois between three eagles' heads erased sable.

Crest.—A demi-horse argent, guttée de sang, maned and hoofed sable.

Rev. Jeremiah Jackson (4th son of Hugh Jackson of Duddington, co. Northampton, by Jane his wife, dau. of James Weldon, by Mary his wife, dau. of Francis Jackson of Duddington); born 29 July 1775; Fellow of St. John's College, Cambridge, B.A. 1797, M.A. 1800; Vicar of Elm-cum-Emneth, co. Cambridge, 1825, and Prebendary of Brecon; J.P. for the counties of Cambridge and Norfolk, and Chairman of Quarter Sessions for the Isle of Ely; died at Elm, aged 82, 24 September, bur. there 29 September 1857. Memorial window and stone in chancel of the church at Elm. Will dated 14 April 1855, with two codicils dated respectively 21 June 1856 and 20 August 1857, proved (P.C.C., 761, 57) 20 October 1857, by Edward Jackson, the Rev. Henry Jackson and Francis Jackson, the sons, the Exors.

= Mary Ann, dau. of the Rev. Robert Willan, 3rd Wrangler and Fellow of Trinity College, Cambridge, Vicar of Cardington, co. Bedford, by Ann his wife, only child and heiress of Sir Charles Smijth of Hill Hall, co. Essex, Bart. (sister of Sarah, wife of the Rev. Charles Swann, Rector of Ridlington, co. Rutland [*see Pedigree of Swann, Vol. 1, page 95*], and of Emma, wife of John Goldsmith of Ampthill, co. Bedford [*see Pedigree of Goldsmith, Vol. 5, page 106*]); born at Cardington 2 November, bapt. there 28 November 1779; marr. at St. Mary's, Stamford, co. Lincoln, 9 June 1801; died at Elm, aged 68, 8 January, bur. there 12 January 1849. Memorial window and stone in chancel of the church at Elm.

A

Edward Jackson of Wisbech, co. Cambridge, and of Walsoken House, co. Norfolk; born 30 March, bapt. privately 31 March 1802 (baptism registered at Uffington, co. Lincoln); died at Walsoken House, in his 70th year, on Tuesday, 4 April, bur. at Elm 10 April 1871. Memorial window in the church at Elm. Will dated 3 December 1869, with two codicils dated respectively 15 December 1869 and 6 April 1870, proved (Prin. Reg., 256, 71) 24 April 1871, by Edward Hugh Jackson of Wisbech, co. Cambridge, and Arthur Jackson of 10 Billiter Square, London, the sons, the Exors.

= Caroline Jane, only dau. of John Goddard Marshall of Elm, by Caroline Mary his wife, dau. of Hugh Jackson of Duddington; born 6 February 1807; marr. at Elm 26 April 1827; died at Cumberland Terrace, Regent's Park, London, in her 60th year, on Friday, 22 June, bur. at Elm 28 June 1866. Memorial window in the church at Elm.

Edwd. Jackson

B

Edward Hugh Jackson of Wisbech; born 30 January 1829; D.L. for co. Cambridge, J.P. of the Isle of Ely.

= Georgiana Sybella, 2nd dau. of the Rev. Richard Macdonald Caunter, Rector of Drayton, co. Oxford, by Ann Harrison his wife; born at the Rectory, Highclere, co. Hants, on Monday, 21 August, bapt. at Highclere 21 September 1843; marr. at Drayton (by the father of the bride) on Thursday, 6 August 1868; died at midnight, aged 31, on Saturday, 3 October, bur. at Elm 9 October 1874.

C

Hugh Jackson, born 24 June, bapt. privately 26 June 1803 (baptism registered at Uffington, co. Lincoln); died 24 December, bur. at Wisbech, co. Cambridge, 27 December 1813.

—

Jeremiah Jackson, born 24 April, bapt. at Wisbech 1 June 1805; died 15 January, bur. at Wisbech 17 January 1806.

William Jackson, born 13 July, bapt. at Wisbech 5 August 1806; died 25 August, bur. at Wisbech 27 August 1822.

—

Emma, born 6 September, bapt. at Wisbech 2 October 1807; died 4 December, bur. at Wisbech 7 December 1810.

Caroline Mary, born 11 April 1831; died at 35 Ventnor Villas, Hove, co. Sussex, aged 54, on Monday, 27 April, bur. at Elm, co. Cambridge, 2 May 1885. Memorial window in the church at Elm. Will dated 3 February 1880, proved at Lewes 6 August 1885, by Edward Hugh Jackson of Wisbech, co. Cambridge, the brother, and Elizabeth Nancy Adair Jackson, the sister, two of the next of kin.

Rev. John Russell Jackson, born 26 July 1832; of St. John's College, Cambridge, matriculated Michaelmas Term, 1853, B.A. 1857, M.A. 1860; Vicar of Moulton, co. Lincoln, 1866, and Rural Dean of West Elloe 1889 until his death; J.P. for co. Lincoln; Chairman Quarter Sessions, Spalding (Holland), January 1877 until his death; died at the Vicarage, Moulton, aged 67, on Friday, 17 November, bur. at Moulton 21 November 1899. Memorial East window in the church at Moulton, and restoration of screen and mosaics in the reredos, erected by public subscription at the cost of £550.

Charlotte, only dau. of William Metcalfe of Woodleigh Vale, St. Marychurch, co. Devon; marr. at St. Marychurch (by the Rev. George Metcalfe, cousin of the bride, assisted by the Rev. Henry Garrett Newland, the Vicar) on Tuesday, 29 June 1858.

J. Russell Jackson

Charlotte Jane, born 17 March, bapt. at Moulton 23 April 1869; marr. there 28 June 1893, the Rev. Edward Henry Bree (son of the Rt. Rev. Herbert Bree, Bishop of Barbadoes, by Jane Sarah his wife, dau. of the Rev. Edgar Rust D'Eye); born at the residence of his grandfather, Abbot's Hall, Stowmarket, co. Suffolk, on Sunday, 31 October, bapt. at Drinkstone, co. Suffolk, on Christmas Day, 25 December 1852; educated at Haileybury; Rector of Stowe-in-Lindsey, co. Lincoln, 1893–1901, Vicar of Edlington, co. Lincoln, since 1901.

Emily Russell, born 4 March, bapt. at Moulton 31 March 1871; marr. at East Dereham, co. Norfolk, 16 October 1902, the Rev. Charles Metcalfe (son of the Rev. William Henry Metcalfe, by Mary his wife, dau. of John Farrer Kensington); born 11 March, bapt. at Kentisbeare, co. Devon, 13 April 1873; educated at Sherborne School, Pembroke College, Cambridge, and at Theological College, Wells; Vicar of Whiteparish, co. Wilts, since December 1902.

—

Marian Edith, born 2 December 1872, bapt. at Moulton 6 January 1873.

Edward Macdonald Caunter Jackson, born at Wisbech on Monday, 27 September, bapt. at Drayton, co. Oxford, 12 December 1869.

Georgiana Sybella Caunter, born at Wisbech on Thursday, 11 January, bapt. there 27 February 1872; marr. at St. Peter's, Wisbech (by the Rev. A. Brandon Whittington, assisted by the Rev. Robert Edward Reginald Watts, the Vicar), on Tuesday, 4 August 1903, Henry Macdonald Caunter, son of George Henry Caunter of Leamington, co. Warwick.

Hugh Macdonald Caunter Jackson, born at Wisbech on Wednesday, 19 March, bapt. at Patcham, co. Sussex, 18 May 1873.

—

Isabel Mary Jane Caunter, born at Wisbech on Thursday, 24 September, bapt. privately at Wisbech 8 October 1874, and received into the church there 18 February 1875.

Rev. Henry Jackson, born 31 July, bapt. privately 1 August 1808 (baptism registered at Wisbech, co. Cambridge); of Magdalen College, Cambridge, B.A. 1830, M.A. 1833; Vicar of Wisbech St. Mary; died there, aged 54, 24 March, bur. at Elm, co. Cambridge, 28 March 1863. Memorial window and tombstone in chancel of the church at Elm. Will dated 27 February 1863, proved (Prin. Reg., 545, 63) 18 September 1863, by Edward Jackson and Francis Jackson, both of Wisbech St. Peter, co. Cambridge, the brothers, the Exors.

Frances, born 26 October, bapt. at Wisbech 27 November 1809; died 24 December, bur. at Elm 28 December 1847. Memorial window and tombstone in chancel of the church at Elm.

Charles Thomas Jackson, born 29 August, bapt. at Wisbech 27 September 1811; died 29 May, bur. at Wisbech 31 May 1817.

Rev. Frederick Jackson, born 10 September 1834; of Trinity College, Cambridge, matriculated Michaelmas Term, 1853, B.A. 1858, M.A. 1862; Curate-in-Charge of Hanwell, co. Oxford, 1862, Rural Dean of Lynn Marshland since 1885, Rector of West Lynn, co. Norfolk, 1863 until his death; died at the Rectory, West Lynn, aged 66, on Saturday, 23 March, bur. at West Lynn 27 March 1901. Will dated 3 August 1871, with two codicils dated respectively 3 August 1871 and 2 December 1899, proved at Norwich 15 May 1901, by Donald Frederick Jackson and Herbert Eustace Russell Jackson, the sons, the Exors.

= Elizabeth Mary Jane, eldest dau. of the Rev. Richard Macdonald Caunter, Rector of Drayton, co. Oxford, by Ann Harrison his wife; born at Highclere, co. Hants, 3 September, bapt. there 9 October 1842; marr. at Drayton (by the father of the bride) on Wednesday, 30 March 1864.

Fanny, born 30 May 1836; marr. at Walsoken, co. Norfolk (by the Rev. Frederick Jackson, Rector of West Lynn, brother of the bride, assisted by the Rev. John Young, the Rector, and the Rev. John Russell Jackson, Vicar of Moulton, co. Lincoln, brother of the bride), on Tuesday, 15 April 1873, the Rev. Sir John Charles Molyneux of Castle Dillon, co. Armagh, Bart. (eldest son of the Rev. Sir John William Henry Molyneux of Castle Dillon, 8th Bart., Rector of Sudbury, co. Suffolk, and Hon. Canon of Ely, by Louisa Dorothy his wife, dau. of John Christian, Deemster of the Isle of Man); born 27 June 1843; of Christ's College, Cambridge, matriculated Michaelmas Term, 1863, LL.B. 1866; Vicar of Portesham, co. Dorset, since 1886; succeeded his father as 9th Bart. 5 March 1879. She died at the Vicarage, Portesham, on Sunday, 23 April 1893, and was bur. at Portesham.

Ethel Mary, born at the Rectory, West Lynn, on Friday, 2 February, bapt. at West Lynn 1 April 1866; marr. at St. Peter's, West Lynn (by the father of the bride, assisted by the Rev. Canon James Lyons, Rector of Fiddown, co. Kilkenny, on Tuesday, 7 June 1892, Arthur Shirley Hamilton, Lieutenant R.N. (retired), and formerly of the Labuan Civil Service.

Donald Frederick Jackson, born 15 March, bapt. at West Lynn 3 May 1868. —

Herbert Eustace Russell Jackson, born 11 July, bapt. at West Lynn 3 October 1869.

Arthur Macdonald Jackson, born 7 November 1870, bapt. at West Lynn 28 May 1871; marr. 21 August 1897, Marie Cookson.

Gwendolen Georgiana Mary, born at the Rectory, West Lynn, on Wednesday, 13 January, bapt. at West Lynn 28 March 1875.

William Edward Russell Jackson, born at the Vicarage, Moulton, on Friday, 21 January, bapt. at Moulton 24 February 1876.

= Ada Frances, dau. of George Dewdney, B.A., J.P., by Eliza his wife, only child of Thomas Spittall; born 28 October, bapt. at Chepstow, co. Monmouth, 14 December 1871; marr. there 28 December 1901.

Mabel Elizabeth, born at the Vicarage, Moulton, on Tuesday, 18 September, bapt. at Moulton 24 October 1877; marr. at East Dereham, co. Norfolk, 26 October 1903, Leonard Hopper, son of Arthur Richard Hopper.

John Metcalfe Jackson, born at the Vicarage, Moulton, on Monday, 3 September, bapt. at Moulton 10 October 1883; Lieutenant R.N. Reserve.

Francis Jackson of Wisbech, co. Cambridge; born 27 July, bapt. at Wisbech 12 August 1812; marr. Lucy, dau. of Joseph Marshall of Waldersea House, Elm, co. Cambridge, High Sheriff for the counties of Cambridge and Huntingdon 1841.

Jane, born 3 June, bapt. at Wisbech 2 July 1813; died 22 June, bur. at Wisbech 24 June 1815.

Robert Jackson, born 8 July, bapt. at Wisbech 19 August 1814; died 29 May, bur. at Wisbech 31 May 1815.

Joseph Frank Jackson, born 26 July 1839, bapt at Wisbech.

Lucy Jane, born 14 May 1843; marr. at SS. Peter and Paul's, Wisbech (by the Very Rev. John Saul Howson, D.D., Dean of Chester, assisted by the Rev. Canon John Scott, the Vicar), on Tuesday, 7 July 1874, the Rev. John Gardiner Brown (only son of the Rev. John Brown of Belfast, formerly Vicar of St. Mary's, Leicester); of Pembroke College, Cambridge; died 30 September 1890.

Mary Anne, born 2 January 1846; died 12 September 1887. —

Helen Elizabeth, born 26 April 1848.

Frances Emily, born 11 September 1849; died 13 November 1903.

Hugh Jackson of Bracebridge, co. Lincoln; born 12 July 1852.

=Alice, youngest dau. of Henry Samson of Brunswick House, Bowdon, co. Chester; marr. at the parish church, Bowdon (by the Rev. John Brown of St. John's, Bournemouth, co. Hants, brother-in-law of the bridegroom, assisted by the Rev. Manners William Hervey), on Wednesday, 26 October 1892.

Charles Ernest Jackson, born 12 October 1854.

B

Arthur Jackson of Preston Park, Brighton, co. Sussex; born 12 February 1839, and bapt. at Wisbech.

=Caroline Edith, dau. of Andrew Steedman of Hampstead, co. Middlesex; born 28 May 1842; marr. at St. John's, Hampstead (by the Rev. John Russell Jackson, brother of the bridegroom, assisted by the Rev. James Joyce Evans, Chaplain of the Home and Colonial Training Schools, Gray's Inn Road, London), on Thursday, 18 August 1864.

B

Edward Mackenzie Jackson, born at 1 Leamington Road Villas, Westbourne Park, London, on Monday, 27 May, bapt. at Walsoken, co. Norfolk, 28 July 1867.

Cyril Hugh Jackson, born at 67 Kensington Gardens Square, Hyde Park, London, on Friday, 24 July, bapt. at St. Mark's, Notting Hill, London, 30 August 1868.

Elinor May, born 8 August, bapt. at St. Mark's, Notting Hill, London, 26 September 1869.

Francis Haines Marshall Jackson, born 13 November 1874, bapt. at the Church of the Annunciation, Chislehurst, co. Kent, 10 January 1875.

Emily, born 10 June, bapt. at Wisbech, co. Cambridge, 30 June 1815; marr. at Elm, co. Cambridge, Augustus Edgar Burch of Canterbury, co. Kent; J.P. for co. Bedford.

Hugh James Jackson, born 9 October, bapt. privately 11 October 1816 (baptism registered at Wisbech); died 10 November, bur. at Wisbech 13 November 1817.

Rev. Frederick Jackson,=Susan, dau. of William Endersby Squire of Outwell, near Wisbech; marr. at Outwell (by Rev. William Gale Townley) 4 July 1848.
born 2 August, bapt. at Wisbech 29 September 1818; of St. John's College, Cambridge, B.A. 1840, M.A. 1843; Vicar of Parson Drove, co. Cambridge, since 1844.

Percy Jackson of=Catherine Marr, dau. of Adderley Howard of Long Sutton, co. Lincoln, J.P. and D.L. for co. Lincoln, by Mary Jane Curteis his wife; marr. at St. George's, Hanover Square, London (by the Rev. Frederick Jackson, Vicar of Parson Drove, father of the bridegroom, assisted by the Rev. Borradaile Savory), on Thursday, 18 January 1883; died 7 September 1888, and bur. at Oakham, co. Rutland.
The Manor House, Scamblesby, co. Lincoln, born 26 October 1850, and bapt. at Parson Drove.

Frederic Howard Jackson, born 17 November 1883; educated at Haileybury.

Adderley Percy Jackson, born 15 August, died 2 September 1888, and bur. at Oakham.

Agatha, dau. of Joseph=Spenser Jackson of Brook House, Riseley,=Lucie, eldest dau. of the Honble Ælian Armstrong King of the Ceylon Civil Service, M.L.C., by Henrietta his wife, dau. of Thomas Atkinson, M.D., Inspector-General A.M.D.; born at Galle, Ceylon, 19 February 1873; marr. at Kandy, Ceylon (by the Bishop of Kandy), on Tuesday, 27 October 1896. 2nd wife.
Hutchinson Hammond, M.D., J.P. for co. Lancaster; born at Preston, co. Lancaster, 12 November 1860, and marr. there; died suddenly at 19 Charlotte Street, Portland Place, London, on Tuesday, 24 June 1884, and bur. in Kensal Green Cemetery, London. 1st wife.
co. Bedford; born 26 January 1853; entered the Army as Lieutenant 81st Regiment of Foot 15 March 1873, Captain The Loyal North Lancashire Regiment 2 May 1881, Major 1st Battalion 10 May 1889, Adjutant Auxiliary Forces 1 October 1881 to 30 April 1885 (retired 20 February 1901); served in Jowaki Expedition 1877, in Afghan War 1878–79, at the operations in Khyber Pass (medal); in South African War 1899–1900 as Station Staff Officer (medal with four clasps); retired.

Agatha Strena, born at Preston 1 January 1899, and bapt. there.

B

Henry Willan Jackson of Cronulla, Petersham, Sydney, New South Wales; born 3 February 1842; marr. 23 April 1873, Tresa Allan Marshall.

Sophia Jane, born 23 November 1843.

—

Elizabeth Nancy Adair, born 13 July 1846.

Emily Weldon, born 1 January 1849; died at "Cliftonville," Brighton, co. Sussex, on Thursday, 17 January 1867.

Edward Marshall Jackson, born 2 February 1875.

Allan Russell Jackson, born 2 June 1877.

Frederick Henry Jackson, born 23 July 1879.

James Birnie Jackson, born 23 March 1887.

Ernest Jackson, born 24 August 1893, and died the following day.

Thomas Jobson Jackson of Bedford; born 12 = Elizabeth Cox, eldest dau. of Richard Francis of Bedford; born 10 February 1818. She marr. 1stly at St. Pancras', London, 7 May 1844, Samuel Wing of Bedford, J.P., who died at his residence in St. Cuthbert's, Bedford, on Thursday, 9 November 1865. | Caroline Elizabeth, born 25 January, bapt. at Wisbech 6 February 1822; died 10 February, bur. at Wisbech 12 February 1822.

February, bapt. at Wisbech, co. Cambridge, 14 March 1820; J.P. for co. Bedford; died s.p. at St. Mary's, Bedford, aged 74, on Saturday, 7 April, bur. in the cemetery at Bedford 13 April 1894. Will dated 23 September 1884, with codicil dated 8 August 1893, proved at Northampton 8 June 1894, by Francis Jackson, gent., the brother, and Adeline Mary Wing, spinster, the step-daughter, the Exors.

Colonel Willan Jackson = Laura, 3rd dau. of Wellingborough, co. Northampton; born at St. Peter's Port, Guernsey, 20 September 1852, and bapt. there; County Councillor for co. Northampton; formerly Lieut.-Colonel and Hon. Colonel (V.D.) 1st Volunteer Battalion Northamptonshire Regiment. | of James Trench of Northampton, by Sophia his wife; born 6 April 1857; marr. at St. Sepulchre's, Northampton (by the Rev. John James Browne), on Tuesday, 30 January 1877. | Rev. Corrie Jackson, = Elizabeth, dau. of Joseph Hall of "Beckthorns," Keswick, co. Cumberland, by Sarah Ann Wilkinson his wife, dau. of Joseph Slack; marr. at St. John's-in-the-Vale, Keswick (by the Rev. John Taylor, assisted by the Rev. John Scott Yardley), on Thursday, 11 January 1877; died in London, aged 40, on Thursday, 22 January, bur. in Highgate Cemetery, London, 26 January 1891.

Rev. Corrie Jackson, born at Wellingborough 19 October 1853; of St. John's College, Cambridge, matriculated Michaelmas Term, 1872, B.A. 1876, M.A. 1879; Chaplain of the Foundling Hospital, London; died at Bournemouth, co. Hants, aged 41, on Sunday, 4 August, bur. in Highgate Cemetery, London, 7 August 1895.

Willan Jackson —

Hugh Willan Jackson, born at Wellingborough 27 October, bapt. there 23 November 1877; Captain 1st Volunteer Battalion Northamptonshire Regiment 13 February 1901, Hon. Lieutenant in the Army 4 June 1901; served in South African War 1900–1901, in the operations in the Orange Free State May to July 1900, and in the Western Transvaal July to October 1900; on lines of communication in North of Cape Colony October 1900 to April 1901 (medal with four clasps). | Francis Willan Jackson, born at Wellingborough 10 July, bapt. there 1 August 1879; Surgeon-Captain 37th Battalion Imperial Yeomanry; served in South African War 1902; Hon. Captain in the Army. | Evelyn Willan Jackson, born at Wellingborough 25 March, bapt. there 18 April 1881; of Trinity Hall, Cambridge, matriculated Michaelmas Term, 1899, B.A. and L.L.B. 1902; Lieutenant 1st Volunteer Battalion Northamptonshire Regiment.

A

William Hugh Jackson of Bedford = Margaret Corrie, youngest dau. of Joseph Keep of Wellingborough, co. Northampton, by Peggie his wife, dau. of Adam Corrie of Senwick, co. Kirkcudbright; born at Wellingborough 11 November 1825, and bapt. there privately; died, aged 66, on Tuesday, 5 April, bur. in the cemetery at Bedford 9 April 1892. M.I.

William Hugh Jackson of Bedford, born 5 July, bapt. at Wisbech, co. Cambridge, 16 July 1823; J.P. for co. Bedford; died at his residence, Bromham Road, Bedford, aged 72, on Wednesday, 14 August, bur. in the cemetery at Bedford 17 August 1895. M.I. Will dated 21 April 1892, proved at Northampton 18 September 1895, by Willan Jackson, gent., the son, the surviving Exor.

Charles Willan Jackson, born at Leverington, co. Cambridge, 13 January, bapt. there privately 14 January 1828 (baptism registered at Leverington); died, aged 13, 19 January, bur. at Elm, co. Cambridge, 22 January 1841. Memorial window and stone in chancel of the church at Elm.

F

Fanny, born at Bedford 20 August 1856, and bapt. at St. Paul's, Bedford; marr. at St. Brides', Fleet Street, London, 22 December 1892, Thomas Hunt of The Old Vicarage, Newport, co. Essex (eldest son of Thomas Hunt, Medical Officer of Health for Port Phillip, Victoria, Australia, by his wife, Mysie Lucy Sweetman of Skibbereen, co. Cork); born at Port Phillip, Victoria, 19 March 1854.

Ada, born at Bedford 7 September 1858, and bapt. at Holy Trinity, Bedford; marr. there (by the Rev. Corrie Jackson, brother of the bride) on Thursday, 19 October 1882, Oswald Fordham Tatham of "The Hawthorns," Framfield, co. Sussex (eldest son of Henry Tatham, by Elizabeth his wife, dau. of John Smith); born in London 13 June 1856, bapt. at St. Mark's, Regent's Park, London, 7 April 1861; entered the Bedfordshire Militia, appointed 2nd Lieutenant 1st Battalion Gloucestershire Regiment of Foot in November 1876, exchanged as Lieutenant to West India Regiment, and again as Captain to Royal Scots Fusiliers in 1889; served in Ashantee Campaign 1881; retired as Captain 1894; served with Royal Scottish Reserve Regiment 1900–1901, and with 8th Provisional Battalion May 1901 to February 1903; Major Reserve of Officers October 1902.

Margaret, born at Bedford 11 November 1861, and bapt. at Holy Trinity, Bedford; marr. at the Embassy Chapel, Paris (by the Rev. Corrie Jackson, brother of the bride), on Wednesday, 11 June 1890, Archibald Joseph Gilbert Tatham of Hunstanton, co. Norfolk (younger son of Henry Tatham, by Elizabeth his wife, dau. of John Smith); born 24 October 1860, bapt. at St. Mark's, Regent's Park, London, 7 April 1861.

G

Sylvia Margaret, born at Toddington, co. Bedford, 3 January, bapt. there 2 February 1878; marr. at Wellingborough (by the Rev. Harry Gillespie Topham of Farnham, co. Surrey, assisted by the Rev. Benjamin Dulley of St. Peter's, London Docks, cousin of the bridegroom, and the Rev. H. L. Arnold of Wellingborough) on Thursday, 1 June 1899, Hereward Reid Sharman of Wellingborough (son of Matthew Reid Sharman of Wellingborough, by Mary Elizabeth his wife, dau. of Benjamin Dulley); born 15 February 1875, and bapt. privately at Wellingborough; formerly Captain 1st Volunteer Battalion Northamptonshire Regiment.

Henry Corrie Jackson, born at Malvern, co. Worcester, 18 June, bapt. at Holy Trinity, Malvern, 25 July 1879; educated at Merchant Taylors' School and at St. John's College, Oxford; served in South African War with 58th Company Imperial Yeomanry (medal); died at Boshof, South Africa, of enteric fever, 26 May 1900, and bur. in the cemetery there.

Phyllis Corrie, born at Hilgay, co. Norfolk, 9 October, bapt. there 6 November 1881.

—

Elsie Muriel, born at Hilgay 5 June, bapt. there 2 December 1883.

143

Fac-simile of a Portrait of Thomas Phillips, Inspector of Ordnance in Scilly, afterwards at Mauritius and Bermuda; born 6 January 1781; died 9 April 1851; in the possession of his son, Rear-Admiral Thomas Tyacke Phillips of " The Hermitage," Paignton, co. Devon.

Phillips.

Thomas Phillips (son of Thomas Phillips of Boscreage, St. Germoe, co. Cornwall); bapt. at St. Germoe 17 October 1749; Captain Scilly Militia and Inspector of Ordnance for the Government; died at Trewithen, co. Cornwall, 14 February, bur. at St. Germoe 19 February 1802. = Sibella, dau. of James Pellowe of Penryn, co. Cornwall, by Sibella his wife, dau. of Richard Dunn of Mylor, co. Cornwall; born at Penryn, and bapt. at St. Gluvias, co. Cornwall, 1 December 1751; marr. there 6 April 1780; died 13 April, bur. at St. Germoe 22 April 1813.

Sibella Phillips

A

Emily, dau. of Captain John Rowland of Penryn, by Harriet his wife, dau. of W. Johns of Penzance, co. Cornwall; marr. at Madron, co. Cornwall, 13 July 1816; died at Bermuda, and bur. at St. George's, Bermuda, 1 September 1819. 1st wife. = Thomas Phillips, born at St. Germoe 6 January, and bapt. there 18 March 1781; succeeded his father as Inspector of Ordnance in Scilly, and afterwards at Newfoundland, Isle of Bourbon, Mauritius and Bermuda; died at Plymouth, co. Devon, aged 70, 9 April, bur. in the cemetery at Plymouth 15 April 1851. Will dated 15 March 1850, proved (P.C.C., 503, 51) 18 June 1851, by Thomas Phillips Tyacke and George Frederick Truscott, the Exors. = Frances Lewis, 4th dau. of the Honble Joseph Hutchison, Member of the Legislative Council of

J Hutchison

Bermuda, by Mary his wife, eldest dau. of John Esten of Paget's Island, Bermuda; born in Bermuda 20 March, bapt. at St. George's, Bermuda, 12 April 1801; marr. at Hammersmith, co. Middlesex, 4 January 1823; died at Shaugh Prior, co. Devon, aged 84, on Wednesday, 6 May, bur. in the cemetery at Plymouth 11 May 1885. 2nd wife.

Frances Phillips

(See Pedigree of Hutchison, Vol. V., page 71.)

Thos Phillips.

B

Laura, born in Bermuda, and bapt. at St. George's, Bermuda, 29 July, died the same day, and bur. at St. George's, Bermuda, 30 July 1824.

Emily Rowland, born 26 September 1817, bapt. at St. George's, Bermuda, 24 August 1825; marr. at St. Mark's, Kennington, co. Surrey (by the Rev. George Greig), 31 December 1855, Henry Sheppard Smyth (son of Charles Smyth of Spanish Town, Jamaica, West Indies, and grandson of Sir Richard Smyth, 1st Sheriff for co. Buckingham); born in Jamaica 10 May 1807; of the Corps of Gentlemen-at-Arms; died at Ellesmere House, Weighton Road, South Penge Park, co. Surrey, aged 58, on Sunday, 7 January, bur. in Norwood Cemetery, co. Surrey, 12 January 1866. Will dated 12 December 1865, proved (Prin. Reg., 117, 66) 9 February 1866, by Emily Rowland Smyth of Ellesmere House, South Penge Park, co. Surrey, the relict, the sole Executrix. She died at Ellesmere House, Weighton Road, South Penge Park, aged 54, on Monday, 10 October, and was bur. in Norwood Cemetery 13 October 1870. Will dated 22 February 1870, proved (Prin. Reg., 690, 70) 28 October 1870, by Frederick Hervey Bathurst Phillips of 2 Lightfoot Road, Hornsey, co. Middlesex, a Captain in the Royal Artillery, and Leigh Churchill Smyth of Heathfield, Tunbridge Wells, co. Kent, the Exors.

Thomas John Phillips, born in Bermuda, and bapt. at St. George's, Bermuda, 5 Sept. 1819; died in Bermuda, and bur. at St. George's, Bermuda, 11 Sept. 1819.

Sibella Pellowe, born 28 December 1782, bapt. at St. Mary's, Scilly, 21 February 1783 ; marr. at Breage, co. Cornwall, 26 January 1802 ; Richard Tyacke of Godolphin, St. Germoe, co. Cornwall (son of Nicholas Tyacke, by Hannah his wife) ; born 19 January 1772, bapt. at St. Germoe 31 January 1773 ; died at Godolphin, St. Germoe, 5 December, bur. at St. Germoe 10 December 1825. Admõn (with will dated 29 November 1825) was granted (P.C.C., 507 *Swabey*) 16 September 1826, to Sibella Tyacke, the relict. She died at Nansloe, near Helston, co. Cornwall, and was bur. at St. Germoe 25 August 1854. Will dated 19 January 1854, proved (P.C.C., 962, 54) 1 December 1854, by Amelia Tyacke, Mary Tyacke and Emily Phillips Tyacke, spinsters, the daughters, the Executrixes.

Hannah, born 19 December 1785, bapt. at St. Mary's, Scilly, 9 February 1786 ; marr. at St. Germoe 2 March 1813, John Tyacke of Merthen, co. Cornwall (son of Nicholas Tyacke, by Hannah his wife) ; born 25 November 1781, bapt. at St. Germoe 13 January 1782 ; died at Merthen 11 August, bur. at St. Germoe 16 August 1858. Will dated 11 June 1855, proved (Prin. Reg., 634, 59), 20 October 1859, by Thomas Phillips Tyacke of the Borough of Helston, co. Cornwall, gent., and John Tyacke of Merthen, co. Cornwall, gent., the son, two of the Exors. She died at Penzance, co. Cornwall, and was bur. at St. Germoe 18 March 1875.

Frances Hastings, born in Bermuda 28 July, bapt. at St. George's, Bermuda, 24 August 1825 ; marr. at Plympton St. Mary, co. Devon, 4 October 1855, George Frederick Truscott of Heavitree, co. Devon (only son of Devon, Commander R.N., by Catherine Rebecca his wife, dau. of the Honble Joseph Hutchison, Member of the Legislative Council of Bermuda (*see Pedigree of Hutchison, Vol. V., page 69*) ; born at Exeter, co. Devon, 16 May,

Francis Truscott of Alphington, co. Devon, Commander

bapt. at Holy Trinity, Exeter, 17 June 1817. She died at Exeter 17 December, and was bur. at St. Michael's, Heavitree, 23 December 1867. He marr. 2ndly at St. Michael's, Heavitree (by the Rev. Charles Dicken, uncle of the bride, assisted by the Rev. Henry Knott Venn), on Thursday, 4 February 1869, Clara Mary, dau. of Henry Perry Dicken, Commander R.N. (*see Pedigree of Dicken, Vol. VII., page 139*), by Emily Ellen his wife, youngest dau. of Henry Williams of Falmouth, co. Cornwall (*see Pedigree of Williams, Vol. X., page 64*) ; born at Falmouth 17 March, bapt. at Budock, co. Cornwall, 6 June 1834 ; died at Heavitree, aged 40, on Wednesday, 15 April, bur. there 20 April 1874. He died 8 January, and was bur. at St. Michael's, Heavitree, 13 January 1898.

(*See Pedigree of Truscott, Vol. IV., page 101.*)

Henrietta, bapt. at St. Mary's, Scilly, 21 August 1789; marr. George George, Commander R.N.; entered the Royal Navy 3 September 1793, as first-class volunteer on board the "Glory," 98 (Captain Francis Pender), Midshipman 1794 of the "Resolution," Acting Lieutenant 1797 in the "Lynx"; assisted at the capture of "Le Mentor" 27 June 1798, saved his ship from destruction during violent hurricane, and made Lieutenant 26 November 1799; captured off St. Domingo, while in command of a boat, a French schooner of 6 guns, and a Dutch sloop mounting 4 swivels; he afterwards in 1802, in the "Chichester" troop-ship, through great presence of mind, saved that vessel from being lost on the rocks off the Isle of Wight; assisted at the reduction, in June 1803, of the Islands of Tobago and St. Lucie; on 8 October 1804, while in the "Albacore," obtained the high approbation of his captain for the very animated part he bore in an attack under very heavy fire near Grosnez de Flamanville; retired as Commander 31 May 1844; died, aged 77, and bur. in Brompton Cemetery, London, 8 February 1855. Will dated 19 August 1854, with codicil dated 19 January 1855, proved (P.C.C., 218, 55) 9 March 1855, by George Francis Nott, William Andrew Tyacke, and George Frederick George and Henry Augustus George, the sons, the Exors. Admon was granted at Bodmin 27 August 1860, to Georgiana Sibella George of Germoe, co. Cornwall, spinster, one of the children. She died at Penzance, co. Cornwall, aged 70, 9 October, and was bur. at St. Germoe 13 October 1859.

Johanna, born 1 May, bapt. at St. Mary's, Scilly, 20 July 1792; marr. at St. Germoe 15 July 1815, James Tilly

(4th son of Tobias Tilly of Penzance, by Sally Tregear his wife, of Treath, near Breage, co. Cornwall; born at Madron, co. Cornwall, 29 May, bapt. there 29 July 1785; died at Flushing-in-Mylor, co. Cornwall, and bur. at Perranwell, co. Cornwall, 16 October 1862. She died 3 April, and was bur. at St. Gluvias, co. Cornwall, 7 April 1880.

Frederick Hervey Bathurst Phillips, born in Bermuda 20 August 1827, bapt. at St. George's, Bermuda, 18 October 1828; entered the Army as 2nd Lieutenant Royal Artillery 1 May 1846, Lieutenant 14 October 1846, Captain 17 February 1854 (retired 1 July 1881).

Catherine, dau. of the Rev. Sir Thomas Francis Fetherston, Bart., by Adeline his 1st wife, dau. of Colonel William Godley (83rd Regiment) of Oaklands, co. Dublin; born at Hackwood, Killeshandra, co. Cavan, 1 May, bapt. at Killeshandra 15 May 1828; marr. at St. Peter's, Dublin, 23 September 1851.

Adeline Elizabeth, born at Hackwood, Killeshandra, co. Cavan, 8 September, bapt. privately 10 September 1852 (baptism registered at Killigar, co. Leitrim).

Frances Margaret, born at Hackwood, Killeshandra, 9 August, bapt. at Killigar 5 November 1854; marr. at Holy Trinity, Penge, co. Surrey (by the Rev. Andrew Augustus Wild Drew, Vicar of St. Antholin's, Nunhead, co. Surrey), on Wednesday, 29 December 1880, John Charles Bois of Shangai, China, son of Henry Bois of Beverley Road, South Penge Park, co. Surrey.

Thomas Frederick Phillips, born at Portaliffe, near Killeshandra, 17 June, bapt. at Killeshandra (by the Rev. J. C. Martin) 13 July 1856.

Amy, dau. of J. Robinson of Robertson, South Africa; marr. at Robertson 1 February 1879.

Catherine Anne, born and bapt. at the Cape of Good Hope.

Gilbert Phillips, born and bapt. at the Cape of Good Hope.

Adeliza Bristowe═Lieut.-Colonel George Hutchison Phillips, born in═Emily Georgina, dau. of
Dyett, born 18 | Bermuda 18 January 1829, bapt. at St. George's, | William Coventry Oak,
January 1837; | Bermuda, 31 January 1838; Lieut.-Colonel in | by Elizabeth Boys his
marr. at Sierra | H.M. Commissariat Department; died at Down- | wife, dau. of John
Leone, West | derry, St. Germans, co. Cornwall, 14 August, bur. | Boys Tucker; born at
Coast of Africa; | at St. Anne's, Hessenford, co. Cornwall, 18 August | Blandford, co. Dorset,
died at Panmure, | 1896. Will dated 8 January 1896, proved (Prin. | 30 August, bapt. there
East London, | Reg., 585, 97) 28 May 1897, by Emily Georgina | 4 December 1846; marr.
South Africa, in | Phillips, the relict, the sole Executrix. | at Holy Trinity, King
July 1864, and | | Williams Town, South
bur. there. 1st | | Africa, 7 April 1866.
wife. | | 2nd wife.

[signature: Geo. S. Phillips]

Maude Eliza, born at Sierra Leone, West Coast of | George Douglas | Arthur Alfred Phillips,
Africa, 8 August 1857; marr. at Battleford, North- | Phillips, born 28 | born at Port Elizabeth,
West Territory, Canada, 1 June 1887, the Rev. | November 1859; | South Africa, 26 August,
Julius Foster Dyke Parker (son of the Rev. Henry | died at East | bapt. at St. Mary's,
Parker, Rector of St. Mary's-in-the-Marsh, Romney, | London, South | Port Elizabeth, 13 No-
co. Kent, by Anne his wife); born at the Rectory, | Africa, 24 Jan- | vember 1861; killed by
St. Mary's-in-the-Marsh, Romney, 17 May, bapt. at | uary 1864, and | Zulus at Roodepoort,
St. Mary's-in-the-Marsh, Romney, 17 July 1859; | bur. there. | South Africa, in 1889,
Missionary (Society for Propagation of the Gospel) | | and bur. at Krugersdorp,
at Prince Albert, North-West Territory, Canada, | | South Africa.
1896–1901, Incumbent of St. George's, Battleford,
since 1901.

Charles Hutchison═Nellie, dau. of Joseph | Rosa Fetherston, born at 22 Barnsbury Park,
Phillips, born at | Bond of Brighton, co. | Islington, co. Middlesex, on Thursday, 14
Portaliffe, near Kille- | Sussex, Captain in the | November 1861; marr. at the Cathedral,
shandra, co. Cavan, | Merchant Service; born | Madras, India, 15 November 1879, Ernest
2 August, bapt. at | 27 January 1861; marr. | Edward MacMahon (son of Brigadier-General
Killeshandra (by the | at St. Nicholas', Brigh- | Patrick William MacMahon, C.B., Commander
Rev. J. C. Martin) | ton, 12 December 1885. | of the Legion d'Honneur, by Ellen his wife,
21 August 1859. | | 3rd dau. of George Savage Curtiss of Eastcliffe,
| | Teignmouth, co. Devon, Lord Lieutenant for
| | co. Devon); born at Sandgate, co. Kent, on
| | Sunday, 4 January, bapt. in the Chapel School,
| | Shorncliffe, co. Kent, 29 January 1857; entered
| | the Army as Lieutenant in the 67th Regiment
Dorothy Margaret, | Herbert Cecil Phillips, | 13 June 1874, Captain 13 June 1885, Wing
born 27 February, | born 25 August, bapt. | Officer 3rd Madras Native Infantry; served in
bapt. at St. Mark's, | at St. Mark's, Dalston, | the Soudan and Burmese Campaigns (medals);
Dalston, co. Middle- | 6 November 1892. | died at Rovapoorum, near Madras, aged 36, on
sex, 27 May 1888. | | Saturday, 4 June, bur. in St. Mary's Cemetery,
| | Madras, 5 June 1892.

Rear-Admiral Thomas Tyacke Phillips of Paignton, co. Devon, R.N.; born=Ellen Annie, dau. of Thomas Hand, in Bermuda 10 March 1832, bapt. at St. George's, Bermuda, 31 January by Ellen Julia his 1838; Naval Cadet of "Avenger," in which Ibraham Pasha returned to Egypt wife, dau. of Benjamin Humphrey in 1846, and received sabre of honour; Midshipman of "Fury," and commanded a boat when in company with "Columbine," two fleets of 84 junks and 2,400 pirates were destroyed in October 1849 (mentioned in despatches); Acting Mate of "Hastings" 1852 in Burmese War, commanded an armed schooner on Irrawaddy (Burmese medal and Pegu clasp); on board the Royal Yacht 28 June to 23 September 1854; Lieutenant 1854, Gunnery Lieutenant to "Esk" in Baltic 1855, constantly employed on boats in cutting out and burning vessels in Gulf of Bothnia (Baltic medal); received Captain's Good Service Pension 1885–89; Commander 1864, Post Captain 1873, Rear-Admiral 1889.

Smart; born at Richmond, co. Surrey, on Friday, 13 April, bapt. at St. Mary's, Richmond, 29 July 1849; marr. at St. Michael's, Heavitree, co. Devon, 10 July 1866.

Tho Phillips. Rear Admiral.

George Percy Achilles Phillips, born at sea on board=Blanche Duval, dau. of William Henry the "Achilles" 9 December 1866, bapt. at St. Craven, Secretary to De Beers Consolidated Mines; born at Aliwal North, George's Cathedral, Hong Kong, China, 13 August 1867; Captain the Western Division (Severn) Royal South Africa, 29 July, bapt. there 15 Engineers (Militia) 13 December 1899; served in August 1865; marr. at the British Consulate, Brussels, Belgium, 6 November, South African War 1902 (mentioned in despatches, "London Gazette," 29 July 1902); now serving as and again at St. Philip's, Kensington, co. Captain Rhodesian Field Force. Middlesex, 27 December 1892.

D

Edith Florine, born at East London, South Africa, 11 March 1863; marr. at Aliwal North, South Africa, 23 February 1884, Octavius Ernest Greathead (son of James Henry Greathead of Graham's Town, South Africa); born at Bayswater, co. Middlesex, 11 November, bapt. at St. Matthew's, Bayswater, 28 December 1859; died from the effects of an accident at Johannesburg, South Africa, 27 December, bur. in the cemetery at Johannesburg 29 December 1890.

Charles Vix Douglas=Minnie, dau. of Phillips, born at East Frederick Semple, London, South Africa, Commander R.N., 8 July 1864; served by Edith Hester through the siege of Mafe-his wife, dau. of king in the South African Daniel Seer; born War, as Sergeant in the at Worcester 17 Protectorate Regiment, February 1868; afterwards promoted for marr. at Johannes-services to be a Lieu-burg 11 November tenant in Driscoll's 1889. Scouts.

Florence Edith, born at Roodepoort, South Africa, 19 December 1890, and bapt. at Krugersdorp, South Africa; died at Roodepoort 27 August 1891, and bur. at St. Nicholas', Krugersdorp.

Norman Arthur Phillips, born at Maraisburg, South Africa, 22 September 1893, and bapt. there.

Constance Alice, born at Florida, near Johannesburg, 2 January 1895, and bapt. at Krugersdorp; died at Maraisburg 11 January 1896, and bur. there.

Cyril Alfred Phillips, born at Maraisburg, South Africa, 12 January 1897, and bapt. there.

Kathleen Sarah Lucy, born at Plympton St. Mary, co. Devon, 22 November 1863; marr. at St. George's, Beckenham, co. Kent (by the Rev. Edward Rivaz Fagan), on Thursday, 18 June 1891, Ernest Thomas Charles Joly (son of Stephen Joly, British Vice-Consul at Smyrna, by Sophie his wife, dau. of Henry Borrell of Smyrna); born in Smyrna 29 January 1859, bapt. at the Consular Chapel, Smyrna, 27 September 1860.

Harriet Sybella, born in Bermuda 4 August 1834, bapt. at St. George's, Bermuda, 31 January 1838; marr. at Newmarket, York County, Ontario, Canada, 11 September 1858, James Hutchison Esten (eldest son of James Christie Palmer Esten, Vice-Chancellor of Toronto, Canada, by Anne Frederick his wife, youngest dau. of the Honble Joseph Hutchison, Member of the Legislative Council of Bermuda [see *Pedigree of Hutchison, Vol. V., page 71*]); born at Exeter, co. Devon, 23 February, bapt. at St. Sidwell's, Exeter, 6 April 1833; died at Toronto 13 June, bur. in St. James' Cemetery, Toronto, 14 June 1892.

Eliza Esten Pellowe, born in Bermuda 5 November 1836, bapt. at St. George's, Bermuda, 31 January 1838; marr. at Grahamstown, Cape of Good Hope, South Africa, 5 May 1860, Edwin Litchfield (son of Charles Litchfield, by Sarah his wife, dau. of Thomas Paget Sharpe); born at 3 Montague Place, Portman Square, London, 13 March 1834. She died at Hong Kong, China, 22 January 1861, and was bur. there in the Happy Valley the same day.

Frank Truscott Phillips, born at Hong Kong 20 November 1867, bapt. at St. George's Cathedral, Hong Kong, 11 March 1868; entered the Royal Marine Light Infantry as 2nd Lieutenant 1 February 1888, Lieutenant 1 April 1889, Assistant Gunnery Instructor 18 August 1893 to 7^a December 1894, Captain (1st Division) 1 April 1897.

Emily May, born at Hong Kong 18 May 1869, and bapt. in St. George's Cathedral, Hong Kong; died 19 June 1870, and bur. at Somerset East, Cape of Good Hope.

Daisy Frances, born at Somerset East, Cape of Good Hope, 10 May 1870, and bapt. in the parish church at Somerset East (by Canon Woodrooffe) June following.

Mary Rose, born at Stoke, Devonport, co. Devon, 14 March, bapt. at Stoke Damerel, co. Devon, 24 May 1872.

Margaret Edith Douglas, born at Avenue Lodge, Hillingdon, co. Middlesex, 16 November 1865, bapt. at the parish church, Hillingdon, 24 March 1866; died at Hornsey, co. Middlesex, aged 4 years and 5 months, on Wednesday, 13 April, bur. in Islington Cemetery, co. Middlesex, 16 April 1870.

Douglas Phillips, born at Tollington Park, co. Middlesex, 22 November 1867, bapt. at the parish church, Tollington Park, 17 February 1868; died 10 January, bur. in Islington Cemetery 13 January 1870.

Georgina Constance, born at South Penge Park, co. Surrey, in October 1873, and died there in April 1875.

Alfred Goldney Phillips, born in Bermuda in 1840, bapt. at St. George's, Bermuda, 13 February 1842; died of yellow fever in Bermuda 26 August 1843, and bur. at St. George's the same day.

Selina Louisa Laurence, born in Bermuda 16 October 1842, bapt. at St. George's, Bermuda, 14 March 1843; marr. at St. Michael's, Heavitree, co. Devon, 12 October 1875, the Rev. James Baxter Strother (eldest son of Anthony Strother of Eastfield Hall, co. Northumberland, by Ann his wife, dau. of William Manderson); born at Woolwich, co. Kent, 30 October, and bapt. privately 24 November 1832; of Magdalen Hall, Oxford, matriculated 3 June 1854, aged 21, B.A. and M.A. 1863; Rector of St. Mary Steps, Exeter, co. Devon, 1864–76, and Vicar of Shaugh Prior, co. Devon, 1878–90; died at Kirknewton, Newton Abbot, co. Devon, aged 67, on Saturday, 9 December, bur. at St. Andrew's, Kenn, co. Devon, 14 December 1899. Will dated 11 March 1895, with codicil dated 7 June 1898, proved (Prin. Reg., 507, 1900) 8 March 1900, by the Rt. Hon[ble] William, Earl of Stamford, one of the Exors.

Violet Oak, born at Stoke, Devonport, co. Devon, 30 January, bapt. at Stoke Damerel, co. Devon, 2 May 1873; marr. at Sheviocke, co. Cornwall (by the Rev. Gerald Pole-Carew), 30 January 1901, the Rev. Arthur Ellis Cleather (only son of the Rev. George Ellis Cleather, Rural Dean, and Rector of Brixton Deverill, co. Wilts, by Jane his wife, dau. of John Russell of Piercefield Park, co. Monmouth, High Sheriff for that county); born at Cherington, co. Wilts, 9 November 1859; educated at Naval College, Portsmouth, and at Wadham College, Oxford, matriculated 21 January 1876, aged 19, B.A. of Charsley Hall 1883, M.A. 1884; Curate-in-Charge of Phillack with Gwithian, co. Cornwall, since 1900.

Thomas William Phillips, born at Stoke, Devonport, 29 March, bapt. at St. James', Keyham, co. Devon, 27 September 1874; 3rd Officer on s.s. "Jason," Ocean Steamship Co., and holds Captain's certificate 1903.

Norman Routh Phillips, born at Plymouth, co. Devon, 12 May, bapt. at St. James'-the-Less, Plymouth, 30 December 1875; entered the London Hospital 1 October 1893; M.R.C.S. Eng. and L.R.C.P. Lond. 29 January 1901; Resident Medical Officer, Queen Adelaide Dispensary, London, 14 February 1901; Assistant House Surgeon Kent and Canterbury Hospital 21 October 1901; Senior House Surgeon 1 March 1902.

B

Rev. Lionel Fremantle Phillips, born at Trelill, near Helston, co. Cornwall,——Anna Rosina, dau.
18 September, bapt. in the parish church of St. Wendron, co. Cornwall, | of Charles Gottlieb
30 November 1845; of Sidney Sussex College, Cambridge, B.A. 1867, M.A. | Niebel, and widow
1873; Curate of West Alvington, co. Devon, 1870–72; Assistant-Master | of Henry Warren
Mussoorie School, India, 1872–77, Officiating Head-Master of St. Paul's | Walker; born at
School, Darjeeling, India, 1877–78, Head-Master Allahabad Boys' High | Darjeeling, India,
School, 1878–80; Chaplain Bengal Ecclesiastical Establishment 1880–1900, | 17 August 1856;
at Allahabad 1880–82, Fyzabad, 1882–85, Landour and Dehra 1885–87, | marr. at St. Andrew's,
Agra 1887–90; Assistant Curate of St. Mary Magdalen's, Launceston, co. | Darjeeling, 20 De-
Cornwall, 1891–92, at Lucknow 1892–94, Muttra 1894–98, Landour and | cember 1877.
Dehra 1898–99; retired in 1900.

Lionel Fremantle Phillips

Frances Hutchison, born at Allahabad, North-West Province, India, 1 August, bapt. at Holy Trinity, Allahabad, 22 August 1879.

George Lionel Esten Phillips, born at Allahabad 11 July, bapt. in Cantonment Church Room 1 August 1881; died at Fyzabad, India, 25 May, bur. in the cemetery at Fyzabad 26 May 1882.

Harriette Hervey, born at Fyzabad 7 June, bapt. privately 15 June 1883; died at Fyzabad 25 September 1885, bur. in the cemetery at Fyzabad the same evening.

Charles Truscott Phillips, born at Landour 7 October, bapt. at St. Paul's, Landour, 29 October 1887.

—

Elfrida Victoria Pellowe, born at Launceston 20 June, bapt. at St. Mary Magdalen's, Launceston, 7 August 1892.

E

Lilian Louise, born at Plymouth, co. Devon, 21 May, bapt. at St. James'-the-Less, Plymouth, 7 October 1876.

John Boys Phillips, born at Plymouth 4 September, bapt. at St. James'-the-Less, Plymouth, 9 December 1877, died at Downderry, co. Cornwall, 19 May, bur. at Hessenford, near St. Germans, co. Cornwall, 23 May 1891.

Claud Hutchison Phillips, born at Mutley, near Plymouth, 7 December 1880, bapt. at St. James'-the-Less, Plymouth, 5 February 1881; joined the training ship "Worcester" 1 February 1895; killed by a fall from the mast of sailing ship "Sardomene," on his homeward voyage, 3 November 1897, and bur at sea the next day.

J. H. B. Phillips

Cave-Browne-Cave of Stanford, co. Northampton.

Arms on record in the College of Arms.— Quarterly : 1st and 4th, Azure, fretty argent, *Cave ;* 2nd and 3rd, Azure, a chevron between three escallops or, all within a bordure engrailed gules, *Browne.*

*Crests.—*1, A greyhound courant sable, collared argent, *Cave;* 2, A stork proper, winged and gorged with a ducal coronet or, beaked and membered gules.

*Motto over Cave crest.—*Gardez.

Sir William Cave-Browne-Cave of Stanford, co. Northampton, and of Stretton Hall, in the parish of Stretton-en-le-Field, co. Derby, Bart. (eldest son and heir of John Cave-Browne of Stretton Hall, by Catherine his 2nd wife, dau. and heiress of Thomas Astley of Wood Eaton, co. Stafford, and of Astley, co. Salop) ; born 19 February, bapt. at Stretton-en-le-Field 25 March 1765 ; succeeded his cousin, the Rev. Sir Charles Cave, as 9th Bart. 21 March 1810 ; assumed the surname of Cave in addition to and after that of Cave-Browne, which surnames were confirmed to his issue, male, together with the arms of Browne quarterly with those of Cave, by Royal Licence dated 18 January 1839 ; marr. 1stly at Croxall, co. Derby, 13 October 1788, Sarah, dau. of Thomas Prinsep of Croxall, who was bur. at Stretton-en-le-Field 21 June 1790, having had issue a son, who died young. Sir William Cave-Browne-Cave died, aged 73, 24 August, and was bur. at Stretton-en-le-Field 29 August 1838. Brass tablet on wall of chancel at Stretton-en-le-Field. Will dated 14 October 1835, proved (P.C.C., 686 *Nicholl*) 12 November 1838, by the Rev. Edward Sacheverell Cave-Browne-Cave, the son, the sole Exor.

=Louisa, 4th dau. of Sir Robert Meade Wilmot of Chaddesden, co. Derby, Bart., by Mary his wife, dau. and heiress of William Woollett ; born 8 February 1771, bapt. privately the same day (baptism registered at Chaddesden); marr. at Stretton-en-le-Field 4 January 1793 ; died, aged 53, 23 April, bur. at Stretton-en-le-Field 30 April 1824. 2nd wife.

A

William Cave-Browne-Cave, bapt. at Stretton-en-le-Field 8 June, and bur. there 30 June 1794. —

Harriot, bapt. at Stretton-en-le-Field 7 July 1795 ; marr. there (by the Rev. John Cave-Browne-Cave) 4 September 1832, William Booth of Beighton, co. Derby ; Major 15th Light Dragoons.

Louisa Catharine, bapt. at Stretton-en-le-Field 19 October 1796 ; bur. there 24 February 1810.

Sir John Robert Cave-Browne-Cave of Stanford, co. Northampton, and of Stretton Hall, in the parish of Stretton-en-le-Field, co. Derby, Bart. ; born at Stretton-en-le-Field 4 March, bapt. there 10 May 1798 ; authorised, with his brothers, by Royal Licence dated 18 January 1839, to continue the use of the surname of Cave and to bear the arms of Browne in the 2nd quarter; High Sheriff for co. Derby 1844 ; succeeded his father as 10th Bart. 24 August 1838 ; died at Stretton Hall, in his 58th year, on Sunday, 11 November, bur. at Stretton-en-le-Field 17 November 1855. M.I. Will dated 23 September 1852, proved (P.C.C., 13, 56) 9 January 1856, by Dame Catharine Penelope Cave-Browne-Cave, the relict, and Sir Mylles Cave-Browne-Cave, Bart., the son, the Exors.

=Catharine Penelope, youngest dau. and coheir of William Mills of Barlaston Hall, co. Stafford ; born 25 June, bapt. at Basford, co. Nottingham, 10 October 1799 ; marr. at Kenilworth, co. Warwick, 22 November 1821 ; died there, aged 71, on Monday, 13 March, bur. at Stretton-en-le-Field 29 March 1871. M.I. Will dated 20 January 1869, with two codicils of same date, proved at Birmingham 10 May 1871, by John Balguy of Longton Hall, Stoke-upon-Trent, co. Stafford, and Thomas Heath of Warwick, the Exors.

B

Eliza Martha, 2nd dau. of Samuel Wathen of New House, co. Gloucester; marr. at Stroud, co. Gloucester (by the Rev. John Williams, D.D.), on Wednesday, 2 May 1828; died s.p., aged 24, 6 November, bur. at Stretton-en-le-Field, co. Derby, 11 November 1828. M.I. 1st wife.	Rev. William Astley Cave-Browne-Cave, born 3 August 1799, bapt. privately the next day (baptism registered at Stretton-en-le-Field); of Brasenose College, Oxford, matriculated 14 January 1818, aged 18, B.A. 1821, M.A. 1824; Rector of Flixton, co. Lancaster, 1823–42, and of Stretton-en-le-Field 1843 until his death; died suddenly at Penmaenmawr, co. Carnarvon, aged 62, on Friday, 13 June, bur. at Stretton-en-le-Field 19 June 1862. Memorial tablet on chancel wall at Stretton-en-le-Field. Will dated 4 July 1860, proved (Prin. Reg., 377, 62) 30 July 1862, by John Campbell of Liverpool, co. Lancaster, and Charles Lee Minton of Newstead, co. Stafford, the Exors.	Julia, dau. of Thomas Minton of Stoke-upon-Trent, co. Stafford; marr. by licence at St. Peter-ad-Vincula, Stoke-upon-Trent (by the Rev. Benjamin Vale), 25 March 1830; died at Colwall Court, Great Malvern, co. Worcester, on Thursday, 6 September 1866. Will dated 24 November 1855, with codicil dated 22 April 1864, proved (Prin. Reg., 693, 66) 21 November 1866, by John Campbell of The Grove, Toxteth Park, Liverpool, co. Lancaster, one of the Exors. 2nd wife.

Louisa Wilmot, bapt. at Flixton 31 March 1833; marr. at Stretton-en-le-Field (by her father) 3 August 1853, Colin Minton Campbell of Hartshill and Woodseat, co. Stafford (eldest son of John Campbell of Liverpool, by Mary his wife, dau. of Thomas Minton of Stoke-upon-Trent); born at Liverpool 27 August 1827; Member Society of Arts 1860; J.P. and D.L. for co. Stafford, High Sheriff 1869; M.P. for North Stafford 10 February 1874 to 24 March 1880; formerly Major 1st Stafford Rifle Volunteers and Captain 20th Staffordshire Yeomanry; died at Woodseat, in the parish of Rocester, co. Stafford, aged 57, on Sunday, 8 February 1885. Bronze statue of him, by Thomas Brock, R.A., unveiled at Stoke-upon-Trent 1 January 1887. Will dated 16 February 1882, proved (Prin. Reg., 320, 85) 23 April 1885, by John Fitzherbert Campbell of Woodseat, in the parish of Rocester, co. Stafford, the son, Herbert Campbell of 43 South Hill Road, Toxteth Park, Liverpool, co. Lancaster, the brother, and Samuel Herbert Cooper of Newcastle-under-Lyme, co. Stafford, the Exors.

B

Sir Mylles Cave-Browne-Cave of Stanford, co. Northampton, and of Stretton-en-le-Field, co. Derby, Bart.; born 1 August, bapt. at Kenilworth, co. Warwick, 31 November 1822; educated at Eton; D.L. for the counties of Derby, Leicester and Warwick, J.P. for co. Derby; formerly Lieutenant 11th Hussars, and Major Derbyshire Yeomanry Cavalry 1864–74; succeeded his father as 11th Bart. 11 November 1855; Patron of the living of Stretton-en-le-Field.	Isabella, youngest dau. and coheiress of John Taylor of "The Newarke," Leicester, and of Stretton Hall, in the parish of Stretton-en-le-Field, co. Derby; marr. at Stretton-en-le-Field (by the Rev. William Astley Cave-Browne-Cave, the Rector, uncle of the bridegroom) on Tuesday, 15 May 1855.	C

Millicent Rosamond, born at the residence of her grandfather, "The Newarke," Leicester, on Friday, 23 May, bapt. at St. Mary's, Leicester, 31 May 1856; marr. at Stretton-en-le-Field (by the Rev. Nigel Gresley, Rector of Over and Nether Seale, co. Derby) 3 February 1885, William Wentworth Clapham of Crumpsall House, co. Lancaster (son of Charles Clapham, by Elizabeth Anne his wife, dau. of William Chadwick); born at Wakefield, co. York, 1 June 1841, and bapt. there.	Geoffrey Lisle Cave-Browne-Cave, born at "The Newarke," Leicester, on Thursday, 5 November, bapt. at St. Mary's, Leicester, 10 November 1857; died at Trevandrum, South India, aged 22, 17 September 1880, and bur. there. M.I. at Stretton-en-le-Field.	Mabel, born at "The Newarke," Leicester, on Friday, 15 May, bapt. at St. Mary's, Leicester, 6 June 1863. —— Genille Cave-Browne-Cave, born 3 September, bapt. at Stretten-en-le-Field 3 October 1869. —— Muriel, born 14 February, bapt. at Stretton-en-le-Field on Easter Day, 28 March 1875.

B

Thomas Cave-Browne-Cave of⊤Anne, eldest dau. of John Walker of Broom House, Levenshulme, Cliff Hall, co. Warwick, and │ and of Stockport and Manchester, all co. Lancaster; born 10 of Repton Lodge, co. Derby; │ March 1806; marr. at Manchester 10 April 1827; died at born 16 June, bapt. privately 21 │ Wellington Lodge, Harborne, co. Stafford, aged 69, on June 1801 (baptism registered at │ Saturday, 27 March, bur. at Harborne 2 April 1875. Will Stretton-en-le-Field, co. Derby); │ dated 21 March 1866, proved (Prin. Reg., 291, 75) 14 April 1875, died, aged 52, 17 April, bur. │ by John Walker Cave-Browne-Cave of Mount Pleasant, Liverpool, at Newton-Solney, co. Derby, │ co. Lancaster, and Thomas Cave-Browne-Cave of 7 Kempshott 22 April 1854. │ Road, Streatham, co. Surrey, the sons, two of the Exors.

Rev. John Walker Cave-Browne-Cave of Lifford Hall, King's⊤Hannah, dau. of Edward Norton, co. Worcester, and of Clarence House, Southport, co. │ Johnson of Full Sutton, co. Lancaster; born 5 September 1828, bapt. privately the next │ York; born 9 June, bapt. at Full day (baptism registered at Stretton-en-le-Field); Hon. Curate of │ Sutton (by the Rev. James Rudd, Birdingbury, co. Warwick, 1900; licenced to officiate in the dioceses │ the Rector) on Monday, 20 of Worcester and Liverpool 1900; died, aged 74, 21 October, bur. │ June 1825; marr. 3 February at King's Norton 24 October 1902. Will dated 20 April 1897, │ 1850; died, aged 70, bur. at proved at Liverpool 27 November 1902, by Henry Wilmot │ King's Norton 29 January 1896. Cave-Browne-Cave, M.D., the son, one of the Exors.

| Edward Johnson Cave-Browne-Cave of Bootle, co. Lancaster; born 14 December 1851; marr. at Balliol Road Wesleyan Chapel, Bootle, 1 July 1880, Phœbe Hannah, dau. of Stephen Andrews of Bootle.

⊤
人

Mary Annie Sophia, born at Armfield Hall, co. York. | Hannah Louisa, marr. at St. Nicholas', King's Norton (by the Rev. Frederick William Barrows, brother-in-law of the bride), on Tuesday, 26 June 1889, the Rev. James Leigh (son of Thomas Leigh of Claughton, co. Chester, by Selina Victoria his wife, dau. of William Vaughan of Liverpool); of Christ's College, Cambridge, M.A.; Curate of Farnworth, co. Lancaster, 1889–91, of Parr, co. Lancaster, 1891–93, of St. Silas', Liverpool, 1893–96, of Holy Trinity, Darwen, co. Lancaster, 1897, of Stanwix, co. Cumberland, 1898–99, and of Kimberworth, co. York, since 1899. | Emily Wilmot, marr. at Liverpool 30 June 1877, George David Welding of Freshfield, King's Norton; born at Liverpool 24 April 1855. ⎯

Amelia Frances Alberta, died unmarried 4 May 1886, and bur. at King's Norton. ⎯

Henry Wilmot Cave-Browne-Cave of King's Norton; born 6 April 1863; educated at St. Thomas' Hospital; M.R.C.S. Eng. 1892, L.R.C.P.I. and L.M., L.R.C.S.I. and L.M. 1892. |

Julia Mead, bapt. at Flixton, co. Lancaster, 17 June 1834; marr. at Stretton-en-le-Field (by her father) 29 March 1854, the Rev. Howard England Tunnicliff Gough of Gorsebrook House, co. Stafford, and of Colwall Court, Great Malvern, co. Worcester (3rd son of Ralph Gough of Gorsebrook House); of St. John's College, Cambridge, matriculated Michaelmas Term, 1848, B.A. 1852, M.A. 1861; Vicar of Hartshill, co. Stafford; died at St. Helier, Jersey, 18 January 1867. Admon (with will dated 31 November 1866) was granted (Prin. Reg., 411, 67) 15 June 1867, to Julia Mead Gough of Leamington Priors, co. Warwick, the relict, the universal legatee in trust and one of the legatees named in the said will.

⊤
人

Louisa Rosamond Sophia, died at Stretton-en-le-Field, aged 23, on Wednesday, 29 September, bur. there 6 October 1847. M.I. | Elizabeth Louisa Maria, died at Kenilworth, co. Warwick, aged 37, on Sunday, 6 August, bur. at Stretton-en-le-Field 12 August 1865. M.I. Will dated 9 November 1861, proved at Birmingham 29 June 1866, by Rowland Cotton of Bentley Hall, Ashbourne, co. Derby, one of the Exors.

Mary, eldest dau. of═Rev. Wilmot Cave-Browne-Cave, born 5 December,═Mary, eldest dau. William Eccles of Daven-ham, co. Chester, and of Eccles, co. Lancaster; marr. 30 October 1824; died, aged 20, and bur. at Stretton-en-le-Field, co. Derby, 26 November 1824. M.I. 1st wife. | bapt. at Stretton-en-le-Field 21 December 1802; of St. Alban Hall, Oxford, matriculated 3 June 1823, aged 20; Vicar of Hope and Perpetual Curate of Derwent, both co. Derby, Perpetual Curate of Altrincham, co. Chester, 14 February 1834, and of Homerton, co. Middlesex, 1856; died s.p., aged 56, 6 May 1857. Will dated 29 June 1849, proved (P.C.C., 361, 57) 25 May 1857, by Mary Cave-Browne-Cave, the relict, the sole Executrix. | of the Rev. Tho-mas Westmoreland, Vicar of Sandal Magna, co. York; marr. at Sandal Magna 27 October 1825. 2nd wife.

D   D

Sarah Wilmot, born 6 June 1830, bapt. privately the next day (baptism registered at Stretton-en-le-Field); marr. at Harborne Heath, co. Stafford (by the Rev. Thomas Smith, assisted by the Rev. Henry Webb Garrett), on Tuesday, 7 April 1863, the Rev. Charles Thomas Cary of Arden House, Fillongley, co. Warwick (3rd son of the Rev. Henry Francis Cary, translator of Dante); of Magdalen Hall, Oxford, matriculated 16 December 1825, aged 19, B.A. 1829, M.A. 1832; Vicar of Kingsbury, co. Warwick, 1832–75; died at Arden House, Fillongley, aged 75, on Wednesday, 15 June, bur. at Nether Whitacre, co. Warwick, 18 June 1881. She died suddenly at Arden House, Fillongley, aged 63, on Wednesday, 3 January, and was bur. at Nether Whitacre 6 January 1894. Will dated 16 December 1892, proved at Birmingham 1 February 1894, by the Rev. Arthur Bicknell Stevenson and Frank Wyamarus Cave-Browne-Cave, the brother, the Exors. | William Cave-═Maria, youngest Browne - Cave | daughter of John of Wellington | Thornicroft of "The Lodge, Har-| Ravenhurst," Har-borne, co. Staf-| borne, by Anne his ford; born 26 | wife, dau. of James October, bapt. | Sadler of Edgbaston, at Stretton-en-| co. Warwick; marr. le-Field 2 No-| at Harborne (by vember 1831. | the Rev. Jordayne | Cave-Browne-Cave, | brother of the | bridegroom) on | Wednesday, 1 Au-| gust 1877.

Stretton Cave-Browne-Cave, born 8 September 1878, and bapt. at Harborne; educated at Malvern College. | Mary, born 28 June 1880, and bapt. at Harborne; marr. there (by the Rev. William James Price, the Vicar, assisted by the Rev. Thomas Cave-Moyle, her cousin, and the Rev. Rupert Stanley Strong) 29 April 1903, Dr. Herbert Vaughan Craster of Stillington, co. York. | Margaret Wilmot, born 15 January, 1884, and bapt. at Harborne.

E

Evelyn Rosamond, marr. at King's Norton, co. Worcester (by the Rev. C. J. Taylor, brother-in-law of the bridegroom), on Monday, 15 February 1886, the Rev. Frederick William Barrows (eldest son of Joseph Barrows of Himley, co. Stafford); of Clare College, Cambridge, matriculated Michaelmas Term, 1880, B.A. 1884, M.A. 1888; Rector of Birdingbury, co. Warwick, since 1892. She died at Lifford Hall, co. Worcester, leaving issue, on Monday, 25 August, and was bur. in the churchyard at King's Norton 28 August 1890. He marr. 2ndly at Old Swinford, co. Worcester, on Tuesday, 4 August 1891, Florence Holmes, 5th dau. of W. J. Turney of Park Hill, Old Swinford. ═

C   C

Rev. William Cecil Cave-Browne-Cave, born 8 October, bapt. at Flixton, co. Lancaster, 13 December 1835; of Magdalen College, Oxford, matriculated 7 December 1854, aged 19, B.A. 1860, M.A. 1862; Vicar of St. Thomas', North Shore, Sydney, New South Wales, 1871; marr. 15 February 1864, Rachel Perrins, dau. of the Rev. Hugh Smith Cumming, Vicar of Seaforde, co. Down.

B   B

Hyacinthe Ellen, marr. at All Saints', Margaret Street, London (by the Rt. Rev. Henry Philpott, D.D., Bishop of Worcester, assisted by the Rev. Charles Henry Christie), on Saturday, 10 July 1875, as his 2nd wife, the Rev. Henry John Torre of Norton Curlieu, co. Warwick (only son of the Rev. Henry Torre, Rector of Thornhill, co. York, by Mary Ellen his 1st wife, eldest dau. of Ellis Leckonby Hodgson of Stapleton Park, co. York); of University College, Oxford, matriculated 8 December 1837, aged 18, B.A. 1841. He marr. 1stly, 30 April 1850, Emma Matilda Wilmot.

A

Rev. Edward Sacheverell Cave-Browne-Cave, born⹀Mary, only surviving dau. of John
3 October 1804, bapt. privately the next day (baptism | (Farsyde) Watson of Bilton Park, co.
registered at Stretton-en-le-Field, co. Derby); of | York, J.P. and D.L.; marr. at Knares-
Brasenose College, Oxford, matriculated 9 April 1823, | borough, co. York, 7 July 1830; died at
aged 18, B.A. 1827, M.A. 1830; Vicar of Stow and | Hereford, aged 68, and bur. in the City
Gayton, co. Stafford, 1837; died, in his 38th year, | Cemetery, Hereford, 12 September
7 August, bur. at Stretton-en-le-Field 12 August 1842. | 1874. M.I. at Stretton-en-le-Field.
M.I. Admͦn was granted (P.C.C., 241, 43) 27 May
1843, to Mary Cave-Browne-Cave, the relict.

F

D   D

Frances Emily, bapt. at | Thomas Cave-Browne-Cave of⹀Blanche Matilda Mary Anne, dau.
Stretton-en-le-Field 20 | "Burnage," Streatham Com- | of Sir John Milton of "High
September 1833; marr. at | mon, co. Surrey; born at | Elms," Streatham Common, C.B.,
Kingsbury, co. Warwick | "Bloomsbury," Charlton-upon- | Accountant-General of the Army,
(by the Rev. Charles | Medlock, co. Lancaster, 11 | by Blanche his wife, dau. of
Thomas Cary, the Vicar, | April, bapt. at Altrincham, co. | Thomas Meyrick Feild of Maid-
brother-in-law of the bride), | Chester, 16 April 1835; entered | stone, co. Kent; born at
on Thursday, 28 April 1864, | the War Office in April 1853, | Lansdowne Villas, West Brompton,
William Hanmer France. | retired as Deputy Accountant- | London, on Friday, 7 March
She died at Sandford Road, | General in April 1900; | 1851; marr. at Immanuel Church,
Moseley, co. Worcester, | Commissioner of the Royal | Streatham (by the Rev. William
aged 48, on Saturday, | Hospital, Chelsea, since 1899, | Milton, uncle of the bride, assisted
8 April, and was bur. at | and a Member of the Central | by the Rev. Stenton Eardley),
Moseley 12 April 1882. | Consultative Council on War | on Saturday, 30 April 1870.
| Relief Funds Organisation.

Blanche Isabelle, born at 7 Kemp- | Beatrice Mabel, born | Thomas Reginald Cave-Browne-
shott Road, Streatham Common, | at 7 Kempshott Road, | Cave, born at "Burnage,"
on Wednesday, 12 July 1871, and | Streatham Common, on | Streatham Common, 11 January,
bapt. privately; died, aged 28 days, | Saturday, 30 May, bapt. | bapt. at the parish church,
and bur. in Norwood Cemetery, | at Immanuel Church, | Streatham, 1 March 1885;
co. Surrey, 12 August 1871. | Streatham, 25 June 1874. | Engineer Cadet R.N.

Jeannette Gertrude, born at | Frances Evelyn, born | Henry Meyrick Cave-Browne-
7 Kempshott Road, Streatham | 21 February, bapt. | Cave, born at "Burnage," Streat-
Common, on Monday, 16 Sep- | at Immanuel Church, | ham Common, 1 February, bapt.
tember, bapt. at Immanuel Church, | Streatham, 23 March | at the parish church, Streatham, 3
Streatham, 8 October 1872. | 1876. | April 1887; Engineer Cadet R.N.

C   C

Charles Wenman Cave-Browne-Cave, bapt. at Flixton, co. Lancaster, 19 May 1837; died at
the Parsonage, Flixton, aged 3 years and 10 months, on Sunday, 17 January, bur. at Flixton
24 January 1841.

B   B

Rev. Verney Cave-Browne-Cave, born 30 January 1833; of Exeter College, Oxford, matriculated
12 June 1851, aged 18, B.A. 1855, M.A. 1859; died at Norton Curlieu, co. Warwick, aged 57,
on Tuesday, 30 September 1890. Will dated 18 March 1890, proved (Prin. Reg., 1091, 90)
16 December 1890, by Hyacinthe Ellen Torre, wife of the Rev. Henry John Torre of Norton
Curlieu, co. Warwick, the sister, the sole Executrix.

F   F

Louisa Mary, born 6 June 1832; died unmarried,
aged 65, on Wednesday, 27 January 1897.

D

Roger Cave-Browne-Cave, born at Barton-under-Needwood, co. Stafford, 10 November 1836,
bapt. at Stretton-en-le-Field, co. Derby, 15 April 1837; lost in the wreck of the "Burmah"
23 November 1859.

C   D

Harriet Ellen, 3rd dau. of William=	Rev. Fitzherbert Astley Cave-=	Frances Esther Anne,
Beckwith of Seacox Heath, co.	Browne-Cave, born 26 October	youngest dau. of
Sussex; marr. at the parish church,	1839, bapt. privately the same	Courtney Kenny
Hove, co. Sussex (by the Rev. James	day (baptism registered at Flix-	Clarke of Larch Hill,
Vaughan, assisted by the Rev. Walter	ton, co. Lancaster); of Brasenose	co. Dublin, by Delia
Kelly), on Tuesday, 5 January 1869;	College, Oxford, matriculated	Priestley his wife, dau.
died suddenly at the Vicarage, Ellel,	16 June 1859, aged 19, B.A.	of Henry Edwards of
co. Lancaster, aged 33, on Saturday,	(Hulmeian Exhibitioner) 1863,	"Pyenest," co. York;
10 May, bur. at Ellel 14 May 1873.	M.A. 1866; Vicar of Horton,	born 25 January
Will dated 6 May 1870, proved at	co. Northampton, 1867–69, of	1848, and bapt. at
Lancaster 23 July 1873, by Mary	Ellel, co. Lancaster, 1869–74,	St. George's, Sowerby,
Jane Longcroft (wife of Thomas	of Padiham, co. Lancaster, 1874	co. York; marr. at
Crawford Longcroft, Deputy Adjutant-	–77, and of Longridge, co. Lan-	St. Stephen's, Upper
General at Madras, India) of 4 Den-	caster, 1877; died 14 January,	Mount, Dublin (by
mark Terrace, Brighton, co. Sussex,	bur. at Longridge 17 January	the Rev. William
the sister, the sole Executrix.	1894. Will dated 12 June 1885,	Robinson, Vicar of
Probate being granted under certain	proved at Lancaster 2 April	Tallaght, co. Dublin,
limitations. Admͦon (with the will)	1894, by Frances Esther Anne	assisted by the Rev.
left unadministered by Mary Jane	Cave-Browne-Cave, the relict,	James Walsh, B.D.),
Longcroft, the sister, the sole Execu-	William Marsden and Henry	on Friday, 23 June
trix, was granted (Prin. Reg., 826, 79)	James Leonard, M.B., the Exͦors.	1875. 2nd wife.
7 April 1879, to the Rev. Fitzherbert		
Astley Cave-Browne-Cave of Long-		
ridge Vicarage, Preston, co. Lancaster		
a legatee. 1st wife.		G

Cecil Beckwith Cave-Browne-Cave of Chesham Bois=	Sarah Eleanor, 2nd dau. of John
Place, co. Buckingham; born at the Vicarage, Ellel, on	W. Nicholson of St. John, New Bruns-
Wednesday, 22 November, bapt. at Ellel 31 December	wick, Canada; marr. at St. George's,
1871; educated at Eton and at Brasenose College,	Hanover Square, London (by the
Oxford, matriculated 1889, B.A. 1894.	Rev. Everard Joseph Haynes), on
	Tuesday, 4 February 1896.

Cecil Fitzherbert Cave-Browne-Cave, born at Chesham
Bois Place on Thursday, 29 August 1901, and bapt.
privately; died in infancy.

B   B

Rev. Ambrose Sneyd Cave-Browne-Cave,=	Caroline Mary Anne Elizabeth, eldest dau. of the
born 31 August 1834; of Corpus Christi	Venble James Saurin, Archdeacon of Dromore;
College, Oxford, matriculated 17 June	born 5 September 1834; marr. at the parish church,
1852, aged 17, B.A. 1856; Rector of	Clontarf, co. Dublin (by the Rev. Edward Brooke,
Stretton-en-le-Field, co. Derby, 1860; died	uncle of the bride), on Thursday, 9 September
suddenly at Virginia Water, co. Surrey,	1858; died at Great Malvern, co. Worcester, in
aged 60, on Monday, 22 July 1895.	her 69th year, on Thursday, 16 April, bur. in the
	cemetery at Great Malvern 18 April 1903.
	H

F

F

Rev. Edward Farsyde Cave-==Sarah Maria, youngest dau. of William Marshall of Penwortham Browne-Cave of 5 The Hall, co. Lancaster, J.P., D.L.; marr. at the parish church, Uplands, St. Leonard's-on- St. Leonard's-on-Sea (by the Rev. Thomas Ross Finch, Rector of Sea, co. Sussex; born 10 Stafford, and the Rev. Fitzherbert Astley Cave-Browne-Cave, October 1833; of Jesus Vicar of Ellel, co. Lancaster, cousin of the bridegroom), on College, Cambridge, ma- Tuesday, 14 October 1873; died at 5 The Uplands, St. Leonard's- triculated Michaelmas Term, on-Sea, aged 63, on Saturday, 23 December, bur. in Hastings 1852, B.A. 1856, M.A. Cemetery at Ore, co. Sussex, 29 December 1899. Will dated 1859; Rector of Bretherton, 27 December 1895, proved at Lewes 6 February 1900, by the co. Lancaster, 1871–74. Rev. Edward Farsyde Cave-Browne-Cave and the Rev. Thomas Ross Finch, the Exors.

D

D

Wilmot Cave-Browne-Cave, born at Cliff Hall, co. Warwick, 3 June, bapt. at Stretton-en-le-Field, co. Derby, 1 July 1838; marr. at Colombo, Ceylon, 24 December 1860, Marie Annie, youngest child of William Skinner of Calcutta, India, and grand-daughter of Sir Robert Rollo Gillespie, K.C.B. He died in New Zealand in 1901.

Frances Catharine Delia, born at the Vicarage, Padiham, co. Lancaster, on Tuesday, 28 March 1876, and bapt. at Padiham.

—

Mary Julia Minton, born 11 July, bapt. at Longridge, co. Lancaster, 12 August 1877.

Violet Gertrude, born 4 April, bapt. at Longridge 11 May 1879.

—

Florence Mabel Fitzherbert, born 17 July, bapt. at Longridge 15 August 1880.

Lucy Wilmot, born 5 September, bapt. at Longridge 29 September 1882.

—

William Astley Cave-Browne-Cave, born 15 November, bapt. at Longridge 14 December 1884; educated at St. Catherine's School, Broxbourne, and at Lancing College.

Elsie Lilian, born 1 February, bapt. at Longridge 13 March 1887; died 21 May 1888, and bur. at Longridge the next day.

—

Courtney Priestley Edward Cave-Browne-Cave, born 4 December 1890, bapt. at Longridge 13 March 1891; educated at Leamington College and at Lancing College.

G

Lieut.-Colonel Bowyer Wenman Cave-Browne-Cave, born 22 March 1837; Captain and Brevet-Major 2nd Dragoon Guards; served with 9th Lancers from January 1861 to September 1874, and as Adjutant Royal Wilts Yeomanry Cavalry 1874–79; retired from the 2nd Dragoon Guards with rank of Lieut.-Colonel 17 December 1879; died in London, aged 61, on Thursday, 7 July, bur. in Kensal Green Cemetery, London, 9 July 1898.

B

H

James Saurin Cave-Browne-Cave, born at Seagoe House, co. Armagh, on Thursday, 21 July 1859; entered the Army as 2nd Lieutenant The King's Own Yorkshire Light Infantry, 13 November 1878, Lieutenant 20 September 1880, Captain 2nd Battalion 28 May 1884; served with his regiment and as Brigade Transport Officer in the Afghan War 1879–80; died unmarried, aged 32, on Sunday, 14 February, bur. in the cemetery at Great Malvern, co. Worcester, 17 February 1892. Admon was granted at the Principal Registry 22 June 1892, to Ambrose Sneyd Cave-Browne-Cave, gent.

H

159

F

Elizabeth, born 18 February 1835; died 31 January 1844.	William Edward Cave-Browne-Cave, born 21 February 1837, bapt. privately the same day (baptism registered at Stretton-en-le-Field, co. Derby; died at 20 King Street, Hereford, aged 65, on Saturday, 20 December, bur. in the cemetery at Hereford 23 December 1902.	Selina, born 19 December 1841; died 31 March 1844.

D   D

Rev. Henry Cave-Browne-Cave, born at=Maria Louisa, youngest dau. of George Chance of
Cliff Hall, co. Warwick, 27 January, bapt. Edgbaston, co. Warwick, and of New York, U.S.A.,
at Kingsbury, co. Warwick, 9 July 1840; by Cornelia Maria his wife, dau. of Arent Schuyler
Vicar of Edington, co. Wilts; died at de Peyster of New York; born in the City of
Edington 4 February, bur. there 8 Feb- New York 22 February 1840, bapt. at St. Mark's,
ruary 1890. Will dated 18 November Birmingham, 5 December 1842; marr. at the parish
1881, proved (Prin. Reg., 228, 90) 13 church, Edgbaston (by the Rev. Thomas Smith,
March 1890, by Arent de Peyster Chance Vicar of St. John's, Harborne Heath, co. Stafford),
of The Manor House, Northfield, co. on Wednesday, 11 October 1865.
Worcester, one of the Exors.

(*See Pedigree of Chance, Vol. 3, page 71.*)

Cornelia Maria, born 28 September, bapt. at St. Luke's, Edgbaston, 30 October 1866.	Maude Evelyn, born 29 May 1872, and bapt. at Clevedon, co. Somerset.	Eustace Henry Cave-Browne-Cave, born 3 February, bapt. at Rotherfield, co. Sussex, 24 February 1876; educated at Lancing College.	Irene de Peyster, born 5 February, bapt. at Edington 5 March 1882.

H   H

Reginald Ambrose Cave-Browne-Cave,=Evelyn, youngest dau. of the | Wilmot Cave-Browne-
born at the Rectory, Stretton-en-le- | Rev. Charles Edward Oakley, | Cave, born at the
Field, on Sunday, 21 October, bapt. at | Rector of Wickwar, co. Glou- | Rectory, Stretton-en-
Stretton-en-le-Field 11 November 1860; | cester, and of St. Paul's, | le-Field, on Friday, 11
entered the Royal Navy as Naval | Covent Garden, London, by | April, bapt. at Stretton-
Cadet 15 January 1873, Midshipman | Lady Georgina Mary Louisa | en-le-Field 4 May 1862.
19 December 1874, Sub-Lieutenant | his wife, eldest dau. of Henry
21 October 1879, Lieutenant 11 July | George Francis, 2nd Earl of | —
1882, Commander 31 December 1896; | Ducie; born at the Rectory,
served as Sub-Lieutenant H.M.S. | St. Paul's, Covent Garden, | Mary Geneviève, born
"Alexandra" at the bombardment of | London, 19 February, bapt. | at the Rectory, Stretton-
Alexandria 11 July 1882, for which he | at St. Paul's, Covent Garden, | en-le-Field, on Satur-
was promoted Lieutenant, and during | 11 May 1865; marr. at | day, 12 September,
Egyptian War (Egyptian medal, | Katoomba, New South Wales, | bapt. there 4 October
Alexandria clasp and Khedive's | 1 October 1890. | 1863; marr. 17 July
bronze star). | | 1894, George Arthur
| | Chenery.

Isabella Louisa Cave-Moyle, born at Cliff Hall, co. Warwick, 10 July 1841, bapt. at Kingsbury, co. Warwick, 8 August 1844; marr. at Harborne Heath, co. Stafford (by the Rev. Thomas Smith, assisted by the Rev. Charles Thomas Cary, Vicar of Kingsbury, brother-in-law of the bride), on Tuesday, 1 June 1869, Thomas Moyle, M.D.; died at "The Beeches," Ladywood Road, Edgbaston, co. Warwick, aged 74, on Friday, 22 May 1891. She assumed the additional surname of Cave before that of Moyle in 1891.

Rev. Jordayne Cave-Browne-Cave, born at Cliff Hall 17 February 1843, bapt. at Kingsbury 8 August 1844; Curate of Kilmington, co. Devon, and a Missionary of British Columbia 1862–70; died s.p. at 20 Wellesley Terrace, Belmont Road, St. Helier, Jersey, 12 December 1879. Will dated 6 October 1875, proved (Prin. Reg., 12, 80) 14 January 1880, by Charlotte Cave-Browne-Cave of 20 Wellesley Terrace, Belmont Road, St. Helier, Jersey, the relict, the sole Executrix.

=Charlotte Dewdney, marr. at St. Mary's, Sapperton (by the Bishop of British Columbia, assisted by the Rev. E. Hayman), on Thursday, 5 December 1867. She marr. 1stly Edward Wright of Penzance, co. Cornwall.

Rowland Henry=Cave-Browne-Cave, born at the Rectory, Stretton-en-le-Field, on Friday, 14 April, bapt. at Stretton-en-le-Field 30 June 1865.

Honora Phebe Gertrude, only surviving child of Benjamin Bright of Barton Court, Colwall, co. Hereford, by Frances Mary his wife, dau. of Fergus J. Graham, Consul at Bayonne; marr. 1 June 1895. She marr. 1stly Edward Seymour Fowler of Barton Court, Colwall, who died, leaving issue a daughter, 22 July 1893. Admon was granted at the Principal Registry 10 November 1893, to Honora Phebe Gertrude Fowler, the relict.

Catharine Penelope, born at the Rectory, Stretton-en-le-Field, on Tuesday, 26 June 1866, and bapt. at Stretton-en-le-Field; marr. at the Priory Church, Great Malvern, co. Worcester (by the Rev. Henry John Torre, uncle of the bride, and the Rev. Gregory Smith, the Vicar), on Thursday, 15 September 1887, William Crewdson Howard, elder son of John Elliot Howard of Tunbridge Wells, co. Kent, by Louisa his wife, dau. of Henry Waterhouse of Manchester.

D

Francis Wyamarus Cave-Browne-Cave of Edgbaston, co. Warwick; born at Cliff Hall, co. Warwick, 1 October, bapt. at Stretton-en-le-Field, co. Derby, 12 October 1844. ╤ Annie Mabel, 3rd dau. of Joseph Barrows of "The Limes," Himley, co. Stafford; bapt. at Himley 27 November 1859; marr. there (by the Rev. Henry Cave-Browne-Cave, Vicar of Edington, co. Wilts, brother of the bridegroom, assisted by the Rev. Edward Davies, the Rector, and the Rev. Charles Jarvis Taylor, brother-in-law of the bride) on Tuesday, 4 December 1883.

Anne, born at Cliff Hall 20 September 1847, bapt. at Stretton-en-le-Field, co. Derby, 12 October 1855; marr. at Harborne, co. Stafford (by the Rev. Edward Roberts, the Vicar), on Thursday, 30 July 1885, William Barnett-Bigley of "Southfield," Harborne, and of "Fairfield," Liverpool, co. Lancaster.

H

Bernard Cave-Browne-Cave, born at Osborn House, Great Malvern, on Saturday, 22 February 1868; Inspector Sierra Leone Frontier Police Force, and Captain Reserve of Officers, formerly Lieutenant 2nd Battalion Wiltshire (The Duke of Edinburgh's) Regiment; served in operations in Sierra Leone 1898–99, at the Mendiland Expedition with the Kwalu Relief Column (severely wounded, medal with clasps); served in South Africa 1900–1902, with rank of Captain, employed with Mounted Infantry (Queen's medal with four clasps, King's medal with two clasps).

—

Edward Lambert Cave-Browne-Cave, born at "The Chase," Great Malvern, on Wednesday, 5 January 1870; marr. Rachel, dau. of the Rev. A. L. Fortin of Brushton, New York, U.S.A.

Clement Andrew Cave-Browne-Cave, born at "Brookside," Bournemouth, co. Hants, on Monday, 7 August 1871.

—

Alfred William Cave-Browne-Cave, born at 1 Coburgh Place, Malvern, co. Worcester, on Sunday, 1 June, bapt. at the parish church, Great Malvern, 1 August 1873; died at 1 Coburgh Place, Malvern, aged 7 months and 7 days, on Thursday, 8 January 1874.

Rosamond Harriette, born at "The Myrtles," Malvern, on Advent Sunday, 29 November 1874, bapt. at the parish church, Great Malvern, 19 January 1875; marr. at the Priory Church, Malvern (by the Rev. George Frederick Woodhouse Munby, Rector of Turvey, co. Bedford, and Rural Dean), on Saturday, 29 April 1899, Edward Mason Munby (elder son of Edward Charles Munby of Oswaldkirk, co. York).

Caroline Emma, born at "The Myrtles," Malvern, on Tuesday, 13 November 1877, bapt. privately the same day (baptism registered at the parish church, Great Malvern); died at "The Myrtles," Malvern, aged 11 weeks, on Tuesday, 29 January, bur. in the cemetery at Great Malvern 31 January 1878.

Anthony Stanhope Cave-Browne-Cave, born at "The Myrtles," Malvern, on Saturday, 4 January, bapt. at the parish church, Great Malvern, 13 March 1879.

Myrtles C. B. Cave

Patchett of Broom Hall, Shrewsbury, co. Salop.

Arms on record in the College of Arms.—
Quarterly, per pale indented, azure and or,
in the 1st and 4th quarters a sword erect
proper, pommel and hilt gold; in the
2nd a leopard's face, and in the 3rd a
demi-dragon couped, wings elevated and
addorsed gules.

Crest.—A dexter arm embowed, couped
at the shoulder, vested argent, resting on a
mount vert, the hand grasping a pickaxe
proper, and between two dragons' wings
azure, each charged with a sword as in
the arms.

Septimus Patchett of Shirley, co. Warwick (son of Richard Patchett of Shirley); born at Shirley 10 August 1797; died at Chester, aged 71, 14 June, bur. in the cemetery at Chester 18 June 1868. = Elizabeth Harris, marr. at Solihull, co. Warwick, 21 July 1821; died at Chester, aged 55, 20 February, bur. in the churchyard of St. Mary's, Shrewsbury, co. Salop, 24 February 1853. M.I.

William Patchett of Broom Hall, Greenfields, Shrewsbury, co. Salop, and of "Allt Fawr," Barmouth, co. Merioneth; born 2 November, bapt. at Solihull 17 November 1822; Major 3rd Battalion King's Shropshire Light Infantry (Militia); J.P. and D.L. for co. Merioneth, and J.P. for co. Salop; High Sheriff for co. Merioneth 1898; died at Broom Hall, Greenfields, Shrewsbury, in his 78th year, on Friday, 29 June, bur. in the cemetery at Shrewsbury 5 July 1900. = Mercy Emily, 2nd dau. of George Townsend of Alcester, co. Warwick, by Lydia his wife, dau. of George Townshend; born 15 December 1816, bapt. at Alcester 6 January 1817; marr. at Stoke Prior, co. Worcester, 27 July 1844; died at Broom Hall, Greenfields, Shrewsbury, 2 November, bur. in the cemetery at Shrewsbury 6 November 1902. Admŏn was granted at Shrewsbury 2 December 1902, to William Gordon Patchett of Broom Hall, Greenfields, Shrewsbury, a retired Colonel in the Army, the natural and lawful son, and one of the next of kin.

A

Kate Arabella, born at Chester 15 October 1845.

Emily Mercy, born at Chester 19 July 1847; marr. at St. Mary's, Shrewsbury, 13 August 1874, the Rev. Thomas Lechmere Tudor Fitzjohn (only surviving son of Henry Fitzjohn of "Highfields," Thorner, co. York, by Anne his wife, dau. of John Heathcote of "Kingsland," Shrewsbury); born at Leeds, co. York, 18 June, bapt. at St. George's, Leeds (by the Rev. Thomas Sturgeon), 16 July 1847 (*Entry in Family Bible of Christenings at St. George's, Leeds:* "Sponsors, George Edensor Heathcote, Esqr, Apedale Hall, Staffordshire, Charles Heathcote"); of Caius College, Cambridge, matriculated Michaelmas Term, 1867, B.A. 1871, M.A. 1874; Vicar of Cardington, co. Salop, since 1883; appointed J.P. for co. Salop 1894.

Ellen Mary, dau. of the Rev. Charles Greene of "The Delles," Great Chesterford, co. Essex, Chaplain to the Forces, by Henrietta Eliza his wife, dau. of Henry Browne-Collison of "New England," Hitchen, co. Hertford; born in London 26 August 1847; marr. at Great Chesterford 16 January 1875; died at St. Servan, Ille-et-Villaine, France, 5 November, bur. at Great Chesterford 10 November 1897. Admon was granted at the Principal Registry 11 December 1897, to William Gordon Patchett, the husband. 1st wife.

= Lieut.-Colonel William Gordon Patchett of Broom Hall, Greenfields, Shrewsbury, co. Salop; born at Shrewsbury 16 October 1848; educated at Shrewsbury and at Trinity College, Dublin; entered the Army as Lieutenant 28 October 1871, Captain 3 October 1877, Major 6 May 1882, Lieut.-Colonel 2nd West India Regiment 2 February 1887, Lieut.-Colonel commanding 29 June 1887 (retired 27 July 1892); served in the Ashanti War 1873–74, including the engagements near Dunquah of 27 October and 3 November (wounded, medal); appointed Officer commanding Troops West Coast of Africa, and Administrator of the Government of Sierra Leone and its dependencies.

= Agatha Josephine Herberta, eldest dau. of Berthold, Baron Gynz von Rekowski, Colonel 77th Regiment Prussian Infantry, of Castle Stebendorf, Ottomachan, Silesia (Baroness in her own right), by his wife, Josephine Fischer of Neuss am Rhine; born at Neuss 26 March 1856; marr. at the parish church, Marylebone, London (by the Rev. Thomas Lechmere Tudor Fitzjohn, Vicar of Cardington, co. Salop, brother-in-law of the bridegroom, assisted by the Rev. Canon William Barker, the Rector), on Tuesday, 9 December 1902. She marr. 1stly Carl, Baron von Ketschendorf of Castle Ketschendorf, Coburg, Reise-Mareschall to H.R.H. Grand Duke Ernst of Saxe-Coburg and Gotha. He died in Paris 8 August 1900. 2nd wife.

Reginald Gordon Patchett, born in Jamaica, West Indies, 26 November, bapt. at the Garrison Chapel, Jamaica, on Christmas Day, 25 December 1875; educated at Wellington College.

Hugh Gordon Patchett, born at the residence of his grandmother, "The Delles," Great Chesterford, on Friday, 23 June, bapt. at Great Chesterford 31 July 1882.

Frederick George Patchett, bapt. at St. Mary's, Shrewsbury, 25 February, died, aged 2 months, 31 March 1850, bur. in the same grave as his grandmother, Elizabeth Patchett, in the churchyard at St. Mary's, Shrewsbury. M.I.

Annie Wylie, born at Shrewsbury 14 February 1853.

Constance Eleanor Margaret Lydia, born 25 August 1857, and bapt. at St. Mary's, Shrewsbury; died 20 April 1860, and bur. in the same grave with her parents at the cemetery, Shrewsbury.

De Chair.

Rev. Richard Blackett De Chair (only son of the Rev. John De Chair, D.C.L., Chaplain to George III., by Julia his wife, 3rd dau. of Sir William Wentworth of Bretton Hall, co. York, Bart.); born 13 June, bapt. 5 July 1760; of St. Mary's Hall, Oxford, matriculated 23 May 1783, aged 21, B.C.L. 1790; Vicar of Sibertswold, Coldred and Postling, co. Kent, and of Hibaldstow, co. Lincoln; died at Sibertswold, in his 90th year, on Wednesday, 26 March, bur. there 2 April 1851. Will dated 19 May 1842, with three codicils dated respectively 2 October 1846, 14 May 1847 and 25 February 1851, proved (P.C.C., 546, 51) 1 July 1851, by the Rev. Frederick De Chair, the son, the Exor named in will, and Chestney Simmons, the Exor named in the first codicil.

═Isabella, 2nd dau. of the Rev. Osmund Beauvoir, D.D., Fellow of St. John's College, Cambridge, Head Master King's School, Canterbury, by Anne his wife, dau. and coheir of John Boys of Hoad Court, Blean, co. Kent; marr. at St. James', Piccadilly, London, 10 July 1786; died at Sibertswold 28 August, bur. there 31 August 1832.

A

Isabella Mary, born at Oxford; died unmarried at Dover, co. Kent, on Sunday, 25 March, bur. at Sibertswold 2 April 1860. Will dated 2 July 1852, with codicil dated 3 March 1853, proved (Prin. Reg., 241, 60) 24 April 1860, by Chestney Simmons of Dover, co. Kent, Commander R.N., one of the Exors.

—

Osmund Blackett De Chair, died 12 June, bur. at Sibertswold 17 July 1801.

Henry William De Chair, Lieutenant Ceylon Regiment; marr. Margaret; died at Douglas, Isle of Man, 23 March 1826, and bur. there. Will dated 31 December 1874, proved (P.C.C., 525 *Swabey*) 10 October 1826, by Margaret De Chair, the relict, the sole Executrix.

B

Rev. Frederick Blackett De Chair, born at Dover 11 February, bapt. at St. James', Dover, 27 February 1838; educated at Marlborough and at Jesus College, Cambridge, matriculated Lent Term, 1857, B.A. 1861, M.A. 1864; Organizing Secretary S.P.G. for co. Norfolk 1874–82; Lecturer at Wymondham, co. Norfolk, 1885–88 and 1891–95, Hon. Canon of Norwich from 1892, Rural Dean of Hingham, Forehoe Division, 1891–1901, Patron and Rector of Morley St. Botolph with St. Peter, co. Norfolk, 1878–98, Rural Dean of Norwich since 1901; J.P. for co. Norfolk.

═Charlotte Elizabeth, only surviving child and heiress of the Rev. Charles Beauchamp Cooper, Rector of Morley, by Harriett his wife, dau. of George Daniel Harvey of Stanmore, co. Middlesex; born at Morley St. Botolph 17 March, bapt. there 11 April 1842; marr. at Morley St. Botolph (by the Rev. William Wigan Harvey, B.D., Rector of Buckland, co. Hertford, uncle of the bride, assisted by the Rev. Francis Raikes, Rector of Carleton Forehoe, co. Norfolk) on Thursday, 23 April 1863.

C

Rev. Frederick Beauchamp Cooper De Chair, born at the Rectory, Morley, on Wednesday, 1 March, bapt. at Morley St. Botolph 9 April 1865; educated at Marlborough and at New College, Oxford, matriculated 10 October 1884, aged 19, B.A. 1888, M.A. 1891; Rector of St. Peter Permountergate, Norwich, 1901–1903, Rector of Spixworth, co. Norfolk, since 1903.

═Brenda Atherton Hustler, younger dau. of George Hustler and Agnes Tuck of Blofield Hall, co. Norfolk, and granddaughter of the Rt. Honble Sir William Atherton, M.P., Attorney-General; born at Salhouse Hall, co. Norfolk, on Tuesday, 28 November 1882, bapt. at Salhouse 4 January 1883; marr. at St. Mark's, Lakenham, co. Norfolk (by the father of the bridegroom, assisted by the Rev. Canon James Percy Garrick, Rector of Blofield, and the Rev. John Huxley, the Vicar), on Tuesday, 7 July 1903.

Dudley De Chair, died at Sibertswold, co. Kent, 12 April, bur. there 17 April 1793.

—

Rev. John De Chair, educated at Eton and at Merton College, Oxford, matriculated 12 October 1810, aged 18, B.A. 1814, M.A. 1818; Vicar of Brixworth, co. Northampton; died 11 April, bur. at Sibertswold 17 April 1832.

Peregrine Edward De Chair, born at Sibertswold 30 June, bapt. there 4 August 1793; died at Sibertswold 21 June, bur. there 26 June 1795. —

Julia, died in infancy, bur. at Sibertswold 1 April 1795.

Osmund Beauvoir De Chair, born at the Rectory, East Langdon, co. Kent, on Saturday, 11 May, bapt. at East Langdon 18 June 1839; Lieutenant 4th Madras Light Cavalry; died at Kamptee, Madras, India, in 1857, and bur. there.

Isabel Louisa, born at Dover, co. Kent, 18 January, bapt. at St. James', Dover, 15 February 1841; marr. there (by the Rev. William Edward Light, the Rector) on Tuesday, 28 February 1865, Augustus William Shawe of the East Indian Civil Service, who was bur. at Ramsgate, co. Kent. She marr. 2ndly James Thomas Foard, eldest son of James Foard of Brighton, co. Sussex.

Richard Blackett De Chair, born at the Rectory, Morley, co. Norfolk, on Thursday, 24 May, bapt. at Morley St. Botolph 14 June 1866; educated at Marlborough; Lieutenant Royal Marine Light Infantry (Chatham Division); died at the Johannesburg Hospital, South Africa, aged 37, on Thursday, 17 September 1903, and bur. at Johannesburg. = Emily Frances, only child of William Standish Wolfe of Ballinswear, co. Tipperary, by Fanny his wife, dau. of Major George Jackson of Rapla, co. Tipperary; born 28 November 1867; marr. at St. Bartholomew's, Sydenham, co. Kent, on Saturday, 14 December 1889.

George Herbert Blackett De Chair, born at Brunswick House, West Hill, Sydenham, on Thursday, 30 July, bapt. at St. Stephen's, Sydenham, 13 September 1891.

Rev. Frederick De Chair, born at ⊤ Louisa Jane, eldest dau. of Richard Mee Raikes, by
Sibertswold, co. Kent, and bapt. there │ Jane his wife, dau. of Samuel Thornton of Albury Park,
8 September 1796; educated at Eton │ co. Surrey, M.P. for co. Surrey; born 10 August
and at Oriel College, Oxford, B.A. │ 1815; marr. at St. James', Dover, co. Kent (by the
1817, M.A. 1820; Rector of East │ Rev. Richard Blackett De Chair, father of the bride-
Langdon, co. Kent, and of Manton, │ groom), on Tuesday, 18 April 1837; died at 4 Marine
co. Lincoln; died at East Langdon │ Place, Dover, aged 51, on Monday, 16 April, bur. in
on Tuesday, 28 September, bur. at │ St. James' Cemetery, Dover, 19 April 1866. Will
Sibertswold 4 October 1852. Will │ dated 18 June 1863, proved (Prin. Reg., 374, 66) 18
dated 6 September 1852, proved │ June 1866, by the Rev. Frederick Blackett De Chair
(P.C.C., 822, 52) 22 November 1852, │ of Morley Rectory, near Wymondham, co. Norfolk,
by Louisa Jane De Chair, the relict, │ the son, the sole Exor.
the sole Executrix.

B

Dudley Raikes De ⊤ Frances Emily, eldest dau. of Christopher │ Georgiana Julia Maria, born
Chair, born at Dover │ Rawson of "The Hurst," Walton-on-Thames, │ at Dover 28 May, bapt. at
8 May, bapt. at East │ co. Surrey, and formerly of Elmwood, │ East Langdon 4 August 1846.
Langdon 5 August │ Lennoxville, Quebec, Canada East, J.P.
1842; died at 6 │ for co. Surrey, by Ellen Frances his wife, │ —
Vereker Road, Ken- │ dau. of John Naylor Wright of Princes
sington, London, in │ Park, Liverpool, co. Lancaster, and of │ Celia Julia Maria, born at
his 56th year, on │ Beaumaris, co. Anglesey; born 14 August │ East Langdon 14 February,
Thursday, 1 March │ 1841; marr. at St. George's, Lennoxville, │ bapt. there 13 April 1848;
1899. │ Quebec (by the Rt. Rev. the Bishop of │ died at Dover, aged 18, on
│ Quebec, assisted by the Rev. A. C. Scarth, │ Thursday, 4 October, bur.
│ the Incumbent), on Thursday, 10 December │ in St. James' Cemetery,
│ 1863. │ Dover, 11 October 1866.

D

Captain Dudley Rawson Stratford De Chair, ═ Enid, dau. of Henry William Struben of
R.N.; born at Lennoxville, Quebec, on │ "Strubenheim," Cape Colony, South Africa,
Tuesday, 30 August 1864, and bapt. at │ formerly of Cowes, Isle of Wight, by Mary Lydia
St. James', Lennoxville; entered the Royal │ his wife, dau. and coheir of the Rev. William
Navy as a Cadet 15 January 1878, served │ Graham Cole, formerly of Enniskillen, co.
with Naval Brigade during Egyptian War │ Fermanagh; born at Pretoria, Transvaal, South
1882, Sub-Lieutenant 19 May 1884 (5 firsts, │ Africa, 24 November 1879, and bapt. there by
Goodenough medal), promoted Lieutenant │ the Rt. Rev. Henry Brougham Bousfield, Bishop
19 May 1885, Commander 22 June 1897, │ of Pretoria; marr. at St. Mark's, Torquay, co.
Captain 26 June 1902; Naval Attaché, │ Devon (by the Rev. Frederick Blackett De Chair,
British Embassy, Washington, U.S.A. │ uncle of the bridegroom, assisted by the Rev.
│ George Herbert Statham, the Vicar), on Tuesday,
│ 21 April 1903.

A

Julia Frances Stanley, born at Sibertswold, co. Kent, in October, bapt. there 1 December 1800 ; marr. at St. Martin-in-the-Fields, Westminster, 13 July 1840, Captain Chestney Simmons, R.N. ; born 23 July 1798 ; died suddenly at 11 Victoria Park, Dover, co. Kent, in his 81st year, on Thursday, 26 June, bur. in St. James' Cemetery, Dover, 2 July 1879. Will dated 3 December 1852, proved (Prin. Reg., 737, 79) 11 August 1879, by Julia Frances Stanley Simmons of 11 Victoria Park, Dover, co. Kent, the relict, the sole Executrix. She died at 11 Victoria Park, Dover, aged 87, on Tuesday, 30 August, and was bur. in St. James' Cemetery, Dover, 2 September 1887. Will dated 16 June 1880, with codicil dated 21 February 1885, proved (Prin. Reg., 895, 87) 12 October 1887, by the Rev. Frederick Blackett De Chair of Morley Rectory, Wymondham, co. Norfolk, the nephew, one of the Exors.

D

Ernest Francis De Chair, born at "The Nest," Lennoxville, Quebec, Canada East, on Wednesday, 27 December 1865, and bapt. at St. James', Lennoxville ; died at Montreal, Canada, 23 July, bur. there 27 July 1902. = Mary Dymphne, youngest dau. of Sydney Yeates, by Dymphne his wife ; marr. at Brisbane, Queensland, Australia, 18 February 1893 ; died 24 February 1901.

Edith Cecilia, born 17 September 1867, and bapt. at St. James', Lennoxville, Quebec ; died 29 February 1868, and bur. at Lennoxville.

—

Henry Beauvoir De Chair (twin with Blanche) ; born at Halifax, Nova Scotia, on Sunday, 1 November 1868, and bapt. there ; died 10 October 1869, and bur. at Halifax.

—

Blanche (twin with Henry Beauvoir), born at Halifax, Nova Scotia, on Sunday, 1 November 1868, and bapt. there ; died 27 April 1870, and bur. at Halifax.

Frances Dymphne, born at Brisbane, Queensland, 8 April 1894.

Dorothy Melville, born at Brisbane, Queensland, on Sunday, 10 May 1896.

Oswald Wentworth De Chair, born 28 February 1870, and bapt. at Halifax, Nova Scotia.

—

Evelyn, born at 8 Nightingale Terrace, Woolwich, co. Kent, on Saturday, 23 March 1872, and bapt. at Christ Church, Woolwich ; died at 8 Nightingale Terrace, Woolwich, aged 8 months, on Friday, 6 December 1872, and bur. in the cemetery at Woolwich.

Beatrice Frances, born 9 May 1873 ; marr. at St. Paul's, Knightsbridge, London (by the Rev. Canon Frederick Blackett De Chair, uncle of the bride, assisted by the Rev. Prebendary Henry Montagu Villiers), on Thursday, 30 October 1902, John Tatchell Studley of Seaborough Park, co. Somerset.

Dorothy Maud, born at 19 Westbourne Square, London, on Tuesday, 17 October 1876.

—

Ella, born 10 March 1880, and bapt. at Rochdale, co. Lancaster ; died 17 June, bur. at Purbrook, co. Hants, 22 June 1885.

F. Hackett De Chair.

Grey of Falloden, co. Northumberland.

Arms on record in the College of Arms.—
Gules, a lion rampant, within a bordure
engrailed argent, a mullet for difference.

Crest.—A scaling ladder in bend sinister
or, hooked and pointed sable.

Motto.—De bon vouloir servir le roy.

The Rt. Honble Sir George Grey, Bart., P.C., G.C.B. (elder son of the Honble Sir George Grey, 1st Bart., K.C.B., Captain R.N. [3rd son of Charles, 1st Earl Grey], by Mary his wife, dau. of Samuel Whitbread of Bedwell Park, co. Hertford); born at Gibraltar 11 May 1799; of Oriel College, Oxford, matriculated 25 June 1817, aged 18, B.A. 1821, M.A. 1824; called to the Bar at Lincoln's Inn 2 May 1826; M.P. for Devonport 1832-47, North Northumberland 1847 -52, and for Morpeth February 1853-74; Under Secretary of State for the Colonies 1834-35 and 1835-39; Judge Advocate General 1839-41; Chancellor of the Duchy of Lancaster in 1841 and April 1859-61; Secretary of State for the Home Department 1846-52, 1855-58, and 1861-66; Secretary of State for the Colonies 1854-55; sworn a Privy Councillor 1 March 1839; Ecclesiastical Commissioner February 1841; G.C.B. 31 March 1849; prevented the Chartists, under Smith O'Brien, invading the House of Commons with their monster petition 10 April 1848; succeeded his father as 2nd Bart. 3 October 1828; died at Falloden, co. Northumberland, in his 84th year, on Saturday, 9 September, bur. at Embleton, co. Northumberland, 15 September 1882. Will dated 21 June 1877, with two codicils dated respectively 6 November 1879 and 5 May 1882, proved at Newcastle-upon-Tyne 12 October 1882, by Harriet Jane Grey of Falloden, co. Northumberland, widow, the Rt. Honble Thomas George, Earl of Northbrook of Stratton, co. Southampton, and George Culley of Fowberry Tower, co. Northumberland, the Exors.

=Anna Sophia, eldest dau. of the Honble and Rt. Rev. Henry Ryder, D.D., Bishop of Lichfield and Coventry (3rd son of Nathaniel Ryder, 1st Baron Harrowby of Harrowby, co. Lincoln), by Sophia his wife, dau. of Thomas March Phillips of Garrendon Park, co. Leicester; born at Lutterworth, co. Leicester, 18 January, bapt. there 22 March 1805; marr. at St. George's, Hanover Square, London, 14 August 1827; died at Wellswood House, Torquay, co. Devon, aged 88, on Saturday, 8 July, bur. at Embleton 14 July 1893. Will dated 11 December 1882, with two codicils dated respectively 15 February 1887 and 28 April 1887, proved (Prin. Reg., 738, 93) 23 August 1893, by Harriet Jane Grey, widow, the daughter-in-law, the sole Executrix.

Lieut.-Colonel George Henry Grey of Falloden; born at Eaton Square, London, 21 March, bapt. at St. Peter's, Eaton Square, London, 9 May 1835; Equerry to H.R.H. the Prince of Wales (now King Edward VII.); Captain Grenadier Guards and Captain Rifle Brigade; Lieut.-Colonel Northumberland Militia; died at Sandringham, co. Norfolk, 11 December, bur. at Embleton 17 December 1874. Admon was granted at the Principal Registry 29 December 1874, to Harriet Jane Grey of Falloden, co. Northumberland, the relict.

=Harriet Jane, youngest dau. of Lieut.-Colonel Charles Pearson, by Jane his wife, dau. of William Eccles; born at Hawford, co. Worcester, 7 January 1839; marr. at St. Luke's, Cheltenham, co. Gloucester (by the Rev. Sir Henry Thompson, Bart., Rector of Frant, co. Sussex), on Tuesday, 20 November 1860.

A

The Rt. Honble Sir Edward Grey = Frances Dorothy, elder dau. of Shalcross Fitzherbert Widdrington of Newton Hall, Felton, and of Hauxley, co. Northumberland; J.P. and D.L. for the counties of Chester and Northumberland, High Sheriff 1874, and Major Northumberland Militia, by Cecilia his wife, eldest dau. of Edward John Gregge Hopwood of Hopwood Hall, co. Lancaster; born at Newton Hall, Felton, on Thursday, 19 January 1865; marr. at Shilbotel, co. Northumberland (by the Honble and Rev. Francis Grey, assisted by the Rev. Joseph Golightly, the Vicar), on Tuesday, 20 October 1885.

of Falloden, co. Northumberland, Bart., P.C.; born at 61 Chester Square, London, on Friday, 25 April, bapt. at St. Michael's, Chester Square, London, 3 June 1862; educated at Winchester and at Balliol College, Oxford, matriculated 21 October 1880, aged 18; J.P. and D.L. for co. Northumberland, M.P. for the Berwick-on-Tweed Division of co. Northumberland since 1885; Under Secretary of State for Foreign Affairs from August 1892 to June 1895; sworn a Privy Councillor 1902; succeeded his grandfather as 3rd Bart. 9 September 1882.

Alice Emma, born at Falloden on Thursday, 9 March, bapt. at Embleton, co. Northumberland, 17 April 1865; marr. at St. Mary Abbott's, Kensington, London (by the Bishop of Limerick, father of the bridegroom), on Tuesday, 30 July 1889, Charles Larcom Graves of 3 Strathmore Gardens, Kensington, London (4th son of the Rt. Rev. Charles Graves, Bishop of Limerick, D.D., D.C.L., F.R.S., formerly Fellow of Trinity College, Dublin, and Dean of the Chapel Royal, Dublin, by Selina his wife, dau. of John Cheyne, M.D., Physician-General to the Forces in Ireland); born 15 December 1856.

A

George Grey, born at Falloden, co. Northumberland, on Saturday, 14 July, bapt. at Embleton co. Northumberland, 16 September 1866; educated at Clifton College.

Jane, born at Falloden on Thursday, 29 October, bapt. at Embleton 13 December 1868; marr. at St. Stephen's, Lewisham, co. Kent (by the Rt. Rev. the Bishop of Peterborough, assisted by the Rev. Roland Errington, Rector of Clewer, co. Berks), on Saturday, 28 November 1891, the Rev. Charles Evelyn Cambridge de Coetlogon (eldest son of the Rev. Charles Prescott de Coetlogon, Rector of Stoke Talmage, co. Oxford, by Henrietta his wife, dau. of the Rev. H. Pickard-Cambridge of Bloxworth House, co. Dorset); born at Lighthorne, co. Warwick, on Saturday, 11 January 1862, and bapt. there; of Selwyn College, Cambridge, matriculated Michaelmas Term, 1882, B.A. 1885, M.A. 1891; Chaplain at Gorpuri, Poona, Bombay, India, 1892, Colaba, Bombay, 1892–95, Aden, Red Sea, 1895–97, Malabar Hill, Bombay, 1897, Nasirabad, Bombay, 1897–99, on furlough 1899, at Ahmedabad, Bombay, 1901–1902, and at St. Mary's, Poona, Bombay, since 1902; Chaplain 1st Infantry Division at Delhi Durbar 1903.

Rev. Alexander Harry Grey, born at Falloden on Friday, 10 June, bapt. at Embleton 18 July 1870; educated at Clifton and at Keble College, Oxford, matriculated 12 October 1889, aged 19; Vicar of St. Alban's, Tortuga, Trinidad, West Indies, since 1900.

=Mabel, dau. of the Rev. Canon Huggins, Rector of San Fernando, Trinidad, by Charlotte his wife; born 18 February 1875; marr. at St. Paul's, Trinidad, on Saturday, 28 July 1900.

Constance Mary, born at Falloden on Wednesday, 31 January, bapt. at Embleton 7 April 1872.

Charles Grey, born at Falloden on Saturday, 23 August, bapt. at Embleton 28 September 1873.

Welch.

Edward Welch of Camden Town, London ;⊤Maria Louisa Jackson ; died at
of the Rolls Office, London ; died at Birkenhead, │ 47 St. Augustine Road, Camden
co. Chester, aged 71, on Thursday, 14 August, │ Town, London, aged 62, on
bur. in the cemetery at Birkenhead 19 August │ Wednesday, 28 January, bur. in
1857.   Will dated 16 November 1849, with │ Highgate Cemetery, London,
codicil of same date, proved (P.C.C., 808, 56) │ 3 February 1857.   Will dated
22 October 1856, by Maria Louisa Welch, the │ 14 January 1857, with codicil
relict, the sole Executrix. │ dated 24 January 1857, proved
│ (P.C.C., 163, 57) 19 February
│ 1857, by Maria Louisa Parbury,
│ the daughter, the sole Executrix.

Edw.ᵈ Welch

A

Maria Louisa, born 20 August, bapt. at St. James', | Edward Welch, born | William Welch, born
Clerkenwell, London, 13 October 1814; marr. there | 18 December 1815, | 18 June 1819, bapt.
by licence 21 November 1837, Charles Parbury (son | bapt. at St. James', | at the parish church,
of Charles Parbury), Lieutenant in Naval Service | Clerkenwell, London, | Islington, London, 9
of the Honble East India Company; died at River | 28 March 1816. | March 1821; died at
Terrace, Islington, London, aged 33, 28 October | | 656 Old Kent Road,
1843.   Admᵒⁿ was granted (P.C.C., 401, 43) | — | London, aged 56,
22 November 1843, to Maria Louisa Parbury, the | | on Wednesday, 24
relict.   She died at Brighton, co. Sussex, aged 50, | John Welch, born | November 1875.
on Sunday, 28 August, and was bur. in Highgate | 24 October 1817,
Cemetery, London, 2 September 1864.   Will | bapt. at Pentonville
dated 7 August 1857, proved (Prin. Reg., 197, 65) | Chapel, London, 21
9 March 1865, by Henry Welch of 1 Tollington | January 1818.
Road, Holloway, co. Middlesex, gent., Frederick
Welch of 4 Addison Gardens, North Kensington,
co. Middlesex, gent., and Septimus Robert Welch
of 22 Brecknock Crescent, Camden Town, co.
Middlesex, the brothers, the Exors.

B

Marianne Jane, born 19 March, | Frederick George Welch,⊤Aileen Kathleen, eldest dau.
bapt. at St. Pancras New Church, | born   at   Kensington, │ of Captain Maurice Power, by
London, 7 May 1856. | London, 4 July 1861, │ Ernestine Neuville his wife;
| bapt. at St. Barnabas', │ marr. at Darjeeling, Bengal,
— | Kensington, 28 November │ India.   She marr. 2ndly at
| 1862 ; died at Calcutta, │ Darjeeling, on Thursday, 16
Ellen Maria, born 18 October 1858. | India, aged 30, 10 January │ June 1898, William Furguson
| 1892, and bur. there. │ Ducat of Calcutta.
—

Arthur Welch, born at Chiswick, | George Frederick Welch, born at
co. Middlesex, in 1860, and died | 3 Upper Wood Street, Calcutta,
aged 3 months. | 28 November 1891, and bapt. at
| Calcutta.

A   Henry Welch, born 14 December 1820, bapt. at the parish church, Islington, London, 9 March 1821; marr. in London, Charlotte Susannah, who died at 2 Harborough Villas, Ramsgate, co. Kent, aged 65, 22 September, and was bur. in the cemetery at Ramsgate 27 September 1893. M.I. Will dated 15 November 1890, proved (Prin. Reg., 1044, 93) 15 November 1893, by Frederick Welch of " Inglemount," Sydenham, the sole Exor. He died s.p. at 10 Canonbury Street, Ramsgate, aged 60, on Thursday, 7 April, and was bur. in the cemetery at Ramsgate 14 April 1881. Will dated 23 December 1859, proved (Prin. Reg., 351, 81) 27 April 1881, by Charlotte Susannah Welch of Florence Villa, Cornwallis Gardens, Hastings, co. Sussex, the relict, the sole Executrix.

Frederick Welch of Balham, co. Surrey; born at Pentonville, London, 10 July 1822, bapt. at Pentonville Chapel 5 October 1823.

Caroline Leah, youngest dau. of William Richardson of Walbrook, in the City of London, and of Pentonville, by Mary King his wife, dau. of James Burbidge of East Knoyle, co. Wilts; born at Pentonville 21 October 1826, bapt. at St. James', Clerkenwell, London, 11 February 1827 (Sponsors: Mrs. Steedman, her sister Ann, and Mr. Steedman); marr. at St. Pancras New Church, London (by the Rev. James Dennett, brother-in-law of the bride), on Thursday, 21 June 1855.

(See Pedigree of Richardson, Vol. 10, page 166.)

Ernest Robert Welch, born at Kensington, London, 20 January, bapt. at St. Barnabas', Kensington, 11 May 1866.

Janet Mary, eldest dau. of William Erskine, M.D., of Sydenham, co. Kent, by Jeanie his wife, dau. of Robert Adam; born at Kincardine, co. Perth, 17 April, bapt. there 14 May 1871; marr. at Christ Church, Southwark, co. Surrey (by the Rev. Alfred Hutchings De Fontaine), on Saturday, 11 June 1898.

Sybil Mary, born at 3 Amesbury Avenue, Streatham Hill, co. Surrey, on Wednesday, 12 December 1900, bapt. at St. Margaret's, Leigham Court, Streatham Hill, 5 April 1902.

B   Charles Welch, born 18 November 1826, bapt. at Pentonville Chapel, London, 16 May 1827; died s.p. at Cape Town, South Africa.

Septimus Robert Welch, born 8 November 1828, bapt. at Pentonville Chapel, London, 6 December 1829; died at his residence, 16 Cambridge Gardens, Notting Hill, London, aged 47, on Thursday, 6 April, bur. in Highgate Cemetery, London, 13 April 1876. Will dated 25 July 1871, proved (Prin. Reg., 447, 76) 1 May 1876, by Helen Welch of 16 Cambridge Gardens, Notting Hill, co. Middlesex, the relict, the sole Executrix.

Helen, 2nd dau. of William Thacker of 10 Cambridge Terrace, Regent's Park, London, by Helen Parbury his wife; marr. at the parish church, St. Pancras, London, on Thursday, 16 April 1868.

Fredk Welch.

Norbury.

John Norbury of Upton and Macclesfield, co. Chester, Silk Throwster; born 16 September 1781; marr. Esther Davenport, who died, aged 37, and was bur. at St. Michael's, Macclesfield, 22 August 1823. He died at Upton Grange, Macclesfield, aged 64, 11 January, and was bur. at Christ Church, Macclesfield, 16 January 1847. M.I. Will dated 24 May 1843, proved at Chester 3 February 1847.

John Norbury

A

Thomas Norbury of Upton Hall, near Macclesfield, Silk Merchant; born at King Edward Street, Macclesfield, 7 May, bapt. at Christ Church, Macclesfield, 1 June 1805; Lieutenant in King's Cheshire Regiment of Yeomanry Cavalry 1829; Mayor of Macclesfield 1841; died at Upton Hall, Macclesfield, 23 May, bur. at Christ Church, Macclesfield, 29 May 1857. M.I. Will dated 7 January 1852, proved at Chester 11 June 1857.

Thos. Norbury

═Frances Elizabeth, eldest dau. of William Binley Dickinson of Macclesfield, Surgeon, by Elizabeth his 1st wife, dau. of the Rev. John Willey of Gilmorton and Willoughby Waterless, co. Leicester; born at Macclesfield 8 January, bapt. at St. Michael's, Macclesfield, 4 February 1818; marr. at Prestbury, co. Chester, 22 April 1841; died at 13 Albert Road, Southport, co. Lancaster, aged 63, on Monday, 14 March, bur. at Christ Church, Macclesfield, on Friday, 18 March 1881. M.I. Admon was granted at the Principal Registry 10 March 1882, to Willoughby Norbury, gent., the son, and one of the next of kin.

(See Pedigree of Dickinson, Vol. I., page 293.)

John Norbury, born 12 February, bapt. at St. Michael's, Macclesfield, 5 March 1807; died, aged 3, bur. at St. Michael's, Macclesfield, 20 January 1811.

—

Henry Norbury, born 24 December 1808, bapt. at Christ Church, Macclesfield, 17 January 1809; marr. at Wybunbury, co. Chester, Elizabeth Morgan; born 23 June 1817; died, aged 47, and bur. at Christ Church, Macclesfield, 13 June 1865. M.I. He died, aged 40, 14 July, and was bur. at Christ Church, Macclesfield, 19 July 1849. M.I. Will dated 28 February 1849, proved at Chester 20 September 1849.

Hester, born 13 April 1847; died, aged 18, 31 August, bur. at Christ Church, Macclesfield, 4 September 1865. M.I.

B

John Frederick Norbury, born at Foden Bank Cottage, Macclesfield, 15 February, bapt. at Christ Church, Macclesfield, 8 June 1842; of Trinity College, Oxford, matriculated 23 May 1860, aged 18, B.A. 1863, M.A. 1866; marr. 1stly by licence at the parish church, Lewisham, co. Kent, 19 August 1882, Ellen Olive, dau. of Charles Rawlins. He died s.p. at 15 Palace Terrace, Fulham, co. Middlesex, aged 58, on Saturday, 28 July, and was bur. in the cemetery at Fulham 1 August 1900. ═Annie, dau. of William Gillies; marr. at St. Peter's, Eaton Square, London, 4 August 1888. 2nd wife.

J. F. Norbury

Catherine, born 8 May, bapt. at St. Michael's, Maccles-field, co. Chester, 30 May 1810; marr. James Pearson (son of Nathaniel and Martha Pearson); born 2 September 1809, bapt. at Macclesfield 2 May 1811; died 19 February 1896, and bur. in the cemetery at Southport, co. Lancaster. Will dated 29 December 1894, proved at Liverpool 25 March 1896, by Frederick Aneurin Jones, the sole Exor. She died s.p. at Southport 17 December, and was bur. in the cemetery at Southport 21 December 1882. Admon (with will dated 2 February 1847, and codicil dated 27 June 1866) was granted, under certain specialities (Prin. Reg., 161, 83), 3 February 1883, to James Pearson of "Glenville," Cambridge Road, Southport, co. Lancaster, gent., the sole Exor.

Elizabeth Davenport, born at Macclesfield in December 1811, bapt. there 24 January 1812; marr. 1stly at Prestbury, co. Chester, Joseph Deane; marr. 2ndly at New York, U.S.A., James Campbell of New York, M.D. (son of the Rev. Robert Campbell, M.A.), who died at New York 12 March 1851; marr. 3rdly at New York, George Glenny of Glenville, co. Down. She died, leaving issue by her 1st and 2nd husbands, 4 December, and was bur. in the cemetery at Southport 7 December 1877. M.I.

B

Fanny Hester, born at Foden Bank Cottage, Macclesfield, 13 June, bapt. at Christ Church, Maccles-field, 2 August 1843; marr. at Prestbury (by the Rev. Willoughby Willey Dickinson, Rector of Wolferton, co. Norfolk, uncle of the bride) on Wednesday, 3 August 1864, John Wright of "Field Bank," Macclesfield, only son of Richard Wright of Macclesfield.

Thomas William Norbury of Stratford-on-Avon, co. Warwick; born at Park House, Macclesfield, 7 July, bapt. at Christ Church, Macclesfield, 8 September 1847; L.R.C.P. Edin. and L.M. 1871, M.R.C.S. Eng. 1871.

Eliza Theresa, 4th dau. of Captain Thomas Colley FitzGerald of Upton Grange, Macclesfield, by Eliza Leggiat his 1st wife; born in India 31 December 1848; marr. at the parish church, Prestbury (by the Rev. Willoughby Willey Dickinson, Rector of Wolferton, uncle of the bridegroom), on Wednesday, 21 July 1875.

Willoughby FitzGerald Norbury, born at Crediton, co. Devon, 10 March, bapt. there 18 April 1877. —

Thomas FitzGerald Norbury, born at "The Heys," Alderley Edge, co. Chester, 30 June, bapt. at Alderley Edge 31 December 1878.

Paul FitzGerald Norbury, born at "The Heys," Alderley Edge, 28 September, bapt. at Alderley Edge 31 December 1879; Lieutenant Royal Irish Regiment 1899, Lieutenant Poona Horse 1903.

Francis Campbell Norbury, born at Winton House, Stratford-on-Avon, 16 January, bapt. at the parish church, Stratford-on-Avon, 9 May 1882; of St. John's College, Cambridge, matriculated October 1901. —

Cicely Alice, born at Winton House, Stratford-on-Avon, 23 January, bapt. at the parish church, Stratford-on-Avon, 31 March 1883

A

| | |

James Norbury, born 24 April, bapt. at Macclesfield, co. Chester, 5 May 1813; died 17 November 1813, and bur. at St. Michael's, Macclesfield, the same day.

Mary, born 10 June 1814, bapt. at Macclesfield 30 June 1815; died 26 January 1818, and bur. the same day.

Joseph Norbury, born at Macclesfield 7 February, bapt. privately 12 March 1817; died 18 January 1818, and bur. the same day.

Maria, bapt. at Macclesfield 17 April 1818; marr. Abraham Downes Abbott of Dublin, Surgeon. She died at Liverpool 3 March 1874. Will dated 28 October 1872, proved (Prin. Reg., 452, 74) 1 July 1874, by James Pearson of 58 Leyland Road, Southport, co. Lancaster, gent., one of the Exors.

Esther, bapt. at Macclesfield 2 August 1820; marr. Edward Bennett of Macclesfield, M.D.; died 18 June 1886. She died at Chapel-en-le-Frith, co. Derby, 30 March 1864. Will dated 18 December 1852, proved at Derby 4 July 1864, by Edward Bennett of Chapel-en-le-Frith, co. Derby, M.D., the sole Exor. Probate being granted under certain limitations.

B

Margaret Louisa, born at Park House, Macclesfield, 28 December 1848, bapt. at St. Michael's, Macclesfield, 30 January 1849; marr. at All Saints', Southport (by the Rev. Frederick Binley Dickinson, Vicar of Ashford, co. Middlesex, uncle of the bride), on Tuesday, 17 April 1883, James Robert Campbell, only son of James Campbell of New York, M.D., by Elizabeth his wife, dau. of John Norbury of Macclesfield.

Willoughby Norbury = Elizabeth Hargreave, only dau. of the Rev. of Wilmcote Hill, Stratford-on-Avon, co. Warwick; born at Park House, Macclesfield, 16 June, bapt. at St. Michael's, Macclesfield, 25 July 1850; of Brasenose College, Oxford, matriculated 4 June 1868, aged 17, B.A. 1871, M.A. 1875; admitted a Solicitor 31 January 1876.

William Brewster of Llandudno, co. Carnarvon, by Ann Jane his 2nd wife, 6th dau. of John Hargreaves of Blackburn, co. Lancaster, Solicitor, and for more than 50 years Coroner for the Hundred of Blackburn; born at "Plâs Trevor," Llandudno, 19 January, bapt. at St. George's, Llandudno, 22 June 1856; marr. at St. Andrew's, Southport (by the Rev. Edward Jones Brewster, LL.D., Vicar of Leyton, co. Essex, uncle of the bride), on Tuesday, 4 June 1878; died at "Fairfield," Brook Lane, Alderley Edge, co. Chester, 5 January, bur. at Llanrhos, near Llandudno, 10 January 1880. Admon (with will dated 3 November 1879, and codicil of same date) was granted (Prin. Reg., 169, 80) 13 February 1880, under certain specialities, to Willoughby Norbury of "Fairfield," Brook Lane, Alderley Edge, co. Chester, the sole Exor.

Brewster Norbury, born at "Fairfield," Brook Lane, Alderley Edge, on Sunday, 21 December 1879, bapt. at Alderley Edge 4 February 1880; of Oriel College, Oxford, matriculated October 1898, aged 18, B.A. 1903.

Sieveking.

Arms.—Gules, two seven-rayed stars waved, argent, and a clover-leaf proper.
Crest.—A seven-rayed and waved star argent between two wings (pinions).
Mottoes.—1, Antiqua fides ; 2, Per aspera ad astra.

Edward Henry Sieveking of 4 Christopher Street, Finsbury Square, and afterwards of Baily's Lane, Stamford Hill, London, and of 65 Fenchurch Street, in the City of London (elder son of Heinrich Christian Sieveking, Senator of Hamburg, by Caroline Luise his wife, dau. of Senator Peter Diedrich Volckmann of Hamburg, and grandson of Peter Nicolaus Sieveking, who became a citizen of the Free State of Hamburg in February 1747); born at Hamburg 2 May 1790; came to England in 1809, returning to Hamburg for War of Liberation; served as 2nd and 1st Lieutenant in Hanseatic Legion, and received medal for campaign of 1813–14; settled permanently in England 23 August 1815; died at 17 Manchester Square, London, 29 November, bur. in Abney Park Cemetery, London, on Thursday, 3 December 1868. M.I., also memorial tablet to his memory in the Lutheran Church of St. Georg, Little Alie Street, Leman Street, London. Admon with will dated 30 May 1859, was granted at the Principal Registry 22 December 1868, to Gustavus Adolphus Sieveking of "The Verandah," Upper Clapton, co. Middlesex, the son, one of the universal legatees substituted in the said will.

═ Emerentia Luise Franciska, dau. of Senator Johann Valentin Meyer of Hamburg; born 4 September 1789; marr. at Hamburg 2 August 1815; died at Stamford Hill, London, in her 73rd year, on Sunday, 24 November, bur. in Abney Park Cemetery, London, 29 November 1861. M.I., also memorial tablet to her memory in the Lutheran Church of St. Georg, Little Alie Street, Leman Street, London.

A

Sir Edward Henry Sieveking of 17 Manchester Square, London, K.B.; born in London 24 August 1816; educated at University College and at Edinburgh; M.D. Edin. 1841, F.R.C.P. Lond. 1852, Physician in Ordinary to H.M. Queen Victoria 1888 till her death, Physician in Ordinary to H.R.H. the Prince of Wales (now King Edward VII.) since 1863, and Physician Extraordinary 1901; Author of various medical works; knighted 1886; Knight of Grace of Order of St. John of Jerusalem, F.S.A., LL.D. Edin.

═ Jane, youngest dau. of John Ray of Finchley, co. Middlesex, J.P.; born 13 September 1825; marr. at St. George's, Hanover Square, London, on Wednesday, 5 September 1849.

B

Henry Edward Sieveking, born at 3 Bentinck Street, Manchester Square, London, on Friday, 21 June 1850; died suddenly, aged 8 months, on Wednesday, 19 February, bur. in Abney Park Cemetery, London, 24 February 1851. M.I.

—

Laurence Ray Sieveking of Nullagine, Western Australia; born at 3 Bentinck Street, Manchester Square, London, on Friday, 11 July 1851; educated at Epsom and at Marlborough College.

Herbert Edward Sieveking, born at 3 Bentinck Street, Manchester Square, London, on Tuesday, 19 April 1853; educated at Marlborough College and at Polytechnic School, Hanover; L.R.C.P. Lond. 1889, M.R.C.S. Eng. 1881, formerly House Physician at St. Mary's Hospital, London; Medical Officer Cape Government Railway Service and Hospital, Fourteen Streams, and of the British South Africa Co.'s Police and Base Hospital, Fort Tuli; Bronze medal, Royal Humane Society, and the order of the Medjidie (4th-class).

A

Gustavus Adolphus Sieveking, = Elizabeth, only dau. of Robert
born at 4 Christopher Street, in | Podmore of Clapton Square,
the City of London, 30 April | Hackney, co. Middlesex, by
1819 ; died at "Loxley," | Jane Soale his wife, dau. of
Headstone Road, Harrow, co. | John Thompson ; born 9 April
Middlesex, aged 77 years and | 1827 ; marr. at St. John's,
10 months, on Saturday, 27 | Hackney (by the Rev. Thomp-
February, bur. in the old | son Podmore, brother of the
churchyard at Chingford, co. | bride), on Saturday, 9 June
Essex, 2 March 1897. | 1849; died at Harrow 21
November, bur. in the old
churchyard at Chingford 25
November 1903. M.I.

Hermann Alfred Sieveking,
born at 4 Christopher Street,
in the City of London, 19
May 1825; died unmarried,
in his 33rd year, on Wed-
nesday, 24 February, bur. in
Abney Park Cemetery, Lon-
don, on Monday, 1 March
1858. M.I.

C

Louisa Jane, born at
17 Manchester Square,
London, on Sunday,
25 July 1858; died at
"The Verandah," Upper
Clapton, co. Middlesex,
aged 17, on Tuesday,
28 September, bur. in
the old churchyard at
Chingford 1 October
1875. M.I.

Rosa Elizabeth, born at "The Verandah," Upper Clapton, on
Saturday, 7 January 1860 ; marr. at Holy Trinity, Marylebone,
London (by the Rev. Hugo Daniel Harper, D.D., Principal of
Jesus College, Oxford, father of the bridegroom, assisted by the
Rev. Canon William Cadman, the Rector), on Thursday, 1 January
1885, Henry Roby Harper (son of the Rev. Hugo Daniel Harper,
D.D., Principal of Jesus College, Oxford, formerly Head-Master of
Sherborne School, by Mary Charlotte his wife, dau. of Sir Henry
Dewey Harness, K.C.B., R.E.) ; born 9 September 1858; of
Trinity College, Oxford, matriculated 12 October 1877, aged 19,
B.A. 1881, M.A. 1884 ; House-Master of Clifton College.

B   B

Arthur Gustavus Sieveking, born at
3 Bentinck Street, Manchester Square,
London, on Sunday, 29 October 1854 ;
educated at Marlborough College and at
Caius College, Cambridge, B.A. 1877, M.A.
1881 ; a Student of the Inner Temple 10
April 1877, called to the Bar 26 January
1880 ; marr. Ann Tucker.

Frederick Seal Sieveking, born at 3 Bentinck
Street, Manchester Square, London, on Sunday,
20 April 1856 ; entered the Royal Navy 1870,
Sub-Lieutenant 1876, Lieutenant 10 August
1881, retired as Commander 1901 ; died at
33 Manchester Street, London, aged 46, on
Sunday, 20 July, bur. in Abney Park Cemetery,
London, on Wednesday, 23 July 1902. M.I.

Alfred Robert Sieveking, born at "The Verandah," Upper Clapton, ┬ Anna Josephine Adeline, co. Middlesex, on Tuesday, 6 January 1863 ; educated at Eastbourne │ youngest dau. of Karl College and at University College School, London, and at │ Stebinger of Stuttgart, St. Mary's Hospital, London ; L.R.C.P., L.R.C.S. Edin., L.M., │ Germany ; born at Baden, L.F.P.S. Glasg. 1889 ; formerly Senior Medical Officer Uganda │ Germany, 21 August 1871 ; Railway, Mombasa, East Africa. │ marr. at Mannheim, Baden
│ (by the Rev. Alfred Gray,
│ Chaplain of the English
│ Church at Heidelberg,
│ Germany), on Saturday,
│ 9 April 1892.

Alfred R. Sieveking

Louisa Marie, born at Gwydir House, Cambridge, on Saturday, 31 December 1892, bapt. at All Souls', Langham Place, London, 21 February 1893.

Marie Rosa Harriette, born at "St. Mary's," Meads Road, Eastbourne, co. Sussex, on Sunday, 28 April, bapt. at St. John's, Eastbourne, 12 May 1895.

Albert Forbes Sieveking ┬ Margaret Julia, elder dau. of Sir George of 12 Seymour Street, │ Campbell of Edenwood, co. Fife, Portman Square, and 34 │ K.C.S.I., of the Bengal Civil Service, Essex Street, Strand, Lon- │ Lieut.-Governor of Bengal, Member of don ; born at 3 Bentinck │ the Indian Council, and afterwards Street, Manchester Square, │ M.P. for Kirkaldy (son of Sir George London, on Friday, 17 │ Campbell of Edenwood, brother of July 1857 ; educated at │ John, 1st Baron Campbell, Lord Felstead School and │ Chancellor of England) ; born at at Marlborough College ; │ Lucknow, India, 8 March 1861, and Solicitor 1881 ; F.S.A. │ bapt. there ; marr. at the British 1894, F.R.Hist.Soc. 1903 ; │ Consulate, and afterwards at the Author of " The Praise of │ English Church, Rue d'Aguesseau, Gardens," 1885 and 1899. │ Paris, on Wednesday, 28 October
│ 1896.

Henry Droop Sieveking, born at 17 Manchester Square, London, on Wednesday, 7 December 1859 ; died at Marlborough College, co. Wilts, aged 13, on Thursday, 2 October, bur. in Abney Park Cemetery, London, 4 October 1873. M.I.

Margaret Eleanor Campbell, born at 12 Seymour Street, Portman Square, London, 18 April, bapt. at St. Mary's, Bryanston Square, London, 24 June 1898 (Sponsors : Elizabeth Jane Campbell, Everilda Gordon [afterwards de Barry Barnett], and Major George Campbell [8th King's]).

C

Edward Gustavus Sieveking of 7 Crosby Square, in the City of London; born at Upper Clapton, co. Middlesex, on Thursday, 27 July, bapt. at St. Thomas', Stamford Hill, co. Middlesex, 12 October 1865.=Isabel, younger dau. of George Giberne of the Honble East India Co.'s Service, and Judge of the Court of Bombay, India, by Maria his wife, dau. of John Sim Smith, M.R.C.S.; born 7 October 1858; marr. at St. Martin's, Epsom, co. Surrey (by the Rev. John Richard Vernon, Rector of St. Audries, co. Somerset, assisted by the Rev. Thompson Podmore, Rector of Aston-le-Walls, co. Northampton, uncle of the bridegroom), on Saturday, 25 April 1891.

Edward G. Sieveking

Valentine Edgar Sieveking, born at 5 Portman Mansions, Baker Street, London, on Friday, 5 February, bapt. at Epsom 23 April 1892.

Lancelot Giberne Sieveking, born at 4 Lyon Road, Harrow, co. Middlesex, 19 March, bapt. at Epsom 25 April 1896.

—

—

Geoffrey Edward Sieveking, born at 5 Portman Mansions, Baker Street, London, on Thursday, 9 March, bapt. at Epsom 25 April 1893.

Elinor Beatrice, born at 4 Lyon Road, Harrow, 14 April, bapt. at the parish church, Harrow, 21 May 1898.

B
                                                                                          B

Florence Amelia, born at 17 Manchester Square, London, on Tuesday, 2 July 1861; marr. at St. Thomas', Orchard Street, London (by the Rev. Henry Geary), on Wednesday, 2 July 1884, Leonard Charles Wooldridge (son of Leonard Wooldridge of Overton, co. Hants, M.R.C.S.); born 11 December 1858; M.D. and D.Sc. Lond., M.R.C.S., Assistant Physician to Guy's Hospital and Lecturer on Physiology; died at 24 Trinity Square, co. Surrey, on Thursday, 6 June, bur. in Norwood Cemetery, co. Surrey, on Wednesday, 12 June 1889. M.I. in Cranleigh School and Guy's Hospital Chapel. Will dated 17 July 1884, proved (Prin. Reg., 648, 89) 1 July 1889, by Florence Amelia Wooldridge of 17 Manchester Square, co. Middlesex, the relict, the sole Executrix. She marr. 2ndly at St. Thomas', Orchard Street, London (by the Rev. Ralph Percy Thompson), on Monday, 23 December 1891, Ernest Henry Starling of 8 Park Square West, Regent's Park, London (son of Matthew Henry Starling of Bombay, India, Barrister-at-Law and Clerk to the Crown, by Ellen Matilda Watkins his wife); born 17 April 1866; educated at Guy's Hospital and at Heidelberg University; M.B., B.Sc. Lond. and M.R.C.S. Eng. 1888, M.D. Lond. (qualified for gold medal) 1890, F.R.C.P. Lond. 1897, F.R.S. and Jodrell Professor of Physiology at University College, London, 1899; Author of "Elements of Human Physiology," 5th Edition, 1902.

180

B

Ella, born at 17 Manchester Square, London, on Thursday, 20 November 1862; marr. at St. Thomas', Orchard Street, London (by the Honble and Rev. John Stafford Northcote), on Saturday, 20 June 1896, Walter Ewing Crum of 33 Manchester Square, London (son of Alexander Crum of Thornlie Bank, co. Renfrew, M.P. for co. Renfrew, by Margaret Stewart his wife, dau. of the Rt. Rev. Alexander Ewing, Bishop of Argyll and the Isles); born at Caplerig, co. Renfrew, on Saturday, 22 July 1865; educated at Eton and at Balliol College, Oxford, matriculated 17 October 1884, aged 19, B.A. 1888, M.A. 1892.

Alexander Edward Sieveking, born 2 February 1864, and bapt. at St. Thomas', Portman Square, London (Sponsors: H.R.H. the Prince of Wales [now King Edward VII.] and H.R.H. the Princess of Wales [now Queen Alexandra]); died at 17 Manchester Square, London, aged 9 months, on Saturday, 3 December 1864, and bur. in Abney Park Cemetery, London. M.I.

Emmeline Wood, born at 17 Manchester Square, London, on Sunday, 1 September 1867; Hon. Secretary of Swanley Horticultural College.

A. Forbes Sieveking.

181

Index.

INDEX.

A

Abbott, Abraham Downes, 176; Maria, 176.
Abercromby, Honble Adèle Wilhelmine Marika, 61; George, Baron, 60; Colonel George Ralph, Baron, 60; George Ralph Campbell, Baron, 61; James, Baron Dumferline, 60; Honble John, 60, 61; Juliet Janet Georgina, Lady, 61; Louisa Penuel, Lady, 60; Honble Mary Anne, 61; Mary Anne, Lady, 60; Honble Montagu, 60, 61; Montagu, Lady, 60; Honble Ralph, 60, 61; Major-General Sir Ralph, 60.
Adair, Rev. Hugh Jenison, 43.
Adam, Jeanie, 173; Robert, 173.
Adcock, Maria, 71.
Adene, Henry John, 103; Isabel, 103.
Adeney, Rev. John, 20.
Agnew, Thomas, 90.
Ailsa, Archibald, Marquess of, 39.
Aislabie, Anne, 121; Benjamin, 121; Louisa, 121; Rev. William John, 121.
Alban, Grace, 6; Samuel, 6.
Aldrich, Philip, 54; Sarah, 54.
Alexander, Nicholas, 14; Sophia Ann, 14.
Alexandra, Queen of England, 181.
Allanson, Dorothy, 120; Rev. George 120.
Allsop, James, 18, 19; Sarah, 18, 19.
Andrewes, Rev. Charles, 48; Frances Jane, 48.
Andrews, Rev. Charles Henry, 1; Phœbe Hannah, 155; Stephen, 155.
Anthony, Amelia Sophia, 68.
Antrim, Hugh Seymour, Earl of, 104.
Argyll and the Isles, Rt. Rev. Alexander Ewing, Bishop of, 181.
Armit, Georgina, 41; Richard, 41.
Armytage, John, 94, 96; Mary Elizabeth, 94, 96.
Arnold, Rev. H. L., 143.
Arnould, Alfred Henry, 24.
Ashley, Atherton Edward, 128; Beryl, 128; Sarah Emily, 128.
Ashley-Cooper, Anthony, Earl of Shaftesbury, 132; Barbara, Countess of Shaftesbury, 132; Lady Barbara, 132.
Astley, Catherine, 153; Thomas, 153.
Atherton, Sir William, 165.
Atkinson, Henrietta, 141; Thomas, M.D., 141; Rev. Thomas, 12.
Awdry, Edmund Mainley, 42.
Awers, John, 108; Mary, 108.
Ayre, Rev. Joseph Watson, 83, 136.

B

Baber, Ann, 49; Rev. Harry, 49, 50; Rev. Henry Harvey, 49.
Babington, Rev. William Peile, 56.
Badcock, Emma Georgiana Bentley, 25; Leah, 87; Martha, 87; Richard, 87; William, 25.
Bagot, Elizabeth, 23; Rev. Walter, 23.
Baker, Hannah Lucy, 24; John Strange, 24; Shirley, 24.

Baldwin, Ann, 107; Georgiana, 107; John, 107.
Balguy, John, 153.
Bambridge, Rev. Joseph John, 108.
Banister, Rev. Charles Litchfield, 126; Eliza Anne, 126; Rev. Edward, 126; Katherine Maude, 126.
Barbadoes, Rt. Rev. Herbert Bree, Bishop of, 138.
Baring, Thomas George, Earl of Northbrook, 169.
Baring-Gould, Rev. Baring, 11.
Barker, Rev. Canon William, 164.
Barlow, Alethea, 62, 66; Algernon, 66; Amelia Sophia, 68; Andrew, 118; Caroline, 63; Cecilia Katherine, 64; Charles John, 68; Charlotte, 68; Charlotte Eliza, 66; Cordelia, 67; Edith Mary, 68; Edmund, 62-66; Edmund Francis Masterman, 64; Eleanor, 67; Eleanor Mary, 68; Elizabeth, 65; Essex Eleanor, 66; Essex Frances, 66; Eustace Hepburn, 62, 64, 67; Florence Marion Rose, 67; Frances Charlotte, 63; Francis, 62, 63; Francis John, 68; Francis Mount, 63; Lieut.-Colonel Frederick, 67; George, 63; Rev. George, 64; George Barne, 63; Rev. George Francis, 62; Rev. George Hilaro Philip, 121; George Thomas, 68; Harold, 67; Harold Everard, 68; Harriet, 62, 65, 118; Lady Harriet Eliza Danvers, 63; Henrietta, 64; Henrietta Rosamund, 67; Rev. Henry Masterman, 65, 67; Rev. John Mount, 62-64, 66, 67; Juliana, 66; Lance Mount, 67; Laura, 68; Laura Frederica, 64; Laura Sarah, 62; Louisa, 64, 65; Louisa (Violet), 63; Lyonell, 66, 67; Marion, 68; Mark Masterman, 67; Mary Cordelia, 67; Millicent Alice, 67; Montague Frederick Harold, 67; Richard, 66; Sophia Sidney, 67; Sybilla Harriet, 67; Vernon Harold, 67; Violet Norah, 67; William Francis, 63.
Barne, Miles, 62.
Barnes-Lawrence, Rev. Arthur Evelyn, 11.
Barnett-Bigley, Anne, 162; William, 162.
Barns, Ann, 90; William, 90.
Barrow, Rev. George Staunton, 124.
Barrows, Annie Mabel, 162; Evelyn Rosamond, 156; Florence Holmes, 156; Rev. Frederick William, 155, 156; Joseph, 156, 162.
Barry, Alice, 115; James, 115.
Battiscombe, Christopher George, 56; Eliza Susan, 56; Rev. Henry, 56; Mary, 56.
Baumbach, Baron de, 102.
Bayley, Rev. Sir Emilius, Bt., 113, 115.
Beardoe, Harriette, 98.
Beauchamp, Frederick, Earl, 103; Henry Beauchamp, Earl, 103; Susan Caroline, Countess, 103.
Beauchamp-Proctor, Emily Charlotte, 111; Major-General George Edward Henry, 111; George Thomas, 111; Hester Maria Fredericka, 111; Louisa Mary Catherine, 111.
Beauclerk, Lady Georgina, 22; William, Duke of St. Albans, 22.
Beaufort, Elizabeth, Duchess of, 102; Henry, K.G., Duke of, 102; Henry Charles, Duke of, 103.
Beaumont, Averil, 22; Captain Richard, R.N., 22; Susan Hussey, 22; Wentworth Blackett, 22.
Beauvoir, Anne, 165; Isabella, 165; Rev. Osmund, D.D., 165.

Becher, Elizabeth Susannah, 50; Honor Henrietta, 50; Rev. John Drake, 50; Rev. William, 50.
Beck, Anna, 73; Herring, 73.
Beckwith, Harriet Ellen, 158; William, 158.
Bell, Dora Laidlaw, 128; Elizabeth, 4; James, 128; Martha Symes, 4; William, 4; William McConbrie, 4.
Bennet, Ann, 113; Rev. Joseph, 113.
Bennett, Edward, M.D., 176; Esther, 176.
Bent, Rev. John Oxenham, 124.
Benwell, Delilah, 72.
Berry, Rev. William, 19, 20.
Bessborough, Frederick, Earl of, 132; Henrietta Frances, Countess of, 132, 134; John William, Earl of, 132; Maria, Countess of, 132; Louisa Susan Cornwallis, Countess of, 103; Rev. Walter William Brabazon, Earl of, 19, 103.
Bews, John, 12; Norah Henrietta, 12; Mary Elizabeth, 12.
Biddell, Arthur, 65; Harriet, 65; Herman, 65; Jane, 65; Manfred, 65.
Bigg-Wither, Rev. Harris Jervoise, 71.
Billing, Amelia Turner, 107; Mary Ann, 107; Thomas Robert, 107.
Binns, Sarah, 117.
Birch, James, 126; Juliana Letitia, 126; Nicoletta Lætitia, 126; Richard Frederick, 120.
Blair, Anne, 9; Lord President Robert, 9.
Blandy, John, 97; Mary, 97.
Bligh, Vice-Admiral Richard Rodney, 5.
Bloomfield, Rev. Father, 9.
Blumer, Clementina, 17; Elizabeth, 17; George, 17; John George, 17; Luke, 17; Margaret, 17.
Bois, Frances Margaret, 147; Henry, 147; John Charles, 147.
Bolton, Elizabeth Henrietta, 108; Gertrude Mary, 108; Lyndon, 108; Rev. Richard Knott, 108.
Bond, Rev. John Wesley, 107; Joseph, 148; Nellie, 148.
Booth, Harriot, 153; William, 153.
Borrell, Henry, 149; Sophie, 149.
Borrer, Mary Anne, 88; William, 88.
Boscawen, Admiral the Honble Edward, 102; Elizabeth, 102.
Bourke, Rear-Admiral Edmund, 39; Rev. Sackville, 135.
Bourne, Elinor Drinkwater, 116; John, 110; Rev. John Bury, 110; Margaret Sophia, 110; Mary, 110; Peter, 116; Robert William, 111.
Bousfield, Rt. Rev. Henry Brougham, Bishop of Pretoria, 167.
Bowden-Smith, Rev. Frederick Hermann, 29.
Bowe, Elizabeth, 42.
Bower, Amelia Mary, 119; Augusta Mary Chivers, 119; Edward Chivers, 119.
Bowling, Henry Paulson, 66, 93.
Bowman, Alice Margaret Perceval, 74; Rev. Arthur Herbert, 3; Cyril, 74; John Eddowes, 74.
Box, Hannah, 47; Mabel Georgina, 47; Stephen Thomas, 47; Rev. William Henry, 47.
Boyle, George, Earl of Glasgow, 60; George Frederick, Earl of Glasgow, 60; Helen Nagle Hill, 71; Henderson, 71; James, Earl of Glasgow, 60; Julia, Countess of Glasgow, 60; Montagu, Countess of Glasgow, 60.
Boys, Anne, 165; John, 165.
Bramston, Clara Isabella Sandford, 64; Rev. John, 64.
Brand, Honble Mrs., 134.
Bree, Charlotte Jane, 138; Rev. Edward Henry, 138; Rt. Rev. Herbert, Bishop of Barbadoes, 138; Jane Sarah, 138.
Brewer, John, 78; Harriet, 78.
Brewis, Robert, 17.
Brewster, Ann Jane, 176; Rev. Edward Jones, LL.D., 176; Elizabeth Hargreave, 176; Rev. William, 176.
Brice, Alexander, 63; Jane, 63.
Bridgman, John, 74; Louisa, 74; Sophia, 74.
Briggs, Elizabeth, 65; Jonas, 65; Mary, 65.

Bright, Benjamin, 161; Frances Mary, 161; Honora Phebe Gertrude, 161.
Bristow, Charles, 108.
Brittain, John, 1; Lavinia Elizabeth, 1; Louisa, 1.
Brock, Thomas, 154.
Brodie, Thomas, 61.
Broke, Elizabeth, 48; Horatio George, 48; Sir Philip, Bt., 48.
Brooke, Rev. Edward, 158.
Brooks, Rev. Harvey, 3.
Brough, Margaret, 92.
Brown, Edith, 91; Rev. George Gibson, 64; Hannah Lax, 32; Harriet, 123; Henry, 91; John, 27; Rev. John, 140; Rev. John Gardiner, 140; Lucy Jane, 140; Margaret Duncan, 98; Margaret Lætitia, 123; Honble Mary Anne, 61; Colonel Nicholas Robert, 61; Sarah Hannah, 91; Rev. Thomas, 32; Rev. Thomas Kenworthy, 126; William, 123; William Williams, 98.
Browne, Rev. John James, 142; Rev. Thirlwall Gore, 31; Sir William, 49, 50.
Browne-Collison, Henrietta Eliza, 164; Henry, 164.
Bryant, Martha, 87; Mary, 87; William, 87.
Buckall, Captain Richard, R.N., 5.
Bucke, Rev. Benjamin Walter, 80.
Bull, Rev. William, 19.
Bunbury, Abraham, 10; Isabella, 10.
Burbidge, James, 173; Mary King, 173.
Burch, Augustus Edgar, 141; Emily, 141.
Burdett, Sophia, 74.
Burnaby, Anne Caroline, 39; Cecilia Florence, 39; Edwyn, 39; Rev. Robert William, 28.
Burne, Rev. John Butler, 97.
Burn-Murdoch, Rev. James McGibbon, 78, 79.
Burrell, Charlotte Joanna, 30; James Fitchett, 30.
Burrows, Sarah, 17; Thomas, 17.
Burton, Harriet Anne, 22; William FitzWilliam, 22.
Bury, John, 110; Mary, 110.
Butler, Honble Charles Augustus, 63; Lady Harriet Eliza Danvers, 63; Honble Letitia Rudyerd Ross, 63; Lady Margaret, 83; Richard, Earl of Glengall, 83.
Byron, Mrs., 25.

C

Caddell, Rev. Henry, 22.
Cadman, Rev. Canon William, 178.
Calcutta, Rt. Rev. John Thomas James, D.D., Bishop of, 26; Rt. Rev. Reginald Heber, D.D., Bishop of, 42.
Cambridge, Duke of, 93.
Cameron, Jane Rose, 40; Mary Frances Lovett, 40; William Lochiel, 40.
Campbell, Colin Minton, 154; Elizabeth, 176; Elizabeth Davenport, 175; Elizabeth Jane, 179; George, 179; Sir George, 179; Herbert, 154; James, M.D., 175, 176; James Robert, 176; John, 154; John, Baron, 179; John Fitzherbert, 154; Louisa Wilmot, 154; Margaret Julia, 179; Margaret Louisa, 176; Mary, 154; Rev. Robert, 175.
Camperdown, Adam, Earl of, 61; Juliana Cavendish, Countess of, 61.
Canterbury, Archbishop of, 49, 89.
Cantrell, Mary Maria, 121.
Cardew, Emma, 38; Rev. John Haydon, 38.
Carlisle, Dean of, 36.
Carrington, Elizabeth, 7.
Cartwright, Rev. Edward Arthur, 96; Lieut.-Colonel Henry, 96; Henry Aubrey, 96; Jane, 96; Maud, 96; Rev. William Digby, 96.
Cary, Rev. Charles Thomas, 156, 157, 161, 167; Rev. Henry Francis, 156; Sarah Wilmot, 156.
Castleden, George, 52; Rev. George, 52; Rev. George Douglas, 52; Jane Packman, 52; Julia Henrietta, 52; Laura, 52.
Castlestewart, Charles Andrew Knox, Earl of, 93.

G

Gale, Lieut.-General Henry Richmond, 81 ; Margaret Elizabeth, 81.

Galloway, Elizabeth, 29 ; James, 29 ; Rev. James, 29 ; Margaret Bridger Goodrich, 29 ; William George, 28, 29, 31, 32.

Gambier, Thomas, 49.

Gandy, Gertrude Emma, 45 ; Rev. James Hunter, 45 ; Marian Jane, 45 ; William Hunter, 45.

Gardiner, Rev. Edward Imber, 38.

Garnett, Rev. Charles, 93.

Garrett, Rev. Henry Webb, 156.

Garrick, Rev. Canon James Percy, 165.

Garritt, Elizabeth, 17 ; William, 17.

Gater, Alice Sarah, 29 ; Caleb Hammond, 29 ; George Henry, 31 ; Margaret, 31 ; Sarah, 29, 31.

Gavin, Rev. Father, 9.

Geary, Rev. Henry, 180.

George, George, 147 ; George Frederick, 147 ; Georgiana Sibella, 147 ; Henrietta, 147 ; Henry Augustus, 147.

George II., King of England, 69.

George III., King of England, 36, 126, 165.

George IV., King of England, 126.

Gervaise-Maude, Frances Charlotte, 63 ; Henrietta, 63 ; John, 63.

Giberne, George, 180 ; Isabel, 180 ; Maria, 180.

Giffard, Edward, 122 ; Jane Mary, 122 ; Rosamond Catherine, 122.

Gill, Rev. J. F. F., 27.

Gillespie, Sir Robert Rollo, 159.

Gillies, Annie, 174 ; William, 174.

Gilpin, Henry, 75 ; Louisa Maria, 75 ; Norcliffe, 75.

Girardot, Rev. Lewis William, 72.

Glasgow, George, Earl of, 60 ; George Frederick, Earl of, 60 ; James, Earl of, 60 ; Julia, Countess of, 60 ; Montagu, Countess of, 60.

Glengall, Richard, Earl of, 83.

Glenny, Elizabeth Davenport, 175 ; George, 175.

Glossop, Rev. G., 26.

Glüber, Florian, 72 ; Margaret Louisa, 72.

Goddard, Ambrose, 21, 23 ; Lieut.-Colonel Ambrose Ayshford, 21 ; Ambrose Lethbridge, 21 ; Ambrose William, 23 ; Rev. Charles Frederick, 21, 23 ; Charles Richard, 23 ; Charlotte, 21 ; Dulcie Gwendoline, 23 ; Edward Hesketh, 23 ; Emma Caroline, 23 ; Eugenia Kathleen, 22 ; FitzRoy Pleydell, 21, 22 ; Colonel Frederick Fitz-Clarence, 24 ; Hannah Lucy, 24 ; Hesketh Pleydell, 23 ; Jessie Dalrymple, 22 ; Jessie Dorothea, 21 ; Jessie Henrietta, 21 ; John Hesketh, 22 ; Julia Margaret, 24 ; Lucy Clarissa, 24 ; Sara Adelaide, 24 ; Sarah, 21 ; Thomas Henry, 22.

Godley, Adeline, 147 ; Colonel William, 147.

Godman, Caroline, 98 ; Joseph, 98 ; Mary, 98.

Goldie, Captain Alexander Taubman, R.N., 117 ; Helen Fredericka, 117 ; Mary, 117.

Goldsmith, Emma, 137 ; John, 137.

Golightly, Rev. Joseph, 170.

Goodall, Katherine, 6 ; Nicholas, 6.

Goodbody, Annie Morris, 116.

Gooden-Chisholm, Anne Elizabeth, 24 ; Hannah Lucy, 24 ; James Chisholm, The Chisholm, 24.

Goodman, Caroline Sarah, 15 ; Thomas, 15.

Goodrich, Agatha Wells, 27 ; Catharine, 27 ; John, 27 ; Mary, 27 ; William, 27.

Gordon, Everilda, 179 ; George, Marquis of Huntly, 135 ; Very Rev. George, Dean of Lincoln, 26 ; George Tomline, 26 ; Gilbert, 61 ; Harriet, 26 ; Lord Henry, 135 ; Rev. John, 26 ; Honble Louisa Frances Charlotte, 135 ; Patricia Heron, 61.

Gordon-Cumming, Sir Alexander Penrose, Bt., 60 ; Francis Hastings Toone, 41 ; Louisa, 60 ; Mary Ada, 41.

Gough, Rev. Howard England Tunnicliff, 155 ; Julia Mead, 155 ; Ralph, 155.

Gould, Captain Davidge, R.N., 5.

Gowers, Ann, 107 ; Samuel, 107.

Graham, Fergus J., 161 ; Frances Mary, 161.

Grant, General Charles, 8 ; Duncan, 70 ; Elizabeth Charlotte, 8 ; Frances Eliza, 8 ; Frederick John, 93 ; Sir Hope, 10 ; Mary, 70 ; Robert, 8.

Graves, Alice Emma, 170 ; Rt. Rev. Charles, D.D., Bishop of Limerick, 170 ; Charles Larcom, 170 ; Selina, 170.

Gray, Rev. Alfred, 179 ; Essex, 66 ; William, 17, 66.

Greathead, Edith Florine, 149 ; James Henry, 149 ; Octavius Ernest, 149.

Green, Charlotte, 65 ; Godfrey Thomas, 110 ; Rev. John, 63 ; Joseph, 65.

Greene, Rev. Charles, 164 ; Ellen Mary, 164 ; Henrietta Eliza, 164.

Greensill, Eliza, 9 ; John, 6, 9.

Greig, Rev. George, 145.

Grenville, Gertrude Agnes, 46 ; Julia Roberta, 46 ; Ralph Neville, 46 ; Robert Neville, 46.

Gresley, Rev. Nigel, 154.

Grey, Rev. Alexander Harry, 171 ; Alice Emma, 170 ; Anna Sophia, Lady, 169 ; Charles, 171 ; Charles, Earl, 169 ; Constance Mary, 171 ; Sir Edward, Bt., 170 ; Frances Dorothy, Lady, 170 ; Honble and Rev. Francis, 170 ; George, 171 ; Sir George, Bt., 169 ; Captain the Honble Sir George, Bt., R.N., 169 ; Lieut.-Colonel George Henry, 169 ; Harriet Jane, 169 ; Jane, 171 ; Mabel, 171 ; Mary, Lady, 169 ; William, Earl of Stamford, 151.

Griffiths, Clara Louisa, 114 ; Emma, 114 ; Frank Bartlett Thomas, 119 ; Helen, 119 ; Lieut.-Colonel, 114.

Gross, Maria Rives, 135 ; Samuel Davis, 135.

Grosvenor, Lady Elizabeth, 37 ; Richard, Marquis of Westminster, K.G., 37.

Gurney, Rev. Joseph John, 83.

H

Hacker, Eliza, 15 ; Thomas, 15.

Hackett, James, 1, 5, 52 ; Katherine, 1, 5 ; Sarah, 52.

Hailes, Charles Montague, 4 ; Isobel Marie, 4.

Haldane-Duncan, Adam, Earl of Camperdown, 61 ; Juliana Cavendish, Countess of Camperdown, 61 ; Lady Julia Janet Georgina, 61.

Halk, Sophia, 74.

Hall, Elizabeth, 142 ; Rev. Frederick, 94 ; Hannah Lax, 32 ; Joseph, 32, 142 ; Rev. Joseph, 32 ; Mary, 32 ; Sarah Ann Wilkinson, 142.

Hamer, Harriet, 118 ; Joshua, 118.

Hamerton, Emily, 8 ; William Henry, 8.

Hamilton, Adela Louisa, 72 ; Anna, 73 ; Anna Christina, 73 ; Archibald George Fuller, 73 ; Arthur Shirley, 139 ; Augusta Christina, 71 ; Augusta Harriet, 69 ; Charles Eliott, 72 ; Cordelia Eleanor, 71 ; Elinor Grace, 73 ; Eliza Euphemia, 70 ; Elizabeth Anna, 69, 70 ; Ethel Mary, 139 ; Euphemia, 69, 71 ; George Frederick, 72 ; George Thomas, 72 ; George Trayton Eliott, 69, 73 ; Helen, 72 ; Henry Francis Trayton, 73 ; Henry Rose, 69, 70 ; James, 71 ; John, 69, 71, 72 ; Rev. John, 69-71 ; Julia Helen, 72 ; Margaret Euphemia, 72 ; Margaret Louisa, 72 ; Mary Grace, 71 ; Mary Susannah Anne, 69 ; Reginald George Eliott, 73 ; Susannah Anne, 70.

Hammond, Agatha, 141 ; Joseph Hutchinson, M.D., 141.

Hamond, Caroline, 28 ; Elizabeth, Lady, 28 ; Admiral Sir Graham Eden, Bt., 28.

Hanbury, Isabella, 4 ; J. Capel, 4.

Hanbury-Tracy, Emily Elizabeth Alicia, Lady Sudeley, 133 ; Honble Madeleine Emily Augusta, 133 ; Thomas Charles, Baron Sudeley, 133.

Hand, Ellen Annie, 149; Ellen Julia, 149; Thomas, 149.
Handsley, Robert, 94.
Hannah, Rev. John Julius, 118.
Hanover, King of, 103; H.R.H. Princess Frederica of, 104.
Harbord, Honble and Rev. John, 41; Mary Ada, 41; Ralph Assheton, 41.
Hardcastle, Emily Augusta, 94; Mary Augusta, 94; Thomas, 94.
Harding, Helen, 119; Samuel Heath, 119; Selina, 119.
Hardinge, Lord, 102.
Hardy, Lieut.-Colonel Jonas Pasley, 6; Katherine, 6; Mary, 6; William Samuel, 6.
Harewood, Henrietta, Countess of, 36; Henry, Earl of, 36.
Hargreaves, Ann Jane, 176; Charlotte Anne, 93; Eleanor Mary, 93; John, 176; Colonel John, 93.
Harington, Rev. Dallas Oldfield, 96.
Harker, Caroline Sarah, 15; Gertrude Clara, 14, 15; John Cooke, 15; Sophia Caroline, 15.
Harness, Sir Henry Dewey, 178; Mary Charlotte, 178; Rev. William, 135.
Harper, Henry Roby, 178; Rev. Hugo Daniel, D.D., 178; Mary Charlotte, 178; Rosa Elizabeth, 178.
Harris, Eliza Bayfield, 72; Elizabeth, 163; Helen Vidal, 43; John, 43, 105; Captain John, R.N., 72; Joseph, 105; Mary Ann, 105.
Harrison, Ann, 137, 139; Anna, 25; Charles, 63; Frances Matilda, 26; Frederick, 63; Harriet, 26; Lady Harriet Eliza Danvers, 63; Jane, 63; Mary, 26; Rachel, 25; Robert, 25; Rev. Robert, 26; Sophia Mary, 25; Thomas, 25; Rev. Thomas, 15, 25; Rev. William Dann, 29.
Harrop, Caroline Mann, 121; Josiah, 121; Mary Maria, 121.
Harrowby, Nathaniel, Baron, 169.
Hartwell, Henrietta, 63.
Harvey, Bridges, 123; George Daniel, 165; Harriett, 165; Rev. William Wigan, B.D., 165.
Hawley, Augusta Harriet, 69; Catherine Elizabeth, Lady, 69; Rev. Charles, 70; Sir Henry, Bt., 69; Rev. James, 69.
Hawthorn, Agatha Wells Bridger, 28; John, 28; Robert, 27, 28; William, 28, 30, 32.
Hayman, Rev. E., 161.
Hayne, Rev. Leighton George, 56.
Haynes, Rev. Everard Joseph, 158.
Hazell, Rev. James Henry, 15.
Heath, Thomas, 153.
Heathcote, Anne, 163; Charles, 163; George Edensor, 163; John, 163.
Heathfield, Major-General Sir George Augustus, Baron, 69.
Heber, Emily, 42; Rt. Rev. Reginald, D.D., Bishop of Calcutta, 42.
Heberden, Rev. William, 103.
Heber-Percy, Alan William, 42; Algernon Charles, 42; Emily, 42; Honble Susan Alice, 42.
Hebert, Rev. Septimus, 114.
Heidenstam, Adèle Wilhelmine Marika, 61; Chevalier Charles von, 61.
Hely-Hutchinson, Honble Harriet, 119; Colonel the Honble Henry, 119; Marianne Christina Isabella, 119.
Hempson, Amis, 19.
Henley, Rev. C., 89.
Hervey, Rev. Manners William, 140.
Hesketh, Jessie Catherine, 21; Thomas, 21; Sir Thomas Dalrymple, 21.
Hessey, Rev. Francis, D.C.L., 3.
Hewitt, Charles, 71; Maria, 71.
Heygate, Rev. Reginald Thomas, 75.
Hickman, Rev. Thomas Greene, 19, 20.
Hill, John, 52; Mary, 52; General Rowland, Viscount, 6; Rt. Rev. Rowley, D.D., Bishop of Sodor and Man, 115.
Hinton, John, 11.

Hitchcock, Arthur, 8; Edward, 8; Emily, 8.
Hoare, Rev. Edward, 88.
Hobbs, Harriet, 70; James, 70.
Hoby, Elise Philippa Salkeld, 107; Jeanie Wilkie, 107; John, 107.
Hocking, Rev. William John, 2.
Hodges, Sydney, 87, 88.
Hodgson, Anne, 121; Rev. Christopher, 65; Ellis Leckonby, 156; John Grant, 104; Louisa Eliza, 104; Mary Ellen, 156; Rose, 104; William, 121.
Hodsoll, Arthur Maxfield Pollock, 53; Caroline, 52; Charles Maxfield, 52, 53; Charles Wilfred Pollock, 53; George Bertram Pollock, 53; Georgiana Katharine, 53; Georgiana Mary, 53; Harold Edward Pollock, 53; James, 52; James Hackett, 52; Julia Henrietta, 52; Laura, 52; Laura Caroline Ethel, 53; Maxfield, 52; Sarah, 52; Susanna, 52.
Holbech, Jane, 96; William, 96.
Holdsworth, Rev. George Kelly, 118; Susan Katherine, 118.
Holgate, John, 90.
Holland, Anne, 91; Rebecca, 91; William, 91.
Holmes, John, 96.
Hood, Henry Fuller Acland, 24.
Hook, Rev. Walter Farquhar (afterwards Dean), 28.
Hooker, Hester, 52.
Hopper, Arthur Richard, 139; Leonard, 139; Mabel Elizabeth, 139.
Hopton, John Dutton, 41.
Hopwood, Cecilia, 170; Edward John Gregge, 170.
Horwitz, Haller, 135; Maria Rives, 135; Orville, 135.
Howard, Adderley, 141; Catharine Penelope, 161; Catherine Marr, 141; Edith Susan Louisa, 134; Lady Fanny, 134; Frederick John, 134; Lady Jane Elizabeth, 132; John Elliot, 161; Louisa, 161; Margaret Fanny, 134; Mary Jane, 141; Thomas, Earl of Suffolk, 132; William Crewdson, 161; William Frederick, 134.
Howarth, Rev. Henry, 119.
Howson, Very Rev. John Saul, D.D., 140.
Hudson, Captain, R.N., 44; Mary, 44, 65.
Huggins, Rev. Canon, 171; Charlotte, 171; Mabel, 171.
Hughes, Elizabeth, 3; Emily Adelaide, 77; John, 3; Rev. John, 77; Margaret, 48; Margaret Frances, 3; Thomas, 93; William, 48; William Hastings, 77.
Hulse, Sir Edward, Bt., 36; Mary, 36; Mary, Lady, 36; Rev. Thomas, 36, 40.
Humfrey, Edward, 87; Martha, 87.
Hunt, Agnes Amelia, 108; Albert Edward, 107; Ambrose Robert, 107; Amelia Turner, 107; Ann, 105; Ann Caroline, 105; Annie Finch, 109; Arthur Joseph, 105; Arthur Rust, 105-107; Beatrice Frances, 109; Catherine Ann, 106; Christmas, 106; Cyril Ernest, 105; Dorothy Ann, 109; Edmund Crisp, 107; Edward Gowers, 108; Elise Philippa Salkeld, 107; Eliza Freeman, 109; Elizabeth, 105; Ella Rose, 109; Emily Jane, 106; Emily Marjorie, 106; Emma Sarah, 106; Ernest Eleazer Cecil, 108; Ethel, 109; Eveline Annie, 105; Fanny, 143; Frederick John, 107; George, 105; George Rust, 107; George Watkins, 106; Georgiana, 107; Gertrude Mary, 108; Harriette Mary, 41; Helen Anne, 109; Herbert Joseph, 106; Hilda Mary, 105, 107; Ida Mary, 106; John, 106, 108; John Dutton, 41; John Ernest, 108; John Henry, 109; Joseph, 105-107; Joseph George, 106; Lucina, 108; Marian, 107; Marian Elizabeth, 109; Marion Elizabeth Gertrude, 108; Mary, 108; Mary Ann, 105, 107; Mysie Lucy, 143; Percy Wright, 105; Rhoda Georgiana, 109; Samuel Denny, 106, 107; Samuel George, 107; Samuel Ling, 106; Sarah, 106, 109; Sarah Ann Phillis, 105; Sarah Elizabeth, 108; Thomas, 143; Thompson, 105; William, 105, 106; William Leonard, 107; William Wright, 105; Winnifred, 109; Wright, 105-107; Wright Albert, 109.

MacMahon, Ellen, 148; Ernest Edward, 148; Brigadier-General Patrick William, 148; Rosa Fetherston, 148.

Maconochie-Welwood, Alexander, Lord Meadowbank, 9; Anne, 9; Maria Isabella, 9; Lieut.-Colonel William Maximilian George, 9.

Madras, Bishop of, 111.

Magrath, Joseph Adolphus, 124; Mary Rosamond, 124; Nony Jane, 124.

Mair, John, 24; Sara Adelaide, 24.

Malet, Dr. Christopher Leycester, 4; Jane Hudson, 4.

Maling, Anne, 6; Lieut.-Colonel Thomas J., 6.

Manders, Caroline, 123; Richard, 123.

Manderson, Ann, 151; William, 151.

Mannering, Caroline, 52; Rev. Edward, 52; Edward Hill, 52; Mary, 52; Walter, 52.

Mari, Marquis di, 126; Nicoletta Letitia, 126.

Marks, Catherine Pickett, 90.

Marriott, Rev. George, 43.

Marsden, Rev. John Howard, 18; William, 158.

Marshall, Caroline Jane, 137; Caroline Mary, 137; John Goddard, 137; Joseph, 140; Lucy, 140; Sarah Maria, 159; Tresa Allan, 141; William, 159.

Martin, Amelia Mary 119; Rev. J. C., 147, 148; William Bennet, 119.

Mason, George Calver, 20; George Godson, 20; Harold Percy, 20; Lætitia Maria, 20; Marion Edith, 20.

Masterman, Alethea, 62; Henry, 62.

Maude, Rev. Arthur, 105, 106; Cordelia, 67; Rev. Thomas, 67.

Maule, William, Baron Panmure, 61; Patricia Heron, Lady Panmure, 61.

Maule-Ramsay, Fox, Baron Panmure, 60, 61; Montagu, Lady Panmure, 61.

Maurice, Rev. John Frederick Denison, 38.

Maxwell, Hamilton George, 10; Isabella, 10.

Maydew, Martha, 91.

Mayhew, John, 89; Mary, 89; Sarah, 89.

McAllister, Rev. James Adair, 2.

McDonnell, Lady Helen Laura, 104; Hugh Seymour, Earl of Antrim, 104.

McGrigor, Elizabeth Anna, 70; Sir James, Bt., 70; Maria Anne, 70; Mary, Lady, 70; Walter James, 70.

McLeod, Agnes Mary, 123; Bentley, 123; Llewellyn Wynn, 123; Nancy Bentley, 123.

McNicol, Rev. Alexander, 125; Marion, 125.

Meade, Honble and Rev. Sidney, 37.

Meadowbank, Alexander, Lord, 9.

Medwyn, John Hay, Lord, 60.

Mellish, Captain, 102; Emilie Marie Louise Wilhelmina, 102.

Melville, Elizabeth, Viscountess, 60; Henry, Viscount, 60; Robert, Viscount, 102; Robert Saunders, Viscount, 60.

Menzies, John, 60; Mary Anne, 60.

Merry, Eugenia Kathleen, 22; Eugenia Mary, 22; Thomas Richard, 22.

Metcalfe, Rev. Charles, 138; Charlotte, 138; Emily Russell, 138; Rev. George, 138; Mary, 138; William, 138; Rev. William Henry, 138.

Meyer, Emerentia Luise Franciska, 177; Johann Valentin, 177.

Mildred, Daniel, 43; Emily, 43; Emma Lucy, 43; Frederick, 43; Henry, 43.

Mill, Rev. Dr., 49.

Mills, Catharine Penelope, 153; Rev. Josias Grant, 80; William, 153.

Milne, Caroline Harriet Margaret, 82; Robert Oswald, 82; William Henry, 82.

Milton, Blanche, Lady, 157; Blanche Matilda Mary Anne, 157; Sir John, 157; Rev. William, 157; William Charles Wentworth-Fitzwilliam, Viscount, 36.

Minchin, Catherine, 97; Rev. Harry Holdsworth, 97.

Minns, Rev. George William Waller, 72.

Minton, Charles Lee, 154; Julia, 154; Mary 154; Thomas, 154.

Mitchell, Eliza Freeman, 109; George Onion, 107, 109; Mary Ann, 107; Rev. Percy Turner, 45; Sarah, 107, 109.

Molloy, Hester, 1; Lieutenant, 1.

Molony, Alice, 115; Chartres Brew, 115; Clara Penrose, 115; Godfrey Massy, 115.

Molyneux, Fanny, Lady, 139; Rev. Sir John Charles, Bt., 139; Rev. Canon Sir John William Henry, Bt., 139; Louisa Dorothy, Lady, 139.

Montgomery, Andrew Castle, 71; Cordelia Eleanor, 71; Helen Nagle Hill, 71; Robert Evans, 71.

Monypenny, Charlotte Jane, 115; Rev. James Isaac, 115.

Moody, Charles, 7; Katherine, 7; Margaret, 7; Thomas, 7.

Moon, Elizabeth, 112; Mary Elizabeth, 112; Richard, 112.

Moor, Rev. Canon Edward James, 65; Rev. Gerald Henry, 45.

Moore, William Armitage, 24.

Mordaunt, Alice, 45; Caroline Sophia, Lady, 45; Sir John, Bt., 45.

Morell, Magdalen, 74.

Moreton, Lady Georgina Mary Louisa, 160; Henry George Francis, Earl of Ducie, 160.

Morgan, Elizabeth, 174.

Mornington, Elizabeth, Countess of, 102; William, Earl of, 102.

Morris, James, 9; Margaret, 9.

Mortimer, George, 63; Hannah, 63.

Morton, Helen, Countess of, 136; Helen Geraldine Maria, Countess of, 136; Sholto George Watson, Earl of, 136.

Moss, Arthur, 64.

Mount, Ven^ble Archdeacon, 97; Christian, 62; Harriet, 62; Jane, 62; John, 62; Laura Sarah, 62; Margaret Emily, 97; Marianne Emily, 97; William, 62; William George, 97.

Moyle, Isabella Louisa, 161; Thomas, M.D., 161.

Munby, Edward Charles, 162; Edward Mason, 162; Rev. George Frederick Woodhouse, 162; Rev. John Pigott, 120; Rosamond Harriette, 162.

Munk, Caroline, 52; Edward, 52.

Munn, Rev. George Shaw, 104.

Munro, Alexander, 40; Charlotte Elizabeth Bell, 128; Dora Laidlaw, 128; Margaret, 40; Surgeon-General William, 128.

Murray, Caroline Sophia, 45; Rev. Francis, 45; Rt. Rev. George, Bishop of Rochester, 45.

Musgrave, Rev. Vernon, 98.

N

Nash, Rev. James Palmer, 75.

Neave, Rev. Henry, 70.

Neeld, Ann Maria, 81; Joseph, 81.

Neuville, Ernestine, 172.

Neville, Rev. William, 46.

Newbery, General Francis, 81; Margaret Elizabeth, 81.

Newland, Rev. Henry Garrett, 138.

Newnham, Caroline, 38; William, M.D., 38.

Newton, Lady Alice Laura Sophia, 39; Cecilia Florence, 39; Charlotte, 38, 39; Emily Charlotte, 38; George, 38, 39; George Douglas Cockrane, 39; George Onslow, 39; Mary, 39.

Nicholls, Sir George, 77; Jane, 77.

Nicholson, Adelaide Robina Winifrede Roddam, 116; Annie Morris, 116; Edward, 116; Lieut.-Colonel James Edward, 116; Jessie Jane, 92; John, 92; John W., 158; Martha, 92; Sarah Eleanor, 158; William Henry, 92.

Niebel, Anna Rosina, 152; Charles Gottlieb, 152.

Additions and Corrections.

ADDITIONS & CORRECTIONS.

AIRY. Vol. 7, page 117.—Hubert Airy died at Stoke House, Woodbridge, co. Suffolk, on Whit-Monday, 1 June, buried at Woodbridge 5 June 1903. Will dated 19 July 1901, proved at Ipswich 25 July 1903, by Osmund Airy, the brother, and Francis Woolnough Wythe Gross, the Executors.

Page 119.—William Shepley Airy was appointed Master at Denstone College 16 May 1900; proceeded M.A. 1901, ordained Deacon 1901, and Priest (by the Bishop of Lichfield) 1903.

Reginald Airy graduated B.A. from Trinity College, Cambridge, 1899.

ALLANBY. Vol. 8, page 17.—Eliza, widow of Erasmus Reginald William Lloyd, died 12 September, buried at Legbourne, co. Lincoln, 15 September 1902.

Page 19 (and Addenda, Vol. 9, page i.)—Commander Frederick Claude Hynman and Edith Mabel Allenby have issue a son, Dudley Jaffray Hynman Allenby, born at Malta on Thursday, 8 January 1903, and baptised there.

ALLCROFT. Vol. 8, page 59.—John Derby Allcroft was married at the Church of the Transfiguration, Fifth Avenue, New York, U.S.A., on Saturday, 13 September 1902, to Marietta, daughter of William Millar Ord, M.D., of Upper Brook Street, London, and widow of David Dwight Wells of Norwich, Connecticut, U.S.A. They have issue a son, John Derby Allcroft, born at Roke Manor, Romsey, co. Hants, on Monday, 28 September 1903, baptised at Roke Manor 14 January 1904.

AMPHLETT. Vol. 1, page 152.—Jane Elizabeth, daughter of John Amphlett, died, aged 53, on Friday, 21 August, buried in the cemetery at Stafford 24 August 1903.

AMPHLETT. Vol. 3, page 157.—Charles Edward Amphlett was gazetted Captain in the 6th (Inniskilling) Dragoons 16 August 1902.

Edward Paul Charlton Amphlett joined the Royal Military College, Sandhurst, as a Gentleman Cadet 19 September 1903.

ARMYTAGE. Vol. 1, page 234 (and Addenda, Vol. 7, page i.)—George Ayscough and Aimée Armytage have further issue a son, Reginald William Armytage, born at 18 Moore Street, Cadogan Square, Chelsea, London, on Monday, 18 May, baptised at St. Simon's, Lennox Gardens, Chelsea, 13 June 1903.

Page 235.—Laura Harriette, widow of the Ven^ble Charles William Holbech, Archdeacon of Coventry, died at Banbury, co. Oxford, in her 80th year, on Thursday, 23 April, buried at Farnborough, co. Warwick, 25 April 1903. Will dated 8 May 1901, proved at Oxford 6 June 1903, by Edward Ambrose Holbech and the Rev. Hugh Holbech, the sons, the Executors.

Page 236.—The Honble Fenella FitzHardinge, widow of Colonel Henry Armytage, died at 67 Warwick Square, London, on Friday, 20 November, buried in Putney Vale Cemetery, co. Surrey, 24 November 1903.

Rosetta Philippa, wife of Percy Armytage, died suddenly at 28 Hans Place, Chelsea, London, on New Year's Eve, Wednesday, 31 December 1902, buried in Putney Vale Cemetery, co. Surrey, 5 January 1903.

ASSHETON. Vol. 1, page 71 (*and Addenda, Vol. 6, page i.*)—Ralph Cockayne and Mildred Estelle Sybella Assheton have further issue a daughter, Mary Monica, born at "Hall Foot," Worston, near Clitheroe, co. Lancaster, on Wednesday, 6 May, baptised at Downham, co. Lancaster, 10 June 1903.

Ralph Cockayne Assheton was appointed J.P. for the West Riding of the county of York 1888, and for the county of Lancaster 1889, and an Alderman of the Lancashire County Council 1902.

Page 72.—Richard and Frances Annette Ellen Assheton have further issue a daughter, Dulcia, born at "Riversdale," Grantchester, co. Cambridge, on Wednesday, 3 December 1902, baptised at Grantchester 3 January 1903.

BACK. Vol. 6, pages 119 and 123.— Hatfield James Back died at Hill House, Dedham, co. Essex, aged 84, on Thursday, 6 November, buried at Ardleigh, co. Essex, on Tuesday, 11 November 1902.

BAILEY. Vol. 7, page 49.—Lieut.-Colonel Edmund Wyndham Grevis and Alberta Sylva Bailey have issue a son, James von Hæstrecht Evelyn Grevis Bailey, born at Nepicar House, Wrotham, co. Kent, on Monday, 24 November 1902, baptised at St. Peter's, Ightham, co. Kent, 15 January 1903.

BARNARDISTON. Vol. 8, page 42.— Nathaniel Walter Barnardiston was appointed Military Attaché, with temporary rank of Lieut.-Colonel to the Courts of Norway, Sweden and Denmark in 1903.

Page 44 (*and Addenda Vol. 10, page ii.*)—Geoffry and Mildred Jane Barnardiston have issue a son, Nathaniel Montague Barnardiston, born at Birstwith, co. York, 16 October, baptised at Henny, co. Essex, 23 December 1903.

Samuel John Barrington Barnardiston, D.S.O., was promoted Captain The Suffolk Regiment 18 April 1903.

BARTLETT. Vol. 1, page 66.—John Adams Bartlett was married at St. Margaret's, Prince's Road, Liverpool, on Tuesday, 21 April 1903, to Ellen Violet Murray, only daughter of the Rev. William Mayor, formerly Vicar of Shotton, co. Durham, by Ellen his wife, daughter of George Murray; born 24 June 1872.

BENTLEY. Vol. 1, page 138.—Edward John, eldest and last surviving son of Edward Bentley, M.D., was born 30 December 1844, and died at 10 Mount Albion Road, Ramsgate, co. Kent, on Wednesday, 18 November, buried in Highgate Cemetery, co. Middlesex, 23 November 1903. Will dated 10 July 1900, proved at the Principal Registry 9 December 1903, by Madeline Isabella Bentley, the sister, and George Edward Hayles, the cousin, the Executors.

Page 140.—Frederick Bentley died suddenly at Streatham Common, co. Surrey, on Sunday, 11 October, buried in Norwood Cemetery, co. Surrey, 16 October 1903. Will dated 3 June 1899, proved (Prin. Reg., 45, 1903) 13 November 1903, by the Rev. Frederick William Bentley, the son, the sole Executor.

BLACKBURNE. Vol. 10, page 144.— Lieut.-Colonel Robert Ireland Blackburne was decorated by H.M. the King as a Companion of the Order of the Bath (military division) at the Levee held at Buckingham Palace on Monday, 18 May 1903, and is now Honorary Colonel (formerly Lieut.-Colonel Commanding) 3rd Battalion Prince of Wales' Volunteer (South Lancashire) Regiment.

BOND. Vol. 3, page 72.—Lewis Charles Powell and Martha Bond have further issue a son, Sydney William Bond, born at Burford, Ontario, Canada, 22 October 1903, and baptised there.

BRINE. Vol. 4, page 21.—Arthur Brine was married at Holy Trinity, Brook Green, co. Middlesex, on Wednesday, 22 July 1903, to Hester Harriet Amelia, elder daughter of Gideon Colquhoun Sconce, late Chief Judge of the Presidency Small Cause Court, Calcutta.

Page 22 (*and Addenda, Vol. 6, page ii*). Henrietta Ina Lindesay Brine, who died, aged 33, 30 July, was buried in the churchyard at Bishops Waltham, co. Hants, 3 August 1897. M.I. and Memorial Window.

Page 22.—The remains of Frederic Bruce Brine, who was buried at Gravesend, co. Kent, 3 June 1884, were re-interred in the churchyard at Bishops Waltham 16 March 1898. M.I. and Memorial Window.

Page 22 (*and Addenda, Vol. 8, page iii.*)—Lieutenant Robert Walter Maxwell Brine, who was killed in action

BRINE, *continued.*

at Belmont, South Africa, 23 November 1899 (medal and clasp), was buried at Belmont. M.I. there and at Garrison Church, Portsmouth, also at Bishops Waltham, where there is a Memorial Window. Memorial Tablets in the St. Clare School Chapel, Walmer, and in Marlborough College Chapel.

Page 22 (*and Addenda, Vol. 7, page ii.*)—Frederic George and Irene Mary Brine have issue a daughter, Mary Sophia Bouverie, born at 2 St. Lawrence Villas, Canterbury, on Sunday, 1 November, baptised at Lower Hardres, co. Kent, on Wednesday, 16 December 1903.

BROCKLEBANK. Vol. 9, page 142.—Richard Moon Brocklebank died at "The Firs," Great Malvern, co. Worcester, aged 60, on Thursday, 27 August, buried in the cemetery at Great Malvern on Saturday, 29 August 1903. Will dated 9 December 1899, proved (Prin. Reg., 47, 1903) 13 November 1903, by Ralph Brocklebank and Thomas Brocklebank, the brothers, the Executors.

BROMLEY. Vol. 5, page 136 (*and Addenda, Vol. 9, page iii.*)—Nathaniel Barrett Warner and Minnie Heather Bromley have issue a daughter, Monica Violet Warner, born at "Mondisfield," The Ridgeway, Enfield, co. Middlesex, on Friday, 16 January, baptised at Christ Church, Enfield, 19 April 1903.

BROOKE. Vol. 1, page 73.—William Henry Rawson died s.p., aged 45, on Friday, 1 December, buried at St. Peter's, Sowerby, co. York, 5 December 1893. Will dated 15 July 1893, proved (Prin. Reg., 370, 94) 21 March 1894, by Frances Jane Rawson, Constance Ellen Rawson, John Selwyn Rawson and William Pickford, the Executors. (*See Pedigree of Rawson, Vol. 8, page 68.*)

Page 74.—Helen Beatrice, wife of John Kendall Brooke, died at Sibton Park, co. Suffolk, 4 February 1897, and buried at Sibton. Administration was granted at the Principal Registry 19 March 1897, to John Kendall Brooke, the husband.

John Kendall Brooke of Sibton Park, was married 2ndly at Hacheston, co. Suffolk, on Tuesday, 24 September 1901, to Katharine Frances, eldest daughter of Arthur Heywood of Glevering, co. Suffolk.

BROOKE, *continued.*

Page 75 (*and Addenda, Vol, 9, page iii.*)—Sir Thomas Brooke, Baronet, was married 3rdly at Armitage Bridge, co. York, 30 September 1902, to Mary, daughter of James Priestley of "Bank Field," Huddersfield, co. York, and widow of the Rev. Charles Farrar Forster, Vicar of Beckwithshaw, co York.

Page 78.—The Rev. Harold John Brooke died at Queenstown, New Zealand, leaving issue three children, 7 October, buried at Queenstown 10 October 1903.

Page 79.—Edward Brooke died at Renfrew, aged 67, 28 July, buried in the cemetery at Scarborough, co. York, 1 August 1898. Will dated 25 November 1892, with codicil dated 31 December 1895, proved (Prin. Reg., 1088, 98) 8 October 1898, by Henry Norman Brooke, the son, Bernard Parker and Annie Maud Hirst (wife of Francis Joseph Hirst) the daughter, the Executors.

Joseph Brooke Turner died at Scarborough, aged 66, 1 October, buried in the cemetery at Scarborough 4 October 1899. Administration was granted at York 25 October 1899, to Joseph Brooke Turner.

Jane, wife of Joseph Brooke Turner, died at Scarborough, aged 64, 25 September, buried in the cemetery at Scarborough 28 September 1896.

Edward Burkill Brooke died at Almondbury, co. York, 11 November 1893, and buried there. Will dated 12 November 1889, proved at Wakefield 9 February 1894, by Edward Brooke, the father, one of the Executors.

The Rev. Riou George Benson died at 53 Bootham, York, in his 62nd year, on Saturday, 18 January, buried at Hope Bowdler, co. Salop, 21 January 1896. Administration (with will dated 5 March 1862) was granted (Prin. Reg., 440, 96) 8 May 1896, to Riou Philip Benson, Captain in the Royal Artillery, the natural and lawful son and one of the next of kin.

Page 80.—William Brooke died at York, aged 60, 3 November, buried in the cemetery at York 6 November 1899.

Elizabeth, youngest daughter of Edward Brooke, died at Hampstead, co. Middlesex, aged 53, on Saturday, 14 July, buried at Honley, co. York, 18 July 1894. Will dated 6 June 1893,

BROOKE, *continued.*
with codicil dated 2 April 1894, proved (Prin. Reg., 850, 94) 25 August 1894, by Henry Brooke, the brother, and Charles Edward Freeman, the Executors.

Page 81.—Henry Brooke died at Warrenfield, Sheepridge, co. York, 11 September, buried at Honley 14 September 1903. Will dated 10 January 1902, proved at Wakefield 6 November 1903, by Hilda Eastwood, the daughter, Harry Arnold Eastwood, the son-in-law, and John Arthur Freeman, the Executors.

BROWN. Vol. 2, page 25.—Henry Forbes Darell-Brown (educated at New College, Oxford, matriculated 23 January 1886, aged 18, from Marlborough College, and is now Captain in the 2nd Oxfordshire Light Infantry), was married at Messing, co. Essex, on Tuesday, 22 December 1903, to Kathleen Edith Maude, only daughter of Charles de Bassyn Fox, formerly of County Cavan, J.P., by Emma Penelope his wife, daughter of Edmund Packe.

The Rev. Otway Darell Darell-Brown was educated at St. Edward's School, Oxford, St. John's College, Oxford, and Scholæ Cancellarii, Lincoln ; Curate of Laceby and Riby, co. Lincoln, 1900 –1902, and of St. Saviour's, Walton Street, London, since 1903.

BRUNKER. Vol. 10, page 115.—Edward George Brunker was married at St. Andrew's, Fulham, co. Middlesex, 15 September 1902, to Louie Elizabeth, youngest daughter of Clement More of 19 Barton Street, Kensington, London, and formerly of Metfield Hall, co. Suffolk. They have issue a son, Edward George Brunker, born at 38 Waldemar Avenue Mansions, Fulham, 11 July, baptised privately at Rathmines, co. Dublin, 10 September 1903.

BUCKLER. Vol. 2, page 165.—Emma Sidney, widow of George Buckler, died at Camberwell New Road, London, in her 86th year, on Tuesday, 12 May, buried in Nunhead Cemetery, co. Surrey, 15 May 1903.

BURKE. Vol 3, page 44.—Kathleen Laura, daughter of Ulick John Burke, was married at Bramdean, co. Hants, on Wednesday, 17 December 1902, to Hugh Nicholson, late Captain King's Royal Rifles, son of William Nicholson of Basing Park, co. Hants.

BURY. Vol. 9, page 117.—Cecil Charles Bury, son of Frederick Maxwell Bury, died at George Town, Demerara, British Guiana, 25 May 1903.

The Rev. William and Eleanor Jane Bury have issue a son, William Gerard Stillingfleet Bury, born at the Rectory, Great Henny, co. Essex, 3 November, baptised at Great Henny 29 November 1903.

BUSH. Vol. 6, page 77 (*and Addenda, page ii.*)—Robert Bush (M. Inst. C.E. 1903) and Beatrice Irene his wife have further issue a son, Herbert Edward Bush, born at Liverpool 3 December 1902, baptised at St. Catherine's, Abercromby Square, Liverpool, 1 January 1903.

CASTLE. Vol. 5, page 45.—Edgar Castle was married at St. Martin-in-the-Fields, London, 18 May 1901, to Ellen Maud, daughter of George Edward Clive and Amy Sarah Griffin of Clapham, co. Surrey; born at 76 South Lambeth Road, London, 7 August 1870, baptised at St. Ann's, South Lambeth Road, 24 November 1871. They have issue two sons, John Edgar Castle, born at 3 Carlton Hill, St. John's Wood, London, on Tuesday, 28 January, baptised at St. Mark's, Hamilton Terrace, St. John's Wood, 8 June 1902, and Desmond William Handley Castle, born at 3 Carlton Hill, St. John's Wood, on Monday, 27 July, baptised at All Saints', St. John's Wood, 26 August 1903.

Page 48.—Septimus Castle was President of the Incorporated Law Society of Liverpool 1902–1903.

CAUDLE. Vol. 8, page 121.—Adolphus William Wisden Caudle died at Millbrook Lodge, Millbrook, co. Hants, in his 63rd year, on Whit-Monday, 1 June, buried in the cemetery at Henfield, co. Sussex, on Thursday, 4 June 1903. Will dated 22 April 1902, proved (Prin. Reg., 25, 1903) 22 June 1903, by Annie Homewood Thornton, the sister, the sole Executrix.

CAVENDISH. Vol. 1, page 132.—Cecil Charles and Maud Henrietta Cavendish have further issue a son, Charles Vernon Balfour Cavendish, born at the residence of his grandfather, Major-General George Thomas Halliday, B.S.C., 65 Redcliffe Gardens, South Kensington, London, on Tuesday, 14 October, baptised at St. Luke's, Redcliffe Gardens, South Kensington, on Saturday, 15 November

CAVENDISH, *continued.*
1902. Major Cecil Charles Cavendish was transferred, 18 April 1902, from the 74th Highland Light Infantry to the 4th Battalion Royal Garrison Regiment at Malta, of which he is second in command.

Page 133.—Spencer Frederick George Cavendish is now of Penhalonga, Umtali, South Rhodesia, South Africa.

Godfrey Lionel John Cavendish was appointed, 22 April 1903, 2nd Lieutenant in the 1st Battalion Manchester (63rd) Regiment, now at Singapore, Straits Settlements.

Page 134.—Ernest Lionel Francis Cavendish was promoted, January 1904, to be Governor of Swansea Prison.

CHAFY. Vol. 7, page 112.—Hugh Edmund Chafy was married at St. Mark's, Swindon, co. Wilts, on Wednesday, 1 July 1903, to Henrietta Sibyl, 5th daughter of George Money Swinhoe of Park House, Swindon, and formerly of the 95th Regiment.

Honor Annette, daughter of the Rev. William Kyle Westwood Chafy, D.D., died at the Midland Nursing Home, aged 20, on Thursday, 2 April, buried at Rous Lench, co. Worcester, 7 April 1903.

CHAMPNEYS. Vol. 10, page 50.—Montague Storr Champneys was buried at Tooting, co. Surrey, 1 August 1868.

CHANCE. Vol. 3, page 67.—George Chance died at his residence, 28 Leinster Gardens, London, aged 84, on Tuesday, 17 February, buried at Harrow Weald, co. Middlesex, on Saturday, 21 February 1903. Will dated 10 July 1889, with codicil dated 27 April 1898, proved (Prin. Reg., 21, 1903) 17 March 1903, by Arthur Frederick Chance, Frank Loftus Wright and Harry Chance, three of the Executors.

Mary, widow of George Chance, died at "The Wainhams," Shrewsbury, co. Salop, in her 75th year, on Thursday, 23 July, buried at Harrow Weald 28 July 1903. Will dated 18 December 1898, proved (Prin. Reg., 65, 1903) 3 September 1903, by Arthur Frederick Chance and Harry Chance, the sons, the surviving Executors.

Page 69.—Lucy Georgina, youngest daughter of Henry Chance, was married at St. George's, Hanover Square,

CHANCE, *continued.*
London, 2 February 1903, to William Francis Bennett, 2nd son of William Henry Massy Bennett of Glenefy, co. Limerick, J.P. for the counties of Limerick and Tipperary, by Fanny his wife, daughter of Thomas Bolton.

Page 71 (*and Addenda, Vol. 9, page iv.*) George Harold de Peyster and Maude Chance have further issue a son, Brian Kesteven de Peyster Chance, born at Sydney, New South Wales, on Friday, 28 August 1903.

Page 71.—Florence Hasted, wife of Alexander Macomb Chance, died at "Lawnside," Edgbaston, co. Warwick, aged 53, on Wednesday, 8 July, buried in the churchyard at Quinton, co. Worcester, 11 July 1903.

CHASE. Vol. 5, page 76.—The Rev. Frederic Henry Chase, D.D., was elected Vice-Chancellor of Cambridge University in 1902, having been appointed Norrisian Professor of Divinity and President of Queen's College in 1901.

CLAPTON. Vol. 10, page 9.—Mary, wife of Edward Clapton, M.D., died at "Towercroft," Lee, co. Kent, in her 70th year, on Sunday, 27 December, buried in the cemetery at Stamford, co. Lincoln, on Thursday, 31 December 1903.

Page 10.—The Rev. Edward Travers Clark (*see Pedigree of Clark, present volume, page 80*) was appointed Vicar of Newnham-on-Severn, co. Gloucester, July 1902, and Surrogate for the diocese of Gloucester 1902.

CLIPPINGDALE. Vol. 9, page 172.—Elizabeth, wife of John Abbott, died at 6 Chichester Terrace, Brighton, co. Sussex, 8 August, buried in the Extra Mural Cemetery, Brighton, 12 August 1903.

COLLINS. Vol. 4, page 114.—Henry John and Jane Frances Leslie Collins have further issue a son, John Ferdinando Collins, born at Caversham, co. Oxford, 7 December, baptised at St. Peter's, Caversham, 30 December 1898; a daughter, Mary Justina, born at Caversham 8 May, baptised at St. Peter's, Caversham, 13 June 1900; and a daughter Patricia, born at Reading, co. Berks, 27 September, baptised at All Saints', Reading, 1 November 1903.

COLMAN. Vol. 9, page 7.—Cecil Colman was married at West Cliff Tabernacle, Bournemouth, co. Hants, 5 August 1903, to Florence Beatrice, 2nd daughter of Henry Laws of "Trefula," Bournemouth, by Elizabeth Ann his wife, daughter of William Caldwell.

COMBER. Vol. 7, page 148.—Eleanor, widow of Edward Comber, died at Myddleton Hall, Warrington, co. Lancaster, in her 85th year, on Sunday, 22 November, buried at Winwick, co. Lancaster, 25 November 1903. Will dated 16 October 1895.

Page 148 (*and Addenda, Vol. 10, page v.*)—Edward and Jane Frances Hartley Comber have issue a son, Thomas Alfred Comber, born at Bombay, India, 19 December 1902.

CONYERS. Vol. 5, page 1.—Marcia Amelia Mary, Baroness Conyers, succeeded as 7th Baroness Fauconberg on the determination of the abeyance of that Barony in her favour by the Committee for Privileges 29 September 1903, and was declared coheir with her sister, the Countess of Powis, 23 July 1903, to the Barony of Darcy.

COODE. Vol. 2, page 18.—Mary, elder daughter of Edward Coode, died at The Old House, St. Austell, co. Cornwall, aged 80, on Wednesday, 3 December, buried at St. Austell 6 December 1902. Will dated 3 October 1898, proved at Bodmin 7 February 1903, by William Melvill Coode and Philip Melvill Coode.

Page 19 (*and Addenda, Vol. 7, page iii.*)—John Melvill and Ruth Caroline Coode have further issue a daughter, Ruth Evelyn Penelope, born at Jubblepore, Central Provinces, India, 13 February 1903, and baptised there.

COOKSON. Vol. 3, page 131.—Frederick William Cookson was married at Bangkok, Siam, 16 January 1903, to Isabella, only child of Frederick Solomon of Bangkok, by Margaret Fitzgerald his wife. They have issue a son, Charles Percival Cookson, born at Bangkok 14 November 1903.

Page 133.—Frederick Nesfield Cookson was married at St. Mary's, Dolgelly, co. Merioneth, 10 June 1903, to Mary MacIver Percival, 2nd daughter of Thomas Parry Jones-Parry of "Tany Gader," Dolgelly, by Sarah his wife,

COOKSON, *continued.* daughter of Hughes Barlow of Avenbury, co. Denbigh; born at Llangollen, co. Denbigh, 13 April 1871.

Cicely Mary, youngest daughter of Thomas Chorley Cookson, was married at St. George's, Leeds, co. York, 10 November 1903, Charles John Tiffen, M.D. Edin. 1885, M.B., C.M. 1882.

Page 134 (*and Addenda, Vol. 9, page iv.*)—Montague Nesfield and Ellen Marie Cookson have further issue a daughter, Edith Joyce Nesfield, born at Nuneaton, co. Warwick, 3 December 1903, baptised at St. Nicholas', Nuneaton, on Sunday, 17 January 1904.

COWPER-ESSEX. Vol. 6, page 11 (*and Addenda, Vol. 10, page v.*)—Henry Swainson and Amy Mary Cowper have issue a son, Christopher Swainson Cowper, born at High House, Hawkshead, co. Lancaster, 13 June 1903, and baptised there the same day.

CRAIG. Vol. 5, page 35.—Algernon Tudor Craig was gazetted Major 4th Battalion Royal Irish Rifles 29 November 1902, and resigned his Adjutancy of the 8th Provisional Battalion 13 January 1903, on his appointment as Secretary of the Incorporated Soldiers' and Sailors' Help Society.

CRANWORTH. Vol. 10, page 93.—Robert Thornhagh, Baron Cranworth, died at his residence, Letton Hall, Thetford, co. Norfolk, aged 73, on Monday, 13 October, buried at Cranworth, co. Norfolk, on Friday, 17 October 1902. Will dated 26 April 1901, with two codicils dated respectively 26 April 1901 and 13 June 1901, proved (Prin. Reg., 1505, 1902) 4 December 1902, by the Rt. Hon[ble] Bertram Francis, Baron Cranworth, the son, one of the Executors.

Bertram Francis, Lord Cranworth, who succeeded his father as 2nd Baron 13 October 1902, was married at St. Peter's, Eaton Square, London, on Saturday, 18 July 1903, to Vera Emily, eldest daughter of Arthur William Ridley of 92 Eaton Place, London, by Adriana Elizabeth his wife, eldest daughter of F. R. Newton.

CRAWFURD. Vol. 2, page 9.—
The Rev. Lionel Payne Crawfurd,
who was instituted Vicar of St.
Cuthbert's, Bensham, Gateshead, co.
Durham, 20 September 1902, was
married at the Church of the Holy
Innocents, Belair, South Australia,
8 January 1902, to Georgina, daughter
of Thomas Kinley Hamilton, M.D., by
Richenda his wife. They have issue
a daughter, Mary Ina, born at St.
Cuthbert's Vicarage, Bensham, Gates-
head, on Monday, 8 June, baptised at
St. Cuthbert's, Bensham, on St. Peter's
Day, 29 June 1903.

Page 9 (*and Addenda, Vol. 6, page iv.*)
Raymond Henry Payne and Ethelberta
Ormrod Crawfurd have further issue a
son, Alan Crawfurd, born at 71 Harley
Street, London, on Saturday, 11 April,
baptised at Christ Church, Harwood,
co. Lancaster, 27 May 1903.

CRIPPS. Vol. 2, page 119.—Wilfred
Joseph Cripps, C.B., died at Cirencester,
co. Gloucester, aged 62, on Monday,
26 October, buried in the cemetery
at Cirencester 29 October 1903.

Page 120 (*and Addenda, Vol. 10,
page v.*)—Egerton Tymewell and Hilda
Katharine Gambier Cripps have issue
a son, William Parry Cripps, born
at "Stratton Firs," Cirencester, on
Tuesday, 23 June, baptised at Ampney
Crucis, co. Gloucester, 26 July 1903.

CURE. Vol. 2, page 22.—George Edward
Capel Cure was married at St. Paul's,
Knightsbridge, London, 5 November
1903, to Ione Catherine Victoria,
daughter of Victor Paley of Freckenham,
co. Sussex, by Augusta Harriet his wife,
daughter of the Rev. Evan Nepean,
Canon of Westminster; born in London,
and baptised at Westminster Abbey.

Page 24.—Margaret, daughter of the
Rev. Laurence George Capel Cure,
died suddenly at Abbess Roding
Rectory, co. Essex, aged 41, on Monday,
20 July, buried at Abbess Roding
24 July 1903.

DARBY. Vol. 4, page 48.—Matilda
Frances, widow of Abraham Darby,
died at "Sunnyside," Coalbrookdale, co.
Salop, in her 93rd year, on Tuesday,
16 December, buried at Coalbrookdale
20 December 1902. Will dated
3 August 1899, with codicil dated
10 October 1900, proved in the Principal
Registry July 1903, by Alfred Edmund
William Darby and W. Blyth.

DARWIN. Vol. 4, page 117.—Richard
Buckley Litchfield died at Cannes,
France, aged 71, on Sunday, 11 January
1903, and buried there. Will dated
27 August 1902, proved (Prin. Reg.,
33, 1903) 26 January 1903, by Leonard
Darwin and Bernard Richard Meirion
Darwin, the Executors.

Page 118.—Ellen Wordsworth, wife
of Francis Darwin, died at Cambridge,
aged 47, on Saturday, 29 August, buried
at Girton, co. Cambridge, 1 September
1903.

DEW. Vol. 1, page 282.—Henry
Monkhouse Dew was married 2ndly
at St. Paul's, Finsbury, London, on
Wednesday, 5 February 1902, to Lena
Mary Meta, only daughter of the Rev.
Thomas James Bewsher, Rector of
Cley-next-the-Sea, co. Norfolk.

Page 285.—Margaret Louise, youngest
daughter of Major Frederick Napleton
Dew, was married at St. Stephen's,
Gloucester Road, London (by the
Rev. Roderick Dew, brother of the
bride), on Tuesday, 18 November 1902,
to Philip James Stopford, Lieutenant
R.N., H.M.S. "Australia," 2nd son of
James Sydney Stopford.

DICKEN. Vol. 7, page 140.—Captain
Charles Gauntlett Dicken, R.N., was
made Inspecting Captain of Torpedo
Boat Destroyers 24 February 1902, and
appointed as Commodore in Charge at
Hong Kong, China, 1 January 1904.

Charles Vernon Dicken was appointed
Mathematical Master at Bishop's
College School, Lennoxville, in the
province of Quebec, Canada, 27 August
1903.

Edward Bernard Cornish Dicken,
R.N., passed from "Britannia," after
cruise in H.M.S. "Aurora," 16 December
1903.

Page 142.—Catherine Lamb, widow
of William Stephens Dicken, died at
St. Leonard's-on-Sea, co. Sussex, aged 91,
on Friday, 17 July, buried in Ocklynge
Cemetery, Eastbourne, co. Sussex,
22 July 1903. Will dated 25 September
1887, with codicil dated 22 November
1902, proved (Prin. Reg., 54, 1903)
7 August 1903, by Florence Elizabeth
Statham, the daughter, the sole
Executrix.

Lord Henry Ulick Browne succeeded
his brother, John Thomas, Marquess of
Sligo, who died 30 December 1903,
as 5th Marquess of Sligo.

DICKEN, *continued.*

Page 143.—Charles Shortt Dicken, C.M.G., died at South Kensington, London, aged 61, on Wednesday, 12 November, buried in Brookwood Cemetery, Woking, co. Surrey, on Monday, 17 November 1902. Will dated 23 May 1878, proved (Prin. Reg., 29, 1903) 12 February 1903, by Emily Augusta Dicken, the relict, the sole Executrix.

DICKINSON. Vol. 1, page 293.—Mary Ann (Henrietta), wife of William Dickinson, died at "Springfield," Bedford Hill, Balham, co. Surrey, 6 October, buried in Paddington Cemetery, Willesden Lane, co. Middlesex, 10 October 1903.

DUGDALE. Vol. 2, page 106.—John Dugdale of Llwyn Llanfyllin, co. Montgomery, died at 9 Hyde Park Gardens, London, in his 83rd year, 9 December, buried in the cemetery at Llanfyllin on Tuesday, 15 December 1903. Will dated 4 February 1897, proved in the Principal Registry 12 January 1904, by John Marshall Dugdale and Charles Tertius Dugdale, the sons, two of the Executors.

John Percy Dugdale died at Mentone, France, aged 23, on Wednesday, 15 April, buried in the cemetery at Llanfyllin 23 April 1903.

Page 107.—Edith, wife of the Rev. Sydney Dugdale, Vicar of Westbury, co. Wilts, died at Westbury, aged 43, on Wednesday, 11 November, buried there 14 November 1903.

Edith Christian, youngest daughter of James Dugdale of Wroxall Abbey, co. Warwick, was married at Wroxall Abbey Chapel on Tuesday, 28 July 1903, to Godfrey Gillson, Captain R.A., 2nd son of Henry Gillson of "Mudeford," Christchurch, co. Hants.

EARLE. Vol. 10, page 112.—Ida Euphemia Bertie, wife of Arthur Earle, died at Childwall Lodge, Wavertree, co. Lancaster, on Wednesday, 1 April, buried at Childwall 4 April 1903.

EDWARDS. Vol. 1, page 259.—Emma, daughter of William Edwards, and wife of the Rev. Thomas William Meller, died at Ipswich, co. Suffolk, aged 83, on Saturday, 31 January, buried in the cemetery at Woodbridge, co. Suffolk, 4 February 1903. Will dated 17 October 1902, proved at Ipswich 31 March 1903, by Alfred Meller, the son, the sole Executor.

EDWARDS, *continued.*

Page 260.—Anne, widow of Thomas William Grimwood, died at her residence, Woodbridge, co. Suffolk, in her 83rd year, on Saturday, 23 May, buried in the cemetery at Woodbridge 27 May 1903. Will dated 30 January 1903, proved at Ipswich 2 July 1903, by Henry Charles Edwards, the nephew, Samuel Stagoll Higham and Thomas Richard Grimwood, godson, the Executors.

EVANS. Vol. 4, page 91.—Margaret Fleming, wife of Edgar Besant, died at 2 St. John's Gardens, Ladbroke Grove, Notting Hill, London, 11 September, buried in the cemetery at Hanwell, co. Middlesex, 15 September 1903.

Page 93.—John Nevett Evans was married at St. Peter's, Eastbourne, co. Sussex, on Thursday, 16 April 1903, to Ethel Louise Gladstone, youngest daughter of Alexander Grant Smith Langhorne, formerly of 44 Holland Park Gardens, London.

FANSHAWE. Vol. 6, page 114.—John Gaspard Fanshawe died at 132 Ebury Street, Pimlico, London, 27 December, buried in Brompton Cemetery, London, 31 December 1903.

Barbara Frederica Beaujolois, wife of John Gaspard Fanshawe, died at 215 Ebury Street, Pimlico, London, 31 January, buried in Brompton Cemetery, London, 5 February 1903.

Basil Thomas and Mary Georgiana Fanshawe have further issue a son, Evelyn Gascoyne Fanshawe, born 16 August, baptised at Bratton Fleming, co. Devon, 13 September 1903. Sponsors: Morland Greig, John Mason Mason, Dowager Lady Clerke and Helen Crawshay.

FAULCONER. Vol. 4, page 83.—Mary, widow of Robert Stephen Faulconer, died at "Fairlawn," Clarence Road, Clapham Park, co. Surrey, in her 83rd year, on Friday, 30 January, buried in Norwood Cemetery, co. Surrey, on Wednesday, 4 February 1903. Will dated 10 March 1899, proved (Prin. Reg., 58, 1903) 20 February 1903, by Frederick Arthur Crisp, the nephew, the sole Executor.

FAWCETT. Vol. 6, page 52.—Eliza Maria, widow of William Fawcett, died 14 February, buried in Fisherton

FAWCETT, *continued.*
Cemetery, Salisbury, co. Wilts, 17 February 1903. Will dated 26 October 1901, proved at Salisbury 25 March 1903, by Sidney Fawcett, the step-son, the sole Executor.

FAWKES. Vol. 7, page 92.—Edith Mary, widow of Ayscough Fawkes, died at Taormina, Sicily, 11 March 1903, and buried at Farnley, co. York. Will dated 18 December 1901, proved (Prin. Reg., 44, 1903) 18 April 1903, by Frederick Robert McClintock, the brother-in-law, one of the Executors.

Page 95.—Rear-Admiral Wilmot Hawksworth Fawkes was created C.V.O. 1902, and K.C.V.O. 1903.

FELLOWES. Vol. 8, page 101.—Dora Mackenzie, daughter of the Rev. Henry John Fellowes, died at "Torridon," Bournemouth West, co. Hants, 29 December 1902, buried at All Saints', Bournemouth, 1 January 1903.

Page 102.—Hilda, daughter of the Rev. Henry John Fellowes, was married at All Saints', Bournemouth, 2 February 1903, to Henry Reginald Hetherington, son of the Rev. Henry Hetherington, formerly Vicar of West Bradenham, co. Norfolk, by Anne Margaret his wife, daughter of the Rev. George Charles Hoste; born at Wetheringsett Rectory, co. Suffolk, on Friday, 17 May, bapt. at Wetheringsett 7 July 1867.

Page 104.—The Rev. Edmund Horace and Lilian Louisa Fellowes have further issue a son, William Hamilton Fellowes, born at the Cloisters, Windsor Castle, co. Berks, on Saturday, 11 July, baptised at St. George's Chapel, Windsor Castle, 23 September 1903.

FIELD. Vol. 3, page 82.—Ellen, widow of Benjamin Field, died at her residence, 4 Calverley Park, Tunbridge Wells, co. Kent, in her 78th year, on Sunday, 5 July, buried at the cemetery, Tunbridge Wells, 9 July 1903. Will dated 19 December 1902, proved (Prin. Reg., 56, 1903) 24 September 1903, by the Rev. Sydney Benjamin Field and Walter Field, the sons, and Margaret Field, the daughter, the Executors.

FIRTH. Vol. 4, page 141.—Frederic Hand Firth died at Place, Ashburton, co. Devon, in his 80th year, on Sunday, 18 October, buried at Widecombe-in-the-Moor, co. Devon, on Thursday, 22 October 1903. Will dated 14 February 1889, proved in the Principal

FIRTH, *continued.*
Registry 23 December 1903, by Frederic William Firth, Walter Alfred Firth and Henry Mallaby Firth of Knowle, Ashburton, the Executors.

FLAVEL. Vol. 1, page 207.—Sidney Reginald Flavel was married at St. Mary Abbott's, Kensington, London, on New Year's Eve, Thursday, 31 December 1903, to Winifred Marion, youngest daughter of Alfred Parkin of Epworth, co. Lincoln, and of Doncaster, co. York, Lord of the Manor of Epworth, by Hannah Maria his 2nd wife, eldest daughter of Alderman John Elwes of Doncaster; born at Doncaster 20 September, baptised at Christ Church, Doncaster, 18 October 1877.

FLETCHER. Vol. 3, page 79.—Ann, widow of the Rev. William Henry Flowers, died at Brigg, co. Lincoln, 10 March, buried at Ulceby, co. Lincoln, 13 March 1903.

FLOYER. Vol. 3, page 116.—Ernest Ayscoghe Floyer died at Cairo, Egypt, aged 51, on Tuesday, 1 December, buried there 2 December 1903.

Page 118 (*and Addenda, Vol. 5, page iv.*)—The Rev. John Kestell and Helen Frances Floyer have further issue a son, Martyn Du Boulay Floyer, born at "The Quillet," Green Hill, Worcester, on Wednesday, 4 February, baptised at Worcester Cathedral 25 March 1903.

FOLJAMBE. Vol. 1, page 49.—The Honble Gerald William Frederick Savile Foljambe of the 1st Battalion Oxfordshire Light Infantry (43rd Light Infantry) was transferred in September 1903, to the 2nd Battalion of the Oxfordshire Light Infantry (52nd Oxfordshire Light Infantry), and is quartered at Chatham.

FREEMAN. Vol. 10, page 121.—The Rev. John Major Freeman, Vicar of Playford, co. Suffolk, for 22 years, died at the Vicarage, Playford, aged 70, on Monday, 10 November, buried at Playford on Thursday, 13 November 1902. Will dated 10 January 1901, proved at Ipswich 26 March 1903, by Herman Biddell and Rosa Crisp, the Executors.

FRY. Vol. 10, page 16.—Francis Charles Miers was baptised at Quintero, Chili [*not* Mexico].

FURNEAUX. Vol. 6, page 34.—The Rev. William Mordaunt Furneaux was appointed Dean of Winchester 16 March 1903, and D.D. Lambeth 20 March 1903.

GARRETT. Vol. 5, page 140.—Louisa, widow of Newson Garrett, died at Aldeburgh, co. Suffolk, aged 89, on Saturday, 17 January, buried at Aldeburgh on Thursday, 22 January 1903. Will dated 13 February 1895, with two codicils dated respectively 4 September 1897 and 16 January 1903, proved (Prin. Reg., 64, 1903) 12 February 1903, by Edmund Garrett, Samuel Garrett and George Herbert Garrett, the sons, the Executors.

Page 144 (*and Addenda, Vol. 7, page v.*)—Frank and Evelyn Rosa Garrett have further issue a daughter, Irene Elizabeth, born at " New Haven," Leiston, co. Suffolk, on Saturday, 2 May, baptised at Leiston 3 June 1903.

Page 144 (*and Addenda, Vol. 8, page ix.*)—Alfred Stead and Winifred Mary Garrett have further issue a son, James Stead Garrett, born at Alma Cottage, Leiston, on Wednesday, 1 July, baptised at Leiston 14 August 1903.

GATTY. Vol. 2, page 153.—The Rev. Alfred Gatty, D.D., died at the Vicarage, Ecclesfield, co. York, in his 90th year, on Tuesday, 20 January, buried at Ecclesfield 24 January 1903. Will dated 22 January 1889, with codicil dated 3 February 1896, proved (Prin. Reg., 12, 1903) 28 February 1903, by Horatia Frances Katharine Eden (formerly Gatty), the daughter, and Francis Patrick Smith, the son-in-law, the Executors.

GIBBONS. Vol. 9, page 48.—Leonard Philip and Gertrude Emma Gibbons have further issue a son, Leonard John Gibbons, born at Uckington, co. Gloucester, on Monday, 23 March, baptised at Elmstone, co. Gloucester, 20 April 1903.

GILBEY. Vol. 3, page 147.—Gilbert Gilbey was married at St. George's, Hanover Square, London, 24 April 1901, to Edith Mary, daughter of John S. and Margaret Barwick. They have issue a daughter, Brenda Mary, born at " Chalklands," Bourne End, co. Buckingham, on Monday, 9 November, baptised at St. Paul's, Wooburn, co. Buckingham, 28 December 1903.

GODDARD. Vol. 6, page 66.—Captain Francis Ambrose D'Oyly [*not* D'Oyley] Goddard of the 2nd Battalion to be Adjutant to 4th Battalion the Royal Munster Fusiliers 5 February 1903. He and his wife, Evelyn Maud, have issue two sons, Denis Gerald Ambrose Goddard, born at Barrackpore, India, 18 January 1898, baptised at St. Bartholomew's, Barrackpore, and Brian Maurice Goddard, born at Queenstown, co. Cork, 14 July, baptised at Christ Church, Rushbrooke, co. Cork, 23 August 1901.

Page 66 (*and Addenda, Vol. 10, page viii.*)—Francis Warren Morrison and Elizabeth Gertrude Goddard have issue a daughter, Imogene Martha May, born at Salida, Colorada, U.S.A., on Saturday, 7 March 1903.

Page 67.—The Rev. Nigel Ernle Goddard was appointed to the sinecure Rectory of Creswell, co. Stafford, 4 June 1903.

GODDARD. Vol. 10, page 27.—Kathleen, 4th daughter of Alfred Courtenay Goddard, was married at Holy Trinity, Paddington, London, on Thursday, 23 July 1903, to Ralph Staples Ellis of 29 Fleet Street, London, youngest son of Joseph Ellis, formerly of Brighton, co. Sussex.

GODDEN. Vol. 3, page 55 (*and Addenda, Vol. 10, page ix.*)—The Rev. Frederick Ernest and Edith Harriet Godden have issue a daughter, Cicely Harriet, born at Hartford House, Blackwater, co. Hants, on Friday, 15 May, baptised at Holy Trinity, Hawley, co. Hants, 3 June 1903.

GOLDSMITH. Vol. 5, page 109.— Emma, wife of Francis Edward Goldsmith, should be described as the daughter of John Hallett [*not* Edward Wallett].

GRESLEY. Vol. 8, page 117.—Arthur Spencer Gresley died at " Green Bank," Turnditch, Derby, aged 35, on Thursday, 10 September, buried at Netherseale, co. Leicester, 14 September 1903. Will dated 30 January 1903, proved (Prin. Reg., 37, 1903) 17 November 1903, by Herbert Nigel Gresley, the brother, the sole Executor.

Page 117 (*and Addenda, Vol. 9, page vi.*)—Herbert Nigel and Ethel Frances Gresley have issue a son, Nigel Gresley, born at Somerset House,

GRESLEY, *continued.*
Newton Heath, co. Lancaster, on Thursday, 25 June, baptised at the parish church, Lytham, co. Lancaster, 9 August 1903.

GUILLE. Vol. 1, page 39.—Mary Elizabeth, eldest and only surviving child of the Very Rev. William Guille, Dean of Guernsey, died at 3 George Place Guernsey, aged 81, on Wednesday, 29 April, buried in Candie Cemetery, Guernsey, 2 May 1903. Will dated 26 June 1902, with codicil dated 30 June 1902, proved (Prin. Reg., 65, 1903) 2 July 1903, by William Lawson Micks, the nephew, and Eleanor Meyrick, the niece, the Executors.

Page 40 (*and Addenda, Vol. 3, page ii*).—The Rev. Hubert George de Carteret and Catherine Lucretia Stevens-Guille have further issue a daughter, Catherine Marion Sophia, born at Beauconnor, in the parish of Monkleigh, North Devon, 22 May, baptised at Monkleigh, 28 June 1903.

HALIFAX. Vol. 10, page 134.—Lieut.-Colonel the Honble Henry John Lindley Wood died at Melton Park, Doncaster, co. York, on Monday, 5 January, buried at High Melton, co. York, 8 January 1903.

The Honble Mary Agnes Emily Wood, youngest daughter of Charles Lindley, Viscount Halifax, was married at Hickleton, co. York, on Thursday, 17 September 1903, to George Richard Lane-Fox, elder son of James Thomas Richard Lane-Fox of Bramham Park and of Hope Hall, co. York, J.P. and D.L., formerly Captain Grenadier Guards, by Lucy Frances Jane his wife, daughter of Humphrey St. John-Mildmay; born 15 December 1870.

HALL. Vol 6, page 110.—Edward Algernon Hall was married at St. Stephen's, Westminster, 27 June 1900, to Annie Maud, daughter of Thomas Gildersleeve.

HARDWICKE. Vol. 4, page 133.—Dorothy Marian, eldest daughter of Richard Reece Hardwicke, died at Bexhill, co. Sussex, aged 15, on Tuesday, 13 January 1903.

Page 134.—Constance Ethel, daughter of Edward Arthur Hardwicke, was married at Howick Falls, Natal, South Africa, 30 September 1903, to William Sandford Cottrill of Heidelberg, Transvaal, South Africa.

HARDWICKE, *continued.*
Page 135.—William Perton Allen Hardwicke was married at Newmarket, co. Cambridge, 1 January 1903, to Elsie Kate, eldest child of Alfred Francis Birbeck of Hexham House, Southport, co. Lancaster, by Elizabeth Chudleigh his wife, daughter of Charles Rees of Newton Abbot, co. Devon, born at Marychurch, Torquay, co. Devon, 18 August 1880.

Herbert Junius Allen Hardwicke was admitted a Solicitor 21 December 1903.

HART-DAVIS. Vol. 9, page 31.—Henry Vaughan Hart Hart-Davis is now of Wardley Hall, Swinton, co. Lancaster, and was appointed Chief Agent to the Earl of Ellesmere for the Bridgwater and Ellesmere estates 20 October 1903.

HASLEWOOD. Vol. 7, page 135.—The Rev. Christopher Francis Beevor Haslewood, Vicar of Pelton, co. Durham, was married at St. Peter's, Harrogate, co. York (by the Rev. Frederick George Haslewood, LL.D., father of the bridegroom), on Thursday, 12 November 1903, to Sibyl Beatrice, elder daughter of Dr. Robert Clark Newton of Eldon Tower, Harrogate.

Page 136.—Eveline Fanny, youngest daughter of the Rev. Francis Haslewood, was married at St. Mary's, Bryanston Square, London, on Thursday, 30 April 1903, to Amédée Eugene Charles Lachenal of Plainpalais, Geneva, Switzerland, son of Joseph Lachenal, by Euphrasine Douquet his wife; born at Geneva 12 April 1869.

HEATHCOTE. Vol. 8, page 2.—Sir William Perceval Heathcote, Baronet, died at "Redvers," Bournemouth, co. Hants, on Thursday, 29 October, buried at Bournemouth on Tuesday, 3 November 1903. Will dated 28 May 1897, with codicil dated 8 July 1897, proved in the Principal Registry 28 December 1903, by Dame Letitia Maria Heathcote, Colonel Gilbert Redvers Heathcote and Sebastian Henry Petre, the Executors.

Page 3.—Mary Forbes, wife of Arthur Malcolm Heathcote, died at "Homestead," Albert Bridge Road, London, aged 50, on Tuesday, 13 January, buried in the churchyard at Hursley, co. Hants, 17 January 1903.

Dorothy, eldest daughter of Arthur Malcolm Heathcote, was married at St. Peter's, Cranley Gardens, London

HEATHCOTE, *continued.*
(by the Rev. James Gavin Young, grandfather of the bride), on Saturday, 8 November 1902, to Arthur Crawford Lee, only son of the Rev. Godfrey Bolles Lee, Warden of Winchester College.

Page 5.—Thomas Richard Frederick Cooke-Trench died at Millicent, co. Kildare, 25 November, buried at St. Michael's, Clane, co. Kildare, 28 November 1902.

HERBERT. Vol. 3, page 123.—Arthur James Herbert has been Consul-General in Budapest, Hungary, since August 1902.

HESKETH. Vol. 1, page 161.—The Rev. Henry Gosse died at "The Firs," Redhill, co. Surrey, aged 87, 3 May, buried at St. John's, Redhill, 7 May 1903. Will dated 4 May 1901, with codicil of same date, proved (Prin. Reg., 48, 1903) 30 May 1903, by James Edmund Maude and John Maude, sons-in-law, the Executors.

HOLE. Vol. 7, page 129.—William Robert Hole, died at "Parke," Bovey Tracey, co. Devon, 7 February, buried at Bovey Tracey 11 February 1903. Will dated 30 January 1901, proved at Exeter 25 April 1903, by William Gerald Hole, the son, and Robert Paul Kitson, the cousin, the Executors. His only son, William Gerald Hole, who was educated at Winchester and at Merton College, Oxford, has now succeeded to "Parke," Bovey Tracey.

HOPKINS. Vol. 8, page 33 (*and Addenda, Vol. 10 page x.*)—Administration of the goods of Francis Henry Hopkins was granted at the Principal Registry 25 November 1902, to Thomas Faulconer Wisden.

HUTCHISON. Vol. 5, page 69.—Alexander Richard Hamilton Hutchison, Captain Royal Marine Light Infantry, was married at Holy Trinity, Gosport, co. Hants, on Wednesday, 7 January 1903, to Georgina Courtenay, daughter of William Henry Haswell, Fleet-Paymaster, R.N., by Henrietta Chetwynd his wife, daughter of George Bernard Knighton Drake of Ipplepen House, Ipplepen, and Goodrington House, Paignton, both co. Devon; born at "Grenofen," Paignton, on Tuesday, 13 April, baptised at St. John's, Paignton, 9 June 1875.

JEAFFRESON. Vol. 2, page 53.—Horace Cavell Jeaffreson, was married at St. Augustine's, Highbury, London, 1 December 1903, to Ettie Louise, daughter of Thomas Ward Turner of Handsworth, co. Stafford.

JERMYN. Vol. 3, page 171.—The Rev. Edmund Jermyn was instituted to the Rectory of Croughton, co. Northampton, 21 September 1903.

Page 172.—The Rt. Rev. Hugh Willoughby Jermyn, Bishop of Brechin, died at his residence, Forbes Court, Broughty Ferry, near Dundee, aged 83, on Thursday, 17 September, and was buried in the churchyard of St. Mary's, Broughty Ferry, 22 September 1903. Confirmation at Dundee, 1 December 1903, of the Rev. Edmund Jermyn, the son, and Agnes Jermyn of Forbes Court, Broughty Ferry, the daughter.

JOHNSON. Vol. 1, page 85.—Elizabeth, wife of Richard Withers, died at her residence "The Uplands," West Derby, co. Lancaster, on Sunday, 7 December, buried at Troutbeck, co. Westmoreland, on Thursday, 11 December 1902.

JOHNSON. Vol. 2, page 6.—The Rev. Robert Johnson, formerly Vicar of Hornchurch, co. Essex, is now of Verandah House, Worlington, co. Suffolk. He married 3rdly at St. John's, Dulwich, co. Surrey, 17 November 1903, to Anna Maria, 2nd daughter of the Rev. Augustus Frederick Padley, formerly Vicar of St. Peter-at-Gowts, co. Lincoln, by Catherine his wife, daughter of Samuel Mather.

JOHNSON. Vol. 3, page 19.—Bertram Vaughan Johnson was married at Skipness, co. Argyll, 7 January 1903, to Dorothy, daughter of Robert Chellas Graham of Skipness, by Emily Eliza his wife, daughter of Joseph Alfred Hardcastle. They have issue a daughter, Margaret Dorothy Vaughan, born at 78 Elm Park Gardens, Chelsea, London, 12 November, baptised privately 12 December 1903, and died the same day.

JUBB. Vol. 2, page 80.—Catherine Favell, wife of Robert Jubb, died at Glaston Hill, Eversley, co. Hants, 17 May, buried at Eversley 22 May 1903.

KITCHENER. Vol. 7, page 6.—Lord Kitchener has been Commander-in-Chief in India and a Member of Viceroy's Council since 1902.

LAW. Vol. 7, page 61.—Henry Charles Hull died at 55 Argyll Road, Kensington, London, aged 68, on Tuesday, 25 February, buried in Brompton Cemetery, London, 1 March 1902. Will dated 16 April 1894, with codicil dated 20 June 1901, proved (Prin. Reg., 492, 1902) 2 April 1902, by Charles Patrick Amyatt Hull, Major in H.M. Army, the son, and Graham Keith, the Executors.

Page 62.—Cecil Arbuthnot Law, Captain The Wiltshire Regiment, was married at Mussoorie, India, 29 April 1902, to Mary Theresa, 2nd daughter of Arthur George Walker, formerly of the Bengal Civil Service, Barrister-at-Law.

Page 63.—Hubert Henry Bingham Law was married at St. James', Spanish Place, Manchester Square, London, 9 July 1902, to Violet, daughter of R. Steuart Muirhead.

LEVESON GOWER. Vol. 1, page 22 (*and Addenda, Vol. 2, page iv.*)—Granville Charles Gresham and Evelyn Mildred Leveson Gower have further issue a son, Thomas Christopher Gresham Leveson Gower, born 19 June, baptised at St. James', Titsey, co. Surrey, 19 July 1903.

LILLINGSTON. Vol. 9, page 35.—Mary Grey, the 2nd wife of Alfred Lillingston, was the eldest daughter of Captain Thomas Monck Mason, R.N., by Mary his wife, eldest child of Captain the Honble Sir George Grey, Baronet, R.N., 3rd son of Sir Charles, 1st Earl Grey.

Charles Alfred Gordon Lillingston was born at Southwold Lodge, co. Suffolk, 30 October 1857, and has retired from the Indian Forest Service. His wife, Mabel Harriet, 6th daughter of the Honble Edward David Stuart Ogilvie of Yulgilbar, New South Wales, and 9 Queen's Gate Place, London, by Theodosia Isabella his wife, daughter of William de Burgh, D.D., was born at Yulgilbar 16 May 1866, and baptised there 19 September 1870. They were married at St. Jude's, South Kensington, London, 9 July 1888, and have issue a daughter, Jessie Mary Grey, born at Ranchi, Chota Nagpur, Bengal, India, 18 April, baptised at Ranchi in May 1889; a son, Edward George Grey

LILLINGSTON, *continued.*
Lillingston, born at Chaibassa, Chota Nagpur, 4 July, baptised at Darjeeling, Bengal, 16 September 1892; and a daughter, Evelyn Mabel Constance, born at Grafton, New South Wales, 22 November 1901, baptised at Yulgilbar, New South Wales, in February 1902.

Page 36.—William George Lillingston was married at Holy Trinity, Sloane Street, London, on New Year's Eve, Thursday, 31 December 1903, to Olive Theodora, daughter of Edmund Theodore Doxat of Woodgreen Park, Cheshunt, co. Hertford, J.P., by Emma his wife, daughter of Frederick Cobb, M.D.; born at "Hollowdens," Frensham, co. Surrey, on Tuesday, 3 October, baptised at Frensham 14 October 1871.

Charlotte Cordelia Tyrelline, widow of the Rev. Edmund John Huntsman, died at Worksop, co. Nottingham, 22 May, buried at Harworth, co. Nottingham, 25 May 1903. Will dated 15 November 1902, proved (Prin. Reg., 124, 1903) 10 July 1903, by George Alexander Irvine Huntsman and Alfred Edmund Francis Fonnereau Huntsman, the Executors.

Page 38.—Violet, daughter of the Rev. Claude Augustus Lillingston, died at Christiania, Norway, on Saturday, 21 November, buried in Vestre Aker's Churchyard, Christiania, 27 November 1903.

The Rev. Frank Lillingston (Rector of Sall, co. Norfolk, since December 1902) was married at the parish church of St. Minver, co. Cornwall, on Monday, 1 December 1902, to Elsie, 3rd daughter of Leveson Granville Campbell, the younger, of Fairfield, co. Ayr, by Mary Douglas his wife, youngest daughter of Walter Angus Bethune. They have issue a daughter, Elsie Yonàthi, born at the Rectory, Sall, on Monday, 21 December 1903.

LITTLE. Vol. 5, page 86.—The Rev. Thomas Palling Little died at the Vicarage, Edge, Stroud, co. Gloucester, in his 87th year, on Christmas Day, Friday, 25 December, buried at Edge 31 December 1903.

The Rev. Thomas Gurney Little proceeded M.A. of Cambridge February 1902.

LLEWELLYN. Vol. 6, page 153.—
The will of William Llewellyn (who died 9 May 1898) was dated 29 September 1894, and proved at Llandaff 28 July 1898, by Robert William Llewellyn, the son.

Page 154.—William Herbert Clydwyn Llewellyn was educated at Eton and at Sandhurst, and gazetted to the South Wales Borderers (24th Regiment) 21 April 1903.

Griffith Robert Poyntz Llewellyn was educated at Winchester.

John Blandy Llewellyn was educated at Winchester.

The following arms were granted to Robert William Llewellyn of Court Colman and Baglan Hall, co. Glamorgan, J.P. and D.L., for co. Glamorgan, by Sir Albert William Woods, K.C.B., K.C.M.G., Garter King of Arms, and George Edward Cokayne, Clarenceux King of Arms, 20 November 1902.

Arms.—Per fesse embattled, azure and or, a javelin erect, between two boars' heads erased in chief, and a like boar's head between two javelins in base, all counterchanged.

Crest.—Upon a rock proper, a boar's head erased or, in front of three javelins, one in pale and two in saltire, also proper.

Motto.—Gwell angau na chywilydd.

LLOYD. Vol. 10, page 98.—The Rev. Robert Watkin Lloyd should be described as the 3rd and youngest [*not* only surviving] son of the Rev. John Lloyd.

Page 99.—Henry Meyric Lloyd died unmarried at Cholsey, co. Berks, 22 November, buried there 26 November 1903.

LOCKETT. Vol. 2, page 109.—Jessie, widow of John Hilton Lockett, died at Grassendale House, Grassendale, co. Lancaster, aged 95, on Monday, 6 April, buried in Smithdown Road Cemetery, Liverpool, on Wednesday, 8 April 1903. Will dated 25 May 1894, with four codicils dated respectively 1 April 1895, 5 November 1896, 3 August 1898, and 6 January 1899, proved at Liverpool 18 May 1903, by William Jeffery Lockett, the son-in-law, E. F. Hicks and Garstang Bradstock Lockett, the nephew, the Executors.

LONGSTAFF. Vol. 6, page 71.—Sara Leam, wife of George Blundell Longstaff, died at "Highlands," Putney Heath, co. Surrey, aged 51, on Thursday, 26 February, cremated, and the ashes deposited in Woking Cemetery, co. Surrey, 2 March 1903. M.I.

Tom George Longstaff proceeded M.A. 1900 and M.B. 1903.

Cedric Llewellyn Longstaff (M.A. 1903, Hon. Captain in the Army 9 July 1901) was married at the parish church, Wimbledon, co. Surrey, on Thursday, 8 October 1903, to Lilias Marow, elder daughter of Sir Thomas Wilmot Peregrine Blomefield of Attleborough, co. Norfolk, Baronet, C.B., by Lilias his wife, daughter of the Honble Charles Napier of "Woodlands," Taunton, co. Somerset; born 30 September 1880.

Page 72.—Ralph Longstaff entered the Army as 2nd Lieutenant Royal Field Artillery 9 May 1900, promoted Lieutenant 3 September 1901.

Cuthbert Dixon Longstaff was promoted Sub-Lieutenant R.N. 15 March 1902.

Frederick Victor Longstaff, who is now of Clare College, Cambridge, matriculated in October 1899.

Gilbert Conrad Longstaff, who is now of Clare College, Cambridge, matriculated in October 1903.

LUKIN. Vol. 7, page 38.—Lieut.-Colonel Henry Timson Lukin, D.S.O., was appointed a Companion of St. Michael and St. George in 1902.

MADDISON. Vol. 5, page 151.—Lionel Maddison died at Spalding, co. Lincoln, aged 29, on Friday, 12 December, buried in the cemetery at Spalding 16 December 1902.

MANT. Vol. 1, page 194.—Arthur French Mant died at "Avenings," Petworth, co. Sussex, aged 41, on Saturday, 20 December, buried in the cemetery at Petworth 23 December 1902. Will dated 7 April 1894, proved (Prin. Reg., 39, 1903) 12 February 1903, by Eva Mant, the relict, the sole Executrix.

MAPLE. Vol. 10, page 54.—Sir John Blundell Maple, Baronet, died at Childwickbury, St. Albans, co. Hertford, on Tuesday, 24 November, buried in the family vault in the chapel at Childwick Green, Childwickbury, on Saturday, 28 November 1903. Will dated 24 November 1897, with three codicils dated respectively 28 July 1903, 15 September 1903 and 17 October 1903, proved in the Principal Registry 5 December 1903, by Arthur Bird, Richard William Evelyn Middleton, Charles Hodges and Clare Henry Regnart, the Executors.

MARKHAM. Vol. 2, page 31 (*and Addenda, Vol. 9, page ix.*)—Gervase Edward and Edith Markham have issue a son, Henry Philip Markham, born at Gloucester Villa, Darlington, co. Durham, on Friday, 14 November 1902, baptised at St. John's, Shildon, co. Durham, on Monday, 9 March 1903.

Page 32 (*and Addenda, Vol. 6, page ix.*)—Arthur Basil and Lucy Bertram Markham have further issue a daughter, Joyous, born at Stuffynwood Hall, Mansfield, co. Nottingham, on Monday, 21 July, baptised at St. Chad's, Stuffynwood, 3 September 1902.

MARSHALL. Vol. 4, page 120.—Allan Walton died at Southport, co. Lancaster, 18 May, buried at Cheadle Hulme, co. Chester, 23 May 1903. Will dated 18 February 1887, proved (Prin. Reg., 42, 1903) 11 July 1903, by Rebecca Anne Walton, the relict, and George Fuller, the surviving Executors.

MARTEN. Vol. 6, page 63.—Alice Anne, wife of the Rev. John Henry Mee, died at Holywell House, Oxford, on Wednesday, 22 July, buried at Westbourne, co. Sussex, on Saturday, 25 July 1903. Will dated 7 June 1897, proved in the Principal Registry

MARTEN, *continued.*
27 November 1903, by the Rev. John Henry Mee, the other Executors having renounced.

MARTYN. Vol. 2, page 83 (*and Addenda, Vol. 10, page xiii.*)—Philip Docton and Agnata Mary Neale Martyn have issue a son, William Lawrence Docton Martyn, born at Roskestal Treen, co. Cornwall, 22 March, baptised at St. Levan, co. Cornwall, 22 April 1903.

MASTER. Vol. 6, page 143.—Charles Onslow and Wilhelmina Master have further issue a daughter, Penelope Wilhelmina, born at Bourton Grange, Flax Bourton, co. Somerset, 2 September, baptised at Flax Bourton 19 October 1902.

Page 144.—Charles Gilbert Master, C.S.I., died at 57 Beaumont Street, Marylebone, London, aged 69, on Monday, 9 March, buried in Reigate Cemetery, co. Surrey, on Friday, 13 March 1903. Will dated 6 December 1899, with codicil dated 29 November 1902, proved (Prin. Reg., 909 1903) 18 April 1903, by Robert Edward Master, the brother, and Charles Onslow Master, the son, two of the Executors.

MELLER. Vol. 7, page 153.—Emma, widow of the Rev. Thomas William Meller, died at Ipswich, co. Suffolk, aged 83, on Saturday, 31 January, buried in the cemetery at Woodbridge, co. Suffolk, 4 February 1903. Will dated 17 October 1902, proved at Ipswich 31 March 1903, by Alfred Meller, the son, the sole Executor.

Page 155.—Lady Helen Blanche, wife of Walter Clifford Meller, died at 20 Cheyne Walk, Chelsea, co. Middlesex, 5 January, buried in the Earl of Galloway's vault, Kensal Green, London, 9 January 1903.

MELLOR. Vol. 3, page 86.—Violet Frances Fenton, 2nd daughter of William Moseley Mellor, was married at Bidston co. Chester, on Friday, 19 December 1902, to the Rev. Ernest Hugh Wright, 2nd son of George Ernest Wright of Skipton-in-Craven, co. York, Barrister-at-Law, by Mary Anne his wife, daughter of William Nutt Field; born at 1 Westgate Terrace, Redcliffe Square, South Kensington, London, on Sunday, 1 December 1872; of Queen's College, Cambridge, matriculated Michaelmas

MELLOR, *continued.*

Term, 1891, B.A. 1895; Assistant Minister at St. Peter's, Vere Street, Cavendish Square, London, 1901, Assistant Master at Dulwich College since 1902.

Page 87 (*and Addenda, Vol. 10, page xiii.*)—Alfred Shaw and the Honble Dora Marion Mellor have issue a daughter, Joan Marion, born on Friday, 6 February, baptised at Christ Church, Lancaster Gate, London, 28 March 1903.

Page 87.—Maria Florence, 3rd daughter of James Robert Mellor, was married at Christ Church, Lancaster Gate, London, on Saturday, 31 January 1903, to Ernest Makins, D.S.O., Major the Royal Dragoons, eldest son of Henry Francis Makins of 180 Queen's Gate, South Kensington, London; born 14 October 1869.

METHOLD. Vol. 1, page 145 (*and Addenda, Vol. 10, page xiii.*)—A window is now placed in the chancel of Hepworth Church, co. Suffolk, to the memory of Mary Ellen, wife of Thomas Tindal Methold, who died 2 October 1902.

MIDDLETON. Vol. 9, page 131.—The Honble Harriet Cassandra, widow of Godfrey Wentworth Bayard Bosville, died at "Noblethorpe," Barnsley, co. York, aged 78, on Monday, 28 September, buried at Rudstone, co. York, 2 October 1903. Will dated 16 October 1886, proved (Prin. Reg., 134, 1903) 9 November 1903, by Alexander Wentworth Macdonald Bosville, the son, the sole Executor.

Page 134.—The Rev. Nesbit Edward and Marjorie Helen Willoughby have issue a son, Guy Willoughby, born at 5 West Parade, Wakefield, co. York, on Friday, 7 November, baptised at Sturton, co. Nottingham, 7 December 1902, and a daughter, Veronica, born at the Vicarage, Sturton, 4 December 1903, baptised at Sturton 3 January 1904.

MIDLETON. Vol. 5, page 97.—Augusta Mary, Viscountess Midleton, died at Peper Harow, Godalming, co. Surrey, in her 75th year, on Whit-Monday, 1 June, buried in the churchyard at Peper Harow on Friday, 5 June 1903. Administration was granted at the Principal Registry 11 July 1903, to the Rt. Honble William, Viscount Midleton, of Peper Harow, Godalming, co. Surrey, the husband.

MIDLETON, *continued.*

The Rt. Honble William St. John Fremantle Brodrick, P.C. (now Secretary of State for India), was married 2ndly at St. George's, Hanover Square, London, on Monday, 5 January 1903, to Madeleine Cecilia Carlyle, elder daughter of the late Colonel the Honble John Constantine Stanley of the Grenadier Guards, by Mary Susan Elizabeth his wife (now Lady Jeune) daughter of Keith William Stewart Mackenzie of Seaforth, co. Lancaster.

Page 98.—The Honble George Charles Brodrick died at Merton College, Oxford, on Sunday, 8 November, buried at Peper Harow on Friday, 13 November 1903. Will dated 30 April 1896, proved in the Principal Registry 8 December 1903, by the Rt. Honble William St. John Fremantle Brodrick and the Honble Laurence Alan Brodrick, the nephews, the Executors.

Page 100 (*and Addenda, Vol. 10, page xiii.*)—William John Henry and Blanche Sophia Emily Brodrick, have issue a son, Trevor Lowther Brodrick, born at Kingsmead, Winchester, co. Hants, on Saturday, 7 March, baptised at St. Cross, Winchester, 11 April 1903.

Page 100.—George Trevor Brodrick died at Rousdon, co. Devon, in his 26th year, on Friday, 26 December, buried at St. Cross, Winchester, 31 December 1902. Administration was granted in the Principal Registry 14 February 1903, to the Rev. Alan Brodrick of Winchester, co. Hants, the father and next of kin.

MOLESWORTH. Vol. 3, page 39.—The Honble Edward Henry Legge died at Holmwood Lodge, Dorking, co. Surrey, aged 66, on Thursday, 16 August, buried in the churchyard at Holmwood, co. Surrey, 21 August 1900. Will dated 18 May 1899, proved (Prin. Reg., 1414, 1900) 10 October 1900, by Cordelia Twysden Legge, the relict, the Honble Charles Gounter Legge, late Captain H.M. Army, and the Honble Heneage Legge, late Colonel H.M. Army, the brother, the Executors.

MONCK. Vol. 2, page 134.—John Bligh Monck died at Coley Park, Reading, co. Berks, aged 91, on Sunday, 22 February, buried at Aldworth, co. Berks, 26 February 1903. Will dated 29 September 1894, proved at Oxford 3 April 1903, by William Berkeley Monck, the son, the sole Executor.

MOORE. Vol. 8, page 106.—Edward James Moore, M. Inst. C.E., late Chief Engineer P.W.D., India, died at 26 Woodville Road, Ealing, co. Middlesex, aged 55 years, on Friday, 20 March, buried at Alvechurch, co. Worcester, 25 March 1903. Will dated 24 December 1902, proved (Prin. Reg., 32, 1903) 7 May 1903, by Frances Eliza Moore, the relict, Richard Aubrey Fitch and Charles Dennis Fitch, brothers-in-law, the Executors.

MOORE-STEVENS. Vol. 8, page 111.—John Curzon Moore-Stevens died at Winscott, Torrington, co. Devon, aged 84, on Tuesday, 4 August, buried at Peters Marland, co. Devon, 10 August 1903. Will dated 15 February 1899, proved at Exeter 16 September 1903, by Richard Arthur Moore-Stevens, the son, the sole Executor.

NEWDIGATE. Vol. 7, page 54.—Francis Alexander Newdigate has assumed the additional name of Newdegate by Royal Licence dated October 1903, in compliance with the will of the Rt. Honble Charles Newdigate-Newdegate, on succeeding to the Harefield and Arbury estates on the death of Lieut.-General Sir Edward Newdigate-Newdegate, K.C.B., 1 August 1902.

NORMANBY. Vol. 9, page 55.—The Rev. Canon the Marquess of Normanby was married at St. Peter's, Eaton Square, London, on Wednesday, 30 December 1903, to Gertrude Stansfeld, youngest daughter of Johnston Jonas Foster of Moor Park, Ludlow, co. Salop, and of Cliffe Hill, Halifax, co. York, J.P., by Hannah Jane his wife, daughter of Robert Stansfeld of Field House, co. York.

OLIVE. Vol. 1, page 233.—The Rt. Honble Frederick Edward Gould, 9th Earl of Cavan, P.C., died at Wheathampstead House, co. Hertford, aged 60, on Saturday, 14 July, buried at Ayott St. Lawrence, co. Hertford, on Wednesday, 18 July 1900. Will dated 4 March 1874, proved (Prin. Reg., 1148, 1900) 30 August 1900, by Mary Sneade, Countess of Cavan, the relict, the sole Executrix.

OLLIVANT. Vol. 6, page 18 (*and Addenda, Vol. 8, page xiv.*)—Lionel Arthur Edward Ollivant was killed in action at Tientsin, China, 13 [*not* 14] July 1900 (medal).

ONSLOW. Vol. 5, page 39.—The Earl of Onslow was appointed President of the Board of Agriculture 19 May 1903.

Page 40.—Lady Gwendolen Florence Mary, elder daughter of Sir William Hillier, 4th Earl of Onslow, G.C.M.G., was married at St. Margaret's, Westminster, on Thursday, 8 October 1903, to the Honble Rupert Edward Cecil Guinness, C.M.G. (*See Pedigree of Guinness, "Visitation of Ireland," Vol. 2, page 79.*)

OUVRY. Vol. 3, page 169.—Ernest Carrington Ouvry was married at the parish church, Marylebone, London (by the Rev. Canon Page Roberts and the Rev. John Delahaize Ouvry, Rector of Elston, co. Nottingham), on Saturday, 25 April 1903, to Elinor Southwood, youngest daughter of Charles Lee Lewes of 6 Cambridge Terrace, Regent's Park, London, by Gertrude his wife, daughter of James Hill of Wisbech, co. Cambridge.

PARLBY. Vol. 8, page 16.—Captain Reginald John Hall and Violet Agatha Margaret Parlby have further issue a daughter, Cynthia Geraldine Hall, born 4 July, baptised at Pennycross, co. Devon, 5 August 1903.

PEARCE-EDGCUMBE. Vol. 5, page 16.—Administration of the effects of Louisa, wife of the Rev. William Iago, who died at Bodmin, co. Cornwall, on Saturday, 2 June 1900, was granted at Bodmin 6 July 1900, to the Rev. William Iago, the husband.

Preston Wallis Pearce died at Sterkstroom, Cape Colony, on Sunday, 27 September 1903, and was buried there. Will dated at Maclear, in Griqualand East, Cape Colony, 29 July 1895, proved at Cape Town, Cape Colony, about November 1903, by Annie Stick Pearse, the relict, the sole Executrix.

Preston Richard Pearse died at Qumbu, Cape Colony, on Sunday, 29 October 1899, and was buried there.

PEARSON. Vol. 10, page 74.—Vice-Admiral Hugo Lewis Pearson was appointed Commander-in-Chief at the Nore 1 January 1904.

Page 77.—Edith Mary, youngest daughter of Colonel Hugh Pearce Pearson, C.B., was married at St. Mark's, Southampton, on Tuesday, 13 January 1903, to Charles Gordon Spencer, 4th son of the Rev. Charles Vere Spencer of Wheatfield, co. Oxford, by Emma Frederica his wife, daughter of John Robert A'Court Gray; born at Wheatfield 23 February 1869; educated at Marlborough and at Keble College, Oxford, matriculated 13 October 1888, aged 19, Exhibitioner 1887; of the Indian Civil Service, Madras Presidency.

PENRUDDOCKE. Vol. 2, page 44.—Flora Henrietta Penruddocke died at Teffont Evias, co. Wilts, 7 November, buried at Compton Chamberlayne, co. Wilts, 13 November 1902. Will dated 24 May 1900, proved (Prin. Reg., 97, 1903) 15 April 1903, by Constance Henrietta Lowther Penruddocke and Sybil Katharine Penruddocke, the daughters, and Reginald Gambier Long, the son-in-law, the Executors.

Page 45.—Clara Albertina, wife of John Powys Penruddocke, died at Eastbourne, co. Sussex, 20 October, buried at Eastbourne 23 October 1901. John Powys Penruddocke of Winchester House, Meads, Eastbourne, co. Sussex, was married 2ndly at Marshfield, co. Gloucester, on Thursday, 8 January 1903, to Margaret Anne, eldest daughter of the Rev. Canon Edward Fiennes Trotman, Vicar of Marshfield. (*See Pedigree of Trotman, Vol. 3, page 161.*)

Page 45 (*and Addenda, Vol. 8, page xv.*)—Edward Wyndham and Muriel Turner Penruddocke of Wiltshire Lodge, Bransgore, co. Hants, have issue a daughter, Joan Teresa Powys, born at Kirkleatham Hall, Redcar, co. York, on Tuesday, 3 March 1903.

Charles Penruddocke, who succeeded, on his father's death, 30 October 1899, to the family estates, is now of Compton Park, Baverstock and Fyfield, all co. Wilts, and of Bratton St. Maur, co. Somerset. He was educated at Clifton College, and at Pembroke College, Cambridge, matriculated Michaelmas Term, 1878; is Lord of the Manors of Compton Chamberlayne, Baverstock, and Fyfield, and a Magistrate for the counties of Wilts and Somerset.

PIXLEY. Vol. 7, page 30.—A Memorial Window to Thomas William and Caroline Pixley was dedicated in the parish church, Freshwater, Isle of Wight, 14 April 1903.

Francis William Pixley was gazetted Major in the 1st Cadet Battalion King's Royal Rifles 24 February 1903.

Page 31.—Jocelyn Francis Renton Pixley, after serving as Lieutenant with the King's Royal Rifles in the South African War, for which he received Queen's medal with three clasps and King's medal with two clasps, died at the Barracks, Cork, aged 22, on Friday, 28 August, buried in the Military Cemetery, Cork, with full military honours, 31 August 1903. M.I. Administration was granted in Cork District Registry, 29 September 1903, to Francis William Pixley, the father.

PLATT-HIGGINS. Vol. 1, page 100.—Cicely, youngest daughter of Frederick Platt-Higgins, was married at St. Margaret's, Westminster, on Thursday, 25 June 1903, to Robert Marsland Groves, 2nd son of James Grimble Groves of Oldfield Hall, Altrincham, co. Chester, J.P., M.P. for Salford (South Division), by Anna Eva his wife, daughter of Robert Marsland of Manchester; born 3 January, baptised at Manchester Cathedral 28 January 1880; entered as a Cadet in the Royal Navy 15 January 1894, Midshipman 15 February 1896, Sub-Lieutenant 15 August 1899, promoted Lieutenant (5 firsts) 15 February 1900, of H.M.S. "Vernon" 30 September 1902.

Page 101.—An Organ with inscription to the memory of Martha Elizabeth, wife of Edward Platt-Higgins, was dedicated at St. Peter's, Belfast, on Sunday, 26 April 1903.

Page 104.—Arthur Platt-Higgins died 7 March, buried at Cheadle, co. Chester, 11 March 1903. Will dated 7 March 1903, proved at Chester 9 May 1903, by Frances Platt-Higgins, the relict, the sole Executrix.

PRIDEAUX-BRUNE. Vol. 2, page 99.—The Rev. Edward Shapland and Sophia Prideaux-Brune have further issue a son, Amyas Molesworth Prideaux-Brune, born at the Rectory, Rowner, co. Hants, on Thursday, 16 April, baptised at Rowner 20 April 1903.

PRIOR. Vol. 1, page 9.—Richard Chandler Alexander Prior, M.D., died at 48 York Terrace, Regent's Park, London, in his 94th year, on Friday, 5 December 1902. Will dated 21 September 1885, with two codicils dated respectively 4 November 1891 and 20 November 1901, proved (Prin. Reg., 56, 1903) 21 February 1903, by Sir Gabriel Prior Goldney, the nephew, the sole Executor.

PRITCHETT. Vol. 1, page 197.—George Edward Barker Pritchett was married at St. Catherine's, Feltham, co. Middlesex, on Thursday, 23 April 1903, to Violet Octavia, 2nd daughter of the Rev. John Francis Jemmett, B.C.L., Vicar of Feltham.

REYNELL-PACK. Vol. 8, page 167.—Elizabeth Catherine, widow of Sir John William Hamilton Anson, Baronet, died at her residence, 41 Eaton Square, London, in her 82nd year, on Friday, 3 July 1903. Will dated 11 April 1900, with three codicils dated respectively 7 November 1900, 21 December 1901 and 24 July 1902, proved (Prin. Reg., 47, 1903) 8 August 1903, by Sir William Reynell Anson, the son, Gertrude Christina Anson, the daughter, and Charles William Dunbar Buller, the Executors.

RIVINGTON. Vol. 3, page 23.—Florence Mary Hill, only daughter of Charles Robert Rivington, was married at St. Paul's, Avenue Road, Regent's Park, London, on Tuesday, 21 July 1903, to Charles John Holmes of 58 Kensington Park Road, London, only surviving son of the Rev. Charles Rivington Holmes (born 25 April 1834, died 22 May 1873), and grandson of John Holmes, Assistant Keeper of Manuscripts in the British Museum (*see "Dictionary of National Biography," Vol. 27, page 192*); born at Preston, co. Lancaster, 11 November 1868; educated at Eton and at Brasenose College, Oxford, matriculated 20 October 1887, aged 18, Scholar 1887, Honours: 2 Classical Mods. 89.

Page 24 (*and Addenda, Vol. 8, page xvi.*)—Arthur William and Rosamund Emma Herbert Rivington have issue a son, Charles Arthur Rivington, born at Chipperfield, co. Hertford, on Sunday, 23 November 1902, baptised at St. Paul's, Chipperfield, 3 January 1903.

ROBERTS. Vol. 7, page 160.—Henry Ellis Harvey died at James House, Hadlow, co. Kent, on Thursday, 1 October, buried in the cemetery at Tonbridge, co. Kent, on Monday, 5 October 1903. Will dated 30 October 1890, proved (Prin. Reg., 62, 1903) 23 November 1903, by Mary Ann Langridge and Frederick Norman Harvey, the brother, the surviving Executors.

ROGERS. Vol. 6, page 132.—William Hender Molesworth Rogers is now of Hertford College, Oxford.

Page 137.—The Rev. Enys Henry and Sarah Louisa Rogers have further issue a daughter, Catherine Gilbert, born at 15 Granville Road, Hove, co. Sussex, on Sunday, 28 December 1902, baptised at St. Stephen's, Brighton, co. Sussex, 26 February 1903.

ROPE. Vol. 2, page 95.—Edward Mingay and Emma Morley Rope have further issue a son, William Morley Rope, born at Te Kopuru, Auckland, New Zealand, 8 September 1903.

Page 95 (*and Addenda, Vol. 3, page v.*)—Walter Henry and Celia Mary Rope have further issue a daughter, Elizabeth Celia, born at Orford, co. Suffolk, 30 November 1902, baptised there 9 January 1903.

Page 96.—James Thomas Rope died at Pietermaritzburg, Natal, South Africa, 25 July 1902.

ROYDS. Vol. 8, page 28.—Frances, daughter of the Rev. Canon Francis Coulman Royds, died at the Rectory, Coddington, co. Chester, on Sunday, 8 March, buried at Coddington 12 March 1903.

ROYDS. Vol. 9, page 3.—Smith Byrom Royds died at Craven Terrace, Morecambe, co. Lancaster, on Thursday, 4 December, buried at Haughton, co. Stafford, 9 December 1902. Will dated 15 March 1902, proved (Prin. Reg., 12, 1903) 14 January 1903, by Frances Harriett Thompson, wife of Reginald Thompson, the sister, the sole Executrix.

SCARLETT. Vol. 3, page 53.—Shelley Leopold Laurence Scarlett succeeded his cousin, James Yorke Macgregor, 4th Baron Abinger, who died 11 December 1903, as 5th Baron Abinger.

SHADWELL. Vol. 3, page 108.—Charlotte, widow of the Rev. Arthur Thomas Whitmore Shadwell, died at Shippon, co. Berks, aged 83, on Friday, 23 January, buried there 26 January 1903. Will dated 14 December 1902, proved (Prin. Reg., 171, 1903) 19 March 1903, by Bernard Shadwell and Arthur Shadwell, the sons, and Ronald Stanley Clarke, the son-in-law, the Executors.

SHERBORNE. Vol. 10, page 24.—Mary Laura, daughter of Colonel the Honble Charles Dutton, died suddenly in London on Wednesday, 26 November, buried at Sherborne, co. Gloucester, 2 December 1902.

Mabel Honor, youngest daughter of Colonel the Honble Charles Dutton, was married at the parish church, Sherborne, on Wednesday, 19 August 1903, to George James Robert Clerk, only child of Colonel Sir George Douglas Clerk of Penicuik, co. Edinburgh, Baronet, V.D., J.P., by Aymée Elizabeth Georgiana Milliken his wife, 2nd daughter of Sir Robert John Milliken Napier, Baronet; born 4 October 1876.

SIMPSON. Vol. 10, page 150.—Freda Frances Margaret Simpson was buried at Townstall, co. Devon, 3 May 1877.

Page 151.—Louisa, youngest daughter of the Rev. Francis Simpson, died at Claybrooke Hall, Rugby, co. Warwick, aged 79, on Saturday, 7 March, buried at Claybrooke 11 March 1903. Will dated 13 September 1897, proved (Prin. Reg., 136, 1903) 21 July 1903, by Digby Charles Legard, the sole Executor.

SKINNER. Vol. 10, page 128.—Alan Cameron and Cœline Skinner have further issue a daughter, Pamela Mary Stopford, born at St. Benedict's Priory, Tenterden, co. Kent, on Thursday, 9 April, baptised at St. Mildred's, Tenterden, on Friday, 8 May 1903.

SPARKS. Vol. 3, page 127.—Sarah Louisa, widow of Isaac Sparks, died at "Ivyside," Grove Park, Denmark Hill, co. Surrey, aged 80, on Monday, 10 November, buried in Nunhead Cemetery, co. Surrey, on Thursday, 13 November 1902. Will dated 10 June 1896, proved (Prin. Reg., 1591, 1902) 24 December 1902, by Arthur Edward Sparks, the son, the sole Executor.

SPENCER. Vol. 9, page 122.—Charles Tallent Spencer, who is now of Harmondsworth Hall, co. Middlesex, was elected a Fellow of the Royal Geographical Society 25 November 1901, and of the Royal Astronomical Society 10 January 1902.

Page 123.—Harrison Spencer, Captain Royal Field Artillery, and Jane Maria his wife, have issue a son, Samuel Edward Harrison Spencer, born at Kirkee, India, 8 February 1902, and baptised there.

STANFORD. Vol. 9, page 94.—Arthur Henry and Georgina Emma Augusta Stanford have further issue a son, Kenneth Wilfred Huét Stanford, born at Beaumont Hall, Colchester, co. Essex, on Monday, 11 May, baptised at Beaumont 30 August 1903.

STRICKLAND. Vol. 9, page 99.—Frederick Strickland was married at the parish church, Chiswick, co. Middlesex, on Tuesday, 21 July 1903, to Mary Beatrix, 3rd daughter of Sir John Isaac Thornycroft, F.R.S., LL.D., of "Steyne," Bembridge, Isle of Wight, and of Eyot Villa, The Mall, Chiswick, by Blanche his wife, daughter of Frederick Coules of Gloucester.

TADDY. Vol. 3, page 103.—Edward Latham died suddenly at 17 Kent Terrace, Regent's Park, London, aged 82, on Monday, 30 March, buried in Kensal Green Cemetery, London, 4 April 1903. Will dated 10 December 1900, with codicil dated 8 April 1902, proved (Prin. Reg., 27, 1903) 15 May 1903, by Annie May Latham, the surviving Executor.

Evelyn Frances, only daughter of Edward Glynn Taddy, was married at St. Andrew's, Biggleswade, co. Bedford, on Tuesday, 29 September 1903, to Charles William Archdale, only surviving son of Charles Archdale of Coltishall, co. Norfolk, formerly Major 85th Regiment.

TAYLOR. Vol. 3, page 95.—William Francis Kyffin Taylor, K.C., was appointed, by Royal Warrant, Presiding Judge of the Court of Passage of the City of Liverpool, 1 October 1903, and resigned the Recordership of Bolton.

THURBURN. Vol. 5, page 117.—Arthur Hugh Thurburn was married at Holy Trinity, Sloane Street, Chelsea, London, on Thursday, 25 June 1903, to Minna Frederica Bradley, 2nd daughter of Vice-Admiral Frederick Charles Bryan Robinson, by Williamina his wife, daughter of William Bradley.

Page 120.—Charles Alexander Thurburn, formerly of Alexandria, Egypt, died at 16 Kensington Park Gardens, London, aged 77, on Tuesday, 19 May, buried in St. James' Cemetery, Dover, co. Kent, on Friday, 22 May 1903. Memorial service same day at St. John's, Notting Hill, London. Will dated 4 November 1901, proved (Prin. Reg., 18, 1903) 15 June 1903, by Sharon Grote Turner, Charles Hannay and Frederick William Mann, the Executors.

TOWER. Vol. 2, page 33.—Lucy Sophia, 2nd daughter of Christopher Tower, died at Hillingdon, co. Middlesex, on Wednesday, 4 February, buried there 9 February 1903. Will dated 4 July 1896, proved (Prin. Reg., 93, 1903) 25 March 1903, by Brownlow Richard Christopher Tower, the brother, one of the Executors.

TROTMAN. Vol. 3, page 161.—Margaret Anne, eldest daughter of the Rev. Canon Edward Fiennes Trotman, B.C.L., was married at Marshfield, co. Gloucester, on Thursday, 8 January 1903, as his 2nd wife, to John Powys Penruddocke of Winchester House, Meads, Eastbourne, co. Sussex. (*See Pedigree of Penruddocke, Vol. 2, page 45.*)

Page 161 (*and Addenda, Vol. 8, page xviii.*)—Fiennes and Hilda Fanny Banger Trotman have issue a daughter, Hilda Mary, born at Beaminster, co. Dorset, 18 March, baptised there 25 April 1902, and a son Fiennes Trotman, born at Beaminster 15 September, baptised there 16 October 1903.

TUKE. Vol. 2, page 85 (*and Addenda, Vol. 6, page xiii.*)—Samuel and Violet Tuke have further issue a son, Edward Christopher William Tuke, born at Netherton Hall, Honiton, co. Devon, on Tuesday, 7 April, baptised at Farway, co. Devon, 1 June 1903.

Page 86.—William Murray Tuke died at Saffron Walden, co. Essex, in

TUKE, *continued.* his 81st year, on Monday, 11 May, buried at Saffron Walden on Thursday, 14 May 1903. Will dated 22 July 1896, proved at Ipswich 7 July 1903, by Emma Tuke, the relict, Henry Tuke Mennell, the nephew, William Favill Tuke, and Henry Samuel Tuke, the sons, and Douglas Day Taylor, the son-in-law, the Executors.

WADE. Vol. 4, page 139.—Ellis Wade died at Hove, Brighton, co. Sussex, aged 67, on Tuesday, 21 April, buried in the cemetery at Hove 24 April 1903. Will dated 11 May 1882, proved (Prin. Reg., 56, 1903) 19 August 1903, by Robert Goulding Ledger, the brother-in-law, the sole Executor.

WALKER. Vol. 6, page 7.—John William and Constance Elizabeth Walker have further issue a son, Robert Milnes Walker, born at "The Elms," Wakefield, co. York, 2 August, baptised at Wakefield Cathedral 31 August 1903.

The Rev. Herbert Milnes and Annie Harriet Walker have further issue a daughter, Margaret Elisabeth Milnes, born at the Vicarage, Littleover, co. Derby, 29 November 1903, baptised at Littleover 6 February 1904.

WALLER. Vol. 9, page 178.—Thomas Naunton and Frances Ellen Waller, who are now of "Rushmere," Wylam-on-Tyne, co. Northumberland, have further issue a son, Cyril Arthur Pretyman Waller, born at "Rushmere," Wylam-on-Tyne, 18 November, baptised at Wylam-on-Tyne 14 December 1902.

Page 179.—The Rev. Arthur Pretyman Waller was married at Boroughbridge, co. Somerset, 27 January 1903, to Constance Julia, daughter of the Rev. George Trevor, Vicar of Boroughbridge.

WARD. Vol. 9, page 119.—The Rev. Samuel and Sarah Ward had another son, James Ward, born at Nottingham 29 July 1809, and died in infancy.

WARDE. Vol. 4, page 62.—William Henry Warde died at Ouray, Colorado, U.S.A., aged 48, on Tuesday, 11 August, buried there on Thursday, 13 August 1903.

WEBB. Vol. 8, page 11.—Major William Wilfrid Webb is now of Bridge House, Berkhamsted, co. Hertford.

Page 12.—James Bertrand Webb was married at Christ Church, Launceston, Cornwall County, Tasmania, 9 August 1899, to Lila Blanche, daughter of Thomas Lockwood of Beaconfield, Tasmania. They have issue a daughter, Schröder Frances, born 29 July 1902.

Eustace Bertrand Stephen Webb, died, aged 10, 2 April, buried at St. Martin-by-Looe, co. Cornwall, 7 April 1903.

WEBB. Vol. 9, page 25.—Aston Webb was elected an Academician of the Royal Academy on Wednesday, 17 June 1903.

WEBBER. Vol. 4, page 159.—The Most Rev. William Thomas Thornhill Webber, Bishop of Brisbane, died at Bishopsbourne, Brisbane, Queensland, 3 August, buried at Brisbane 8 August 1903. Will dated 16 March 1897, proved at the High Court, Queensland, September 1903, by Archdeacon David.

WELMAN. Vol. 3, page 36.—Mary, wife of Frederick Tristram Welman, died at "Nunthorpe," Guildford, co. Surrey, aged 43, on Saturday, 6 December, buried at Woodchester, co. Gloucester, 11 December 1902.

WHELER. Vol. 8, page 83.—Colonel Sir Edward Wheler, Baronet, died on board the P. and O. s.s. "Persia" when entering Marseilles, on his voyage home from India, aged 46, on Tuesday, 11 August, buried at Leamington Hastings, co. Warwick, 19 August 1903.

WHITAKER. Vol. 10, page 162.—Ruth Helen Whitaker was born at Edinburgh 26 November 1858.

Page 163.—George Reginald Whitaker died 10 August 1882. Percy Duncomb Whitaker was born at Colchester, co. Essex, 8 November 1886 [*not* 1885], and baptised there. Noel Ralph Whitaker was born at Colchester 26 [*not* 27] December 1887 [*not* 1886].

WHITBY. Vol. 6, page 57.—Hilda, daughter of the Rev. Canon Thomas Whitby, died 25 November, buried at Christ Church, Sandown, Isle of Wight, 28 November 1903.

WICKHAM. Vol. 1, page 250.—William Joseph Wickham has been promoted from 2nd Lieutenant to Lieutenant in the Scots Guards.

WILDER. Vol. 2, page 128.—Francis Langham Wilder was married at the parish church, Chalfont St. Peter, co. Buckingham, on Wednesday, 28 October 1903, to Beatrice, 5th daughter of Frederick Drummond Hibbert of Bucknell Manor, Bicester, co. Oxford, and formerly of Chalfont Park, co. Buckingham.

WILLIAMS. Vol. 1, page 41.—Sir William Robert Williams, Baronet, died suddenly at his residence, Oare House, Lynton, North Devon, aged 43, on Saturday, 16 May, buried at Heanton Punchardon, co. Devon, 21 May 1903. Will dated 29 April 1903, proved (Prin. Reg., 79, 1903) 29 June 1903, by William Edwin Pitts Tucker and Charles Marwood Tucker, the Executors.

WILLOUGHBY DE BROKE. Vol. 8, page 38.—Henry, Baron Willoughby de Broke, died at sea, between Colombo and Aden, on board P. and O. s.s. "Australia," on his homeward voyage, aged 58, on Friday, 19 December 1902, buried at sea the same day. Will dated 9 October 1897, proved (Prin. Reg., 6, 1903) 3 August 1903, by Richard Greville, Baron Willoughby de Broke, the son, the sole Executor.

WILSON. Vol. 6, page 23.—Catherine Roberta, youngest daughter of Robert Wilson, was married at Croydon, co. Surrey, 16 March 1903, to William Burton Watts, son of Major-General William Henry Watts of the Madras Army; born 17 February 1856; Major (retired) South Wales Borderers.

WISDEN. Vol. 3, page 9 (and *Addenda, Vol. 8, page xix*).—Arthur Patrick and Ethel Charlotte Piggott Wisden have further issue a son, Thomas Patrick Wisden, born at "Baldocks," Penshurst, co. Kent, on Wednesday, 16 December 1903.

WOOD. Vol. 10, page 7.—Graham Wood, now of 200 Denmark Hill, co. Surrey, was married 2ndly at St. George's Chapel, Albemarle Street, London, on Tuesday, 5 May 1903, to Ida, 2nd daughter of Edward Liljewalch of Stockholm, Sweden, and widow of Carl A. Hellstrand of Stockholm; born at Wisby, Gotland, Sweden, 29 May 1861.

WOODD. Vol. 9, page 70.—The Rev. Charles Hampden Basil Woodd, Principal of Momoyama College, Osaka, Japan, was married at Singapore Cathedral, Straits Settlements, on Monday, 5 January 1903, to Elfrida Mary, elder daughter of the Rt. Rev. George Frederick Hose, D.D., Bishop of Singapore, Labuan and Sarawak.

WOODROOFFE. Vol. 2, page 12 (*and Addenda, Vol. 6, page xiv*).— George Borries and Elizabeth Macfarlane Woodrooffe have further issue a son, Arnold Walter Woodrooffe, born at 14 West Shrubbery, Redland, Bristol, on Tuesday, 14 April, baptised in the chapel of Dulwich College, co. Surrey, 13 June 1903.

WORTHINGTON. Vol. 1, page 223 (*and Addenda, Vol. 9, page xiv*).— William Worthington and Lady Muriel Gladwys Worthington have issue a son, William Greville Worthington, born 26 February, baptised at Netherseale, co. Derby, 14 April 1903.

WORTHINGTON, *continued.*
Dorothy Hilda, daughter of Albert Octavius Worthington, was married at The Oratory, Brompton, London, 20 April 1903, to Colonel Francis Edward Fitzherbert, D.S.O., eldest son of Basil Thomas Fitzherbert of Swynnerton Park, co. Stafford, J.P. and D.L., by Emily Charlotte his 1st wife, elder daughter of the Hon[ble] Edward Stafford Jerningham, 2nd son of Sir George William, 8th Baron Stafford; born on Sunday, 28 August 1859; J.P. for co. Stafford, Lieut.-Colonel 3rd Battalion Lancaster Regiment, formerly Major Staffordshire Yeomanry Cavalry; heir presumptive to the Barony of Stafford.

WRINCH. Vol. 8, page 115.—Charlotte, daughter of Leonard Wrinch, died at Eastbourne, co. Sussex, 23 March, buried at Erwarton, co. Suffolk, 26 March 1903. Will dated 16 April 1901, proved at Ipswich 15 April 1903, by Walter Wrinch, the Executor.

www.ingramcontent.com/pod-product-compliance
Lightning Source LLC
Chambersburg PA
CBHW080235270326
41926CB00020B/4243